BTEC National
2nd Edition

Travel & Tourism
Book 1

Gillian Dale

www.harcourt.co.uk
✓ Free online support
✓ Useful weblinks
✓ 24 hour online ordering

01865 888058

Heinemann

From Harcourt

Heinemann is an imprint of Harcourt Education Limited, a company incorporated in England and Wales, having its registered office: Halley Court, Jordan Hill, Oxford OX2 8EJ. Registered company number: 3099304

www.harcourt.co.uk

Heinemann is the registered trademark of Harcourt Education Limited

Text © Gillian Dale and Helen Oliver 2007

First published 2007

12 11 10 09 08 07
10 9 8 7 6 5 4 3 2 1

British Library Cataloguing in Publication Data is available from the British Library on request.

ISBN 978 0 435445 88 1

Typeset and illustrated by 𝒯\ Tek-Art, Croydon, Surrey, UK
Original illustrations © Harcourt Education Limited 2007
Picture research by Kay Altwegg
Cover photo © Corbis
Printed by Scotprint, Haddington, Scotland, UK

Websites
The websites used in this book were correct and up-to-date at the time of publication. It is essential for tutors to preview each website before using it in class so as to ensure that the URL is still accurate, relevant and appropriate. We suggest that tutors bookmark useful websites and consider enabling students to access them through the school/college intranet.

Contents

Acknowledgements

This book is for my dad for love and support

Photographs

The authors and publisher would like to thank the following individuals and organisations for permission to reproduce photographs:

Alamy/AA World Travel Library – page 83
Alamy/Anthony Wiles – page 175
Alamy/David Frazier Photography, Inc. – pages 2–3
Alamy/Doug Houghton – page 344
Alamy/FAN travelstock – page 278
Alamy/Ferruccio – page 166
Alamy/Images of Africa Photobank – page 163
Alamy/Jeff Greenberg – page 113
Alamy/Jon Arnold Images – pages 158, 253
Alamy/Jon Sturrock – page 45
Alamy/M. Timothy O'Keefe – pages 336–7
Alamy/Martin Mayer – page 171
Alamy/Stock Connection Blue – page 310
Alamy/Suzy Bennett – page 391
Alamy/The Flight Collection – pages 306–7
Alamy/TNT MAGAZINE – pages 108–9
Alamy/vario images GmbH & Co.KG – page 392
Alton Towers – page 64
BAA/Simon Kreitem – pages 386–7
BAA/Steve Bates – pages 72–3, 194, 321
Brand X Pictures – page 134
britainonview/Jon Spaull – page 89
britainonview/V K Guy/Mike Guy – page 81
Center Parcs Ltd – page 24
Corbis – pages 32, 40–1, 126, 134, 240–1, 261, 297
Digital Vision – pages 134, 342
easyJet airline company limited – page 52
Getty Images – page 117
Getty Images/PhotoDisc – pages 261, 293, 329, 356, 376
Harcourt Ltd/Debbie Rowe – pages 62, 150–1
Harcourt Ltd/Devon Olugbena Shaw – page 340

Harcourt Ltd/Philip Bratt – page 355
Intercontinental Hotel Group – page 5
John Birdsall – pages 190–1, 318
Photo courtesy of Princess Cruises – pages 11, 195
Photofusion/Jacky Chapman – pages 372–3
Picture courtesy of YHA – page 7
Robert Harding/Amanda Hall – page 280
Robert Harding/Gavin Hellier – page 254
Robert Harding/John Miller – page 346
Robert Harding/Peter Scholey – page 276
Robert Harding/Robert Francis – pages 270–1
Robert Harding/Roy Rainford – page 389
Robert Harding/Sylvain Grandadam – page 402
SNCF/Cumulus – page 28
*The Birth of Venus, c.*1485 (tempera on canvas) (for detail see 85293) by Botticelli, Sandro (1444/5–1510)/Galleria degli Uffizi, Florence, Italy/Giraudon/The Bridgeman Art Library – page 255

Artwork/text
Gillian Dale gives grateful thanks to:

Helen Oliver for Unit 4
Liz Atwal for the benefit of her expertise in human resource management
Rebecca Hammond for sharing her residential study project and information about her job at the Tourist Information Centre
Lisa Carmentari for telling us about her job at *Sound on Sound* Canvas Holidays and particularly Michele Bretenoux for providing information and patiently answering questions
Chris Fidler for helping with cash flow forecasting

The authors and publisher would like to thank the following individuals and organisations for permission to reproduce copyright material:

A2 Media Group – page 275
ABTA – pages 17, 165, 259–60, 308, 313, 320

Introduction

Welcome to this BTEC National Travel and Tourism course book, specifically designed to support students on the following programmes:

- BTEC National Award in Travel and Tourism
- BTEC National Certificate in Travel and Tourism
- BTEC National Diploma in Travel and Tourism.

For the BTEC National Award the book covers all four core units, that is:

- Investigating travel and tourism
- The business of travel and tourism
- The UK as a destination
- Customer service in travel and tourism.

It also provides five specialist units from which you can choose two to complete the qualification. These are:

- Preparing for employment in the travel and tourism industry
- The European travel market
- Long haul travel destinations
- Retail and business travel operations
- Work experience in the travel and tourism industry.

For the BTEC National Certificate and Diploma programmes, the book covers the four core units, that is:

- Investigating travel and tourism
- The business of travel and tourism
- The UK as a destination
- Customer service in travel and tourism.

It also provides eight of the specialist units to complete the qualification. These are:

- Marketing travel and tourism products and services
- Preparing for employment in the travel and tourism industry
- The European travel market
- Long haul travel destinations

- Retail and business travel operations
- Sustainable tourism development
- Work experience in the travel and tourism industry
- Residential study visit.

You will find further specialist units in Book 2. These are:

- Investigating the cruise sector
- Tour operations
- Roles and responsibilities of holiday respresentatives
- Events, conferences and exhibitions
- The appeal and importance of UK visitor attractions
- Hospitality operations in travel and tourism
- Handling air passengers
- Current issues in travel and tourism.

The aim of this book is to provide a comprehensive source of information for your course. It follows the BTEC specification closely, so that you can easily see what you have covered and quickly find the information you need. Examples and case studies from travel and tourism are used to bring your course to life and make it enjoyable to study. We hope you will be encouraged to find your own examples of current practice too.

You will often be asked to carry out research for activities in the text, and this will develop your research skills and enable you to find many sources of interesting travel and tourism information, particularly on the internet.

In some units of the book you will find information about jobs in travel and tourism and how to apply, which will be of great practical help to you.

The book is also a suitable core text for students on HND, foundation degree and first-year degree programmes. To help you plan your study, an overview of each unit and its outcomes is given at the beginning of each unit.

Guide to learning and assessment features

This book has a number of features to help you relate theory to practice and reinforce your learning. It also aims to help you gather evidence for assessment. You will find the features identified in the sample spread below in each unit.

Your teacher or tutor should check that you have completed enough activities to meet all the assessment criteria for the unit, whether from this book or from other tasks.

Teachers/tutors and students should refer to the BTEC standards for the qualification for the full BTEC grading criteria for each unit (www.edexcel.org.uk).

Assessment features

Activities and assessment practice

Activities are also provided throughout each unit. These are linked to real situations and case studies and they can be used for practice before tackling the preparation for assessment. Alternatively, some can contribute to your unit assessment if you choose to do these instead of the preparation for assessment at the end of each unit.

Grading icons

Throughout the book you will see the **P**, **M** and **D** icons. These show you where the tasks fit in with the grading criteria. If you do these tasks you will be building up your evidence to achieve your desired qualification. If you are aiming for a Merit, make sure you complete all the Pass **P** and Merit **M** tasks. If you are aiming for a Distinction, you will also need to complete all the Distinction **D** tasks. **P1** means the first of the Pass criteria listed in the specification, **M1** the first of the Merit criteria, **D1** the first of the Distinction criteria, and so on.

Preparation for assessment

Each unit concludes with a full unit assessment, which taken as a whole fulfils all the unit requirements from Pass to Distinction. Each task is matched to the relevant criteria in the specification.

Accommodation

There are many different types of accommodation available in the travel and tourism industry. We will look at the different types but remember that accommodation can be serviced which means that meals are on offer and your room will be cleaned for you, or it can be non-serviced where you look after yourself and do your own cleaning, shopping and cooking.

Hotels

Hotels may be independently owned or part of large chains. The chains tend to be more impersonal, but they do provide consistency of quality throughout the world. For example, if you were to stay in a Mercure hotel in London or in Paris, the room would offer exactly the same facilities, and even the layout is often the same.

Assessment practice

1 List the hotels in your town or local area. Find out which ones belong to which group. Are there any independent hotels?

2 Choose one of the hotels in your area. Describe how the hotel appeals to different tourists **P1 M1**

Many hotels are owned by international groups who encompass several chains within them, aiming at different types of customers. An example is InterContinental Hotels Group, a large international group that has 3,500 hotels. They are not all owned outright – some are run on a franchise arrangement. This means that the owner pays for the right to use the hotel name, but in return must follow corporate policies.

Guest accommodation

This includes bed and breakfast accommodation, guesthouses and farmhouses. Homeowners who wish to capitalise on having extra space available often run this type of accommodation. Many tourists consider it charming and an opportunity to experience local culture. This type of accommodation is very popular in France, where gites are rented out for holidays.

Holiday parks and campsites

Holiday parks and campsites are popular with British tourists heading for France and Spain, although camping is probably less popular in the UK because of the unreliable weather. Holiday parks offer chalets and mobile homes so that tourists do not have to worry so much about the weather.

Self-catering

Self-catering accommodation may be in holiday parks or in rented apartments or houses. Cooking facilities will be provided.

Rail travel

Network Rail owns and operates the national rail network in the UK. Its role is to maintain the infrastructure and renew tracks as necessary.

The train-operating companies (TOCs) lease trains from rolling-stock companies. There are 25 TOCs in the UK, and they compete for franchises to run each service.

The Strategic Rail Authority issues these franchises. This body also monitors the train-operating companies to make sure the interests of rail passengers are protected; they can fine the TOCs if they fail to meet agreed standards. The TOCs are commercial companies and aim to make a profit, but they do receive government grants.

Examples of TOCs are Virgin Trains and Central Trains. The National Express Group, a British-owned transport group, owns Central Trains.

Other important aspects of the rail system are the London Underground, Docklands Light Railway and, of course, Eurostar. Eurostar is the passenger train service through the Channel Tunnel. It operates from London Waterloo and Ashford in Kent to Paris, Lille and Brussels. Eurostar is owned by London and Continental Railways, and run by a management company.

Helen Oliver, an experienced writer and travel and tourism professional, has contributed Unit 4, Customer Service in Travel and Tourism. I have worked with Helen for many years and am very grateful to her for lending her expertise and specialist knowledge to this book.

In addition, a number of travel and tourism industry people have shared their company policies and procedures with us to allow you to develop your knowledge. Many have allowed us to use company information for case studies, and we are grateful for their help.

I do hope that you enjoy your course and find this book an excellent support for your studies.

Good luck!

Gillian Dale

Learning features

Case study

In summer 2004, an investigation was undertaken by the Rail Passenger Council, the watchdog for the rail sector. Passengers had complained that advance tickets, normally much cheaper, were not always available. For example, passengers travelling from London to Manchester should be able to buy tickets for £22. Instead they were forced to book later at higher prices – an open return from London to Manchester costs £182.

The problem occurs because Network Rail does not give the TOCs advance notice of engineering works, so timetables cannot be confirmed. Customers telephone to book advance tickets and are told they are not yet available as train times cannot be confirmed until engineering works are scheduled.

Sceptics have suggested that Network Rail is disregarding passenger interests and that the TOCs are profiting from the situation by receiving higher fares.

1 **Describe the roles and responsibilities of the organisations mentioned.**

2 **Describe how the problems outlined affect the travel and tourism industry.**

3 **What is your opinion of this situation? How can it be resolved? Recommend a course of action, with justifications. Discuss it with your group and write up the findings.**

Theory into practice

Visit your local Tourist Information Centre. Your tutor may wish to organise a group visit. Find out about the services it offers, and try to determine how many of its services generate revenue for the TIC. Discuss your findings with the group when you return.

Consider this

Sometimes trade associations have a code of ethics. These are not compulsory but members are asked to abide by them. Numbers employed in travel and tourism.

There are an estimated 1.4 million jobs in tourism in the UK, some 5% of all people in employment. Approximately 130,400 of these jobs are in self-employment.

	Total (millions)	Tourism-related (millions)
Total employment	28.4	1.42
Employee jobs	24.6	1.29
Self-employment	3.6	0.13

Table 1.4 Employment in tourism-related jobs

Theory into practice

These practical activities allow you to apply theoretical knowledge to travel and tourism tasks or research. Make sure you complete these activities as you work through each unit, to reinforce your learning.

Case studies

Interesting examples of real situations or companies are described in case studies that link theory to practice. They will show you how the topics you are studying affect real people and businesses.

Consider this

These are points for individual reflection or group discussion. They will widen your knowledge and help you reflect on issues that impact on travel and tourism.

Key term

▪ – the body representing the sector. It also has tour operators as members. According to ABTA figures, in 2005 it had 866 tour operator members and 1468 travel agency members with 6164 travel agency offices.

Roles and responsibilities

We have looked at the roles and responsibilities of various organisations as we have discussed the various components of the travel and tourism industry. However there are some general points to be made about how roles and responsibilities may differ from sector to sector.

Knowledge check

1 How did the development of low-cost airlines impact on travel and tourism?

2 What is meant by deregulation?

3 What are the elements of a package holiday?

4 Give an example of legislation affecting tourism in the UK?

5 What are the problems affecting the UK railways?

6 Describe the different methods of distributing travel and tourism products to consumers.

Key terms

Issues and terms that you need to be aware of are summarised under these headings. They will help you check your knowledge as you learn, and will prove to be a useful quick-reference tool.

Knowledge check

At the end of each unit is a set of quick questions to test your knowledge of the information you have been studying. Use these to check your progress, and also as a revision tool.

Investigating travel and tourism

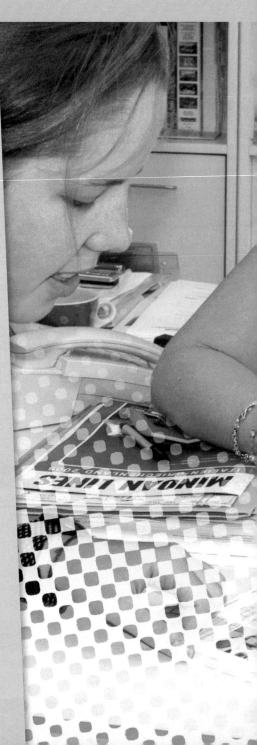

Introduction

The travel and tourism industry is dynamic, exciting and provides a challenging working environment. If you're reading this book, it's likely that you're considering a career in travel and tourism and that you're beginning your studies of the industry.

This unit aims to give you a sound introduction to the industry so that you gain an overview of its various components and how they link together. You will also study the roles and responsibilities of travel and tourism organisations within the different sectors of the industry.

You will learn about the development of the industry, particularly from the 1960s to the present day. You will find out how changes in demand, new travel and tourism products and changes in the distribution of products have affected the industry.

You will also look at the factors which currently affect the travel and tourism industry and are likely to affect future trends in its development.

After completing this unit you should be able to achieve the following outcomes:

1   Know the components of travel and tourism and how they interrelate

2   Know the roles and responsibilities of travel and tourism organisations within the different sectors

3   Understand how recent developments have shaped the present-day travel and tourism industry

4   Understand the trends and factors affecting the development of travel and tourism.

Thinking points

You need to understand what is meant by the travel and tourism industry before you start your studies, and hopefully you will realise that it is not just about exotic holidays – although they are covered!

Tourism is the provision of services to tourists. Everything that tourists do while they are away is considered part of the travel and tourism industry. Tourism is a significant contributor to the UK economy; many businesses depend on tourism, directly or indirectly. Many businesses in tourism are very small. Government figures show that the tourism industry consists of 127,000 businesses and that 80 per cent of these have a turnover of less than £250,000 per year. Five per cent of all people in employment work in tourism, that is 1.5 million people.

The businesses which make up the travel industry are complex and diverse. In this section of the unit we will examine the various components which make up the industry.

Who do you think make up the travel and tourism industry?

How many travel and tourism organisations can you name?

By components of travel and tourism we mean the different parts of the industry that provide travel and tourism products and services. None of these components is able to work in isolation. Each one relies on one or more of the other component parts to be able to operate.

▲ Figure 1.1 Components of the travel and tourism industry

Tourists

There are many types of tourists, but for statistical purposes they are categorised according to their purpose of travel, broadly as follows:

- leisure
- business
- visiting friends and relatives (VFR).

Leisure travel includes travel for holidays, cultural events, recreation, sports, religion and study.

Business travel includes all travel for business reasons, such as meetings, conferences and exhibitions. Usually business travellers have their expenses paid by their company, which can make a difference to the services they choose or have chosen on their behalf.

VFR accounts for many trips, particularly within the UK.

In addition you should know about some other types of tourists.

Inbound tourists are those coming in to visit a country which is not their country of residence, for the purposes of tourism. If a tourist comes from the USA to the UK, then they are inbound to the UK. This also means that they are an *outbound tourist* from their own country. In the same way, you are an outbound tourist from the UK if you go to Spain on holiday. Inbound tourists to the UK spent about £14.25 billion in 2005.

Domestic tourists are those people who are travelling within their own country for tourism purposes. People on day trips are not officially tourists as they are not staying away from home. Statistics consider tourists to be people who stay away for at least one night. However, as day trippers spend a lot of money in the tourism sector, particularly on travel and in the visitor attractions sector, it is important to measure the value of their spending. In England, this is measured in the Leisure Visits Survey. Day visitors spent almost £37.4 billion in 2005.

Accommodation

There are many different types of accommodation available in the travel and tourism industry. We will look at the different types. Remember that accommodation can be serviced, which means that meals are on offer and your room will be cleaned for you, or it can be non-serviced where you look after yourself and do your own cleaning, shopping and cooking.

Hotels

Hotels may be independently owned or part of large chains. The chains tend to be more impersonal, but they do provide consistency of quality throughout the world. For example, if you were to stay in a Mercure hotel in London or in Paris, the room would offer exactly the same facilities, and often the layout is exactly the same.

Activity

Study each of the examples below. What kind of tourists are they? Note that some examples might fit into more than one category.

Example	Type of tourist
Marianne is taking a holiday in the UK. She lives in Austria.	
Raj is going on holiday to Bournemouth. He lives in Leicester.	
Year 11 at Chichester Village College are going to visit Leeds Castle for the day.	
Sheena and Donald are going to Madrid for a weekend break. They live in Glasgow.	
Mary is a sales director. She is going to a sales conference in Barcelona.	
The Patel family are going on holiday to Disneyland, Paris.	
Jerry goes to visit his father in Dublin every Christmas.	
Mario is visiting the UK to undertake a language course.	

Many hotels are owned by international groups who encompass several chains within them, aiming at different types of customers. An example is InterContinental Hotels Group, a large international group that has 3500 hotels. They are not all owned outright – some are run on a franchise arrangement. This means that the owner pays for the right to use the hotel name, but in return must follow corporate policies.

InterContinental Hotels brands are:

- Crowne Plaza
- Holiday Inn
- Express by Holiday Inn
- Holiday Inn Express
- Staybridge Suites
- Candlewood Suites.

There are many more hotel groups, and you will be familiar with names like Best Western and Moat House.

Hotels offer many products and services, catering for different customers, and the prestigous and more expensive hotels like Sofitel, offer greater luxury. In addition, hotels cater for both business and leisure customers so they need a range of products to suit each type. Conference customers may come for just a day and will need different services from the residents.

Figure 1.2 Express by Holiday Inn is part of the InterContinental hotel group and aims to provide comfortable, modern accommodation at affordable prices

Assessment practice

1 List the hotels in your town or local area. Find out which ones belong to which group. Are there any independent hotels? **P1**

2 Choose one of the hotels in your area. Describe how the hotel appeals to different tourists.

3 Explain how your chosen hotel interrelates with other areas of travel and tourism, for example tour operators or transport providers. Make sure your examples include domestic, inbound and outbound tourism. **P2 M1**

Grading tips

To reach Pass level, you would need to describe the facilities of the hotel and say what type of tourist it appeals to.

To reach Merit level, you would need to think about all the other organisations the hotel works with and how they are interdependent. You could draw a diagram illustrating the relationships, along with explanatory notes.

Guest accommodation

This includes bed and breakfast accommodation, guesthouses and farmhouses. Homeowners who wish to capitalise on the extra space they might have available often run this type of accommodation. Many tourists consider it charming and an opportunity to experience local culture. This type of accommodation is very popular in France, where gîtes are rented out for holidays.

Holiday parks and campsites

Holiday parks and campsites are popular with British tourists heading for France and Spain, although camping is probably less popular in the UK because of the unreliable weather. Holiday parks offer chalets and mobile homes so that tourists do not have to worry so much about weather conditions.

Self-catering

Self-catering accommodation may be in holiday parks or in rented apartments or houses. Cooking facilities will be provided.

Youth hostels

The Youth Hostel Association (YHA), which is a charity serving the needs of young people, runs hostels in the UK. However, you do not have to be a young person to be a member. It is very cheap to join the YHA and some of the hostels are of a very high standard, almost like hotels.

There are 226 youth hostels in both city and rural locations in the UK. The original aim of the YHA was to promote love, care and understanding of the countryside in principle and in practice.

There is also an International Youth Hostel Federation, with 5000 hostels in 60 countries. The YHA provides not only accommodation but a range of activity holidays.

Campus accommodation

Universities are keen to rent out their halls of residence outside term time. They encourage conference trade as they can also offer meeting rooms and catering facilities. This is an excellent means of using empty rooms and increasing revenue during students' holidays.

Grading standards

VisitBritain has created quality standards for a wide range of accommodation in England. Scotland, Wales and Northern Ireland have their own schemes. Trained assessors determine these gradings.

Hotels are given a rating from one to five stars – the more stars, the higher the quality and the greater the range of facilities and level of service provided.

Guest accommodation is rated from one to five diamonds. The more diamonds, the higher the overall quality in areas such as cleanliness, service and hospitality, bedrooms, bathrooms and food quality.

Self-catering accommodation is also star-rated from one to five. The more stars awarded to an establishment, the higher the level of quality. Establishments at higher rating levels also have to meet some additional requirements for facilities.

Holiday parks and campsites are also assessed using stars. One star denotes acceptable quality. Five stars denotes exceptional quality.

The aim of the grading system is to make it easier for tourists to compare the quality of visitor accommodation offered around the country. However, as the Scottish and Welsh tourist boards use different systems and the English system uses a diamond system and a star system, it is still confusing.

When you travel abroad, you will find that there is no standard system. The star grading system is more or less accepted in Europe but cannot be wholly relied upon. Tour operators tend to use their own grading standards so that they can indicate a level of quality to their customers. An example is the 'T' system adopted by Thomson.

Transport provision

Airports

The British Airports Authority (BAA) is the major organisation in airport ownership in the UK. In 2006, the company was taken over by a Spanish airport operator and engineering company Ferrovial SA at a cost of £10 billion. BAA owns the airports at:

- London Heathrow
- London Gatwick
- London Stansted
- Glasgow.
- Edinburgh
- Aberdeen
- Southampton

BAA also has management contracts or stakes in ten other airports outside the UK, plus retail management contracts at two airports in the USA. There are 144 million passengers travelling through BAA airports every year.

Other major UK airports are Birmingham, Manchester and London Luton, all owned by different consortia.

Running an airport is a complex but profitable operation. The airport provides products and services to various groups of people and businesses:

- airlines are provided with the infrastructure and services to operate their flights
- customers are provided with facilities, such as restaurants and shops
- it provides a location in which other businesses can operate, for example, car hire, retailing or ground handling.

The airport earns revenue from all these sources but also has to work hard at keeping all its groups of customers happy.

Assessment practice

Study an airport of your choice. This might be one that you are able to visit or one that you can examine via its website.

1 Describe the role and responsibilities of the airport in relation to its customer groups, airlines, freight companies and passengers. You could make this into a wall display with explanatory notes. **P1**

2 Explain how an airport interrelates with other organisations from the travel and tourism industry, giving examples that include domestic, inbound and outbound tourism. **P2 M1**

All UK airlines are privately owned. British Airways (BA) is one of the world's most famous airlines and one of the largest in terms of international scheduled services. It is the largest in the UK and flies to more than 200 destinations around the world. In 2005, around 36 million people chose to fly with the airline.

British Airways' main bases are at the London airports of Heathrow and Gatwick. The airline's products include four different types of cabin service ranging from Economy to Club World. It also fully owns subsidiaries such as British Airways CitiExpress.

The role and responsibilities of BA are:

- to meet the needs of passengers by providing travel on the routes demanded and good in-flight service
- to meet the needs of freight customers. The airline carried 877,000 tonnes of cargo in 2005
- a responsibility to its shareholders, who expect British Airways to make a profit and provide a return on investment
- a responsibility to provide sufficient remuneration and good working conditions to staff. The airline employs nearly 50,000 people.

Theory into practice

Find out about the products and services available to British Airways customers. Compare Economy with Club World and make a table charting your comparison. This information is available on the BA website (www.ba.com).

Other major UK airlines include British Midland and Virgin Atlantic – these airlines are scheduled airlines. The UK also has many charter airlines, such as Monarch and Thomsonfly. Hundreds of other airlines from all over the world fly in and out of UK airports, paying for the services they use.

■ Low-cost airlines

The principle behind the operation of a low-cost airline is to keep costs as low as possible, with few or no 'extras'

Key terms

Scheduled – these airlines run to a regular timetable that is changed only for the winter and summer seasons. The flights depart even if not all the seats have been booked.

Charter – these aircraft are usually contracted for a specific holiday season and run to a timetable set by the operator. For example, each major tour operator will need seats for its summer passengers flying to the Mediterranean. They fill every seat on the contracted aircraft and each seat forms part of the holiday package. The major tour operators own their own charter airlines, for example TUI owns Thomsonfly airline.

offered to the customer without further charge. In this way the low-cost operators are able to offer very cheap fares. The low-cost airlines are scheduled airlines.

They practise a system known as 'yield management' which means that bookings are constantly monitored and prices are adjusted accordingly. In periods of high demand, such as school holidays or weekends, prices will be higher and can even be more expensive than traditional airlines like BA.

One of the most successful low-cost airlines is Irish-based Ryanair, which reported record quarterly profits of €116 million to 30 June 2006.

Airport charges are paid per passenger and vary depending on who owns the airport and the deal negotiated by the airline. Low-cost airlines often fly to regional airports because of lower charges. Ryanair recently moved its business from Birmingham to East Midlands airport, to take advantage of lower charges. It is also currently in dispute with Stansted over airport charges.

Low-cost airlines usually have a fleet of aircraft all of the same type, often Boeing 737s. This gives flexibility, as the planes can be moved to any route as needed, and it also means that maintenance is simpler.

There is no business class on a low-cost flight, allowing more seats to be put in the plane. Ryanair's new planes do not have reclining seats or pockets for magazines, resulting in further savings.

The airlines rely heavily on newspaper advertising, which is costly, but they gain revenue by carrying advertising on their own websites. Ryanair carries advertisements on seatback covers, bringing an extra source of revenue.

The airlines charge the customer extra for food, drink or paying by credit card, and even sell lottery tickets on board some flights. The airlines also sell hotel rooms, car hire and insurance on a commission basis.

Regulation of air travel

The Civil Aviation Authority (CAA) regulates the UK aviation sector. The CAA is an independent statutory body. The responsibilities of the CAA are to:

- ensure that UK civil aviation standards are set and achieved
- regulate airlines, airports and National Air Traffic Services' economic activities and encourage a diverse and competitive industry
- manage the UK's principal travel protection scheme, the Air Travel Organisers' Licensing (ATOL) scheme, license UK airlines and manage consumer issues
- bring civil and military interests together to ensure that the airspace needs of all users are met as equitably as possible.

The CAA also advises the government on aviation issues. It receives no government funding but is funded by the charges it makes for its services.

The Air Transport Users Council (AUC) is the UK's consumer council for air travellers. It receives its funding from the CAA. It acts as the independent representative of air passengers and aims to complement and assist the CAA in furthering the reasonable interests of passengers.

National Air Traffic Services (NATS) is the organisation responsible for air traffic control. It is a public/private partnership owned by the government, a consortium of seven airlines and NATS staff. It looks after UK airspace but also the eastern part of the North Atlantic. NATS handles more than 2 million flights a year carrying over 180 million passengers.

The major air traffic control centres are at Swanwick, Hampshire; West Drayton, Middlesex; and Prestwick, Ayrshire. There are also air traffic control services at the country's major airports.

Sea travel

As residents of the UK we live on an island, sea transport has always been an important part of the travel and tourism industry. Historically, the main mode of transport to the Continent was by sea across the English Channel. When the Channel Tunnel opened, it was expected that ferry services across the Channel would be threatened. The tunnel did take about 50 per cent of the market, but passenger ferries have also been severely hit by low-cost airlines offering cheap fares to the Continent. It is often cheaper to fly and drive rather than take your own car.

In 1997, over 21 million passengers passed through Dover, which is the biggest port in the UK. By 2004, numbers had declined to fewer than 15 million. The first full year of Channel Tunnel operation was 1995.

The Channel Tunnel and low-cost flights are not the only competition faced by the ferry operators – there is also a high-speed catamaran operated by SpeedFerries. SpeedFerries is offering low fares to attract customers.

Other operators in the Channel include Sea France and Brittany Ferries. Brittany Ferries operates on longer routes to France and Spain, for example Poole to Cherbourg, Plymouth to Santander and Portsmouth to Caen, St Malo or Cherbourg. Ferries also operate to the Channel islands, for example Jersey and Guernsey.

The established ferry operator P&O revealed that its ferries lost £40 million in the financial year 2003–4, because of competition in the Channel and from low-cost airlines. The company announced 1200 job losses in September 2004 as it cut its routes from Portsmouth to Cherbourg, Le Havre and Caen and from Rosslare to Cherbourg. Hoverspeed also ceased trading.

Not all ferry travel is across the Channel. Here are some examples of other important routes:

Stranraer – Belfast	Hull – Rotterdam
Fleetwood – Larne	Holyhead – Dublin
Fishguard – Rosslare	Pembroke – Rosslare
Holyhead – Dun Laoghaire	Isle of Man – Liverpool
Hull – Zeebrugge	Isle of Wight – Portsmouth.

Theory into practice

1 Check the ports listed on page 9 on a map and make sure you know the location and the country of each.

2 Choose one route and find out which ferry operators serve it. Produce an information sheet detailing the services provided and extra products available on that route. A ferry brochure will help you.

The Scottish islands are accessible by ferry, both from the mainland and via inter-island services.

Figure 1.4 ▶ **Map showing some of the Scottish islands**

Consider this

Irish Ferries advertises its ferries as 'cruise ferries'. Do you think this makes them more appealing?

In the event of business failure, the Passenger Shipping Association provides financial protection to the customers of some tour operators who offer cruise and ferry-based holidays.

■ The cruise market

The cruise sector has enjoyed steady growth over the past decade or more. In 2003–4, 28 new ships including the *Queen Mary 2* were launched, as companies invested in new liners. Seven new ships were delivered in 2006 including Royal Caribbean International's *Freedom of the Seas,* the largest passenger ship ever built, carrying more than 4000 passengers.

In 2005, 1.21 million British people went on cruise holidays. Cruise companies are doing their utmost to reach new markets, such as families and younger people, rather than just the older age groups who traditionally take cruises.

One newcomer is Easycruise. The company aims to attract young, independent travellers who can embark or disembark at any port on the ship's route as long as they stay on board at least two nights. The ships are in port during the day and sail at night so that passengers can make the most of time ashore.

Most cruises take place on the sea and most passengers from the UK take fly-cruises. This means they fly to the ship's starting point. The Mediterranean and the Caribbean are very popular cruise destinations. Those people who are looking for something different might take a cruise to a colder place like the Arctic to experience the beautiful scenery and the wildlife.

River cruises are also growing in popularity; destinations include the rivers Rhine, Moselle, Danube and Nile.

Major cruise companies you may have heard of are P&O Cruises, Cunard, Royal Caribbean and Princess.

Theory into practice

Choose a cruise from a brochure. Outline all the facilities and services included in the price of the cruise.

▶ Figure 1.5 The cruise sector has enjoyed steady growth over the last decade

Road travel

The private car dominates road travel. Car ownership is very high in the UK, and most domestic holidays and day trips are taken by car. In addition, many people choose to hire a car when abroad, and this has led to the growth of the car-hire sector.

■ Car hire

Major car-hire groups in the UK include Hertz, Avis and Europcar. All have international operations. Their products and services have become very sophisticated, making car hire very easy and convenient for customers. They offer:

- online or telephone pre-booking
- airport pick-up or drop-off
- a wide range of choice of vehicles
- all insurances included in fixed prices
- one-way rentals – you don't have to return the car to the place where you picked it up.

One of the largest companies in car hire is Holiday Autos, which claims to be the world's largest car-rental service with access to over 750,000 cars worldwide. Holiday Autos is part of the Lastminute.com group.

■ Coaches

Coach operators have adapted their products to meet consumers' changing needs and coaches today are very luxurious. Fly-coach holidays are offered so that customers do not have a lengthy initial journey but have the benefits of coach travel for touring, for example in California.

There are extensive coach networks operating in the UK offering scheduled services between towns and also into Europe. Eurolines claims to connect to 500 destinations within Europe. Its services are very comfortable with toilets, refreshments and video available on board.

Rail travel

Network Rail owns and operates the national rail network in the UK. Its role is to maintain the infrastructure and renew tracks as necessary.

The train-operating companies (TOCs) lease trains from rolling-stock companies. There are 25 TOCs in the UK, and they compete for franchises to run each service.

The Strategic Rail Authority issues these franchises. This body also monitors the train-operating companies to make sure the interests of rail passengers are protected; they can fine the TOCs if they fail to meet agreed standards. The TOCs are commercial companies and aim to make a profit, but they do receive government grants.

Examples of TOCs are Virgin Trains and Central Trains. The National Express Group, a British-owned transport group, owns Central Trains.

Other important aspects of the rail system are the London Underground, Docklands Light Railway and, of course, Eurostar. Eurostar is the passenger train service through the Channel Tunnel. It operates from London Waterloo and Ashford in Kent to Paris, Lille and Brussels. Eurostar is owned by London and Continental Railways, and run by a management company.

Case study: Rail Passenger Council

In summer 2004, an investigation was undertaken by the Rail Passenger Council, the watchdog for the rail sector. Passengers had complained that advance tickets, normally much cheaper, were not always available. For example, passengers travelling from London to Manchester should be able to buy tickets for £22. Instead they were forced to book later at higher prices – an open return from London to Manchester costs £182.

The problem occurs because Network Rail does not give the TOCs advance notice of engineering works, so timetables cannot be confirmed. Customers telephone to book advance tickets and are told they are not yet available as train times cannot be confirmed until engineering works are scheduled.

Sceptics have suggested that Network Rail is disregarding passenger interests and that the TOCs are profiting from the situation by receiving higher fares.

1. **Describe the roles and responsibilities of the organisations mentioned.** **P3**

2. **Compare these with the roles and responsibilities of organisations from different sectors.** **M2**

3. **Describe how the problems outlined affect the travel and tourism industry.** **D1**

4. **What is your opinion of this situation? How can it be resolved? Recommend a course of action, with justifications. Discuss it with your group and write up the findings.** **D2**

You could use this case study for assessment practice. If you do, follow the grading tip.

Grading tip

To reach Distinction level, you should think about how other transport companies look after passenger interests and see if their strategies are suitable for this sector.

Visitor attractions

The UK officially has 6500 visitor attractions. These UK attractions are important to both the domestic tourism market and the inbound tourism market. There are, of course, hundreds of different types of attractions, but they can be broadly divided as follows.

Natural attractions

These include beautiful beaches, lakes and landscapes. In order to protect them, some are designated Areas of Outstanding Natural Beauty (AONBs), National Parks or Heritage Coasts.

Heritage attractions

In the UK we have a wealth of historic houses, often cared for by the National Trust or English Heritage. We also have museums and galleries such as Tate Britain and Tate Modern, the Victoria and Albert Museum. These examples are in London, but there are museums throughout the country, for example the National Museum of Photography, Film and Television in Bradford.

Purpose-built attractions

Purpose-built attractions may be historic also, for example most museums are purpose built. Favourite purpose-built attractions include theme parks, for example the theme park resort Alton Towers.

Events

Events such as the Edinburgh Festival or the Notting Hill Carnival attract many visitors. There are events in the business tourism sector too, such as the World Travel Market.

Paying and non-paying

Another way of categorising attractions is to divide them into paying and non-paying. Museums, for example, are usually free, as the principle is that we should all be able to view the nation's heritage. It is usually difficult to charge visitors to natural attractions as it would mean creating barriers to access.

Non-paying attractions are still important for the economics of tourism, as they attract visitors to an area where they spend money on food, accommodation and shopping. Blackpool Pleasure Beach is the most popular free attraction with an estimated 6.5 million visits per year. However, although it is free to enter the Pleasure Beach, you have to pay to go on a ride.

Attraction	Location	2004	2005	Percentage change
British Airways London Eye	London	3,700,000	3,250,000	–12
Tower of London	London	2,139,366	1,931,093	–10
Flamingo Land Theme Park & Zoo	Yorkshire	1,380,110	1,400,210est.	1
Kew Gardens	London	1,063,384	1,354,928	27
Windermere Lake Cruises	Cumbria	1,289,866	1,282,702	–1
Drayton Manor Family Theme Park	Staffordshire	1,100,000	1,200,000	9
Eden Project	Cornwall	1,223,959	1,177,189	–4
Chester Zoo	Cheshire	1,161,684	1,089,576	–6
Canterbury Cathedral	Kent	1,091,684	1,054,886est.	–3

Table 1.1 Major paid admission attractions   est. = estimate   (Source: http://www.tourismtrade.org.uk)

Attraction	Location	2004	2005	Percentage change
Blackpool Pleasure Beach	Lancashire	6,200,000	6,000,000	–3
British Museum	London	4,868,127	4,536,064est.	–7
Brighton Pier	Brighton	4,500,000	4,500,000est.	0
National Gallery	London	4,959,946	4,202,020est.	–15
Tate Modern	London	4,441,225	3,902,017	–12
Natural History Museum	London	3,240,344	3,078,346	–5
Science Museum	London	2,154,366	2,019,940	–7
Victoria & Albert Museum	London	2,010,825	1,920,200	–5

Table 1.2 Major free admission attractions   est. = estimate   (Source: http://www.tourismtrade.org.uk)

Activity

To improve your knowledge of the UK visitor attractions sector, create a table similar to the one below. Use your local Tourist Information Centre and the VisitBritain website (www.visitbritain.com) to help you complete it. Check your answers with your teacher or tutor.

Type of attraction	Two national examples	A local example
Historic house		
Garden		
Museum		
Art gallery		
Wildlife attraction		
Theme park		
Historic monument		
Religious building		

Associations

The British Association of Leisure Parks, Piers and Attractions (BALPPA) was founded in 1936. It is non-profit-making and its role is to represent the interests of owners, managers, suppliers and developers in the UK's commercial leisure parks, piers, zoos and static attractions sector. It has about 300 members.

The International Association of Amusement Parks and Attractions (IAAPA) is a similar organisation to BALPPA but it is an international association and has members all over the world. The mission of the association is to promote safe operations, global development, professional growth and commercial success in the amusement industry.

Consider this

Sometimes trade associations have a code of ethics. These are not compulsory but members are asked to abide by them. The IAAPA includes in its code of ethics the aim 'to fill the hearts of children and all those young in spirit with joy while spending their hours of play and recreation'.

Tour operations

The role of tour operators is to put together all the different components that make up a holiday and sell them as packages to the consumer. They make contracts with hoteliers, airlines and other transport companies to put the package together. All the holiday details are described in a brochure which is distributed either to travel agents or directly to customers. There are three main types of tour operators catering for the different categories of tourism:

- outbound
- inbound
- domestic.

Outbound tour operators

Four major tour operators have dominated the outbound market for years. These are often referred to as the 'big four'. They are TUI, MyTravel, First Choice and Thomas Cook. In 2007, Thomas Cook and MyTravel merged and First Choice and TUI merged, forming two dominant organisations rather than four. Traditionally, these major tour operators were considered to be mass market tour operators as they sold similar holidays in packages that appealed to the majority of holidaymakers. In contrast, specialist tour operators sold more individually tailored holidays or specialised in one destination or activity. Today, the large tour operators also offer many specialised products.

TUI UK was the UK's largest holiday company until the merger and includes the leading UK brand Thomson Holidays. Thomson employs around 10,000 people, 7000 of whom work overseas in around 40 holiday destinations. The parent company, World of TUI, is the largest travel group in the world. MyTravel is a major player in the market for air-inclusive holidays and other leisure travel services. It also has travel agents, hotels and airlines in its group. First Choice has a major travel agent in its portfolio and an airline. It offers holidays in destinations such as Majorca, Menorca, the Canaries, Spain, Turkey, Greece and the Caribbean. Winter sports destinations include France, Austria, Italy, Andorra, Bulgaria and Switzerland, and many specialist brands such as Twentys, aimed at young people, and Sunstart, aimed at budget holidaymakers. Thomas Cook also has travel agencies, airlines and hotels as well as tour operator brands, including JMC, Thomas Cook Holidays and Club 18–30.

These companies produce an astonishing range of different holidays packaged in brochures according to type of holiday or type of customer. Here are the brochures selling holidays within the Thomson organisation:

- Jetsave & Jersey Travel
- Simply Travel
- Headwater Holidays
- Magic Travel Group
- Crystal Holidays
- Thomson Ski and Snowboarding
- Thomson Lakes and Mountains.

There are many other tour operators in the market; some specialise in particular destinations, for example Simply Spain, or in a product, for example diving holidays. Cosmos is the UK's largest independent tour operator and part of the Globus group of companies, a family-run organisation established in 1928 which encompasses Cosmos Tourama, Avro, Monarch Airlines and Archers Direct, along with Cosmos.

Case study: Thomson cuts Turkey capacity by one-fifth

Thomson and Thomas Cook have cut their Turkey capacity in response to a lapse in demand following the bird flu outbreak.

Thomson's 20 per cent cut means its summer 2006 programme has been reduced to a similar capacity as last year.

A Thomson spokesman said the Turkey programme was still under review and capacity could be increased quickly if demand picked up.

'We trimmed back the programme slightly because of the decline in demand, although in the last couple of weeks we have seen it picking up again,' he said.

'There is nothing to stop us putting flights back in.'

Thomas Cook chief executive, Manny Fontenla-Novoa, said it had cut back in response to falling demand, adding that Spain appeared to be a favoured alternative destination. However, he said Thomas Cook could quickly reinstate capacity in Turkey if necessary.

Some specialist operators say demand for the country is returning to normal.

Upmarket Turkey specialist, Exclusive Escapes, said sales had returned to 2005 levels after a surge in bookings during the past two weeks.

Until Christmas, Exclusive Escapes had reported Turkey sales up by 50 per cent on the previous year, but sales collapsed after reports of the outbreak.

Managing director Andrew Lee said: 'Bird flu certainly had a very negative impact on bookings to Turkey at the start of the year. In recent weeks, however, as bird flu has emerged just across the Channel, there

has been greater understanding of the situation and bookings have resumed normal levels.'

Nick Wrightman, managing director of Tapestry Holidays, said Turkey bookings had been strong recently but were still down on last year.

Meanwhile, research by Trip-Vision showed that 16 per cent of travellers polled said bird flu considerations had influenced their travel plans in the week to 1 March.

Just over 2 per cent of the whole sample said they had ruled out some countries and decided on another location. Spain was the most popular alternative, chosen by 26 per cent.

Trip-Vision managing director David Jones said 6.4 per cent of travellers polled said they still planned to go to one of the infected countries.

(Source: *Travel Trade Gazette*, 10 March 2006)

1 Why did Thomson and Thomas Cook cut capacity to Turkey?

2 Do you think this was the right decision?

3 Thomson say they could put flights back if necessary. How would they do this?

Taking it further

Research some current events which are impacting on demand for specific destinations. Give examples of what tour operators are doing in response to changes in demand. **P4**

Key term

Air Travel Organisers' Licensing (ATOL) – a scheme that protects air travellers and package holiday makers from losing money or being stranded abroad if air travel firms go out of business. When a tourist books a holiday the cost of this financial protection is included in the price. Any package firm that includes a flight should by law hold a licence. ATOL is managed by the Civil Aviation Authority.

Inbound tour operators

Inbound tour operators cater for the needs of overseas visitors to the UK. An example is British Tours Ltd, which claims to be the longest-established inbound operator. It offers tours for different sizes of groups and has a wide variety of products, including a Harry Potter tour. The tours are available in many languages.

An example is a 'fun for children' tour, which includes Robin Hood and his Merry Men, Maid Marion and the bad Sheriff of Nottingham; HMS *Victory*, where Nelson lay wounded; Henry VIII's battleship the *Mary Rose*; HMS *Warrior*, England's first armoured battleship; a lively and noisy fort where children can 'fire' guns and handle swords; and Legoland, a short drive from Windsor Castle, or one of the many theme parks.

Domestic tour operators

Domestic tour operators package holidays within the UK for UK residents. They include coach companies which place advertisements in the local newspapers. Like outbound operators, they offer beach, city, touring and special-interest holidays.

Tour operators' associations

UKinbound is the trade body which represents tour operators and tourism suppliers to the UK. It was founded in 1977 to represent the commercial and political interests of incoming tour operators and suppliers to the British inbound tourism industry. It is a non profit-making body governed by an elected council and funded by subscriptions from its members and from revenue-generating activities.

The Association of Independent Tour Operators (AITO) is an organisation which represents about 160 of the UK's specialist tour operators. AITO members are independent companies, most of them owner-managed, specialising in particular destinations or types of holiday.

The Federation of Tour Operators (FTO) is an organisation for outbound tour operators. It aims to ensure the long-term success of the air-inclusive holiday by influencing governments and opinion formers on the benefits to consumers of air-inclusive holidays compared with other types of holiday. Members pay an annual subscription based on the size of their organisation. All current members are also members of ABTA, and the two organisations work very closely together.

Travel agents

The role of travel agents is to give advice and information, and sell and administer bookings for a number of tour operators. They also sell flights, ferry bookings, car hire, insurance and accommodation as separate products.

Thus, they are distributors of products.

Travel agents may operate through:

- retail shops
- business shops
- a call centre
- online.

Most travel agents are part of a multiple chain, and these dominate the business. Examples you will be familiar with are Thomas Cook, Thomson and Going Places. These particular chains are linked to tour operators and may try to prioritise their own company's products.

There has been a slight reduction in the number of branches of multiple chains in the past few years as customers choose to buy travel and tourism products through other means, particularly through travel websites.

Independent travel agents are usually run by their owner and a small team, and may have only one or two outlets. There are also independent chains – an example is Travelcare.

Travelcare is the UK's largest independent travel chain with branches nationwide The chain is very successful with profits rising by £0.9m to £1m in 2004. The chain was voted favourite major high street travel agent in the *Guardian/Observer* 2004. This company is part of the Co-operative Group.

Key term

Association of British Travel Agents – the body representing the sector. It also has tour operators as members. According to ABTA figures, in 2005 it had 866 tour operator members and 1468 travel agency members with 6164 travel agency offices.

Business travel agents

Business travel agents specialise in the business market. They aim to handle all the travel arrangements for large companies.

'Implants' are travel agents located within another business. They set up office within a company so that they are on hand to deal with the travel requirements of the company's personnel.

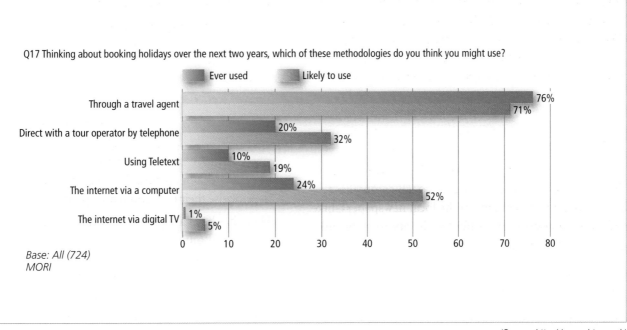

Q17 Thinking about booking holidays over the next two years, which of these methodologies do you think you might use?

Ever used   Likely to use

Through a travel agent	76% / 71%
Direct with a tour operator by telephone	20% / 32%
Using Teletext	10% / 19%
The internet via a computer	24% / 52%
The internet via digital TV	1% / 5%

Base: All (724)
MORI

(Source: http://www.abta.co.uk)

▲ Figure 1.6 Changing booking methods in the travel and tourism industry

Call centres

Almost everyone has experience of speaking to staff in call centres – they are widely used by banks and insurance companies as well as in the travel and tourism industry. Increasingly customers prefer to book travel by telephone or the internet rather than by visiting a travel agent. Figure 1.6 shows that 52 per cent of people polled are likely to book their holiday over the internet in the next 2 years, a big increase on those who have booked on it before. However, travel agents are still the most popular option.

Call centres are often in out-of-town locations where rents, rates and labour are cheaper. Some banks and other companies have relocated their call centres to India to take advantage of lower costs. Some call centres are operator- or airline-owned and sell on behalf of that company exclusively; others are specialist call centres and handle calls and bookings for many companies.

Call centres rely on high staff productivity to be successful. They motivate staff through incentives such as bonuses on sales targets reached. Call answering time, call durations, sales and complaints ratios are carefully monitored.

Online

Websites are the most up-to-date means of distributing travel and tourism products and services. Table 1.3 shows visits to some popular travel websites between 2005 and 2006.

You will learn more about travel agents in Unit 9.

Climbers: the old rockers	Jan 06	Jan 05	% Growth
• Thomson	• 5.92%	• 4.53%	• +31
• Thomas Cook	• 4.46%	• 2.45%	• +82
• First Choice	• 4.37%	• 3.11%	• +41
• MyTravel	• 4.18%	• 2.30%	• +82
Fallers: the new wave			
• Expedia	• 9.23%	• 9.27%	• –0.4
• Lastminute	• 5.30%	• 6.10%	• –13
• Ebookers	• 1.83%	• 2.44%	• –25
• Opodo UK	• 1.47%	• 1.68%	• –13

(Source: http://www.hitwise.co.uk/)

Table 1.3 Share of visits to selected travel websites, January 2006

Tourism development and promotion

The development and promotion of tourism in the UK is mostly undertaken by organisations in the public sector such as VisitBritain and VisitWales. Their role is described on pages 20–21. In addition, trade associations and regulatory bodies have a role to play in development and promotion as they represent the interests of their members and help them operate successfully in business. The relevant trade associations for each component of the travel and tourism industry have been discussed as we have studied each sector. In each sector of the industry, we have seen that there are regulatory and trade bodies whose role it is to advise members and represent them, particularly to the government. Ensure you have understood the role of each of these associations or regulatory bodies.

Ancillary services

This term refers to organisations who do not have a direct role in travel and tourism but play a supporting role, perhaps offering related products and services. Examples include insurance companies who offer travel insurance and car parks who operate parking facilities at airports as well as in other locations.

Interrelationships and interdependencies in the industry

We have examined the different components of the travel and tourism industry, and it is obvious that the various businesses cannot work in isolation. Each of them relies on others for its success. In this section of the unit we will examine how businesses work together, and who needs whom.

The chain of distribution is the means of getting the product to the consumer. It applies in any industry, and traditionally takes this form:

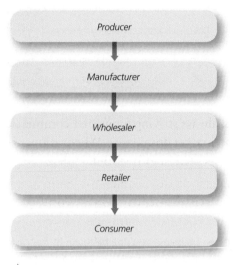

▲ Figure 1.7 Chain of distribution

In the travel and tourism industry there is also a traditional chain of distribution:

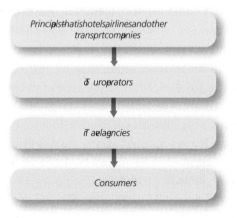

▲ Figure 1.8 Simple chain of distribution in the travel and tourism industry

In this traditional chain of distribution, businesses fit neatly into a category such as 'travel agency' and perform the role of that business. However, the industry is much more complex than that and in many cases the traditional chain has been shortened. Figure 1.9 gives some examples.

In addition, companies do not stick rigidly to one line of business. They tend to buy or merge with other

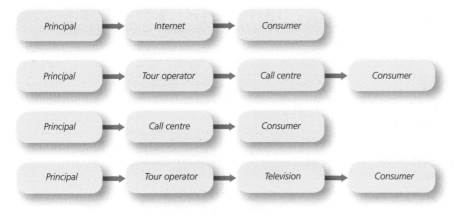

Figure 1.9 Chain of distribution in the travel and tourism industry

agencies, airlines and often hotels besides different tour-operating businesses. In fact, their operations are not limited to the UK; all are global operations.

The Thomas Cook Group has companies in all parts of the chain of distribution: airlines, hotels, tour operators, travel and incoming agencies. Its global and UK operations are described on its website.

The group encompasses 33 tour operators, about 3600 travel agencies, a portfolio of 76,000 controlled hotel beds, a fleet of 77 aircraft and a workforce numbering some 24,000. The company is represented in the sales markets of Germany, Great Britain, Ireland, France, Belgium, Luxembourg, the Netherlands, Austria, Hungary, Poland, Slovakia, Slovenia, Egypt, India and Canada.

The UK's third-largest vertically integrated leisure business comprises the tour operator brands Thomas Cook, Thomas Cook Signature, JMC, Neilson, Style, Club 18–30, Cultura, Time Off, Sunset, Sunworld Ireland and roomsandhotels.com. Under the tour operator brand, Thomas Cook, the company offers package holidays.

With more then 1500 outlets, ThomasCook UK is the market leader in the British travel agency business. It also owns Thomas Cook Airlines UK, Britain's second-biggest charter carrier with 24 aircraft.

(Source: http://www.thomascook.info/tck/de/en/nws; Thomas Cook Jobs website 2006)

businesses, always striving for greater commercial success and market dominance. When companies do this it is known as vertical or horizontal integration.

Vertical integration occurs when two companies at different levels in the chain of distribution merge or are bought. This may be backwards integration – for example, a tour operator buys a hotel – or forwards integration, for example a tour operator may buy a travel agency.

Tour operators have bought or created airlines, hotels and travel agencies. This means they own all the different components in the chain of distribution and are able to control the whole operation. They claim that this gives them economies of scale and allows them to offer better prices to customers. It can also mean that smaller operators are forced out of business.

Key term

Economies of scale – these occur when a company is able to spread its costs over mass-produced goods or services. Savings can be achieved through discounts for bulk purchasing, rationalisation of administration systems and management, and lower production costs.

If a tour operator buys another tour operator at the same level in the chain of distribution, this is known as horizontal integration. A recent example was the acquisition of the specialist schools tour operator Travel Class by First Choice in 2006. First Choice already runs a schools ski programme in France and owns a North American student tour operator.

All of the major tour operators in the UK are vertically and horizontally integrated, owning their own travel

At an Institute of Travel and Tourism conference in 2004, the chief executive of Thomas Cook UK explained why Thomas Cook had become a vertically integrated company: 'We were a successful retailer, but felt vulnerable without our own product. We also wanted to control the quality of the holidays we were selling – that was important for the brand.'

There are those, however, who think that vertical integration is no longer suitable for today's market, because it means that capital is tied up in assets and is subject to risk. Also, if customers do not want to buy from the high street agencies, many of the chain stores will close as tour operators invest in other types of distribution.

The not-for-profit sector

This sector includes public sector organisations, regulatory bodies and conservation groups.

The role of the not-for-profit sector is one of supporting and guiding different businesses so that everyone, including tourists, employees and management, can benefit from tourism while minimising problems.

Public sector organisations receive their funds from local or central government and usually aim to provide a service. Examples include the national and regional tourist boards and some visitor attractions. Funds for public sector tourism organisations come from central government through the Department for Culture, Media and Sport (DCMS) or from local councils. These organisations are judged on issues such as numbers of visitors achieved and quality, rather than on financial success.

In some countries the state owns and runs companies, re-investing the profits into other state ventures. Many transport facilities are state-owned, although not in the UK where privatisation has taken place. Privatisation means the state selling assets previously in the public sector to the private sector, to raise money.

Within the public sector in the UK, the DCMS is responsible for supporting the tourism industry at national level. In 1999, the government's overall strategy for the development of tourism was published in the report *Tomorrow's Tourism Today*. This policy was reviewed and updated in 2004 and a new statement of the roles and responsibilities in tourism of the DCMS, VisitBritain, Regional Development Agencies, local government and the Tourism Alliance was issued, covering the following areas for action:

- marketing and e-tourism
- product quality – introducing common standards for accommodation grading schemes
- workforce skills, supporting People First, the sector skills council
- improved data and statistics.

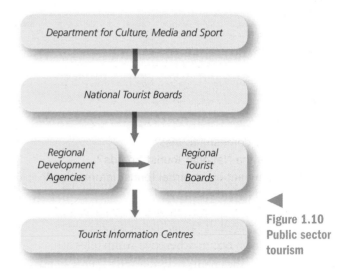

Figure 1.10 Public sector tourism

Other government departments have responsibilities for areas of tourism. The Department for Transport looks after aviation, railways, roads and the London Underground. The Department for Education and Skills (DfES) has responsibility for sector skills councils and training organisations. The Department for the Environment, Food and Rural Affairs (DEFRA) is responsible for issues affecting the countryside, wildlife and waterways, among others.

The structure of public sector tourism is shown in Figure 1.10.

The UK has four tourist boards: VisitBritain, VisitScotland, the Northern Ireland Tourist Board and VisitWales.

VisitBritain reports to the DCMS. VisitWales reports to the National Assembly for Wales and VisitScotland reports to the Scottish Executive.

VisitBritain

The role of VisitBritain is to market the UK to the British and the rest of the world. Formed by the merger of the British Tourist Authority and the English Tourism Council, its mission is to build the value of tourism by creating world-class destination brands and marketing campaigns. It also aims to build partnerships with other organisations which have a stake in British tourism.

Theory into practice

You will use the VisitBritain website (www.visitbritain.com) a lot during your studies as it is an invaluable tourism resource. Look at it now to find out the objectives of the organisation. Make a note of them and ensure you understand the terminology used. You should be able to answer the following questions.

- What is a domestic tourist?
- What are the National Tourist Boards?
- What is meant by impartial tourist information?
- Who funds VisitBritain?
- What is the current grant given to VisitBritain?
- What are Regional Development Agencies?
- Where are VisitBritain's overseas offices?

These organisations include the British Council, UKinbound, the British Hospitality Association and the UK Immigration Service.

Part of VisitBritain's role is to advise the government and other bodies on issues that might affect the British tourism industry. The aim is to provide advice that reflects the needs of both the tourism industry and the tourist, and to recommend courses of action to the government.

The overseas offices work closely with British diplomatic and cultural staff, the local travel trade and media, to stimulate interest in the UK.

Another example of the role of VisitBritain is its campaign to persuade high-spending tourists to come to the UK. It is important that inbound tourists spend money and boost the UK economy.

VisitBritain has launched a magazine called *So British*, aimed chiefly at high-spending US tourists, but also at emerging markets like Russia. The magazine features luxury British brands like Harrods, Barbour and Wedgwood, and carries articles on destinations in the UK.

VisitBritain owns the VB grading scheme, which is administered by the Regional Tourist Boards.

Regional Development Agencies (RDAs) and Regional Tourist Boards (RTBs)

Regional Development Agencies (RDAs) have responsibility for tourism in their regions and usually work closely with Regional Tourist Boards (RTBs).

From 2003 to 2006, the RDAs received £3.6 million per year from the DCMS specifically for tourism. This money was to be passed on to the RTBs until the end of 2005–6. The RDAs determined the objectives and targets the RTBs should meet in return for the funds. There is overlap between the roles of the RDAs and RTBs. Sometimes the tourist boards adopt a different name to explain more precisely what they actually do. An example is Marketing Manchester, the tourist board for Greater Manchester. Its role is to:

- provide destination leadership
- attract the visitor
- support the industry
- service the visitor.

These organisations are not totally dependent on government funding. Funds can be raised from business membership fees and from the provision of training courses to tourism organisations and employees.

Local authority tourism departments

Local authorities play an important role in supporting the tourism industry because of their statutory duties and because they recognise that tourism is a major contributor towards the economy. They have tourism departments and plans. Most towns also have a Tourist Information Centre (TIC). These are run independently – most are subsidised by the local council. They all rely heavily on generating income to ensure their financial viability.

The TIC provides a full information service for both residents and visitors. It gives information on visitor attractions and on accommodation. It usually provides a booking service for accommodation, and often incorporates a shop selling locally made crafts and gifts, as well as books of local interest. The shop is more than a service for visitors – it is an important means of generating funds.

Theory into practice

Visit your local Tourist Information Centre. Your teacher or tutor may wish to organise a group visit. Find out about the services it offers, and try to determine how many of its services generate revenue for the TIC. Discuss your findings with the group when you return.

Key term

Public limited company – a business that is owned by shareholders. Its shares are bought and sold on the London Stock Exchange. Avoid confusing this type of business with one which is 'in the public sector'. It is not the same thing. A business in the public sector is owned and usually financed and run by national or local government.

Conservation groups

Conservation groups are usually voluntary organisations with charitable status. Many are run by volunteers, although some have paid employees. They may be pressure groups, such as Greenpeace and Tourism Concern. Others, for example the National Trust, aim to preserve and protect historic buildings and landscapes.

Conservation groups do not aim to make a profit, but this does not mean they cannot be commercial. Any revenue they gain will be re-invested to further the aims of the group.

Profit sector

Most organisations in the travel and tourism industry are privately owned. These organisations may be huge companies like British Airways or small businesses. They usually aim to make a profit and are commercial companies. When they fail to make a profit over a period of time they are likely to cease trading. All theme parks, restaurants, tour operators and travel agents in the UK are privately owned. There are different types of private ownership ranging from sole trader to public limited companies. Sole traders are small and run by one person, as the name suggests. A public limited company is listed on the stock market and is owned by its shareholders who may buy and sell shares as they see fit.

Roles and responsibilities

We have looked at the roles and responsibilities of various organisations as we have discussed the various components of the travel and tourism industry. However there are some general points to be made about how roles and responsibilities may differ from sector to sector.

The not-for-profit sector:

- Provides services which benefit the public or the community
- Provides the services at rates that make them accessible to all – often subsidised
- Provides services which are beneficial to society, e.g. promote health
- Reinvests any profits in the organisation
- Depends mainly on government grants or donations for funding.

The profit sector:

- Makes profits for shareholders
- Remains competitive
- Achieves company objectives, e.g. growth in market share or improved company image.

Since the 1960s, the travel and tourism industry has changed dramatically. It is unlikely that your grandparents had regular holidays abroad unless they were quite wealthy, but today foreign travel is within the reach of almost all segments of society. In this part of the unit we are going to look at the key developments that have made the possibility of travel open to almost all of us.

Legislation

The UK government has always recognised the importance of tourism to the economy and has introduced new policies and laws over the years.

Development of Tourism Act 1969

The Act established a British Tourist Authority and tourist boards for England, Scotland and Wales. The British Tourist Authority and the English Tourism Council have now been merged to form VisitBritain, which is described earlier in this unit. The Act's aim was to co-ordinate all the organisations that make up the tourism industry and provide it with a single voice. Since this Act was passed the responsibility for tourism funding and development in Scotland and Wales has been devolved to the Scottish Parliament and the Welsh Assembly. Also, VisitScotland and VisitWales have been given the power to market overseas independently of VisitBritain. This has caused a lack of clarity in the role of VisitBritain, as its role is to market Scotland and Wales as well as England.

Transport Acts 1980 and 1985

The 1980 Transport Act ended licensing regulations affecting express coach routes and tours of over 30 miles. It led to competition between National Bus (then a public company) and private companies. The 1985 Transport Act brought about wholesale deregulation. This meant private companies could operate on any route.

Key term

Deregulation – this occurs when a government decides to remove restrictions on the operation of a business to allow greater competition and hopefully greater efficiency and reduced prices for customers.

Air passenger duty

In 1996, air passenger duty was reduced on economy flights, removing a barrier to the growth of inbound tourism. However, in 2006 it was greatly increased.

Tourism strategy

In 1999, *Tomorrow's Tourism Today*, the government's tourism strategy, was published. It is still valid, although it has been reviewed.

Package Travel, Package Holidays and Package Tours Regulations 1992

As a result of an EC Directive, since 1992 all UK tour operators offering package holidays have been subject to the Package Travel Regulations. The regulations set out the tour operators' responsibilities to their customers and what those customers can do if the regulations are breached.

Product development

Holiday camps

Billy Butlin was on holiday in Skegness in the 1930s when he noticed a group of miserable holiday makers, sitting on a bench in the rain. They had nowhere to go as, in those days, when you stayed in a boarding house you were expected to leave in the morning and not come home until the evening, rain or shine. He saw the opportunity of providing for these people and decided to open a holiday camp. It opened in Skegness in 1936.

The concept was very popular and attracted about 2 million visitors a year. The appeal of Butlins was that it provided, on one site, all the facilities and entertainment a family could wish for, including childcare, swimming lessons, bingo and ballroom dancing. Between 1945 and 1960, holiday camps were at their peak, catering for about 60 per cent of the holiday market. Warners and Pontins were other important names in the market. The holiday camp went into decline in the 1970s as demand for sunshine and package holidays abroad grew.

Butlins still exists and is owned by the Bourne Leisure Group. See the case study in Unit 3 to find out what has happened to Butlins.

Holiday parks

A forerunner to Center Parcs was opened in 1968. It was in Holland and named De Lommerbergen. Piet Derksen developed the concept. Derksen liked to escape from everyday life and get back to nature. His idea was for 'a villa in the forest'. He built 30 luxury villas and an outdoor pool in a forest in Limburg, constructing everything to harmonise with nature, a rule which still applies today. This park was the birth of a company which has since expanded throughout Europe, Center Parcs.

Center Parcs leads the short-break holiday market in the UK. The first park was opened in 1987 at Sherwood Forest. It offers short-break holidays, with midweek or weekend breaks all year round, and longer stays if desired. Center Parcs achieves occupancy figures of over 90 per cent at all its villages and repeat bookings of more than 60 per cent within a year. Elveden Forest opened in August 1989 and Longleat in 1994. A competitor, Oasis, was acquired in 1997. The following case study gives a description of one of the parks from the Center Parcs website.

Case study: Sherwood Forest

Opened July 1987, 786 villas, 39 apartments, 400 acres, up to 4206 guests per break. Eleven themed restaurants and bars, five retail outlets and an extensive range of indoor and outdoor sport and leisure facilities. Most of the restaurants, bars and shops are in and around the Village Square, the open centre of the Village, where the Subtropical Swimming Paradise is also located. The newly opened Aqua Sauna is an outstanding Spa facility. Indoor sports facilities are mainly located in the Jardin des Sports, quite close to the Village Square and also containing the Time Out Club for children and teenagers. There is a separate Country Club in another part of the Village, with an additional restaurant and bar and sports facilities including a golf driving range.

(Source: http://www.centerparcs.co.uk)

▲ Figure 1.11 Sherwood Forest village

1 Carry out some research to find out what Center Parcs' future plans are. Try looking on the internet at the websites of publications such as *Leisure Opportunities* (www.leisuremedia.com) or *Business Week* (www.businessweek.com), or at the BBC News website (news.bbc.co.uk/). You might find out what has happenned to plans for a fifth Center Parc at Warren Wood near Woburn, where a £160 million development was planned.

2 What changes in society and consumer expectations have contributed to the success of Center Parcs? **P4**

3 Find out about another holiday centre (not Butlins) and compare it with Center Parcs.

Package holidays

Thomas Cook is credited with being the first person to organise a package holiday. That was a trip from Loughborough to Leicester by train – not very far at all! It was in 1841. The first package as we know it today was in 1949 and was organised by Vladimir Raitz. He took 32 passengers to Corsica on a DC3 aeroplane. He charged them £32.50. The package included accommodation in tents, return flights, transfers and full board. He established Horizon Holidays in the same year, and by the end of the 1950s the company had grown to be one of the UK's major tour operators.

Other companies followed Horizon's example and package tours grew in popularity. The major growth came in the 1970s as people became more prosperous and keen to see new places. Most of the package holidays were to Spain and its islands, where hotels were built rapidly to fulfil the demand from British and German tourists.

Currency restrictions were lifted in the 1970s; before this, tourists were allowed to take only £50 in sterling out of the country. This led to an increase in the appeal of the package holiday as tourists could take more spending money with them.

Destination development

As the world realises the economic benefits tourism brings, more and more governments plough money into attracting tourists from overseas.

Dubai has constructed hotels, residential developments and shopping centres to attract tourists and added the infrastructure and transport links to bring the tourists in. There are few places in the world where tourists have yet to venture. Some more examples of 'new destinations' are given on page 32.

Technological development

One of the areas of greatest impact through new technology has been in the way bookings are made. Bookings in the period following the Second World War (1939–45) were simple to make, as airlines and tour operators had charts on the walls of their offices and took bookings by telephone or by post. These charts were fairly efficient but were of course subject to human error, and double bookings could easily arise.

As demand for travel grew, reservations departments were introduced. With the advent of computers, tour operators and airlines developed their own systems. Eventually these systems were linked to travel agencies via terminals, and travel agents could make bookings in their offices. These are known as 'Viewdata' systems. Thomson decided to accept bookings only through Viewdata, which meant that the system was essential for any travel agent. By today's standards Viewdata is unsophisticated technology, although it is still used.

Meanwhile, airlines developed computer reservation systems (CRS). Airlines started to use computers in the 1950s to store the huge amount of information they needed to access. The CRS was used internally by airlines, and agents would use a publication called *OAG* (the *Official Airline Guide*) to look up flight times and details, then telephone the airline to make a booking. Today travel agencies have direct access to the CRS systems. Global Distribution Systems (GDS) link up several CRS systems and present them to the travel agent.

Internet booking – unpackaging

The internet is growing rapidly as a means of booking holidays and flights. The growth in internet booking can be attributed to the low-cost airlines, which educated passengers in how to book quickly and easily via the internet and offered discounts for doing so. With increased confidence and access to information, travellers happily book all aspects of their holiday online and in effect make their own packages. Travel agencies will have to redefine their role as this trend continues.

Theory into practice

Use the internet to package your own imaginary holiday to Majorca. You will be travelling with a friend for a week. You will need to find a flight, a suitable hotel and car hire. Do not use any resources other than the internet. Make notes on the products available, the web addresses and the costs. (Stop before you get to the final booking page!)

Self check-in at airports

Where this service is available, passengers can save time by checking in at a kiosk where they can choose their seat and print their own boarding pass. From there they can go to a 'fast bag drop' and leave their hold baggage. Passengers without baggage can go straight to the boarding gate.

On line check-in for airlines

Using this system, passengers can check in without even being at the airport. From home or the office they go online and follow instructions to check in, choosing their seats and printing their boarding passes. Online check-in is used by several airlines including Ryanair, reducing queues at check-in desks.

Transport development

Aviation

The aviation sector in travel and tourism includes airlines and airports, and the industry is heavily dependent on this sector for transporting passengers to their destinations.

During the Second World War great advances were made in the development of aviation – in the building of planes, in navigation and communication, and in flight procedures. When peace returned to Europe it was possible to put these resources into civilian travel. There were also many RAF-trained pilots available for employment. These developments meant that aircraft became important for leisure travel.

The first British fully jet-powered passenger aircraft, the de Havilland Comet, was put into service in 1949. In 1954, two of the earlier models crashed in the Mediterranean, and services using the plane were suspended. In 1954, Boeing introduced its new passenger jet aircraft, the Boeing 707, and when it began commercial service in 1959 it dominated the market. In 1963, the Boeing 727 was introduced, one of the most successful series of passenger jetliners of the past 50 years.

In 1969, Boeing produced the 747 Jumbo Jet, a wide-bodied jet. The 747 can seat 500 passengers, though it usually holds 385. It cruises at about 965 kilometres per hour and has a non-stop range of just over 11,500 kilometres. It usually has a forward first class (or 'business class') section and a second level on which the cockpit and a lounge are located. This aircraft had the following impact on the package holiday market:

- it became possible to fly further in less time, making long haul destinations more accessible
- increased capacity on the jet led to a decrease in the price per seat, bringing the price of holidays down
- as jumbo jets were used more, smaller aircraft were available for charter operations.

In 1976, British Airways, in collaboration with Air France, started the first supersonic airliner service, Concorde. Concorde ceased flying in 2003 but it had set the standard for luxury air travel.

■ Introduction and growth of low-cost airlines

Deregulation of air travel in Europe led to the development of low-cost airlines. The European Union (EU) started the liberalisation process in 1987, when cost-related fares and certain types of discount fares were first allowed. The final stage of deregulation came in 1993.

What deregulation meant was that EU airlines could establish themselves in any EU member state and obtain an operating licence. All routes within the EU are available to all EU carriers. Thus an airline such as Ryanair can have a base in Frankfurt Hahn and fly to and from countries all over the EU. In 1994, easyJet launched a low-cost airline offering two routes from Luton to Glasgow and Edinburgh. Now there are about 77 low-cost airlines flying travellers all over Europe.

In 2004 there was much expansion in routes as the EU grew to 25 states. The new member states in eastern Europe brought opportunities for travel to and from these countries. EasyJet introduced flights to Budapest (Hungary), Ljubljana (Slovenia) and Bratislava (Slovakia). Ryanair flies to Riga in Latvia.

The impact of the low-cost airlines on the travel and tourism industry has been to encourage people to travel more and to gain new travellers – that is, people who were unused to travelling abroad but were attracted by the low prices. Many of the low-cost airlines operate from regional airports, so travel is even more convenient for people in the regions, who now have direct flights to many destinations.

In December 2001, the first non-stop flight went around the world without refuelling. In 2004, the longest non-stop passenger flight yet was launched by Singapore Airlines. It flies from Singapore to New York, over the North Pole, in 18 hours, with no need for a refuelling stop.

In 2001, the unmanned aircraft Global Hawk flew automatically from Edwards Air Force Base in the USA to Australia non-stop and without refuelling . Although the technology will soon be in place for passenger aircraft to fly unmanned, it remains to be seen whether people will accept this.

■ Super planes

The Airbus A380 is on its way. The aircraft can seat between 555 and 800 passengers. It is expected that there will be a range of activities on offer on board, including Jacuzzis! Virgin Atlantic has ordered six of these to start delivery in 2007. However, airports which accept the aircraft have to make changes to infrastructure in order to accommodate the large plane and the large numbers of passengers boarding and disembarking. Some airports are reluctant to make such changes until major American airlines have committed themselves to these huge aircraft.

Another new aircraft is the 7E7 Dreamliner introduced by Boeing. It has lower operating costs and fuel consumption than the current Boeing 767 and a greater flight range, so it is expected to be a popular choice for airline fleets. For example, this plane can fly from the UK to Hawaii non-stop. First Choice, the tour operator, has ordered six.

Consider this

How long do you want to be in the air without stopping? Do you think such long flights will cause health problems for passengers and crew?

Sea

■ Channel Tunnel

A tunnel under the English Channel between France and England was just an idea for many years. But in 1986 the Anglo-French Channel Tunnel Treaty was signed and the idea became reality. The tunnel would allow the British to leave their island without flying and without risking seasickness, and encourage our continental neighbours to visit the UK.

In 1987, the boring for the tunnel began in the UK. The tunnel opened in 1994. Its original budget was £4.8 billion but its final cost exceeded £10 billion. Ten major British and French construction companies were involved in the building of the tunnel, collectively known as 'Transmanche'.

Theory into practice

The French call the English Channel 'La Manche'. Do you know, or can you find out, what this word means?

■ Super ships

A new £36-million passenger ferry has been created by a French naval architect, Gilles Vaton. It is called a Bateau à Grande Vitesse (BGV), which means high-speed boat. The biggest boat will carry 1200 people and 250 cars, or 1000 lorries as a cargo ship. Because of its high speed, the ferry cuts the journey from Portsmouth to Caen in France from 6 hours to under 3, and the 20-hour journey from Marseilles to Algiers to 9 hours. High speed is not the boat's only advantage – there are already fast catamarans operating as ferries – but the BGV can maintain its speed in all weathers, whereas the catamarans have to stay in port in rough weather.

On the French Riviera, the local council is thinking of buying a small version of the BGV, carrying 350 passengers, as a means of sea transport between Monaco and St Tropez. The aim is to reduce congestion on the Riviera's roads.

Figure 1.12 The TGV high-speed train offers fast travel across France

Rail

■ High-speed trains

High-speed train lines, such as France's extensive Train à Grande Vitesse (TGV) network, have helped maintain the success of the railways in some countries. The TGV is operated by the French nationally owned and subsidised rail company, the SNCF. The TGV travels at speeds of over 300 kilometres per hour.

The European high-speed rail network has been extended and TGV services now run direct from Paris, the Channel Tunnel and Brussels towards Germany. The Belgian high-speed trains are known as Thalys. It is important to note that such trains require new tracks to run on, which means substantial investment.

The Eurostar service through the Channel Tunnel is operated with TGV trains, but the track on the UK side of the tunnel has only recently been renewed. New track reduces the journey time of the UK leg from London by almost half.

For the future, in order to compete with low-cost airlines, international train services in Europe will need to be overhauled. The European Commission wishes to open up competition in cross-border passenger rail links, including high-speed links like Eurostar and Thalys, to increase price competition between rival operators by 2010.

Rail's proportion of the total EU passenger travel market has been falling for some time: it dropped from 10 per cent in 1970 to 6 per cent in 1998, according to European Commission data.

Lifestyle changes

Pattern of taking holidays

In 2004, the then education minister Charles Clarke gave the go-ahead for plans to change the school year to a six-term year. The school year is now divided into terms of more equal length than the old three-term system. This will impact on holiday seasons for tour operators and should lead to more even prices during July and August. It is hoped there will be less demand in the summer as parents have more choice of when to take a holiday. It is a recognised problem that children are being taken out of school to go on family holidays during cheaper periods, and the new arrangement of terms in the school year may solve this to some extent.

Another change in holiday patterns is that people are taking more short breaks. There has been an immense growth in this market, both within the UK and with people travelling abroad. Cities are very popular destinations, especially London, New York and Amsterdam.

Increased income and expectations

We are wealthier as a nation and have higher expectations than in the past. Most people have been abroad and most expect to take at least one holiday a year; this is in contrast to previous generations. People's income can be described as follows:

- gross income – pay before deductions like tax, National Insurance, etc.
- net income – pay in hand after deductions (also known as disposable income)
- spending money – the amount left over after essential outgoings such as rent or mortgage payments (also known as discretionary income).

Discretionary income is important in the travel and tourism industry because without it people are less likely to go on holiday or travel. Fortunately, most people have a greater discretionary income these days, and travel is relatively cheap.

Official figures show disposable income rather than discretionary income, as it is easier to measure.

Key terms

Disposable income – what's left after tax, National Insurance and pension contributions are deducted from pay.

Discretionary income – what's left after essentials like rent or mortgage, food and the cost of travel to work are deducted from disposable income.

Improved education

The government aims to improve the level of education achieved by people from all sectors of society. It aims to get more students into university and more of the population achieving at least a Level 2 qualification, for example a GCSE.

The more educated we are, the more we are aware of the world and its possibilities. We are curious about different cultures and languages and keen to experience them. As we live in a multicultural society we are more familiar with different religions, foods and cultures and less anxious about the unfamiliarity involved in travelling to new places.

More leisure time

The increase in leisure time can be attributed to several factors.

Most households have a range of labour-saving appliances, including dishwasher, washing machine and microwave. This means the household chores are not the drudgery they once were and we are free to use our time to do other things.

People are also living longer. One of the most important markets in travel and tourism is the 'grey' market. This refers to older people who have plenty of time and available funds and want to travel. Older people these days are usually in good health due to the success of the National Health Service and the availability of good food. Contributing to private pension schemes over their working years has led to a good income in retirement for many people. If the mortgage has been paid off and the children have left home, older people can party! Saga is the most famous tour operator catering for older people, but all tour operators are aware of and market to this group.

It has become common for people to retire earlier, even in their fifties, and take advantage of good pension arrangements. This trend will reverse in the future as many pension schemes have experienced difficulties, and the government is also encouraging people to work longer. As the older section of the population increases, the younger working people cannot generate enough in taxes to support a large section of the population not working. This is a concern for the British government, which is constantly reviewing pension schemes to find ways around the problem.

It is a legal requirement for employers to give their staff paid holidays, and now most UK employees receive at least four weeks' holiday a year. This had led to people being able to take more holidays than the traditional summer break, and many people also take a winter holiday and/or several short breaks. Those who benefit from flexitime working can arrange their hours so that they are able to take weekend breaks.

How we spend our leisure time varies greatly according to taste, age, income and expectations. There is, however, an increase in demand for travel and attractions to visit.

Numbers employed in travel and tourism

There are an estimated 1.4 million jobs in tourism in the UK, some 5 per cent of all people in employment. Approximately 130,400 of these jobs are in self-employment.

	Total (millions)	Tourism-related (millions)
Total employment	28.4	1.42
Employee jobs	24.6	1.29
Self-employment	3.6	0.13

(Source: Labour Market Trends, April 2005; http://www.tourismtrade.org. uk/MarketIntelligenceResearch/KeyTourismFacts.asp)

Table 1.4 Employment in tourism-related jobs

Table 1.5 shows where most jobs are in travel and tourism and in hospitality.

	2003–4
Restaurants	518,700
Hospitality services	402,000
Contract food service provision	179,600
Gambling	74,000
Hotels	247,100
Youth hostels	2300
Visitor attractions	10,600
Holiday parks/self-catering accommodation	51,400
Travel and tourist services	114,700
Pubs, bars and nightclubs	368,400
Sector total	**1,968,800**

(Source: Labour Force Survey, average of four quarters)

Table 1.5 Workforce by industry

Contribution to countries GDP

Key terms

Gross Domestic Product (GDP) – the value of all final goods and services produced within a country in a given period of time.

Balance of payments – one of the UK's key economic statistics. It measures the economic transactions between the UK and the rest of the world. It tells us the difference between spending on imports and exports.

Tourism contributes to the economy and therefore to the GDP as visitors spend money on goods and services and also on transport to enter a country.

The impact on the economy of incoming and outbound tourism is recorded in the balance of payments. Each sector of the economy is measured in terms of its imports and exports. Travel services have their own balance which contributes to the overall balance of payments. Unfortunately, the travel services balance shows a deficit (£15.8 billion in 2003) and has done for some years. This means that more money is spent by UK residents travelling overseas than by inbound tourists and domestic tourists. Transport is shown separately from travel services.

Activity

Find out what the current travel balance is. You can find this in *The Pink Book*, a government publication, in your library or online. Look at the transport balance also. Is there a deficit or a surplus? Discuss your findings with your teacher or tutor.

Trends affecting development

As people become more affluent they are able to take more frequent holidays. This had led to the popularity of the short break, often to a city.

Nights	Percentage of trips
1	29
2	27
3	15
4	9
5	5
6	3
7	6
8–13	3
14	2
15+	2
Average	3.37

(Source: United Kingdom Tourism Survey 2004)

Table 1.6 Duration of all domestic tourism trips taken by UK residents, 2004

Paris, Amsterdam, Bruges and Rome were 2004's top four destinations.

Greater flexibility of booking

As people become more confident about travel and more used to travelling abroad and seeing different cultures, they are able to book the component parts of their holiday themselves rather than go to a travel agent. This is most likely to happen for more frequent lower-priced trips. When people are spending a lot of money, for example on a wedding or cruise, they are more likely to seek expert advice from a travel agent. Many people now have access to the internet at home and are able to carry out research into travel and destinations and make their own bookings online. Websites like Expedia have profited from internet growth by providing the ability to make up holiday packages, selecting flights and accommodation as desired. In spite of this ABTA still reported sales of 18.5 million package holidays sold in 2005.

More independent travellers

According to a 2004 Mintel report ('Independent Holidays UK'), the number of independently booked holidays exceeded the number of package holidays taken for the first time in 2003. The rise in independent travel is set to continue to an estimated 55 per cent of all holidays. This is almost entirely due to the internet. It is not only young travellers who go independently but also more upmarket customers who plan their own luxury trips but want value for money. However, it is not expected that the package holiday market will decline completely as it offers convenience and in some instances cheaper packages.

Adventure travel

There is no one definition of adventure travel. Surveys have shown that some adventure holidays include activities such as birdwatching and cultural activities. Others perceive adventure holidays to include extreme sports and risk taking. In spite of the difficulty of defining adventure travel, it is clear that organisations offering 'adventure travel' report increased interest and increased bookings.

Tour operators are aware of the trend and have created or acquired activity or adventure holiday businesses. An example is TUI UK who acquired Explorers, the dive operator, in 2006. TUI UK has a specialist active and adventure division.

Consider this

What is your idea of an adventurous holiday? Birdwatching or extreme sport?

New destinations

Tourists are constantly looking for new and more exciting destinations. These days there are very few new

▲ Figure 1.13 Tourists on a diving holiday

destinations to visit as improved transport has made almost everywhere accessible. ABTA carries out its own research through its members and predicts that the following destinations will rise in popularity, but for different reasons.

■ New Zealand

According to ABTA the islands regularly top travel surveys and more and more British people are choosing to visit them. New Zealand offers beautiful scenery with rainforests, glaciers, fjords and geothermal pools. It has a lot to offer for adventure tourists, as white-water rafting, jetboating and bungee jumping are all available. The *Lord of the Rings* films have also been an influence in attracting visitors to New Zealand.

■ Croatia

Croatia could be described as a revamped destination as it was a popular resort for UK travellers before the Balkan wars in the 1990s. At that time Croatia was part of Yugoslavia. Now that the area is peaceful again more and more tourists are going, not only for its beauty but because it is relatively cheap. The popular areas are the beautiful resorts of Dubrovnik, Split and Rovign on the Dalmatian coast. There are also hundreds of idyllic islands dotted along the coast and it is ideal for sailing.

■ Bulgaria

The UK is Bulgaria's third-largest market after Germany and Greece. Bulgaria has a lot to offer; it has beaches along the Black Sea coast, lively cities and skiing in the winter. It is improving all the time with investment in infrastructure and new hotels.

■ Tasmania

Another destination growing in popularity according to ABTA is Tasmania. It lies off the coast of south-east Australia. Tasmania has one of the most beautiful beaches in the world, Wineglass Bay. It also has a World Heritage site, Cradle Mountain Lake St Clair.

Theory into practice

ABTA reports that eastern European destinations are seeing a surge in demand. Write a short informal report for a travel agent. Make sure you give examples of specific destinations.

1 Describe the key trends and factors that have led to an increase in demand for eastern European destinations. **P5**

2 Analyse the effect of these factors on the future development of the travel and tourism industry. **M3**

Taking it further

Recommend how travel and tourism organisations could adapt to the increase in demand for eastern European destinations. **D2**

Growth and expansion of regional airports

The UK government has a policy of expansion for regional airports, demonstrated by growth at Stansted, Manchester, and at smaller airports like Coventry or Robin Hood airport in Doncaster. Such expansion has advantages in that it takes some pressure off London airports and brings tourists into the regions, boosting their economy. Much of the increased capacity at Stansted and Liverpool is due to the growth of the low-cost airlines.

Factors affecting development

Natural disasters

Natural disasters, such as hurricanes and earthquakes, bring about a decline in tourism. They are considered an 'Act of God' and not covered by insurance, so, if a flight is delayed for technical reasons passengers will be compensated, but if a plane is struck by lightning, they will not.

Climatic disasters have a devastating impact on destinations and on their tourist industry. Recent examples include the hurricane of 2003 which hit Grenada badly, the hurricane of 2005 in New Orleans and the tsunami in the Far East in late 2004. The tsunami resulted in thousands of deaths across twelve countries. The human death toll was appalling but the livelihood of the survivors is also threatened because of the devastation of infrastructure and the hesitation of tourists to return to the area.

Health warnings and epidemics

Foot and mouth disease had a devastating effect on travel and tourism in the UK in 2001. Animal, rural and farm-based attractions were badly affected by the crisis caused by the disease. Overall, 26 per cent of attractions were forced to close for part of their normal opening season in 2001.

Fortunately, figures from the following year saw a large increase in visits to farms, gardens and countryside attractions, as tourism recovered from the outbreak: farm visits were up 50 per cent.

In the winter of 2002–3 an outbreak of the respiratory disease SARS affected tourism, particularly in the Far East. People were discouraged from travelling to and from countries which were affected, such as Hong Kong and Canada. This had an impact on the UK economy as these countries provide many of the UK's inbound tourists.

Terrorism

The devastating terrorist attacks of 11 September 2001 in the USA also had an impact on the UK and the worldwide tourism industry. People were afraid to fly, particularly American tourists, resulting in a decline in visitors to the UK and a decline in worldwide travel for leisure and for business.

The impact of 9/11 has been long term. Security is high priority at airports, passengers easily become alarmed and there are many incidents of planes diverting or being delayed due to zealous security checks or panic incidents. Travel insurance has risen as some companies have reviewed their policies to include terrorist incidents which are normally excluded. On a positive note, international organisations have had to work together to respond to security threats.

In October 2002, a terrorist bomb in Bali resulted in over 200 deaths. The tourism industry in Bali was ruined, and only began to pick up again 2 years later.

There have been similar bombings in Istanbul, elsewhere in Turkey, in Kenya, Madrid and London over the past few years. Each of these events results in a loss of tourism for the area involved until travellers begin to forget about the incidents and feel safer.

Environmental issues

As society and government policy become more 'green', the awareness of tourists about environmental issues grows. This leads to a demand for responsible travel and an expectation that travel and tourism companies will act in an environmentally friendly way. These issues are explored in detail in Unit 11.

Cost of travel

Travel is relatively cheap today, particularly air travel. The advent of low-cost airlines has brought down the price of air travel and many people take advantage of this to take frequent short breaks in addition to their main holidays. Long haul travel prices are more fluid but there are often bargains to be had. For example, tight security restrictions in the summer of 2006 and the inconvenience of travelling without travel essentials on flights to the USA led to a reduction in bookings for transatlantic airlines. Fares were reduced to entice passengers back and the resulting fares were some of the lowest ever, with returns to New York from £160.

New products and services

Different holiday products have been developed to meet changing consumer demand. Demand for shorter, more frequent holidays has led to city break products. As consumers have become more aware about the dangers of sunbathing, they demand active or adventure holidays. Those seeking safety and reassurance about the cost of a holiday before they go can choose an all-inclusive holiday.

Another area of growth is the 'spa' holiday. Massage and special treatments and activities like yoga are included in the price of the holiday. Many hotels are now described as 'spa hotels'.

The increase in car ownership has meant that people choose to drive to their destination rather than take a train or a coach. It also led to a demand for car use on holidays. If you have access to a car at home why not when you are away? This demand has brought about the growth of a huge car hire industry operating internationally. Tour operators developed 'fly drive' holidays to give customers flexibility.

The wedding market has been developd into an extensive product range. About 50,000 couples get married abroad each year, according to ABTA. Although exotic holidays are expensive, they are much cheaper than a traditional wedding at home. Some couples persuade a few friends to holiday with them to attend the wedding. The top destinations for weddings abroad are the Caribbean, Sri Lanka, Mauritius and Florida.

Some companies have found their niche in catering for particular types of activity holidays. One example is Cycling for Softies. It provides bikes and all the equipment you might need at the starting point of your holiday. The cycling is fairly gentle and each night is spent in a different hotel along the route where the holidaymakers can relax and enjoy dinner.

Assessment practice

Look in the quality newspapers and find examples of events, trends or factors that have affected the travel and tourism industry in the past week.

1 Describe these events, trends or factors and how they have affected the industry. **P4** **P5**

2 Explain how such events, trends or factors are likely to affect future development of travel and tourism. **M3**

Taking it further

Say what you think the industry could do in response to such events or factors. Recommend courses of action and give your justifications. **D2**

Grading tips

Examples of events to look for include natural disasters, heatwaves, transport strikes, the introduction of new products or technology and outbreaks of war.

To reach Merit level you need to think about whether the event will impact on demand for products, how products and services are delivered and the profitabilty of travel and tourism companies.

Knowledge check

1 How did the development of low-cost airlines impact on travel and tourism?

2 What is meant by deregulation?

3 What are the elements of a package holiday?

4 Give an example of legislation affecting tourism in the UK.

5 What are the problems affecting the UK railways?

6 Describe the different methods of distributing travel and tourism products to consumers.

7 Why is Croatia increasing in popularity as a holiday destination?

8 What is the difference between scheduled and charter airlines?

9 What are the drawbacks of accommodation grading schemes?

◆ How do call centres motivate their staff?

1 Who are the major tour operators?

2 What is horizontal integration?

3 What is vertical integration?

◆ Which government department is responsible for tourism?

5 What is the role of a Tourist Information Centre?

◆ What is the role of the AUC?

End of unit assessment

Preparation for assessment

Your college has a thriving travel and tourism department and wishes to ensure its continued success. In order to do this it wants to carry on recruiting students who are enthusiastic about the industry and interested in pursuing a career in one of its diverse sectors. Each year the college holds two open days and these are well attended and efficiently organised, but the students who come have already decided they are interested in travel and tourism and are easy to recruit.

Your tutor thinks it would be a good idea to 'spread the word' about travel and tourism, and proposes a road show for local secondary schools. The purpose is to spend half a day in each school mounting an exhibition/information session/interactive activities for Year 10 pupils. This will differ from the usual careers evening sessions in that it will be organised by students and it will be about the travel and tourism industry, not just the courses. It is hoped that the students will be so enthused by what you tell them that they will come flocking to college to study travel and tourism.

For the following tasks you might produce a display with illustrations and explanatory notes, and an information sheet to be distributed to students.

1   To give students an overview of the industry, describe the components of the industry. To do this effectively you should include the following:
   - a description of the different components   **P1**
   - an explanation of the ways that the components interrelate.   **P2** **M1**

Grading tip

To reach Merit level on this task you must ensure you have examples of organisations within the components that cover domestic, outbound and inbound tourism.

2   Students need to understand the roles and responsibilities of organisations in travel and tourism. Add the following to your display:
   - a description of the roles and responsibilities of travel and tourism organisations, including at least one from each sector   **P1**
   - a comparison of the roles and responsibilities of travel and tourism organisations from different sectors   **M2**
   - an assessment of how the roles and responsibilities of organisations from different sectors affect their operations.   **D1**

Grading tips

To reach Merit level, you could produce a comparative chart with explanatory notes.

To reach Distinction level, you need to give examples of organisations and how their aims impact on what they do, for example an organisation in the not-for-profit sector will not spend extravagantly on advertising and will have to account for all spending very carefully. Any surplus will be re-invested in projects.

3   Students need to know about the development of the travel and tourism industry. Add to your display:

- an explanation of recent developments that have shaped the present-day travel and tourism industry **P4** **M3**
- an explanation of key trends and factors that will affect the development of travel and tourism **P5** **M3**
- recommendations with justifications on how the industry could respond to key trends and issues affecting the future development of travel and tourism. **D2**

Grading tip

To reach Merit level, analyse how developments have shaped travel and tourism. **M3**

This could be represented in a timeline with pictures and detailed explanatory notes. The difference between a Pass and a Merit is that to reach Pass level you need to say what the key developments were and when they occurred. To reach Merit level you must show an understanding of the effect of the development. For example, to reach Pass level you should mention the introduction of low-cost airlines, to reach Merit level you must say that this has led to an increase in demand for short haul holidays as passengers can access cheap flights from regional airports such as Stansted and Liverpool.

To reach Distinction level, you might discuss how rising fuel prices affect airlines, the prices of seats and consequently holidays. You should recommend courses of action for airlines or tour operators to deal with this problem and justify your recommendations. **D2**

Grading criteria

To achieve a pass grade the evidence must show that the learner is able to:	To achieve a merit grade the evidence must show that, in addition to the pass criteria, the learner is able to:	To achieve a distinction grade the evidence must show that, in addition to the pass and merit criteria, the learner is able to:
P1 describe (giving examples including domestic, inbound and outbound tourism) the components of the travel and tourism industry **Assessment practice page 6**	**M1** explain how the components of travel and tourism interrelate, giving examples that include domestic, inbound and outbound tourism **Assessment practice page 6**	**D1** assess how the roles and responsibilities of travel and tourism organisations from different sectors affect their operations **Case study page 12**
P2 describe the ways that components of travel and tourism interrelate **Assessment practice page 6**	**M2** compare the roles and responsibilities of travel and tourism organisations from different sectors **Case study page 12**	**D2** recommend and justify how the travel and tourism industry could respond to key trends and issues affecting the future development of travel and tourism **Case study page 12**
P3 describe the roles and responsibilities of travel and tourism organisations from different sectors **Case study page 12**	**M3** explain how recent developments have shaped the present day travel and tourism industry and how key trends and factors are likely to shape the industry in the future **Theory into practice page 33**	
P4 describe recent developments (from the 1960s onwards) that have shaped the present day travel and tourism industry **Taking it further page 15**		
P5 describe the key trends and factors that will affect the development of travel and tourism **Assessment practice page 33**		

The business of travel and tourism

Introduction

In Unit 1 you were introduced to the different sectors in the travel and tourism industry and you looked at some examples of organisations within the sectors. This unit investigates features of organisations in terms of their operation and the importance of good financial performance.

The management of cash flow is very important to an organisation's success. In this unit you will learn how to complete a cash flow forecast. You will look at how to interpret figures in a cash flow forecast and analyse problems within it, and you will be given the opportunity to consider solutions for such problems.

You will also have an opportunity to plan a travel and tourism project taking into account financial constraints.

Finally, you will investigate how travel and tourism organisations seek to gain competitive advantage over each other.

After completing this unit you should be able to achieve the following outcomes:

1   Know the features of different types of travel and tourism organisations

2   Be able to complete a cash flow forecast

3   Be able to plan a travel and tourism project within financial constraints

4   Understand how a travel and tourism organisation gains competitive advantage to achieve its aims.

Thinking points

This unit provides you with an introduction to the business world that will be invaluable to your understanding of how travel and tourism businesses operate, and how any business operates. Although you are studying travel and tourism now, you may find yourself in another industry one day – for example, there is much overlap between the IT industry and others. Everyone needs to learn about technology these days, and what you learn here will stand you in good stead and help you understand business affairs.

You may decide in the future to start your own business. Does that seem very ambitious? As you proceed through this unit you will find out about some very enterprising people who started up businesses; some are small operations and others have grown into multinational companies. You, too, might one day start your own travel and tourism business and this unit will give you the basic information you need. On the other hand, if you decide to work for a major company, you will have an understanding of how it operates and the support systems it needs.

A good example of a successful set-up can be found in the story of Lastminute.com. Have you heard of the organisation? If not, look at its website before you read on.

Case study: Lastminute.com

The idea for a website selling holidays at the last minute at cheap prices came from Brent Hoberman. Martha Lane Fox was a colleague of his and became involved in the idea; the two of them worked together on the company's business plan for 8 months. Lane Fox and Hoberman bought the Lastminute.com domain name for £5000 in 1998. They needed to raise capital to start their business and this proved to be difficult as, at that time, people didn't fully understand the internet and its potential. Hoberman and Lane Fox had to reassure investors that the internet would take off.

It did, and the company now offers customers everything to do with going away, going out and staying in, including package holidays, short breaks, hotels, flights, train tickets, theatre tickets, restaurants and sports events. It also offers home food delivery, DVD rentals and personalised TV listings. Everything is available at the last minute, which is defined as within 3 months.

Martha Lane Fox attracted a lot of publicity and was interviewed in papers and magazines, gaining interest in the new venture. In March 2000, at the height of the dot.com boom, Lastminute.com was floated on the stock market. The company's share price rose to a high of 487.5p. Lastminute.com shares rose 28 per cent on the first day of trading, representing a valuation of £732 million and earning the company £113.5 million. Lane Fox personally had a fortune of £40 million. However, in 2001 the dot.com bubble burst, and the Lastminute share price fell to an all-time low of 18.75p. Lane Fox's fortune was now only £9 million.

At this point many dot.com businesses went bust, but Lastminute.com staged a strong recovery. In 2003,

Lastminute.com announced its first full-year profit, £200,000, against losses of £16.2 million a year earlier. Martha Lane Fox decided to resign from her post as managing director. She was only 30 years old, and her 3.6 per cent stake in the company, which she still has, was then worth about £26 million.

Since those exciting early days, Lastminute.com has become the most recognised e-commerce brand in London and the second most recognised in the UK. The company owns and operates online brands holidayautos.com, travelprice.com, degriftour.com, travelselect.com, travel4less.co.uk, eXhilaration.co.uk, medhotels.com, first-option.co.uk, gemstonetravel.com, onlinetravel.com. In July 2005, the company was acquired by Travelocity Europe Limited, part of the Sabre Holdings Corporation. Brent Hoberman remained as Chief Executive.

1 **Lastminute.com is an intermediary (middleman). What do you think might happen to it as more and more suppliers, such as airlines, sell their products directly on the internet?**

2 **Why do you think Lastminute.com has a policy of acquiring different companies?**

3 **Why was it, in turn, bought by Travelocity?**

Taking it further

Find out who Lastminute's competitors are – compare the services and products on offer and find out how they are performing financially. Make a chart comparing the organisations.

Types of organisation

Non-profit sector

In Unit 1 you were introduced to the profit-making and non-profit-making sectors.

Many not-for-profit organisations are public sector organisations who receive their funds from local or central government and usually aim to provide a service. Examples include the tourist boards and some visitor attractions. (Many examples are given in Unit 1.)

Not-for-profit organisations are judged on issues such as numbers of visitors achieved and quality, rather than on financial success. In some countries the state owns and runs companies, re-investing the profits into other state ventures. Many transport facilities are state-owned, although not in the UK where privatisation has taken place. Privatisation means the state selling assets previously in the public sector to the private sector, to raise money. The following case study gives an example.

Theory into practice

Find out which travel and tourism organisations in your area are in the public sector. Compare your findings with your group.

Profit sector

Most organisations in the travel and tourism industry are privately owned and aim to make a profit. These organisations may be huge companies like British Airways, or small businesses. When they fail to make a profit over a period of time they are likely to cease trading.

All theme parks, restaurants, tour operators and travel agents in the UK are privately owned. There are different types of private ownership, ranging from sole trader to public limited companies. Organisations can have many different forms of ownership affecting liability, how profits are distributed and control. We will look at the different types in this section, remembering that they are not mutually exclusive.

Case study: privatisation of hotel chain

Dublin Airports to sell €150 m+ hotel portfolio
22 May 2006

The state-owned Dublin Authority Airport has put its eight-strong Great Southern Hotels chain up for sale.

The six four-star and two three-star hotels for sale are located at the DAA-owned Dublin, Shannon and Cork Airports, Parknasilla and Killarney in County Kerry, Eyre Square and the Corrib in Galway city and Rosslare Harbour in County Wexford.

The sale process, which will be carried out by public tender with a deadline for bids of 23 June 2006, is expected to conclude in late August or early September.

In a statement the GSH board said it was 'pleased with the level of informal expressions of interest in the hotels to date as recorded by the agents for the properties, CBRE'.

According to the *Sunday Business Post*, more than 100 enquiries have been received, with the hotels expected to fetch a total of €150 m–€200 m (£102 m–£136 m). The paper reports that the DAA is selling the chain because of its continuing losses – it is forecast to lose €8 m this year – which are hindering the authority's ability to fund the construction of a second terminal at Dublin Airport.

1 Why do you think the Irish government is allowing the sale of these hotels?

2 What is meant by 'public tender'?

3 What are the advantages and disadvantages of privatisation?

Types of ownership

A small independent firm usually operates as a sole trader. This means that the owner is personally responsible for all amounts owed to creditors and the government. It also means that should the sole trader not be able to make suitable arrangements to settle any debts, personal possessions will be taken by creditors. Although this is a simple business set-up, sole traders are very vulnerable because if their ventures fail, they can lose everything including their homes. A sole trader has the advantage of full control over their business.

Partnership

This is when two or more people combine to form a company; the maximum number of partners allowed by law is 20. Each partner receives a percentage of the return of the business, depending upon how much they invested. Each partner is responsible for all the debts incurred by the business, no matter which partner incurred them. The partners usually retain the profits in the business and pay themselves a regular salary.

If you were to set up in business, would you be prepared to risk everything you have? Many people do as they are so sure they will be successful.

Co-operatives

Co-operatives belong to members rather than to share-holders. They operate for the benefit of their members. Co-operatives are democratically controlled by their members, and they believe in supporting the community and campaigning for a fairer world – these are just some examples of how the co-operatives' values and principles, which are shared by all co-operatives, are put into practice. A list of co-ops in the UK can be found at www.cooponline.coop.

Key term

Co-operative – a co-operative is an autonomous association of persons united voluntarily to meet their common economic, social and cultural needs and aspirations through a jointly owned and democratically controlled enterprise (The International Co-operative Alliance Statement on the Co-operative Identity, Manchester 1995).

Private limited company

There are different types of private companies – the differences lie in the amount of liability the owners have if the company goes bankrupt. Private limited companies issue shares that can be bought and sold only with the permission of the board of directors. If the company goes bust each shareholder's liability to pay the company's debts is limited to the amount of company shares that they own. This means that they cannot be asked to put any further money into paying the company's debts. It is also possible to set up a private company limited by guarantee. In this case, the owners agree on liability limits when they set up the company. This structure is often used to limit the personal liability of directors.

There are also private unlimited companies, where there is no limit to liability. This is very dangerous as if the company goes bust the directors will be liable for the debt and could lose all their assets including their homes.

Most small businesses are private rather than public limited companies.

A private limited company has to have at least one director and a company secretary – these cannot be the same person.

At the end of the year, the board of directors decides whether to pay dividends to shareholders depending on how much money the company has made. Dividends are paid in relation to the number of shares held by an individual. Shareholders have to pay tax on dividends.

Key terms

Private limited company – a company which is not listed on the Stock Exchange and usually has limited liability.

Public limited company (plc) – a public company which is limited by shares and has share capital. Shares are offered for purchase by the general public. Only public limited companies may qualify for listing or trading on the Stock Exchange.

Share capital – the money raised by selling shares in a business.

▲ Figure 2.1 London Stock Exchange

Public limited companies and flotation

The shares of a plc can be traded on the Stock Exchange.

A company can become a plc only if it has share capital of £50,000, at least two shareholders, two directors and a qualified company secretary.

A business is said to be floated when it enters the stock market for the first time. It first has to meet the criteria described above. The advantages of floating your company are:

- you get back the money you invested in the company and hopefully a lot more – remember Martha Lane Fox!
- you issue shares and therefore raise new capital to develop your business
- you can motivate your employees by issuing shares to them
- it is good for your reputation – it shows you are an established company
- it is easier to acquire other businesses – you can use shares in your existing company to trade, as well as cash.

Of course, there are also disadvantages:

- share prices can go down as well as up and the value of your business fluctuates with them
- you will need a lot of professional advice to carry out the flotation, and this is expensive
- there is always a risk of a takeover
- shareholders will have a say in the running of the company
- public accounts have to be issued.

■ Board of directors

The board of directors is a group of people who are elected by the shareholders of an organisation and have the responsibility of overseeing the running of the organisation. Public companies usually have executive and non-executive directors. One member of the board will be appointed chairman. Sometimes the board may be referred to as a board of trustees or a board of governors. If you are studying at a college, for example, you will hear of governors rather than directors but their function is the same. Charities usually have trustees, for example Earthwatch Institute (Europe) has a board of trustees who are responsible for the governance of the charity and overseeing its strategy and direction.

Key terms

Executive director – usually a full-time employee of the company who also has management responsibilities.

Non-executive director – someone paid an annual fee to attend a number of board meetings and contribute to decision-making. They are invited onto the board because of their experience and skills.

Case study: Holidaybreak

The Board of Directors

The Board of Directors is currently made up of six Executive Directors, three Non-executive Directors and the Chairman. Each Non-executive Director and the Chairman is considered to be independent of management and free from any business or other relationship which could materially interfere with the exercise of their independent judgement. The positions of Chairman and Chief Executive are not combined, ensuring a clear division of responsibility at the head of the Company. Collectively, the Non-executive Directors provide broadly-based knowledge and experience to the Board's deliberations. The complementary range of financial, operational and entrepreneurial experience ensures that no one Director or viewpoint is dominant in the decision-making process. Appointments to the Board are made after receiving recommendations from the Nomination Committee.

The practice is to appoint Non-executive Directors for specified terms of 3 years, subject to 3 months' notice within that period and also subject to re-election and to Companies Act provisions relating to the removal of a Director. Re-appointment is not automatic. New Directors appointed by the Board must submit themselves for re-election by shareholders at the Annual General Meeting following their appointment.

Thereafter the Company's Articles of Association require that all Directors stand for re-election at intervals of not more than 3 years. The Chairman will confirm to shareholders when proposing re-election that, following formal evaluation, the individual's performance continues to be effective and they continue to demonstrate commitment to the role. Procedures are in place to ensure that all Directors are provided with appropriate and timely information, and Directors have access at all times to the advice and services of the Company Secretary. The Company Secretary is responsible for ensuring good information flow, that Board procedures are followed and that applicable laws and regulations are complied with. Directors are able to take independent professional advice, if necessary, at the expense of the Company.

(Source: Holidaybreak plc Annual Report and Financial Statements 2005. © Holidaybreak plc)

1 What type of organisation is Holidaybreak?

2 Describe the features of Holidaybreak. **P1**

3 Describe the features of a co-op (see page 44). **P2**

4 Compare the features of Holidaybreak and a co-op. **M1**

5 Explain the difference between executive and non-executive directors at Holidaybreak. **P1**

6 What are Articles of Association? **P1**

7 Why do you think it is important that directors are not dominant in the decision-making process? **M1**

Taking it further

1 Find out what the role of a company secretary is.

2 Choose another travel and tourism company and find out (from the annual report) how the board is made up.

Consider this

The annual report also tells you how much directors get paid and how many shares in the company they hold.

Franchise

A franchise is a type of ownership which allows an individual to start up their own business but to minimise the risks by being part of an existing organisation. An organisation, the franchisor, sets up a contract with the person wanting to enter the business, the franchisee. The contract includes the following:

- permission to trade under the corporate name

Case study: travel and tourism franchise

The Global Travel Group is an example of a travel and tourism franchise. It offers franchisees the chance to start their own travel businesses from home or an office. The Global website shows what is on offer:

- a complete induction to The Global Travel Group, including an introduction to the travel industry for those who require it
- an introduction to Global technology, sales, marketing and customer service
- follow-up training and regular workshop seminars covering a wide range of topics including business management, industry developments and NVQs in most travel-related subjects.

(Source: http://www.globaltravelgroup.com)

1 **What are the benefits of taking on a franchise?**
2 **What are the drawbacks of taking on a franchise?**

You can find out more about franchising from the British Franchise Association.

- assistance and advice in running the business
- provision of stock and trading materials
- help in finding premises.

In return the franchisee must pay a premium, and a percentage of the revenue earned by the new business.

Business policies

Takeovers

Sometimes a business has a policy of acquisition, of buying out other companies. Look back to the case study on Lastminute.com for an example. Companies take over other businesses to grow and to reduce the competition.

Takeovers happen constantly in travel and tourism. Recent examples include the purchase of the Southlands Hotel in Scarborough by the coach company Shearings. Shearings already owns 37 hotels in the UK. This is an example of vertical integration.

Takeovers can be friendly or hostile – a hostile bid means that a company management does not want the company to be taken over, but the decision must be made by the shareholders.

Key term

Vertical integration – when companies merge or one takes over another at different levels in the chain of distribution.

Mergers

A merger differs from a takeover in that two companies agree to become one. Mergers can, however, result from takeovers. An example is the merger in 2004 of two city-break companies: Bridge and Cresta. Both companies had previously been taken over by the MyTravel Group. Cresta and Bridge were rivals and this had not changed since they became part of MyTravel. The two companies were located in separate parts of the country with their own managements. The merger will help avoid duplication as the companies share one management team in one location, and costs are reduced. There is no reason to get rid of the brand names, as both can be retained.

Theory into practice

Find out what the current situation is with Cresta and Bridge. Research on the internet and find out if both brands still exist and whether they are in competition. Check also on the parent company. Discuss your findings with your group.

Public–private partnerships

This type of partnership is a collaboration between a public body, such as a local authority or central government, and a private company.

The Labour government in the UK wants to expand the range of public–private partnerships because it believes it is the best way to secure the improvements in public services that Labour promises. The government believes private companies are often more efficient and better run than bureaucratic public bodies. Some consider that management skills and financial expertise from the private sector can create better value for money for taxpayers. These partnerships are in services like health, but there are often public–private partnerships in tourism as governments cannot afford to resource new developments by themselves. Many local Tourist Information Centres form public–private partnerships to offer a conference organisation service to business. The TICs liaise with contacts in the private sector and charge a fee for arranging venues and facilities.

Distribution of profits

If an organisation makes a profit, the directors have to decide what to do with it. The usual course of action is to distribute the profits amongst the shareholders but the board must recommend how much to pay, as in the extract from the Holidaybreak Annual Report below. They may wish to retain some of the profits to expand the company or invest in new projects. Payments made to shareholders are called dividends and are paid each year or half year. Sometimes, if a company is doing badly, they are not paid at all.

> *The Board is recommending a final dividend of 19.35p (2004: 17.6p) payable on 25 April 2006, to shareholders on the register on 31 March 2006, making a total of 26.6p (2004: 24.2p) for the year.*
>
> *The 10 per cent increase in the annual dividend reflects the Board's confidence in future prospects. The Group is financially strong and has a clear strategy to grow, both organically and by acquisition, adapting to and exploiting the rapidly changing market place. The Board intends to continue to pay ordinary dividends that are appropriate in light of the growth prospects and the underlying performance of the Group.*
>
> (Source: Holidaybreak plc Annual Report and Financial Statements 2005. © Holidaybreak plc)

Key term

Dividend – a share of profits made as a payment to a shareholder.

Sources of finance

If you are setting up in business you will need enough set-up capital to run the business until it begins to make a profit. Companies of all sizes also have to raise funds from time to time to finance growth, new ventures or takeovers. Various sources of finance are available according to the nature of the business and its ownership.

Family and friends

Many small businesses are financed by families and can grow to be huge family enterprises. Friends may wish to invest in a business and reap profits without hands-on commitment.

Banks

Banks are an obvious source of funds and they can offer loans. A loan is an amount of money borrowed for a set period and with an agreed repayment schedule. The repayment amount will depend on the loan size and the interest rate. The bank will lend only if the money is guaranteed, which may mean using a house as security or a family member as guarantor. Banks will also probably ask to see a business plan.

Overdraft facilities are also available from banks. These are more flexible than a loan as an individual has an agreed overdraft amount and can borrow what they need up to that limit. It is very quick to arrange an overdraft and you don't need to provide so much security, but if you do exceed the agreed limit you will have to pay penalties and this can be expensive.

Grants

There are many sources of grants and in travel and tourism the Regional Tourist Board is able to advise on possible sources. Grants are usually from government or EU funds; they are one-off payments and do not have to be repaid, nor does interest have to be paid. There are strict criteria for eligibility when applying for grants, and a grant will not usually be given for the full cost of a project or venture.

Case study Tourism Capital Grants Scheme

An example of a grants scheme was the Tourism Capital Grants Scheme in the East of England region. The scheme finished in 2006. To be eligible for a grant, the proposed development had to:

- involve capital spending and a tangible new asset (maintenance and repairs not included)
- provide facilities for tourists, as opposed to the local community
- have planning permission
- have a total eligible capital cost of over £6000
- conform to VisitBritain minimum quality standards on completion of the project
- be a member of, or join, a marketing organisation
- be committed to training
- provide paid employment

.(Source: http://www.eetb.org.uk/)

1 **Discuss with your group the kind of projects you think would be eligible for this grant scheme.**

2 **Why is it necessary to join a marketing organisation?**

3 **Why is training mentioned?**

Taking it further

East of England has introduced another grant scheme relating to training. Visit the website and find out if tourism businesses would be eligible for this funding.

UK finance

The National Lottery is a source of grants. The DCMS has responsibility within government for National Lottery policy but does not award the grants. There are six lottery distributors: the Arts Council of England, Sport England, the Heritage Lottery Fund, the Millennium Commission, the National Lottery Charities Board and the New Opportunities Fund.

The extract below describes how the Heritage Lottery Fund aims to distribute the Grant it is responsible for.

> *The Heritage Lottery Fund helps groups and organisations of all sizes with projects that aim to conserve and enhance the UK's diverse heritage; encourage more people to be involved in, and make decisions about, their heritage; and make sure that everyone can learn about, have access to and enjoy their heritage. Heritage includes many different things and places that have been and can be passed on from one generation to another. Among these are the countryside, parks and gardens; objects and sites that are linked to our industrial, transport and maritime history; records such as local history archives, photographic collections or oral history; historic buildings; and museums and gallery collections.*

(Source: http://www.hlf.org.uk/English/AboutUs/)

Camelot runs the lottery games and is responsible for the provision of lottery terminals and promoting the National Lottery. Camelot takes no part in awarding lottery grants.

Commercial companies whose aim is to make a profit are rarely eligible for grants as grants come from public funds.

European finance

The European Regional Development Fund was set up in 1975 to stimulate economic development in the least prosperous regions of the EU.

The EU has three other funds within it. These are the European Social Fund (ESF), the European Agricultural Guidance and Guarantee Fund and the Financial Instrument for Fisheries Guidance. It is the ESF that is relevant to tourism as it provides opportunities for business support and development through training.

Theory into practice

Go to the National Lottery website (www.national-lottery.co.uk) and find out which organisations related to travel and tourism have been awarded lottery grants. Remember they are likely to be in the heritage sector. Discuss with your group what the funds were spent on.

Shareholders

One way of raising funds is to issue shares in a company. Individuals buy shares and become part owners of the business with voting rights. When profits are distributed they are shared amongst the shareholders as dividends. If the company does not make any profit there are no dividends. Issuing shares is a type of private equity finance. As stated earlier, public companies must have at least £50,000 of share capital. If a company needs more money to expand or undertake a new venture, it can issue new shares to raise the finance.

Companies can hold shares in other companies too. Table 2.1 shows the main shareholders in MyTravel. Remember that these often change as shares are bought and sold.

Goldman Sachs	9.70%
JP Morgan Chase & Co.	8.21%
Legal & General	6.63%
Morgan Stanley Securities	5.98%
Credit Suisse First Boston	5.93%
Pardus Capital Management	5.10%
Barclays	4.78%
Merrill Lynch	4.27%
Standard Life Investments	3.84%
Deutsche Bank	3.47%

(Source: *Travel Trade Gazette*, 11 August 2006)

Table 2.1 MyTravel's main shareholders

Venture capital

Venture capital is also known as private equity finance. Venture capitalists are often major companies which will invest large sums of money in return for shares in a business. They are looking for a high earning potential and a return on investment within a specified time. In other words, they expect the company to grow and be sold on very quickly at a large profit.

Venture capitalists are experienced at business and bring expertise and advice. They will require financial projections and will exert a great deal of control over the business. The former airline Go was at one time owned by the venture capitalists 3I. They backed a management buyout of £110 million to buy the airline from the founder, British Airways. About a year later, they sold it to easyJet for £374 million.

The British Venture Capital Association helps larger businesses locate venture capital companies.

Business angels

Shareholders may be business angels. These are wealthy individuals interested in investing their own funds in growing companies. They do not usually invest in very large corporations, but in start-ups. Most investments are less than £75,000.

They are often people who have experience of running a business and therefore are a source of advice. There is a National Business Angels Network whose role is to bring potential angels and businesses together.

Documentation needed to set up a business

If you decide to set up a limited company then you will need to complete several documents and submit them to Companies House.

Key term

Companies House – an executive agency of the Department of Trade and Industry responsible for company registration in the UK. There are more than 2 million limited companies registered in the UK.

Certificate of Incorporation

Incorporation is the means of registering a business as a company with Companies House. An application is completed and submitted with all the company details. If the application is successful the registrar of companies issues a Certificate of Incorporation – from this point the limited company is formed. In Northern Ireland the process is handled by the Companies Registry.

Memorandum of Association

This document gives the name and location of the company and describes the nature of its business. It also shows the amount of share capital in a company and how it is divided. If you are setting up a business with others you decide on how many shares each will have and sign the memorandum. The money paid for the shares is kept by the company and does not have to be repaid – although dividends from profits will be paid to shareholders. Employees are sometimes given shares in a business or an option to buy shares at a preferential price.

The following extract from the Holidaybreak Annual Report explains the company's Sharesave scheme.

Sharesave Scheme

The Company runs an annual Sharesave Scheme that allows employees of Holidaybreak to save regularly for a period of three or five years. Options over shares in Holidaybreak plc are granted at a discount to the share price at the time the contract is entered into. On maturity, employees receive a tax-free bonus on savings and are able to use the savings and bonus to buy shares in the company.

Folllowing maturity of two schemes this year, Superbreak employees were featured in a national newspaper. The article highlighted the benefits to employees of joining employee share ownership schemes.

(Source: Holidaybreak plc Annual Report and Financial Statements 2005. © Holidaybreak plc)

Consider this

Why might it be advantageous for employees to have shares in a business? Do you think they would have greater loyalty to the company?

Articles of Association

This document explains how the company will be run, what rights the shareholders have and what rights the company directors have.

Support on setting up a business can be found from the following sources:

- Stockbrokers offer general financial advice on corporate finance-related transactions. They can advise on mergers and acquisitions, disposals, equity issues and flotation.
- Solicitors advise on legal matters and ensure the company operates according to current legislation. Some large companies employ their own solicitors.
- Banks are not only a source of funds but handle all financial transactions and can give advice on financial matters.

- Auditors check the final accounts and accounting systems of companies.
- Registrars deal with all matters relating to registration and certification of shares and making dividend payments.
- Business Link is managed by the Department for Trade and Industry, a government department. It provides invaluable advice for those setting up their own businesses. It is also possible to attend subsidised training courses run by Business Link on many aspects of business.
- Trade associations are very important for business support, particularly for small and medium-sized businesses which are less likely to employ experts in the different areas of business. The associations represent the interests of their members and press for changes needed in trading conditions or legislation by consulting with relevant bodies and lobbying government. In addition the associations provide advice and information to their members and try to keep them up to date with events which may affect their businesses. Examples of trade associations include the Association of British Travel Agents (ABTA) and Air Travel Organisers' Licensing (ATOL). The relevant trade associations for each sector can be found in Unit 1.
- Enterprise bodies are usually set up by government but are not government departments. They operate independently from ministers, although ministers remain accountable to Parliament for their performance. Scottish Enterprise and Highlands and Islands Enterprise are examples of enterprise bodies set up to deliver economic development policies through a network of 22 local enterprise companies. They are funded by the Scottish Executive and aim to help new businesses get under way and support and develop existing businesses. These do not have to be travel and tourism businesses.

Theory into practice

Regional Development Agencies are enterprise bodies and support business development. Find out about your local Regional Development Agency and whether it supports any travel and tourism projects. Other members of your group could investigate different regions. Compare notes and discuss your findings.

EasyJet has its main base at Luton airport, and its offices are named 'Easyland'. EasyJet is a low-cost airline and offers over 170 routes from 50 European airports.

The airline was started in 1995 by Stelios Haji-Ioannou. He started with two routes from Luton to Glasgow and Edinburgh. His father owned a shipping line and he received money from his father to start up the airline. Although it is now a listed company on the Stock Exchange, the family remains the major shareholder.

In August 2002, easyJet bought another low-cost airline, Go, at a cost of £375 million, boosting the growth of easyJet.

During the financial year to 30 September 2005, the company reported pre-tax profits of £67.9 million on a turnover of £1341 million and carried 30 million passengers. Haji-Ioannou has started up several other 'easy' brands and has sold £19 million of his shares to do so. He calls this 'selling his past to finance his future'. His start-up businesses included easyInternetcafé and easyCar.

Haji-Ioannou could have raised finance from banks, business angels or venture capitalists but these sources would have meant letting go of control of his businesses.

1 Describe the features of the easyJet organisation, including its ownership, distribution of profits, sources of finance and how it is controlled. **P**

2 Compare the features of the easyJet organisation with those of a non-profit-making company. Draw up a comparative chart. **M**

The easyJet annual report is available on the internet.

Grading tip

To reach Merit level, make sure you explain the differences between the two types of organisation.

Figure 2.2 An easyJet plane

In this section you will be introduced to the principles of cash flow forecasting and learn why cash flow is important to the success of a business. If you are setting up a business you will be expected to present a cash flow forecast as part of your business plan.

Key term

Cash flow – the assessment of money coming into a business and money going out at any given time.

You will have heard of the expression 'strapped for cash'. It may refer to you when you are waiting to get paid for a Saturday job and yet you need money to buy a birthday present or have a night out. In business terms it may mean that you are waiting for payments due in from customers and yet you don't have the cash right now to buy stock or pay an essential bill.

What happens to you in this situation? Do you decide to manage better next month and either borrow money or forego the night out? A business might not have the opportunity to do better next month as by then it may have gone bust. It is essential that it manages cash flow so that these difficult cash situations don't occur.

If you are setting up a business you will need some cash reserves to keep you going until payments from customers start to come in.

Consider this

Cash flow and profit are not the same thing. Think of your bank balance at the end of the year – you may be in the black but have had occasions during the year where you struggled to pay for things.

Companies may make a profit when everything owed is paid in but have problems throughout the trading period. These problems can be significant in the travel business when flights, hotels, etc. have to be booked a long time before the customers pay for them.

What does cash inflow include?

- Payments for sales from customers – that is, receipts from sales and VAT on sales
- The cash put aside to start up the business – start-up capital
- Interest on savings
- Shareholder investments
- Overdrafts or loans.

Cash outflow includes:

- Payments to suppliers, e.g. hoteliers, transport
- Payments on fixed assets, e.g. company office
- Loan repayments
- Overheads, e.g. rent, wages, electricity and telephone bills
- Purchase of fixed assets, e.g. computers
- Stock, e.g. stationery or raw materials.

Key terms

Balance brought forward – money carried over from the previous month.

Balance carried forward – difference between net cash flow and the balance brought forward. The net cash flow shows the difference between total payments and income.

Preparing a cash flow forecast

The forecast can be divided into three parts:

- forecast revenue – that is, cash inflow
- forecast expenses – that is, cash outflow
- the balance.

We will look at an example of a travel website designer whose trading follows the tax year from 1 April to 31 March the following year. We will look at cash flow for 6 months.

Sales are forecast to be £5500 per month. Customers are given credit terms of one month, so the cash inflow occurs one month after the sale.

Expenses will be:

- Rent £1000 per month – no arrears
- Computers, printing, stationery, etc. £250 per month
- Salary £2000 per month – payable each month
- Electricity £75 per quarter – first payment in June
- Travelling £200 per month.

The carried forward bank balance is £3000.

This information can be entered into a table or spreadsheet.

Below is an example of a cash flow consolidated account from the Accor Group Annual Report 2005. Consolidated means that it is no longer a forecast but an actual account of cash inflow and outflow for the year. (Note that figures in brackets represent expenditure.)

	2004	2005
Funds from operations	853	935
Renovation and maintenance expenditure	(314)	(449)
Free cash flow	539	486
Expansion capex*	(680)	(479)
Proceeds from asset disposals	429	313
Dividends paid	(284)	(287)
Proceeds from issue of share capital	312	822
Other	75	(31)
Decrease in net debt	391	824

*Capital expenditure which includes purchase of new equipment.

(Source: Accor Group Annual Report 2005)

Table 2.2 Cash flow consolidated account (sums in million euros)

▼ **Figure 2.3 Cash flow forecast for a website designer**

	April	May	June	July	Aug	Sept
Revenue (inflow)						
Sales	–	5500	5500	5500	5500	5500
Expenses (outflow)						
Rent	1000	1000	1000	1000	1000	1000
Computers etc.	250	250	250	250	250	250
Salary	2000	2000	2000	2000	2000	2000
Electricity	0	0	75	0	0	75
Travelling	200	200	200	200	200	200
Total expenses	3450	3450	3525	3450	3450	3525
Net cash flow	–3450	2050	1975	2050	2050	1975
Opening balance	3000	–450	600	3575	5625	7675
Net cash flow	–3450	2050	1975	2050	2050	1975
Closing balance	–450	1600	3575	5625	7675	9650

Note there is no revenue in the first month — Sales

All the monthly expenses added up — Net cash flow

Opening balance is always the same as the closing balance from the month before — Opening balance

The difference between inflow and outflow — Net cash flow

Closing balance is the difference between opening balance and net cash flow — Closing balance

Assessment practice

1 Study the example shown in Figure 2.3 and make sure you understand it. Then think about the following.

What would happen if:
- sales are expected to dip to £500 in June
- the company decides that from May it will advertise at a cost of £700 every 2 months
- the car is scheduled for service at a cost of £1000 in August?

2 Update the cash flow forecast using a table or a spreadsheet. **P3**

Consider this

Accounting software is available to help with completing cash flow forecasts. See if your teacher or tutor has a package you can practise on.

Cash flow management

Cash flow has to be controlled – businesses can't afford to wait and see what happens and hope for the best. Keeping an eye on cash flow means that potential problems can be identified and dealt with. Before making any major buying decisions you can make sure you have enough cash and, if necessary, arrange to borrow. It is a good idea for a business to have a contingency fund so that there is some cash for emergencies.

Ways to improve cash flow

Improving cash flow means getting money in as quickly as possible and delaying payments out as long as possible.

Getting the money in

Ask for information. A business needs to know if its customers are credit worthy. For example, if a customer pays for a holiday by credit card the travel agent is assured of payment – the credit card company has already vetted the customer's credit worthiness. For business customers, a company can get a credit reference from a bank. This doesn't guarantee payment but does give some confidence in ability to pay.

- Ask customers to pay upfront.
- Chase non-payers immediately.
- Borrow money (if you can afford to pay it back!).

Stopping the money going out

- Keep a tight control on stock and orders from suppliers.
- Check payment terms with suppliers – ask for good credit terms.
- Don't buy equipment and assets, lease them.

Case study: Safari Specials

Joe Jensen, the managing director of Safari Specials, was devastated to report to his staff that the company had gone bust after 12 years in business. Jensen was unable to pay his bills and tried in vain to secure a rescue package from the banks. Trade had been going very well about 4 years ago and Jensen decided to move into a new office and employ new staff. Overheads increased from £900,000 in 2003 to £1.6 million in 2004. Just after, a key manager left and set up in competition with Safari Specials taking staff with her. Jensen decided to take action. He cut staff and cut capacity, reducing the number of safari destinations on offer. However, it was too late, Jensen had accommodation bills that were due, as he had committed to long-term contracts for accommodation that had to be paid for in advance, as well as flights to pay for. The company folded with debts of about £4 million. A competitor suggested that the company had overcommitted on flight seats for May and June, many of which remained unsold.

1 **Identify the cash flow problems experienced by Safari Specials.** **M2**

2 **Suggest how Jensen might have managed the cash flow situation.** **D1**

Case study: changing circumstances may affect cash flow

Ticketing site gives agents a 10 per cent rate

AGENTS can make up to 10 per cent commission by selling tickets and city breaks from Concierge Desk's new online service.

The site offers tickets to shows such as the West End production of *Billy Elliott*, and to attractions such as the Tower of London and the London Eye.

Coach and guided tours of London, Bath and Oxford are also available.

Agents can register for free at conciergedesk.co.uk.

They can then use the password-protected site to sell and print out tickets, and earn commission for every booking.

(Source: *Travel Trade Gazette*, 14 April 2006)

Princess refunds bug-hit cruise

PRINCESS Cruises has given partial refunds to all 2200 passengers on a ship that was struck by an outbreak of vomiting bug norovirus.

Agents were asked to pass the 30 per cent refunds on to all passengers on *Sea Princess*, which returned to Southampton a day early after 250 people were hit by the bug.

Princess Cruises UK director Peter Shanks said 'every inch' of the ship was disinfected after she returned to port, and it had since embarked on a fourteen-night Mediterranean cruise.

There was also a small outbreak on the ship's previous cruise, in the same week that Travelscope and Fred Olsen ships were hit by infections.

Shanks said there was no evidence the two outbreaks on *Sea Princess* were linked and it was possible the virus, which was widespread in the UK, could have been brought onboard by a passenger.

(Source: *Travel Trade Gazette*, 9 June 2006)

Interest rise spells gloom

HARD-pressed agents struggling to make a living could find the screw tightening further as interest rate rises force prices even lower.

David Pope, a financial analyst specialising in travel for Brewin Dolphin Securities, warned that the Bank of England's decision last week to increase the cost of borrowing from 4.5 per cent to 4.75 per cent could be the start of an economic trend that would hit agents' pay packets hard.

Pope said if interest rates were to go up again, the value of the pound would strengthen, which could in turn lead to yet cheaper holidays as prices are adjusted to account for a more valuable UK currency.

'If the world's markets believe UK interest rates will continue to rise, sterling will get stronger, making holidays cheaper,' he said.

The price of holidays – and the amount of commission agents get for selling them – could also be squeezed if potential customers who borrowed heavily while interest rates were low tightened their belts to pay off more expensive loans, overdrafts and credit card charges.

(Source: *Travel Trade Gazette*, 11 August 2006)

Study these extracts from the travel trade press. Explain the impact on cash flow of each of the situations described. Discuss your ideas with your colleagues.

Financial records

Every organisation, from the sole trader to the largest company, has to produce financial records. A sole trader must, at least, record incoming cash and outgoings and produce a tax return. A plc is required to publish a full set of formal accounts.

Case study: fuel price rises cause concern for airlines

Fuel price rises have caused anxiety amongst airline shareholders worried about dividends and loss of profits. Jet fuel is the second biggest cost for airlines after staff costs, accounting for up to 20 per cent of operating expenses.

The Iraq war is blamed for the rise in oil prices and according to estimates from the International Air Travel Association, the airline industry will break even this year only if the average price of oil is $33 a barrel. At an average price of $40 a barrel, the industry will lose $6.9 billion.

BA has carried out some hedging but has still added fuel surcharges to fares. Other airlines are reviewing their fuel-hedging policies as the rise in oil prices forces carriers to choose either to lock in now before oil climbs higher, or wait and hope prices fall.

Lufthansa is one of the most comfortably hedged major airlines. It hedged about 89 per cent of its fuel requirements this year and 35 per cent of fuel needs for 2005.

1 **Find out what is meant by fuel-hedging policies.**

2 **Find out whether airlines still have fuel surcharges.**

3 **How will fuel surcharges affect an airline's cash flow?**

Taking it further

What can airlines do to improve their general cash flow situation?

All financial transactions within a business have to be recorded. The organisation's management need up-to-date financial information to help them run the business efficiently. In very small organisations paper systems may be sufficient, but most companies rely on information technology to produce financial information.

- Petty cash is needed for small day-to-day purchases and expenses. An amount of cash is kept for these purposes and any amounts spent are recorded in the petty cash book, with receipts.

- The sales ledger records the sales the company has made, the amount of money received for goods or services, and the money still outstanding from debtors. Copies of invoices are kept alongside the sales ledger. These have to be kept for 6 years.

- The purchase ledger records outgoing payments to suppliers or money still owed to suppliers, against their invoices. It allows the business to see how much money is owed at any one time.

- Cash books record all the money that comes into and goes out of a business. The cash book should record all transactions, however made, and be divided into two separate sections, receipts and payments.

- Profit and loss accounts show the income received and the expenses and overheads paid over a period of time, leaving a profit or loss figure for the period. Not all income is from sales – it may be from rentals or the sale of assets, for example.

- The balance sheet gives a view of the state of the company's finances at a given point in time. It shows all the assets of an organisation including any property and equipment, which are known as fixed assets. Any money in the bank is a financial asset. The assets are set against liabilities and must balance each other. Liabilities are the owner's capital or the shareholders' capital in the business. Other liabilities are any debts the company owes.

All of these accounts can be kept on a computer rather than in books. All large companies use computerised accounting. Those who can afford it have tailor-made packages and their own accounting departments, employing expertise in both accountancy and IT systems.

Smaller companies are more likely to buy accounting software. Bought-in systems are cheaper than tailor-made ones but will have some features that are not needed and perhaps some that do not entirely fit the needs of the business. Sage is a popular accounting package.

Computerised systems should provide all the necessary information for annual returns, tax returns and value added tax (VAT) returns. Any reports needed should be easily accessible as long as the data have been input correctly.

External accounts

Financial information about an organisation is of interest to many people. Shareholders and potential shareholders are interested in dividends to be paid and the value of their shares. Employees want to know if the company, and therefore their job, is secure. Any creditors, including banks, are interested in the ability of the organisation to pay its debts. The government will expect to receive taxes from a profitable company.

Sole traders do not have to make their annual accounts public, although they are likely to keep them for their own use. Private and public limited companies, however, must comply with the Companies Act and complete an annual return. They must also supply a signed set of accounts to Companies House every year.

Most large organisations incorporate their annual accounts into an annual report. This gives information about the current activities in the business as well as the figures in the accounts. All shareholders receive a copy of the annual report. All companies in the UK have to have their final accounts audited by a professional accountant from outside the company.

From January 2005, Europe's listed companies have to conform to International Financial Reporting Standards. The aim of these standards is to create one single set of accounting standards that can be applied anywhere in the world. This will make it easier for investors to compare the performance of companies across international boundaries. But the new rules will cause a lot of work for companies, and particularly their accountants, as they prepare accounts that meet the standards.

Key terms

Annual return – record of key company information which must be provided annually. Annual returns are filed at Companies House in London and are made publicly available.

Audit – check on the accounts and accounting system of an organisation. An audit checks that the accounts show a true and fair view of the affairs of the company.

Tax returns

Every sole trader must complete a self-assessment tax return. Tax has to be paid on profits from the business. Expenses can be deducted from income to calculate how much profit is left (if any). If all the internal accounting systems have been properly managed, it is relatively easy to complete the tax return.

Corporation tax has to be paid by companies on their profits. The company must file tax returns with the Inland Revenue.

Theory into practice

Study the annual report of a company that interests you. You can ask for a free copy of any annual report from the *Financial Times* Annual Reports service or you can find an annual report on a company's website. Perhaps you would like to study the annual report from Lastminute.com – it is on the website.

Look at cash flow. Can you make any judgements about the financial status of the company? Who are the major shareholders? Make some notes and compare your findings with other companies researched by your group.

Value added tax (VAT)

VAT is a tax on sales of goods and services. The current rate of VAT in the UK is 17.5 per cent. Some goods, for example foods, are exempt.

All VAT-registered businesses have to complete a VAT return form for each tax period, usually every three months. A business must be registered for VAT once its turnover reaches £58,000, and must charge VAT on its goods and services, and keep records of VAT paid on purchases. The following information is included in the VAT return:

- VAT charged to customers
- VAT paid by the business to suppliers.

The difference between the amount of VAT received and the amount paid out must be calculated. If a business pays out more than it receives, it can claim this back, but if it receives more than it pays, this amount must be paid to HM Customs and Excise, a government department.

	Apr	May	June	July	Aug	Sep	Oct	Nov	Dec	Jan	Feb	Mar
Revenue (Cash inflow)												
Sales												
Expenses (Cash outflow)												
Net cash flow												
Opening balance												
Net cash flow												
Closing balance												

Stephen and Al Brown run a bed and breakfast business, the St Raphael Guesthouse, with twelve rooms on offer. Al is concerned about the way the business is operating. He has looked at the figures for the last few months and is worried that they will have to borrow more money. Al knows that there is £1000 in the business bank account. He is preparing a cash flow forecast for the coming financial year.

Cash inflow

Room sales	May to October £5000 per month, November and December £3000, January and February £3500, March and April £4000, guests pay immediately
Food and bar	£1000 per month in May to October, £500 per month in other months

Cash outflow

Wages	£4000 per month
Repainting	£900 in May
Maintenance	£100 per month
Heating and lighting	£50 per month
Advertising	£20 per month
Other expenses	£200 per month from May to October and thereafter £150 per month.

1 Use a spreadsheet to prepare the cash flow forecast. **P3**

   Should Al and Stephen be worried? Why have problems occurred? Give a possible explanation. **M2**

   Make realistic recommendations to resolve the problems. **D1**

2 Al suggests to Stephen that they should get an overdraft of £12,000 to refurbish three annex rooms that are not currently used. This would increase monthly room sales by £800 and give another £120 in food sales.

   Update the cash forecast for the month following the refurbishment. **P2**

   What happens if the rooms are not fully booked? **M2**

   How could this situation be resolved? **D1**

In this section of the unit, we are going to concentrate on the practical aspects of planning a project and working to a budget. Ideally, you will plan a real project for which you determine objectives, identify areas of expenditure and keep within your given budget.

Objectives

The objectives of the project must be clear from the outset. The objectives should be tested against the SMART theory to make sure they are feasible.

SMART objectives are:

Specific – clear and concise
Measurable – how will we know if we achieved them?
Achievable – must have the skills and resources to achieve them
Realistic – not overly ambitious
Timed – deadlines.

Case study: day trip project

One group of students organised a day trip to a go-cart track. They had all managed to find sponsors based on the number of laps they managed to achieve. They had to organise transport and entry to the track. They managed to have the track to themselves as they were a group. They took lots of photographs and wrote a press release which they sent to the local newspapers. The funds raised were donated to charity.

What do you think were the objectives of this project?

Timescales

Everyone involved in planning the project must know exactly what they are responsible for. At meetings, tasks must be assigned to individuals with agreed deadlines. Where tasks are not assigned to specific people they will not happen.

These will vary depending on the type of project, but areas of responsibility may include:

- venue liaison and booking
- administration
- finance
- fundraising
- marketing
- catering
- methods of gathering feedback for evaluation.

Organisation on the day

In addition, people will have particular responsibilities on the day the activity takes place. If it were a day trip, for example, these would be:

- registration
- liaising with the driver/transport
- checking documentation
- guiding the trip
- taking photographs
- checking health and safety measures
- gathering feedback
- ensuring everyone has onward travel arrangements.

Theory into practice

You should determine the roles and responsibilities of each group member once you have decided on the nature of your project. Be very specific and write job descriptions which you can include in your plan. Consider the strengths and weaknesses of group members when deciding who will do what and who will work well together in small groups. Decide whether you will have a chairperson for the project. **P4**

Key terms

SWOT – analysis of strengths, weaknesses, opportunities and threats.

PEST – analysis of political, economic, social and technological factors affecting an organisation. These will be explained in Unit 5.

Case study Middleton Railway

Carl Turner recently graduated from Leeds Metropolitan University with a degree in Tourism Management. In his final year he had to carry out a travel and tourism project, producing a 12,000-word report. This was an assessed project and very important to Carl's final grade.

He worked in a group of five students and they were assigned to Middleton Railway near Leeds. The railway is a non-profit-making organisation and claims to be the oldest working railway in the world. It is a tourist attraction as well as being of interest to train enthusiasts, but it does not attract huge numbers of tourists. The Middleton Railway has two coaches and several heritage industrial locomotives and visitors can go for a ride on the trains. It also holds special events such as Santa Claus train journeys. There is a gift shop.

The group was set a brief which had been determined by the tutors at Leeds Metropolitan and agreed with the management of Middleton Railway. The brief was to suggest improvements to the railway and its operation and events, with the aim of increasing visitor numbers. Greater visitor numbers would provide increased revenue which could be re-invested by the railway. Improvements should also lead to a higher and improved company profile.

The students were allocated a budget of £300. This was to enable them to take and print photographs and print and bind their reports, etc.

The group began by visiting Middleton Railway and individually carrying out observations and research.

Afterwards they reconvened and, using their findings, carried out a SWOT and PEST analysis.

They were able to make many practical recommendations to Middleton Railway following their study. These included improved signage, seating, shelters and improvements to the car park. The students also helped with an application for a lottery grant.

By lateral thinking they provided solutions to problems. For example, it was thought that a 'Thomas the Tank Engine' day would attract family visitors. However, the cost of using this name was too high because of the permission fees involved. Instead, they decided on a 'Friendly Engines' day using their own character locomotives. There would be no royalty fees, and yet the associations are the same and still attract visitors.

On completion of the project the team made a PowerPoint presentation to an audience of about 150 people including the chairman of Middleton Railway and three tutors. The presentation lasted about half an hour and the team answered questions afterwards.

You will be pleased to know that Carl achieved a first-class grade for this project! For more information on Middleton Railway go to www.middletonrailway.org.uk.

(Source: http://www.middletonrailway.org.uk)

1 **Identify the objectives and possible outcomes from Carl's project.**

2 **What do you think the budget was used for? Estimate how much money was used for what.**

Theory into practice

You will have to determine the objectives for your own project. You might find it useful to do this as a group. You can record the objectives individually and then determine your own personal objectives depending on your role in the planning of the project.

Producing a budget

A budget must be realistic and include all costs and all sources of revenue. It should include an amount for contingencies. Figure 2.4 shows an example of a budget for a local outdoor festival.

Promotional campaign

You may decide to run a promotional campaign for your event. You can find out how to do this in Unit 5.

You will not be able to spend much money on a tour campaign so you should consider means of promoting your event for free. Think about:

- posters
- flyers
- contacting local newspapers and radio stations with a press release.

Assessment practice

Produce a budget for your project which will form part of your plan. Estimate all the costs you are likely to incur and all the revenue. You are likely to try and keep costs as low as possible and use accommodation and facilities in your school or college as far as possible. Determine where your budget is coming from. Is money allocated for your project? Will you have to fundraise? Will there be any income? Copy the following table to produce your budget, adjusting headings as appropriate. **P4**

Total amount available	
Number of people attending	
Category	**Amount budgeted**
Venue cost	
Catering	
Entertainment	
Audio-visual equipment	
Printed materials and promotion	
Transport	
Gifts/souvenirs	
Overheads	
Contingency	

Figure 2.4 Budget for a local outdoor festival ▶

OUTGOINGS

Site

Toilets:	£6000
Fencing, radios etc.:	£2000
Recycling and litter:	£2500
Site and park crews, vehicle:	£2800
Crew food and drink:	£1200
Total site	**£14,500**

Health and safety

Stewards, security:	£6000
Gate crew, first aid, barriers:	£4000
Total health and safety	**£10,000**

Entertainment

Bands:	£3000
Stage and lighting:	£3600
Marquees:	£5000
Sound:	£900
Total entertainment	**£12,500**

Production

Signs:	£500
Insurance:	£600
Publicity:	£900
Phone, photocopying:	£2000
Other production:	£3000
Total production	**£7000**

Council charges

Entertainment licence:	£3000
Use of park:	£6000
Park deposit:	£1000
Total council charges	**£10,000**

Total expenses	**£54,000**

ESTIMATED INCOME

Stalls:	£20,000
Bar income:	£10,000
Gate donations:	£8000
Muffin and magic stalls:	£3000
Fun make-up stalls:	£400
Sponsorship:	£500
Loans:	£2000
Donations:	£2000
Programme:	£100
Park deposit:	£1000
Total income	**£47,000**
Current estimated shortfall	**£7000**

▲ **Figure 2.5 Tourist Information Centres can provide information about potential venues**

Case study: organising a conference

A group of students at Trenchtown College started their Business of Travel and Tourism unit in September. They were allocated 3 hours a week of class time with a tutor for the unit which was to be completed by February. Part of this time was devoted to planning a travel and tourism project which had to take place by the end of January. They were fortunate in that the local Tourist Information Centre had asked them to help in a consultation process with local tourism businesses to aid with the writing of the Trenchtown tourism strategy. The idea was that the students would organise a one-day conference in January. All details of the organisation of the conference would be left to the students but on the day, discussion and seminar activities would be led by Tourist Information Centre staff.

Planning

The students thought they had plenty of time to prepare. The first couple of meetings went very well. As a group they determined the objectives of the event and then they decided who would be responsible for what and wrote their job descriptions. Graham, their tutor, told them to keep a log of their contributions and to keep copies of whatever they did. They started their logs and were very pleased with what they had achieved so far.

- Sunita, Saul, Tony and Sean were responsible for finding tourism businesses to be represented at the conference.
- Annika and Phillip were in charge of catering – there was to be morning coffee and lunch on the day.
- Lizzie and Selma were in charge of administration and finance and making sure they kept to their budget of £200.
- Raj was to organise a venue.
- Marcy and Chris were the marketing team.
- Helena and Marcus were to oversee the project as chair and deputy chairperson.
- James and Chitra took responsibility for health and safety and equipment.

Four weeks in

Graham, the tutor, had taught the group how to run a formal meeting and they were doing this weekly with an agenda and minutes, etc. It was now the end of October and the students realised that although they had roles, job descriptions and minutes of meetings, they had not actually progressed their event. No one had arranged a venue, contacted any businesses or done anything outside Graham's class. They realised that each of them needed deadlines for specific tasks and that they needed a timeline of planning for the whole event. They spent 3 hours doing their timeline with dates set for each task. They felt much better. The next week they came to class and still no one had done anything, after all, they still had nearly 3 months.

- Helena and Marcus had a talk with Graham and he told them to be more forceful. They started to ask each team member to report on what they had done weekly.
- Sunita and Saul had contacted a whole list of businesses and had four positive replies, but Sunita had left the letters at home. She would bring them next week to show the group.

- Tony and Sean were going to contact some businesses – soon.
- Raj had sprung into action and booked a room in the college. It was fine, although not their first choice, they had missed out on a better venue by a week.
- Marcy and Chris had drawn up a beautiful poster. The others weren't sure what to do with the poster or who it was for.
- Annika and Phillip spent 3 hours a week planning the lunch menu and how much it would cost. Sometimes they went to Sainsbury's to check prices. However they had, as yet, no cash released from the budget to spend and nothing much else to do before the event.

The weeks went on and slowly and surprisingly, with a lot of help from Graham they had: secured delegates; James and Chitra had done a risk assessment; Marcy and Chris had written a press release and sent it to local papers. The meetings continued to be a bit of a shambles as Helena and Marcus – who had been a couple – split up. There was a lot of arguing with members of the group shouting at each other. Sunita was away a lot so Saul had found the delegates by himself. Tony and Sean had found one delegate. Graham thought he might be in the wrong job but decided to persevere.

On the day

All but Tony turned up. They arrived early which was just as well as the room had someone else in it. This was soon sorted out and the group managed to set up in time using the layout plan they had prepared. Saul went to collect their AV equipment from the IT department. It all worked but there was a lead missing. Saul knew there was one in the staff room and found it. Graham appeared and said their delegates were arriving. They had forgotten to put anyone in charge of meeting them so Helena and Marcus went. Helena wished they had thought of having badges for the students and delegates. The conference went well and the Tourist Information people were very happy. At lunchtime, Annika and Phillip produced a wonderful buffet lunch although two delegates went out for lunch appointments as they had not been told lunch was on offer. The lunch alone cost £230. They all stayed to clear up.

The following day

The group met to write thank you letters to delegates. Graham said they would start their evaluation and asked them if they had any feedback. He suggested they could have had a questionnaire, a delegate feedback form, asked the Tourist Information Centre staff for their comments or taken a video or photographs – but they hadn't thought about any of these options!

You could do better than this, couldn't you? Discuss the performance of this group and point out where they went wrong and the few things that went right. Show how they could have done things differently. Look critically at your own group so far and see if you are repeating any of their mistakes. Discuss how you can improve your own performance. Make notes on the discussion points and keep them for reference. **M3**

Your group has decided to arrange a visit to Alton Towers, the theme park resort, for yourselves and another group of travel and tourism students. The trip will take place at the beginning of July and there will be 30 students going. You will need to produce a plan for the trip. You should not charge more than £30 per head and this has to include entrance fee, travel and a packed lunch each.

1 Produce a full plan for this trip within the financial constraints given. Include:
   - objectives
   - timescales
   - actions required by the group and individuals.

This should be an individual piece of work although you may carry out group discussions.

2 Explain how the plan for the trip enables the objectives to be met within the financial constraints.

Grading tip

To reach Merit level you could include a copy of your budget with an explanation of how you decided to spend the money and where you had to cut costs.

▲ Figure 2.6 A visit to Alton Towers can be a useful trip for travel and tourism students to practise planning

Aims

Company aims vary, particularly according to whether they are profit-making or non-profit-making. A profit-making company must make money to stay in business and to satisfy the shareholders, who, after all, have invested in order to make money. However, a profit-making company may have other aims too, although these will be determined with the main aim of making money. Here are some examples of possible aims other than profit-making:

- to be environmentally friendly and support sustainable tourism
- to improve product quality
- to be competitive
- to increase market share.

A non-profit-making company is likely to share some of these aims but will put any money earned back into the company to achieve further aims or will donate it to the cause it supports.

The best way to understand company aims is to look at some specific examples. First, we return to Holidaybreak whom we met earlier in this unit. In its annual report it gives the aims for each division of the business. The aims for the camping division are:

- to maintain strong margins
- to increase campsite occupancy rates
- to continue to generate substantial cash.

In the report, Holidaybreak acknowledges that its camping division faces extensive competition, not only from other camping operators but from alternative types of holidays and destinations. In order to retain competitive advantage it has to employ strategies which help it achieve its expressed aims. These strategies or objectives are:

- to improve occupancy rates, optimise yields and increase margins
- to retain tight control of costs
- to develop e-commerce initiatives and affiliate relationships to target new customer groups in the UK and overseas

Assessment practice

How could Holidaybreak put the first strategy into practice?

They could:

- advertise more to improve occupancy
- optimise yields by making sure all camping customers change over on Saturdays so that pitches and mobile homes do not have empty nights
- increase margins by cutting costs or increasing prices.

You should consider the other strategies by discussing each of them with a partner. Write down your ideas and then join up with another pair. Combine your ideas and then form a larger group. Continue until the group reaches agreement with one combined list of ideas. **P5**

- to increase consumer reach of exisiting brand portfolio and increase differentiation of brands
- to develop mobile home holiday distribution business using camp site owned accommodation.

(Source: Holidaybreak plc Annual Report and Financial Statement 2005. © Holidaybreak plc)

These are the stated aims of a non-profit-making trade association in the Visitor Attractions sector, The British Association of Leisure Parks, Piers and Attractions (BALPPA):

- To promote safe practice throughout the industry
- To promote and defend the interests of the industry
- To represent the needs and concerns of the industry to HM government departments, policy-makers and influencers
- To provide advice, information and services to members, to provide forums for discussion of their interests and concerns, and to promote professionalism, profitability, and best practice in the industry
- To act as an authoritative source of information concerning the industry to the media and other opinion formers.

(Source: http://www.balppa.org/details1.cfm?codeID=1)

Theory into practice

1. Compare the aims of BALPPA with those of the Holidaybreak camping division. How are they similar and how do they differ? Draw up a comparative table.

2. BALPPA is a non-profit-making organisation. Give your ideas on whether it seeks competitive advantage and with whom. **P6**

3. Compare the ways in which Holidaybreak seeks to gain competitive advantage. **M4**

4. Suggest and justify other ways in which either of these organisations could gain competitive advantage. **D2**

Competitive advantage

Key term

Competitive advantage – an advantage gained over competitors by giving better value to customers so that they choose your product and not the competitor's product.

Let's consider some other ways of gaining competitive advantage.

Giving added value

Customers do not always choose a product or service on price alone. If that were the case there would be no business class on airlines, everyone would travel in economy.

Sometimes a company can be more competitive by having a better product. Grand Central Trains is an example.

Total Quality Management (TQM)

This is a business philosophy which arose from the Japanese management approach known as Kaizen. It

Case study: Grand Central trains

A new train company announced plans to introduce services between Sunderland and London Kings Cross at the end of 2006. GNER tried to stop the new operation but failed. The new company will not be receiving any government subsidies. It plans to offer improved seating in ordinary class compartments with power points so that people can work as they travel. In first class it will provide wider, reclining seats and power points.

1. Visit www.grandcentraltrains.com to find out more about the new service.

2. Do you think the service represents added value in comparison with competitors?

3. Suggest what else could be offered to improve the service. **P5**

involves all members of an organisation constantly trying to improve quality in the processes they use, the products and services they produce, and the culture in which they work. It can be summed up as a management approach to long-term success through customer satisfaction.

TQM has three stages:

1. Setting quality targets – to ensure high standards of customer service

2. Quality development – setting up procedures and systems to achieve the standards

3. Quality assurance – monitoring the quality to make sure standards are upheld.

Training and development of staff

Many would argue that this is the most effective means of achieving competitive advantage and that without excellent staff a company will not survive. Staff need to project a favourable company image, know their product and deliver good service. This cannot be achieved without good training.

Advertising

Advertising is an essential tool for being competitive. Travel companies spend a lot of their budgets on advertising. It is impossible to say which adverts contribute to company success, as there are so many other factors involved. Some of the traditional advertising budget might be better diverted to paying for prime positioning on search engines. This will ensure the company's name appears on internet searches, targetting the increasing numbers of customers who research and book travel online.

The key to advertising is reaching the right target audience. For example, if a holiday advertisement appears in the travel section of a newspaper, it is likely that anyone reading this section of the newspaper will also be interested in reading about this product.

Eurotunnel and Eurostar are different companies involved in promoting travel through the Channel tunnel. Eurostar is for foot passengers from London and Ashford International to the Continent, whereas Eurotunnel is for passengers and their vehicles from Folkestone to Calais, as shown in Figure 2.8.

Figure 2.7 Advertisement for Direct Holidays
(Source: Direct Holidays)

Figure 2.8 Advertisement for Eurotunnel
(Source: The Channel Tunnel Group Ltd)

Pricing policies

Competitive pricing is a strategy that is used to great effect in tour operating and in the low-cost airline business. Where products are almost homogenous (that is, there is very little difference perceived between them) price is very important. This is not always the case with a flight. The further people are travelling the more important service and comfort become. With short haul air travel, however, many people are prepared to forego service and comfort for a cheap price.

The problem that often occurs with such a pricing strategy is that competitors continue to undercut each other until prices get so low that they are unrealistic, margins are cut to the bone and businesses start to drop out of the market. There have been many airlines which have failed in recent years.

Mass-market tour operators operate on such low margins that unforeseen events such as a terrorism attack or extreme climatic conditions can wipe out their profits for the year.

Location

Location is most important for travel and tourism companies who depend on customer footfall. Travel agents depend on customers being able to access their services personally, as do Tourist Information Centres. You will therefore notice these types of business in town centres. Call centres and tour operators have no need to be in central locations and can reduce costs by seeking cheap out-of-town locations.

Key term

Footfall – refers to the number of customers walking into retail premises.

Sales techniques

Using high-pressure sales techniques can put customers off, so staff need to be trained in using sales techniques effectively. This is particularly important for call centre staff who are selling over the telephone. In travel agencies, staff concentrate on add-on sales such as insurance, car hire and excursions.

You can learn more about marketing strategies in Unit 5 and find out how travel agencies attain competitive advantage in Unit 9.

Knowledge check

1 What are the differences between public, private and voluntary organisations?

2 What is the difference between an executive director and a non-executive director?

3 What is a dividend?

4 Why might a dividend not be paid?

5 What does 'flotation' mean?

6 Give three examples of sources of finance for setting up a business.

7 What is a Memorandum of Association?

8 Give three examples of cash inflow.

9 Give three examples of cash outflow.

10 Give two examples of overheads.

11 Why is it necessary to manage cash flow?

12 Why are timescales important in planning a travel and tourism project?

13 What is meant by Total Quality Management?

14 What types of travel and tourism organisations need town centre locations?

Preparation for assessment

LEGO

The LEGO Group ended 2005 in the firm belief that it has survived its financial crisis. Results for 2005 indicate that the Company is once more on the right track. The overall result before tax – a surplus of Danish Krone (DKK) 702 million – exceeded all expectations for the year. Despite generally slow growth on global toy markets, the LEGO Group enjoyed an increase in sales and in market share in all major markets. This was the case in the largest toy market, USA, and the Group's core market in Germany where sales were raised significantly. Total Group sales in 2005 increased by approximately 12 per cent.

LEGO Group strategy for the period to 2010 goes under the name of Shared Vision. The strategy is made up of many components – but its core remains unchanged.

Objectives:

- Be the best at creating value for our customers and sales channels.
- Refocus on the value we offer our consumers.
- Increase operational excellence.

The strategy underlines the continued importance of focusing on profitability within the organisation. The situation facing all toy manufacturers at present is that they are pressured from many quarters – by consumers, customers and competitors. The LEGO Group meets this challenge with a determination to bind consumers, fans and retailers even closer to the organisation.

At the same time, the Group will increasingly refine and improve its product range to enable its new products to compete, for example, with the many electronic products on the market.

It continues to be the LEGO Group's primary purpose to supply good, healthy play – developing children and helping them to face the challenges of tomorrow.

(Source: http://www.lego.com/eng/info/default.asp?page=facts; LEGO is a trademark of the LEGO Group, here used with special permission)

Youth Hostel Association (YHA)

The following is an extract from the YHA website.

YHA (England & Wales) Ltd. operates a network of 227 Youth Hostels across England and Wales. Over 310,000 members receive a warm welcome, comfortable accommodation, good food and affordable prices.

YHA's charitable objective forms the basis of all our work:

> To help all, especially young people of limited means, to a greater knowledge, love and care of the countryside, and appreciation of the cultural values of towns and cities, particularly by providing Youth Hostels or other accommodation for them in their travels, and thus to promote their health, recreation and education.

We are committed to building bridges between town and country, and contributing to international understanding. Our plans for the future include increasing the membership and Youth Hostel use and to extend the YHA network to areas where we do not have Youth Hostels at present. YHA has always been a countryside and environmental organisation, founded as part of the 'outdoors' movement. This has further developed into the YHA's adoption of policies that encourage sustainable use of the countryside, Youth Hostels and their local communities.

(Source: http://www.yha.org.uk/Join_YHA/About_YHA/About_YHA.html)

1 Focus particularly on the LEGO Group and carry out research to find out and explain how the LEGO Group seeks to gain competitive advantage in order to meet the company aims. **P5**

2 Carry out research to find out and explain how the YHA seeks to gain competitive advantage in order to meet its aims. **P6**

3 Compare how the LEGO Group and the YHA seek to gain competitive advantage. **M4**

4 Suggest and justify other ways in which *either* the LEGO Group *or* the YHA could gain competitive advantage. **D2**

Taking it further

You might look at other similar companies to see how they gain competitive advantage and whether their ideas could apply to the LEGO Group or the YHA.

Grading criteria

To achieve a pass grade the evidence must show that the learner is able to:	To achieve a merit grade the evidence must show that, in addition to the pass criteria, the learner is able to:	To achieve a distinction grade the evidence must show that, in addition to the pass and merit criteria, the learner is able to:
P1 describe the features of a selected profit-making travel and tourism organisation **Case study page 46**	**M1** compare the features of a profit-making and a non-profit-making travel and tourism organisation **Case study page 46**	**D1** make realistic recommendations to resolve cash flow problems **Case study page 55**
P2 describe the features of a selected non-profit-making travel and tourism organisation **Case study page 46**	**M2** interpret the cash flow forecast explaining how problems have occurred **Case study page 55**	**D2** suggest and justify other ways either a profit-making or non-profit-making organisation could gain competitive advantage **Theory into practice page 66**
P3 complete a cash flow forecast for a travel and tourism organisation for a minimum of a six month period **Assessment practice page 55**	**M3** explain how a plan for a travel and tourism project enables the objectives to be met within the financial constraints **Case study page 63**	
P4 plan a travel and tourism project within financial constraints **Theory into practice page 60**	**M4** compare how specified profit-making and non-profit-making organisations seek to gain competitive advantage **Theory into practice page 66**	
P5 explain how a chosen profit-making organisation seeks to gain competitive advantage to meet its aims **Theory into practice page 65**		
P6 explain how a chosen non-profit-making organisation seeks to gain competitive advantage to meet its aims **Theory into practice page 66**		

The UK as a destination

Introduction

This unit will provide you with the opportunity to explore tourism in the UK. It will build on the knowledge you already have about the UK, and introduce you to key tourism products and customers.

You will learn how to use different reference materials so that you can locate key destinations, gateways and geographical features.

You will study the factors that contribute to the appeal of destinations, including the natural appeal, the location and access and the attractions to be found in a destination.

You will also explore the differing needs of domestic and inbound tourists and how the UK travel and tourism industry meets those needs.

After completing this unit you should be able to achieve the following outcomes:

1   Be able to use sources of reference to provide information on UK destinations

2   Know the location of the main UK gateways, tourist destinations and geographical features

3   Understand the appeal of UK destinations

4   Understand the needs of UK domestic and inbound tourism markets and the ways in which the UK meets those needs

5   Understand key trends and factors affecting the UK inbound and domestic tourism markets.

Thinking points

In 2005, the *Daily Telegraph* newspaper published its annual survey to find out the opinions of British travellers and holidaymakers. Of those surveyed, 75 per cent said they had chosen to travel within the UK as well as abroad in the previous 2 years. The reasons given for the appeal of the UK included ease, history and walking: 36 per cent said culture was improving, 60 per cent felt that shopping is comparable or better than in foreign destinations and 45 per cent thought the UK offered a safer holiday.

Where do you take your holidays? In the UK or abroad?

What do you think the UK can offer holidaymakers?

You will need to become proficient in using a range of reference materials to investigate UK destinations.

Atlases

A good atlas is essential to anyone working in travel and tourism. Any library will have a selection of good atlases. The *World Travel Atlas* (Columbus Press) has been designed for the travel trade and for students. It is also available online and is a good source of facts and figures which are updated every year.

The internet

The internet is a wonderful source of information. However, there are so many sites that you will have to learn how to search properly to find what you want, and to make sure the information is reliable.

You should first make sure you are familiar with search engines such as Yahoo and Google. You have the option of searching UK or worldwide, and it is often easier to limit yourself to UK searches to begin with. If you enter 'Travel and tourism' you will find thousands of sites listed and many will have little relevance to you. However, it is worth spending some time surfing these sites and bookmarking those which are useful in your favourites list. (If you do not have your own computer, make a note of the addresses.)

Some websites are themselves directories and link to other useful tourism information sites. Examples are www.altis.ac.uk and www.tourismeducation.org.

If you are searching for information on UK destinations the following websites will help you:

www.visitbritain.com
www.enjoyengland.com
www.visitwales.com
www.visitscotland.com
www.discovernorthernireland.com

Set some time aside to familiarise yourself with these websites so that you know what can be found on them.

Brochures

These give a lot of destination information. They are visually appealing and easy to understand. But remember that their purpose is to sell, and therefore they are likely to give a biased view, always positive. Brochures are produced by tour operators, often with several editions in a year. The brochures are distributed to travel agents who use them to sell holidays. You will need them for your studies and you can collect them free at any travel agency. It is best not to take too many at one time! You can also order brochures from tour operators online or by telephone.

Statistical data

The internet means that you can easily access data about UK tourism. Star UK (www.staruk.co.uk) publishes useful statistics and this should be your starting point. You should also familiarise yourself with the website for official UK statistics (www.statistics.gov.uk). You will look at statistics later in this unit when examining key trends affecting UK tourism.

Timetables

Timetables are published by all transport carriers and are readily available in published form and on the internet. Airports amalgamate the timetables of their carriers and post them on their websites. All transport providers' timetables can be accessed on the internet. You can look up routes and times for coaches, ferries and trains as well as airlines. Useful websites are:

www.thetrainline.com
www.nationalrail,co.uk
wwww.nationalexpress.com
www.ferrybooker.com.

Travel guides

These are extensively available in bookshops and libraries. They are constantly updated, so do check the dates of library editions as many libraries cannot afford to update their whole collection of travel guides regularly.

Some of these guides are very well produced and include maps, hotel and restaurant recommendations, and plenty of information on what to see and do. They are ideal for finding out what there is to do in a destination and how to get there.

Hotel guides

All major chains produce their own guides listing their hotel locations, facilities and services. Remember that these are sales tools like brochures and will present only positive information.

There are travel trade hotel guides which travel agents refer to. These give independent reviews of hotels and are useful for checking hotels before you visit them.

Travel trade press

Your library should have copies of travel trade journals, which give up-to-date features on the industry and on specific destinations. If you wish you can subscribe to these publications with a student subscription.

Newspaper reports

The national and regional press also carry regular travel pages, which are full of informative features and advertising.

Television programmes

Holiday programmes feature reports on UK destinations as well as those abroad.

Assessment practice

To achieve P1 in this unit you must keep records of all the sources of information you use for your research on UK destinations. You should give details of every source and say how and where you used each source. Start this now. Get a notebook for this purpose or start a Word file. If you are working electronically, make sure you keep a back-up file.

An example of an entry might be:

> 12/9 Carried out research on the VisitBritain website (www.visitbritain.com). I looked at the section on royal palaces and their location in the UK. This was an example of how Visit Britain helps meet the needs of inbound tourists.

When you submit each section of your assignment, you should add a bibliography, that is, a comprehensive list of all the sources you have used. If you keep a detailed log throughout the unit and complete your bibliographies, you will have achieved **P1**

Gateways

UK airports

Airports are gateways to travel destinations. London is served by four major airports: Heathrow, Gatwick, Stansted and Luton. There is also a small airport in the Docklands area of London, London City Airport. This airport is used mainly by business travellers.

Gateway airports are always the busiest. Sometimes the gateway is to another flight. Transfer passengers are those who fly to a hub airport and transfer to another flight. To cope with increased demand for air travel, many gateway airports have had to expand capacity. For London, Heathrow is building a fifth terminal, and Stansted has plans for a second runway. There are over 50 regional airports in the UK, but distances are not so great as to make air travel a preferred option within the UK. However, services from cities in Scotland and Ireland to London do very well. Air travel is the most favoured form of travel for inbound tourists to the UK. Airports are identified by three-letter codes.

1	Heathrow	67 million
2	Gatwick	32 million
3	Manchester	22 million
4	Stansted	22 million
5	Birmingham	9.4 million
6	Luton	9.1 million
7	Glasgow	8.8 million
8	Edinburgh	8.5 million
9	Bristol	5.2 million
10	Newcastle	5.2 million

(Source: Civil Aviation Authority – UK Airport Statistics)

Table 3.1 Top ten UK airports (by passenger numbers) in 2005

Assessment practice

1 Locate each of the airports from Table 3.1 on the map of the UK (Figure 3.1).

2 Find out the airport codes for each of the airports.

3 You will note that Heathrow is by far the busiest airport. Visit Heathrow's website (www.heathrowairport.com/) and find out the following.

- Who owns Heathrow airport?
- What other airports does this company own?
- Find five examples of domestic (inside the UK) cities linked by air to Heathrow. For each example state the airline operating the flight. **P2**

Taking it further

Do some research on the Internet and find out how the ownership of Heathrow has changed. Assess the impact of this change on the operation of Heathrow.

Key terms

Airport code – every airport in the world has a unique three-letter code to identify it. You can find these codes at The Airline Codes Web Site at www.airlinecodes.co.uk.

Hub – an airport, usually major, that serves many outlying destinations and allows passengers to fly in and transfer to other flights. The outlying airports are known as 'spokes'.

Figure 3.1
Map of the UK

Seaports

Like airports, ports are gateways. They are embarkation points for ferry services and also for cruise passengers. UK-originating cruise passengers may fly to a port to start their cruise or may leave by sea from the UK, usually Southampton.

Major passenger ports are situated along the south coast, providing Channel crossings to France, Spain and the Channel Islands, and along the east coast, providing crossings to Belgium, Germany, Holland, Denmark, Norway and Sweden. There are also numerous crossings between Wales and Ireland, and Scotland and Ireland.

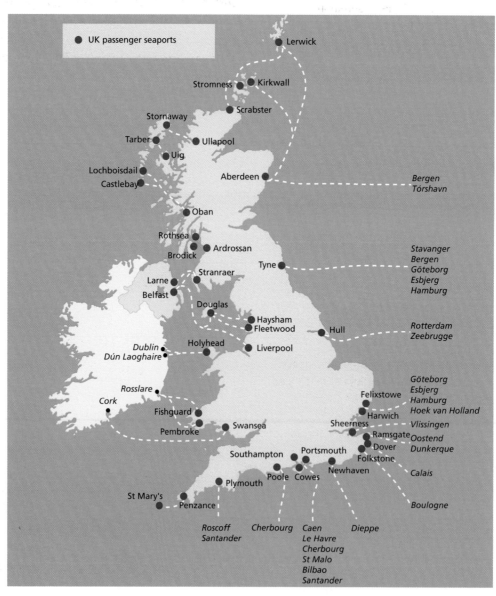

Figure 3.2 ▶
Main sea routes

Tourist destinations

Capital cities

The UK's capital cities, Belfast, Cardiff, Edinburgh and London, are important destinations for domestic and inbound tourists alike, with London receiving the most tourists.

Assessment practice

1 Choose one of the capital cities and find a guide for that city. You will find guides in your library.

2 Describe three main features of the destination that would appeal to inbound tourists. **P3**

3 Consider whether these features would also appeal to domestic tourists and say why. **P3**

Coastal resorts

Coastal resorts provide something for all the family – the sea, a beach and some form of entertainment. Later you will need to be able to locate coastal towns on a map of the UK. Some are important for business tourism as they provide extensive conference facilities. Examples include Brighton, Bournemouth and Blackpool.

Towns and cities

Cities and towns have traditionally been on the 'tourist trail' for incoming tourists because of their cultural and historic appeal. London is the most popular but overseas visitors are usually keen to see places such as Bath, Stratford, Oxford and Edinburgh. City breaks are one of the fastest-growing sectors in UK domestic and inbound tourism.

Activity

Figure 3.3 shows the top towns, outside London, visited by overseas residents in 2004. London received over 13 million visits.

1 Locate and name these destinations on the map of the UK (Figure 3.1). **P2**

2 For each town and city name the nearest airport and motorway or major road. Locate these on the map. **P2**

3 Choose one of the towns and try to find out the visitor numbers for that town. You should be able to find these on the local government website or via the Tourist Information Centre. Produce a short report with tables on numbers of visitors, length of stay, purpose of visit, etc. Draw conclusions from your findings. Ask your teacher or tutor to check your work.

Figure 3.3 Top 20 UK towns visited (excluding London) by number of overnight visits ▶

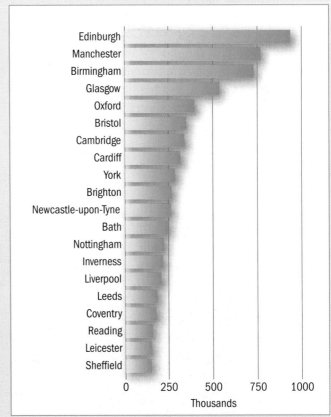

(Source: Travel Trends 2004)

Geographical features

Later you will need to be able to locate various geographical features. These include rivers, lakes, mountain ranges and upland areas. The appeal of these features is discussed in the next section.

3.3 Understand the appeal of UK destinations

Natural appeal

Natural attractions appeal to tourists who want to appreciate and enjoy the world's wonders, such as the lakes and mountains in the UK's Lake District. Lakes, rivers and mountains can provide the setting for a wide variety of leisure and sporting activities, for example walking, mountaineering and fishing. Every tourist area will have some kind of natural attraction in or near to the destination that can be promoted to tourists. It may be beaches, lakes, mountains or rolling countryside. Particular features of the topography will appeal to different types of visitors.

Key term

Topography – the shape and composition of the landscape, including mountains and valleys, the pattern of rivers, roads and railways.

Coastlines

Much of the coastline in the UK is protected. About 31 per cent of the coast in England and 42 per cent in Wales is protected under the heritage coast scheme. In England, the heritage coasts are managed by the

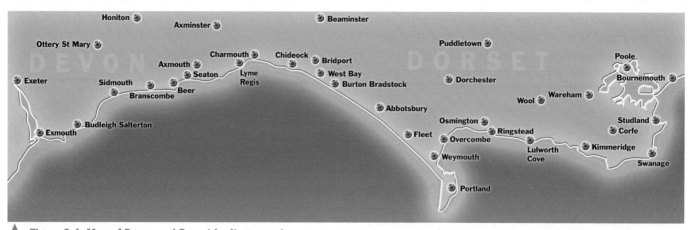

▲ **Figure 3.4 Map of Devon and Dorset heritage coast**

(Source: http://www.worldheritagecoast.net)

▲ Figure 3.5 The Lake District

Countryside Agency, while the Countryside Council for Wales (CCW) administers the coasts in Wales. The United Nations Educational, Scientific and Cultural Organisation (UNESCO) awarded Natural World Heritage Status to the coast of Dorset and East Devon in December 2001 in recognition of its unique pedigree which spans 185 million years.

The coast appeals to many types of tourists as there is so much to do. If it is sunny adults and children can relax on the beach enjoying the sea and sand. The more active can go rock climbing, fishing, walking and cycling. In the south west (Cornwall) the beaches are famous for surfing. Coasteering is a new extreme sport. It combines swimming and climbing with cliff jumping. The aim is to climb along rocks by the sea, and when it is impossible to go any further on the rocks to jump into the sea and swim to the next set of rocks. **This is a potentially dangerous sport not to be undertaken by amateurs but under the guidance of a qualified instructor.**

Rivers and lakes

In the UK there are nearly 6500 kilometres of rivers and canals. Many of these waterways are managed by British Waterways, a public corporation. It looks after more than 3220 kilometres of canals and rivers in the UK. Its role is to conserve and enhance the waterways.

Rivers also provide lots of scope for activities such as boating, including using motor boats, canoeing and rowing. In Oxford and Cambridge, tourists love to go punting on the rivers. British Waterways is trying to enhance our canals and rivers and encourage people to visit them as part of their day-to-day business as well as for leisure activities.

The Lake District in Cumbria attracts tourists for walking and admiring the spectacular scenery or boating on the lakes. The largest lake is Windermere which is 17 kilometres long. The largest lake in the UK is in Northern Ireland. It is called Lough Neagh and covers 383 square kilometres.

National Parks

About 9 per cent of the land area of the UK is designated as National Park. These parks were created in the 1950s and 1960s to protect areas of particular beauty and areas with special ecological features. They provide valuable recreational areas for visitors. In England and Wales there are twelve National Parks.

In recent years some new National Parks have been designated: Cairngorm National Park and Loch Lomond

Activity

Choose one of the National Parks and describe the features that attract tourists. See if you can find statistics about numbers of visitors to the park. Does the park attract more inbound or more domestic tourists and why? What might be the negative impacts of attracting tourists?

▲ **Figure 3.6 National Parks in the UK**

and the Trossachs National Park, both in Scotland.

The parks are not publicly owned. In fact, large areas are owned by private landowners. The National Trust owns about 12 per cent of the Peak District National Park and more than 25 per cent of the Lake District National Park: the organisation also owns areas of other parks.

National Park Authorities run National Parks and are given funding to do so by the government. The Authorities have powers to control development and manage tourism.

Areas of Outstanding Natural Beauty (AONB)

An AONB is a landscape which has such great beauty that it is important to protect it. It may be coastline, water meadow, moors or downland. There are 41 AONBs in England and Wales. About 18 per cent of the countryside of England and Wales is protected in this way. The AONBs are important national resources and were given further protection under the Countryside and Rights of Way Act of 2000.

In addition there are many botanical parks in the UK, possibly the most famous is Kew Gardens near London. Also in London there are several royal parks, for example St James Park, and vast areas of heath such as Hampstead Heath. The heaths are most popular with local people for recreational activities and walking but some are also attractive to tourists. Greenwich Park with its observatory is one of the most popular London attractions.

Mountains

The UK has several mountainous areas. These include Ben Nevis in Scotland which is the highest at 1343 metres. In Wales, Snowdon is 1085 metres high and in England the highest mountain is Scafell Pike at 987 metres.

Mountainous areas are popular with walkers, although the terrain can be tricky so it suits experienced walkers best.

Gorges and waterfalls

A gorge is a deep ravine created by water running through it. It has steep sides and often has waterfalls.

These features provide spectacular scenery. Examples in the UK include the Falls of Glomach in the Highlands of Scotland, one of the highest waterfalls in the UK. In Wales the gorge at Ceunant Llennyrch, in the Brecon Beacons, has sides 30 metres high and a waterfall called Rhaeadr Ddu. Some of the water from this waterfall was once used for hydroelectricity. North Yorkshire also has many gorges and waterfalls.

Lydford Gorge in Devon offers:

- woodland trails through a deep-cut ravine alongside the river Lyd
- a 30-metre Whitelady waterfall
- 'walk the plank' over the Devil's Cauldron whirlpools
- wildlife-watching hides located along the Railway Trail
- organised children's activities.

Case study: river revival

The Bow Back rivers of East London could be set for a glowing revival in time for the 2012 Olympics.

Plans have been put forward by British Waterways to take over a million tonnes of traffic off local roads and make this hidden network of rivers a vibrant visitor destination.

The move follows the publication in May 2006 of the Lower Lea Valley Vision by the London Thames Gateway Development Corporation (LTGDC), London Development Agency and Greater London Authority. It sets out a blueprint for the sustainable restoration of the waterways and underlines their strategic importance to the life, economy and environment of the area.

The first practical step would be the construction of a £15 m new lock and flood control structure close to Three Mills. The structure, which could be operational as early as December 2007, would restore navigation on the waterways above Three Mills for the first time in 40 years and create a major new transport link between the Thames and the planned developments of the Olympic Park and Stratford City. The lock would be able to accommodate 350-tonne barges, helping to save at least 100,000 journeys before 2012 and providing a green transport system for waste and recyclates in the future.

(Source: http://www.waterscape.com)

1 **How will the restoration take traffic off roads?**

2 **What is meant by the term 'sustainable restoration'?**

3 **Why do you think a lock and flood control structure is needed if there isn't one now?**

4 **What kind of things do you think will be transported on the waterways?**

5 **How will the project be funded?**

Taking it further

Find out what other restoration projects are underway in East London in preparation for the Olympics.

Theory into practice

Find a natural attraction close to where you live. It may be something that already attracts tourists. If this is so, find out how many tourists visit, when they visit and what the appeal is. If the attraction does not yet appeal to tourists, consider the potential and suggest what developments could be made to encourage tourists to visit. Prepare some notes for a presentation on your findings to the rest of your group. **P3 P4 D1**

Figure 3.7 Lydford Gorge ▶

Location of destinations

The map of the UK road network shows how easy it is to reach destinations by road in the UK. However, in northern Scotland the roads become more sparse and access becomes more difficult. There is also an extensive rail network in the UK with fast and frequent journeys available, particularly from north to south.

Once inbound tourists arrive at a gateway (a seaport or an airport), they can easily reach their destination by private or public transport.

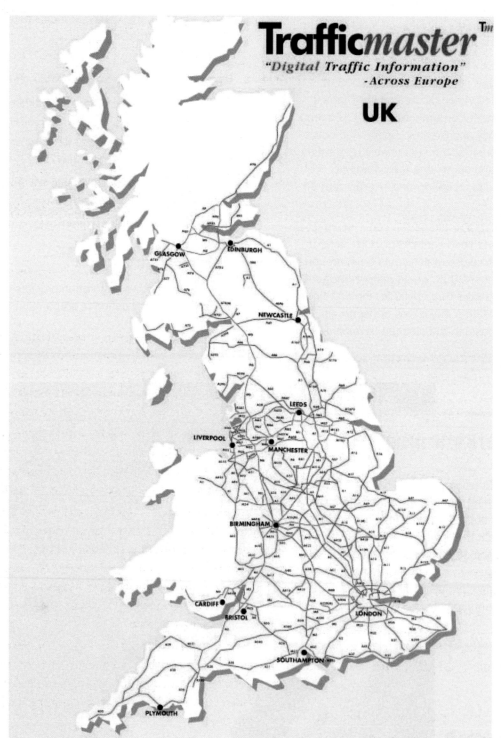

▲
Figure 3.8
UK road map

(Source: http://www.trafficmaster.co.uk; © Trafficmaster plc)

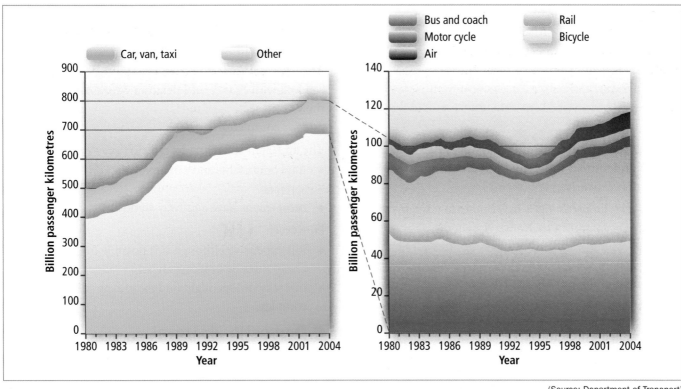

Figure 3.9 Passenger travel by car and other modes 1980–2004

(Source: Department of Transport)

Transport

When travelling by road different types of tourists will have different requirements. Those with plenty of time and no small children may make the journey an integral part of the trip, enjoying driving and stopovers en route. Others want to arrive at their end destination as quickly as possible. Tourists also have to consider what transport is available within the destination as well as getting to the destination.

According to Transport Trends 2005, car use has continued to increase as disposable income has risen, as there has been little rise in the cost of motoring.

The number of bus journeys has declined from the mid-1980s to the mid-1990s, but has shown some increase over the last few years, mainly because of increased bus use in London. Rail travel has increased by over 40 per cent over the 10 years to 2005 despite the effects of the Hatfield crash in October 2000. Investment in national rail infrastructure has increased significantly since privatisation.

■ Roads

Domestic travellers within the UK are more likely to travel by road than by any other means. Car ownership is at its highest ever – 44 per cent of households own one car, 23 per cent own two cars and 5 per cent have three or more cars, according to the 2001 census. Results from the United Kingdom Tourism Survey 2004 show that 73 per cent of domestic tourism trips are made by car.

As our roads are also used for transporting goods, this means that the network is under a lot of pressure. The UK has a good network of motorways but they are frequently congested, particularly the M1, M6 and M25.

In general, using the road network is free, apart from road tax and petrol. Petrol is very expensive in the UK, so it is an important cost consideration. There are a few toll roads, for example the Dartford crossings via the M25, and the M6 north of Birmingham which has an optional toll section for motorists to avoid congestion on the main M6 route.

Even when tourists are to travel to their destination by air they may use the road network to reach the airport. Possible hold-ups from traffic congestion have to be taken into consideration when planning the journey to the airport.

The appeal of travelling by road in the UK is:

- there is an extensive road network with few tolls
- it is easy to find petrol stops and services
- roads are well signed
- you can carry whatever baggage you want
- it is easy and comfortable for families with children.

However:

- roads can be congested in holiday periods
- inbound tourists may have trouble driving on the left
- petrol is expensive.

Tourists with limited budgets may choose to travel by coach. There are some excellent services in the UK, especially for longer distance express services across the country where coach travel offers a good alternative to rail travel at competitive fares. For journeys between about 120 and 560 kilometres, coaches and railways enjoy a similar market share. The leisure and holiday market is vital to the success of coach operators, with organised coach tours and holiday journeys accounting for about 60 per cent of all coach travel in UK. Services to airports are an important element of coach travel.

The major coach operator, National Express, carries over 16 million passengers a year to 1000 different places in the UK. It also runs services to and from UK airports and operates special services to festivals like Glastonbury.

The appeal of travelling by coach in the UK is that:

- there are services from all major towns
- it is cheaper than other forms of road transport.

However, journeys take longer compared with other modes of transport.

■ Rail

The rail network in the UK is complex and beleaguered by problems. Serious crashes like the one at Potters Bar in May 2002 undermine public confidence, and some services have a reputation for being expensive and unpunctual.

There are different train-operating companies (TOCs) for different regions, and another company, Network Rail, is responsible for all the tracks and systems. Network Rail is a not-for-profit company. There are 25 TOCs which hold franchises to run each service. Examples include Virgin Trains and Stagecoach.

London has a comprehensive underground rail system, and Glasgow and Newcastle have metro systems.

The London Docklands Light Railway has been very successful in improving transport links and reducing road congestion.

The Channel Tunnel opened in 1994 and provides a vital rail link with France and Belgium. Work continues on the second section of the UK high-speed rail line and is due for completion in 2007.

The appeal of travelling by rail is:

- it is comfortable and can be very fast on express services
- most towns have a railway station.

However:

- it is expensive although it is possible to get some very cheap rates by booking ahead
- overseas visitors might find the pricing of tickets complex.

■ Domestic air travel

In terms of fatalities per passenger kilometre, air is the safest mode of transport.

There were 26 million passengers on UK domestic flights in 2005, up by 4 per cent from the previous year. It is possible to travel from most regional airports to London and there are excellent daily connections between Scotland and London.

The following extract explains the trends.

Airports that enjoyed large traffic increases last year included Kent International at Manston (104 per cent more passengers), Bournemouth (up 68 per cent) and Coventry (up 56 per cent).

Passenger numbers at the London area airports increased 4 per cent to nearly 134 million, with Heathrow handling nearly 68 million customers in 2005.

Traffic at regional airports last year rose 9 per cent to 95 million, with Blackpool numbers up 42 per cent, Exeter up 36 per cent and Liverpool up 32 per cent. Regional airport passenger numbers have now doubled from the 47 million handled in 1995.

Air transport movements (landings and take-offs of commercial aircraft) increased 6 per cent last year to 2.3 million. The biggest increase was at Luton where movements rose 17 per cent to 75.4 million passengers, an increase of 11.2 million.

(Source: Civil Aviation Authority – UK Airport Statistics)

Theory into practice

Find out the numbers of passengers at your nearest airport. You should be able to find them on the airport's website. Find out where tourists are coming from. Are they domestic travellers, inbound or outbound? Compare your findings with another member of the group.

The appeal of air travel is:
- it is often cheap
- the journey is fast.

However:
- onward connections are also needed
- airport check-in and travel to and from adds time to the journey.

■ Sea

The UK is linked by ferry to its neighbours in Ireland and also to France, Holland and Scandinavia. Because of competition from air travel and the Channel Tunnel, operators have added many extras to their services to entice people to travel by ferry.

Domestic tourists who travel by sea are most likely to be leisure or VFR (visiting friends and relatives) travellers. They may be going to the Channel Islands, the Isle of Wight or the Isle of Man on holiday. Many tourists cross to Ireland to visit family, although these routes face competition from the low-cost airlines.

The following is a description of a ferry service operating from Holyhead to Dublin.

Irish routes

When Irish Ferries' flagship Ulysses *was launched in 2001 on the Holyhead–Dublin route it seemed almost too good to be a ferry. While other new ships may have matched or outshone it since, it is still an impressive vessel.*

The fact that many of the ship's attractions are named after characters in James Joyce's legendary novel Ulysses *gives it a touch of added class. Facilities include both self- and table-service restaurants, several lounges, the Cyclops Family Entertainment Centre and a cinema.*

Rival Stena Line has recently spent about £1 million on upgrading services on the Stena Adventurer, *which operated on the same route. Improvements include the addition of a Stena Plus lounge.*

(Source: *Travel Trade Gazette*, 19 May 2006)

The appeal of sea travel is:
- the journey is relaxing and part of the holiday experience
- it is relatively cheap.

However:
- it takes a long time
- connections are needed to and from the seaport.

Attractions

Purpose-built attractions

Buildings that attract tourists may be historic, like the colleges of Oxford and Cambridge, or purpose built, for example theme parks. Attractions are also built to enhance the existing tourism potential of a destination such as water parks and fairgrounds at a seaside resort.

A purpose-built resort is an area that has been developed solely for tourism. It has accommodation, transport links and tourist facilities and entertainment. Examples are Center Parcs and Butlins.

Historic attractions

These attractions include monuments and ruins, castles, palaces and churches.

Unoccupied royal palaces are looked after by the Historic Royal Palaces Agency, a charitable organisation set up by DCMS. The organisation must care for the upkeep and conservation and also manage public opening.

The palaces it takes care of are:
- The Tower of London
- Hampton Court Palace
- Kensington Palace State Apartments
- Royal Ceremonial Dress Collection
- The Banqueting House
- Whitehall
- Kew Palace with Queen Charlotte's Cottage.

Case study: Butlins

There are three Butlins resorts in the UK, all situated in seaside locations: Bognor Regis, Minehead and Skegness. Each resort offers different kinds of accommodation, eating places, shops, swimming pools and plenty of entertainment. The main target is families on a limited budget, although Butlins has worked hard at expanding this by offering specialist short breaks and catering for the conference market.

Traditionally, Butlins was known as a holiday 'camp' rather than holiday centre, and it had an image of being cheap and cheerful. Billy Butlin opened the first camp in 1936. It remained a family operation until 1972 when it was bought by Rank.

Butlins now belongs to Bourne Leisure, one of Britain's largest holiday companies. It was acquired from Rank as part of a package of several holiday companies.

Rank spent £139 million refurbishing the three resorts over 2 years from 1998. One thousand new chalets were built, and a huge pavilion was added to each site with indoor shops and entertainment. In spite of this investment Butlins did not attract enough customers and losses were made.

Bourne Leisure considered selling the operation but decided to try to turn around the business. Families are now the main target only in peak season, the rest of the time Butlins offers 'entertainment breaks' aimed at adults.

Bourne has also invested £30 million in upgrading accommodation, landscaping, and updating the Redcoats' uniforms. In 2004 a spa centre opened at the Skegness resort. So far the results have been good, with turnover and spend per head increasing. Bourne has further plans – it intends to give each resort its own theme and to attract more conference business, as a Butlins resort can accommodate at least 5000 people.

In 2006, Butlins decided to enter the timeshare market, this means that loyal Butlins customers can now buy a timeshare at BlueSkies, the new timeshare resort at Minehead. Butlins joined forces with the timeshare exchange company, RCI, so that those with timeshares in other parts of the world can exchange their weeks for some at Butlins.

Find out more about the conference market at Butlins. Look at Butlins brochures and search for the Butlins and Bourne Leisure sites on the internet.

1 **Choose one of the three Butlins resorts and describe the features that attract tourists. Remember to include transport links and location.** **P3**

2 **Describe the appeal of a Butlins resort to a conference customer. Your customer is likely to be a large company or public sector operation which needs a large venue for a conference. Compare your findings with the appeal of another conference venue in the UK.** **P3**

Case study: Burghley House

Burghley House is the largest and grandest house of the first Elizabethan age built between 1555 and 1587. As well as 35 major rooms on the ground and first floors, there are more than 80 lesser rooms and numerous halls, corridors, bathrooms and service areas. It also has beautiful walks around the historic parkland laid out by Capability Brown.

Investigate Burghley House on the internet (www.burghley.co.uk) and answer the following questions.

1 **What is the appeal to visitors of Burghley House?** **P3**

2 **What kind of visitors are most likely to visit and why? Are they domestic tourists, incoming tourists or day visitors?** **M1**

3 **Which organisation(s) are involved in running the house?**

Taking it further

Choose a historic property in your area and answer the same questions.

Figure 3.10 Notting Hill Carnival ▶

Modern attractions

These are usually purpose built-attractions. Examples include theme parks, new museums and galleries, such as the Tate Modern on the South Bank in London. Some modern attractions are visitor centres. Visitor centres give tourists an opportunity to get an overview of what is on offer at an attraction in a specially built environment. They usually have an exhibition illustrating the attraction's features, a cafe and a shop. Sometimes tourists go to the visitor centre and decide not to go to the actual attraction!

Educational attractions

Some attractions deliberately market to schools and colleges and offer special rates and educational tours. Examples include the Science Museum in London and the Eden Project in Cornwall.

Theory into practice

Choose an attraction which provides special tours for educational groups. Explain how it meets the needs of these tourists. Gather information and photos which can be used for a display.

Cultural attractions

The many music festivals in the UK are more likely to attract domestic rather than incoming tourists. In the summer, 'V' festivals in Reading and Leeds attract rock music lovers to those areas. Glastonbury is also a famous music festival venue. In addition, events such as the Notting Hill Carnival attract domestic tourists to London. Other events feature pageantry or historical anniversaries. VisitBritain uses such events whenever possible to aid in its marketing to tourists. Often the marketing campaigns link events and attractions to a theme to give added impetus to the campaign.

The Notting Hill Carnival takes place in Ladbroke Grove in London every August Bank Holiday weekend. The festivities last for three days. The first carnival was in 1966, and was started by West Indian immigrants in the area. These were mainly Trinidadians who wanted to replicate the flavour of their wonderful carnivals at home. The first carnival was fairly small, but now it is a massive spectacular attracting up to 2 million people.

The carnival reflects the multicultural nature of British society, with people celebrating their own musical and artistic traditions from around the world, for example the Philippines, Central and South America and Bangladesh as well as the Caribbean.

For two days of the carnival there are three live stages featuring local bands, as well as song artists from other countries. Visitors can buy exotic foods at street stalls or buy traditional arts and crafts.

Perhaps the most exciting part of the carnival is the long procession which takes place. People parade in magnificent costumes, alongside soca and steel bands.

Theory into practice

If you can, visit the Notting Hill Carnival. Otherwise, find out about a similar (possibly much smaller-scale) event in your area that represents the local culture. Describe the event in detail. Find out if the event attracts tourists and if that is its purpose. Compile some facts and figures on the event and share your findings with your group.

Case study: the appeal of York

York is a popular city destination for both domestic and overseas tourists.

Most visitors arrive in York by car as it is easily accessible by road. It does, however, also have good rail links. There are regional airports within reach but international visitors are likely to travel via London or Manchester.

The city has many historic and cultural attractions, the most famous being York Minster, the Jorvik Centre and the Castle Museum. The last two are purpose-built attractions.

Motivation for travel to the city varies according to the type of tourist. Many visit to see a historic city but there are those who come for the good shopping or to be entertained at the horse races.

Geographically, York benefits from its proximity to beautiful countryside – the Yorkshire Moors and the Yorkshire Dales. Many tourists combine a visit to the countryside with their city visit.

Local attractions include:

- Jorvik Centre – a ride back to life more than 1000 years ago, with many items on display that were discovered in an archaeological dig on the site
- York Minster – the largest gothic church in England
- medieval city walls
- Barley Hall – a timber-framed house dating form the Wars of the Roses
- nearby stately homes – Bishopthorpe Palace and Sutton Park
- shopping in the streets of Stonegate and Petergate.

Repeat business is important to York, otherwise overall visitor numbers would fall. A series of one-off or annual events is arranged in order to attract visitors. Look at the York Tourism website (www.visityork.org) for the latest examples.

Information about tourism in York provided by City of York Council for 2005:

- 3.84 million visitors to York
- £311.8 million spent by visitors to York

- 9570 jobs in York created by tourism
- 65 per cent travel to York by car, 23 per cent by train and 2 per cent by regular bus.

The following information is for the year 2005 following a visitor survey:

- 11,000 year-round and seasonal bedspaces
- 48 per cent bed occupancy, 62.9 per cent room occupancy
- the largest number of visitors is in the 35–64 age groups and in the ABC1 socio-economic groups
- the great majority are independent travellers (90 per cent). However, there is a trend towards older (over 55) visitors
- over 1.3 million of the visitors to York have been, or will go, to other parts of Yorkshire during their current visit to York, using York as a gateway
- 74 per cent of visitors have been to York before – a strong showing for repeat business and up from 58 per cent in 1996–7
- 24.4 per cent of visitors are from overseas with the greatest increases from the Far East and Australasia.

(Source: City of York Council)

1 **What is another term for the amount of money spent by tourists?**

2 **Why is there a difference between bed occupancy and room occupancy?**

3 **How could York attract more young people?**

4 **Fewer overseas visitors went to York between 1996 and 2005. Can you suggest why this was so?**

5 **Do some research and identify five attractions in York or the surrounding area that might appeal to a visiting couple in their fifties from the USA.** M1

Taking it further

Analyse why the attractions appeal to both domestic and inbound tourists.

Key terms

Domestic tourists – people who are travelling in their own country for tourism purposes.

Inbound tourists – people who visit a country which is not their country of residence for the purposes of tourism. If the tourist comes from France to the UK then they are outbound from France and inbound to the UK.

Assessment practice

Working in your group debate the motion 'Holidays in the UK are preferable to going abroad'. Your tutor will assign you to speak either for or against the motion. You should prepare your arguments from the point of view of domestic tourists. Usual debating rules apply. Points to consider include:

- natural attractions
- acess to destinations
- transport
- cultural attractions
- safety and security
- language
- events.

Domestic tourism markets

Families

Families can be difficult to cater for as needs differ according to the age of children. Those with small children may prefer the flexibility of self-catering. They may require early meal times in hotels and babysitting facilities. Those with older children will probably look for the provision of entertainment and children's clubs.

The UK has a great deal to offer families on holiday, but the perception is often that going abroad is cheaper and the weather is better.

In 2006, Enjoy England set out to show that this was not the case.

Cheaper to go abroad?

We don't think so. That's why we accepted the BBC's challenge to find a 2 week holiday in England cheaper than an equivalent holiday abroad for under £1100 and we went back with a number of options. Last Friday a guest family selected their winner … Having taken this holiday in the East of England, when asked to compare it with their holiday abroad, and whether they would prefer to travel abroad or stay in England next time, the children said they would choose England!

(Source: http://www.enjoyengland.com/ideas/whats_on/june/feature_page/bbc-breakfast-challenge.aspx)

School trips

School trips are an important element in the domestic tourism market. It is becoming increasingly difficult for schools to organise trips, as parents and teachers become more conscious of health and safety and parents are often prepared to sue if something goes wrong. This has led to an increase in bureaucracy and risk assessments for schools planning trips. However, most schools still organise some outings, and attractions and destinations provide special rates and facilities for them. Group organisers will expect some kind of educational activity organised for them. Even if the visit is to a theme park, a talk may be requested. They will also often request a space to meet and a place to eat their packed lunches!

Business

The sectors contributing to business tourism include conferences, exhibitions, corporate hospitality and individual business travel. By 2001, expenditure by business travellers exceeded that of leisure travellers. The sector is estimated to be worth more than £16 billion.

Business customers require many of the same services as holiday customers but there are some differences:

- Business services are needed, for example fax and internet
- High-quality products and services are needed
- There is less seasonal variation – facilities are required all year round
- Corporate entertainment or catering may be needed.

Honeymoons

Some domestic tourists choose to take their honeymoon in the UK for reasons of cost or convenience. Not everyone wants a sunny honeymoon. The UK can offer all sorts of more active honeymoons, such as walking and cycling holidays. Romance is also available in five-star hotels or even Scottish castles. Inbound honeymooners may be looking for a cultural experience and wish to spend a few nights in London, enjoying theatre, shopping and good restaurants.

Groups

Groups have particular needs in that there are a lot of people at one time trying to access the same facilities, for example entering an attraction, using toilets or catering facilities, or moving around a tourist area. Visitor attractions, in particular, have strategies in place for managing groups. Otherwise, the needs of the group depend on what type of group it is, for example it may be a school group or a group of senior citizens.

VisitBritain carried out some research in 2004 to try and establish who England's customers are and what their expectations are. The study was entitled 'Destination England – How well does it deliver?' The British public was grouped into eight main segments as shown in the pie graph in Figure 3.11. The labels describe the type of people and the percentage relates to the percentage of the population in that category.

Three of the groups were chosen as specific targets for marketing campaigns. They were chosen on the basis of taking frequent short breaks and on the likelihood of their receptiveness to enjoy British marketing campaigns. The three chosen groups are described in Table 3.2.

Segment	Core values	Market size and lifestage	Holiday habits
Cosmopolitan	Independent, individual risk-takers who seek new experiences and challenges, both physical and intellectual	15 per cent of the population, with high ethnic representation. Relatively young, average income is £26,000 and over a third of them are post-family	On average take over four short breaks a year. Enjoy a wide variety of types of holiday, especially activity/themed holidays
Discoverers	Independent of mind and keen on value for money. Little influenced by style or brand, but value good service	12 per cent of the population, predominantly C1 with average income of £25,000. Most likely to be aged 26–35, with kids at home, and high internet users	Likely to take bargain break/late deal rather than package holiday. Much more likely to weekend in England than abroad
High Street	Fashion victims (rather than pioneers) who care what others think. Will pay more for quality as long as tried and tested	21 per cent of the population, predominantly ABC1 with average income of £22,000. Physically active, representing wide range of ages	Attracted to bargain breaks and unlikely to go off the beaten track. Much more likely to take long holiday abroad than in England

Table 3.2 VisitBritain survey: characteristics of targeted groups

(Source: VisitBritain, 'Destination England')

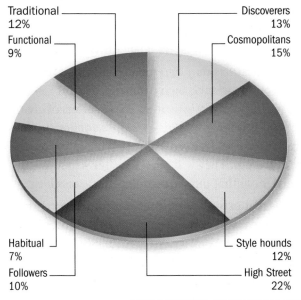

Traditional 12%
Functional 9%
Discoverers 13%
Cosmopolitans 15%
Habitual 7%
Followers 10%
High Street 22%
Style hounds 12%

(Source: VisitBritain, 'Destination England')

▲ Figure 3.11 VisitBritain survey: types of people

Inbound tourist markets

Business

Business tourism is a very important product for the UK inbound tourist market. It brings in a lot of revenue but also allows regeneration of urban areas when hotels are built for business tourism. In seaside areas, resorts which might be lifeless in the winter are often used for conferences out of season. London and Cardiff have been pinpointed by the government as locations for the development of major international conference facilities.

Leisure

Leisure tourists from abroad are attracted by the British culture and visitor attractions. Many inbound tourists come on short breaks, visiting major towns and cities, particularly London. They may want to indulge a special interest: VisitBritain offers lots of ideas for leisure tourists and categorises them to appeal to different interests and age groups, for example youth or gay. For families, outings to attractions such as steam trains or zoos are recommended and child-friendly accommodation is also recommended.

A function of VisitBritain is to attract overseas tourists. An important market is Japan. VisitBritain provides market profiles of different countries to aid organisations who wish to market to them. This extract describes a market segment from Japan.

VB Key Consumer Segment – MAKEINU – 'Office Ladies'

Basically a Japanese version of 'Bridget Jones' – single and childless working women older than 30.

According to Japan Tourism Marketing (JTM), there is a new group of women that is being watched by the travel industry: the 'ohitorisama' (single – not young – lady) who travels alone by choice. The 'Makeinu' label best describes these women and their attitudes.

More people are travelling alone, either by choice or out of necessity, such as for business. According to the research carried out by the advertising agency Hakuhodo, Britain ranked second as the most preferred destination to visit alone, first was New York.

Ohitorisama, according to this research, tend to be women in their 30s and 40s, many of them are highly successful career women, who see travelling alone as a way of rejuvenating themselves. They prefer to visit attractions at their own pace, enjoy dining and having a drink on their own and prefer staying at a hotel alone.

As more women gain financial independence and choose a career before marriage, spending habits, lifestyles and leisure demands will change. Travel firms have begun to target these women. ANA Sales said that an increasing number of 'ohitorisama', especially women in their 30s, travel to Europe. The agency said that women in this age group who travel alone tend to be very selective about the location of the hotel and even the type of room they want to stay in. They want to be pampered and spend quality time alone. The JTB Chikyu Club introduced a short-term overseas language study tour targeting this group. Jalpak has another for language learning combined with cooking classes in London.

(Adapted from http://www.visitbritain.com)

Grading tips

To reach Pass level, you need to produce four information sheets, for example descriptions of the needs of:

- families
- business tourists
- visitors from the USA
- European students who want to study English.

To reach Merit level, you must do more than describe the needs of the tourists. You must clearly link the features of four destinations to the characteristics of each of your chosen group. For example, in Stratford, tourists can watch productions of Shakespeare plays by the Royal Shakespeare Company. This meets the needs of tourists from the USA who want to experience traditional British culture firsthand.

Meeting domestic and inbound tourist needs

Access to information

The internet can help all travellers in planning their journeys and holidays. Incoming tourists need information on transport, accommodation, attractions and events. The VisitBritain website and the national and regional tourism board websites and their links allow inbound tourists to do a lot of research before they arrive in the country.

Inbound tourists cannot always access information in English. It needs to be available in their own language.

VisitBritain has added a local language websites facility with new websites recently added for the Czech Republic, Greece, Hungary, Malaysia and Thailand.

Inbound tourists may also require information from other sources in their own countries. The provision of overseas offices by VisitBritain is one means of giving access to this information. Tour operators in overseas countries are also a means of supplying information about the UK. They will print brochures in local languages so that information is easily accessible.

Domestic tourists need the same information and can get it from travel agents, tourist boards, direct from attractions and from Tourist Information Centres.

The British are not best known for their linguistic abilities and yet our inbound tourists cannot always be expected to speak English. They need to have information readily available in their own language. This does not often happen, even with common languages like French and Spanish. Few restaurants provide translated menus and transport information is not often available in other languages. Hotel staff with languages are only found in large cities. In addition, cultural differences between visitors and UK residents should be recognised.

The sector that performs best in terms of language interpretation is the attractions sector where, in order to appeal to inbound tourists, information in the form of leaflets and tapes is often in several languages.

The importance of welcoming visitors in their own language is recognised by the *Welcome to Excellence* training programme provided for tourist staff by tourist boards. The course also raises awareness of cultural differences. The following is an example from the Welcome International course language module.

The objectives are that by the end of the training, you will be able to:

- *meet, greet and inform visitors in nine languages – Arabic, Chinese (Mandarin), Dutch, French, German, Italian, Japanese, Norwegian and Spanish*
- *be able to help visitors with a range of requests*
- *promote your facilities and services*
- *enhance the positive image of your organisation*
- *make overseas visitors especially welcome – so hopefully they will want to return.*

(Source: *Welcome to Excellence*, Regional Tourist Board Partnership Limited)

Accommodation

Hotels and other accommodation providers wish to attract inbound and domestic tourists. Those hotels in international groups often have an advantage as they can market globally, and visitors to the UK who are familiar with a brand in their home company may look for it here. Smaller establishments can use the services of tourist organisations to help them promote themselves to tourists.

Providers of accommodation should be aware of the expectations of different groups. The Japanese women referred to earlier would expect good security in the hotel and places to eat and drink where they feel comfortable. Tourists from the USA may be used to very spacious rooms with high standards of cleanliness and service. London hotels tend to have smaller rooms and because of pressure on space may not provide facilities like gyms and swimming pools.

Transport

Airlines and ferry companies cater for outbound and inbound tourists but UK-based companies have to make greater marketing efforts in foreign countries to establish their reputation. Some low-cost airlines have had success in this way to the extent that they have established bases in other countries, for example Ryanair has a base in Frankfurt-Hahn.

Inbound-tour operators will be less familiar to you than outbound ones as their marketing activity takes place overseas attracting tourists to the UK. These tour operators are represented by Ukinbound, a trade organisation. It has over 260 members in all sectors of tourism.

When inbound tourists arrive at the airport they will find tourist information services, transport information and accommodation desks to help them move on to their destination.

Tourists, like all of us, need a safe, efficient and clean transport system. Most domestic tourists travel by car (71 per cent of day trips are taken by car according to the Leisure Visits Survey). The car traveller needs an adequate, uncongested road network and services at regular intervals en route.

In terms of public transport, domestic tourists are familiar with our systems and are more likely to get to grips with booking tickets on different forms of transport than overseas visitors. Overseas visitors are much more dependent on public transport than domestic tourists. Driving is not such a popular option as drivers have to contend with driving on the left-hand side of the road and having a steering wheel on the right if they are in a hire car. Transport systems which met the needs and expectations of inbound tourists, especially those coming from countries with excellent train services, would certainly meet the needs of domestic tourists.

Inbound tourists need:

- good public transport directly from airports to cities and towns – Heathrow and Gatwick are quite well served but some regional airports are not
- access by lift and escalator, space for luggage
- clear information about services – across transport systems
- the ability to buy tickets which can be used for through journeys across transport systems
- catering en route, for example buffet cars on trains.

At the end of 2004, the Department of Transport launched a new website. The aim was to provide in one place everything anyone needs to know about getting round the UK. It forms part of the government's integrated transport strategy. Travellers can enter their departure point and their destination and get a breakdown of the journey by public transport with details of trains and buses, times and even walking times between connections. Information for air routes is also given. Details of the equivalent car journey can also be found for comparison. Some have already criticised the website saying it does not have complete information, but it is still in its infancy. The website had a budget of £40 million allocated up to 2006.

Figure 3.12 shows the route by public transport for a visitor arriving at Gatwick and travelling to Manchester.

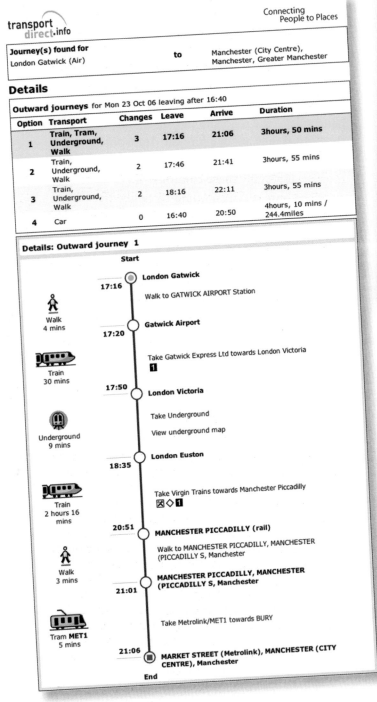

Theory into practice

Go to the website at www.transportdirect.info. Imagine you are a visitor arriving at Heathrow and find out how you would get to Lancaster by public transport. Are there any limitations to the website from the incoming tourist's point of view? Discuss your use of the website with your group.

Both inbound and domestic tourists will welcome a new development by National Express coaches. The company accepts that it can't be the fastest form of travel but aims to be the most relaxing. They have found that a big cause of stress for travellers is worrying that someone will sit next to them. Psychologists say that a typical person has a comfort zone which extends to just over 1 metre around them and they don't like this space being intruded upon. The National Express Solution – book two seats together, a 'supersized' seat!

Facilities

Most tourists require similar facilities such as entertainment, restaurants and activities for children. Different religious groups may have special needs because of their culture. Examples include separate swimming times, dietary requirements and information about religious services.

Special events and attractions

VisitBritain has campaigns aimed at overseas tourists to try to encourage them to come to the UK. You can find current examples on the VisitBritain website. Some of them relate to royal palaces and events. Many tourists from overseas are fascinated by the British royal family and the pomp and ceremony that goes with it. Remember that many of the UK's visitors are from republics and therefore have no royalty. There are numerous royal palaces to visit and some of them put on events to attract people. Many such events provide an opportunity to see local or national customes, such as bonfires on 5 November or Christmas celebrations.

(Source: http://www.transportdirect.info)

▲ **Figure 3.12 Page from Department of Transport website**

World Heritage sites also attract tourists. The United Nations Educational, Scientific and Cultural Organisation (UNESCO) seeks to encourage the identification, protection and preservation of cultural and natural heritage around the world considered to be of outstanding value to humanity. It does this under the World Heritage Convention of 1972 and has over 700 World Heritage Sites designated worldwide. UNESCO is a global organisation and not specific to the UK. In the UK the DCMS makes sure that the UK complies with the convention. It can also nominate sites in England as potential World Heritage Sites. Nominations in Wales, Scotland and Northern Ireland are made by the respective administrations.

The UK currently has 25 World Heritage Sites. Here are some examples:

- City of Bath
- Hadrian's Wall
- Heart of Neolithic Orkney
- Giant's Causeway and Causeway Coast
- St Kilda.

Theory into practice

Find the list of UK World Heritage Sites from the UNESCO website (portal.unesco.org/). Make sure you know what and where each of them is. Choose one in the UK and try to decide what makes it outstanding. Discuss your findings with your group.

Theory into practice

Discuss the differences in needs of these two groups of tourists on a short break to London.

- A couple visiting London from Sheffield travelling by train. They have been twice before.
- A couple visiting London from Frankfurt (Germany). They do not speak English and this is their first visit.

Prepare a PowerPoint presentation which describes the needs of each of these couples. **P4**

Case study: Enjoy England Quality Rose

The Enjoy England Quality Rose reassures you before you check into your holiday accommodation that it will be just what you want, because it's been checked out by independent assessors. Enjoy England assessors work all year round, ensuring that the standards you find are what you would expect. And since we've done all the work, you can relax, book with confidence and get on with the real business of having a fantastic break.

The Quality Rose is the mark of England's official, nationwide quality assessment scheme and is an independent, reliable, impartial assessment of quality covering just about every type of place you might want to stay. The variety of accommodation on offer is truly astonishing: from caravan parks to stylish boutique hotels, farmhouse B&Bs to country house retreats, self-catering cottages by the sea to comfy narrowboats perfect for getting away from it all. There are nine main types of accommodation, with a host of different options in each. But whatever your budget or preference, you can be sure of finding something

to suit. Think of the Quality Rose as your personal guarantee that your expectations will be met.

Our objective quality ratings give you a clear indication of accommodation standard, cleanliness, ambience, hospitality, service and food. Using a clear star and diamond rating system (1–5 stars or diamonds), they provide the reassurance you need about what to expect before you arrive. Generally, the more stars or diamonds, the higher the level of quality. For individual types of accommodation, the quality rating allows you to distinguish between both the quality of the accommodation and the facilities on offer. In fact, we'd like to make things even more simple for you in future – so very soon Enjoy England star ratings will be exactly the same as those awarded by the AA and the RAC because we've all used the same rigorous criteria. That way, you know where you are.

(Source: http://www.enjoyengland.com)

1. **Explain how a system such as the Quality Rose is reassuring for tourists.**

2. **Why do you think the ratings used by the AA and the RAC are currently different?**

Quality assurance

All tourists have a right to know that the transport and travel services that they use meet particular quality standards. It is unlikely that inbound tourists will want to know the detailed grading schemes, rather they want to know that three-star or four-star rated accommodation can be relied on to be of a particular standard wherever they go in the UK or elsewhere. Inbound tourists will also use guides for quality recommendations on places to visit and for restaurants. These may be international guides such as Michelin or Fodor.

3.5 Understand key trends and factors affecting the UK inbound and domestic tourism markets

Key trends

Before use consider the factors affecting the UK inbound and domestic market, carry out your own investigation.

Assessment practice

For this activity you should research the International Passenger Survey. This can be found online at www.statistics.gov.uk. You should investigate:

- numbers of inbound tourists
- numbers of outbound tourists
- countries of origin of inbound tourists
- purpose of visit.

Include graphs as appropriate and draw some conclusions. In particular, you should comment on trends and say why you think the UK is gaining or losing appeal as a tourist destination. Produce a report of your findings.

Length of stay

Domestic tourist trips tend to be short in length with more than half of trips lasting one or two nights. This is explained by the growth of short leisure breaks and the decline of the traditional British seaside holiday. Business tourism trips also tend to be short.

Generating countries and regions

It is visitors from eastern European countries and from long haul destinations outside the USA who have provided the increase in visits of inbound tourists. The expansion of the EU with ten new members in 2004 has meant that residents of those states have easier access to European travel. Asian tourists are returning as the Asian economy improves.

Country	Visits (000)	Country	Spend (£m)
USA	3438	USA	2400
France	3324	Germany	825
Germany	3294	France	769
Irish Republic	2806	Irish Republic	760
Spain	1786	Spain	618
Netherlands	1720	Australia	588

(Source: International Passenger Survey, Office for National Statistics)

Table 3.3 Top six overseas markets for the UK in 2005

There are a number of points that can be noted from these figures.

- The countries generating the most visitors are not necessarily those who generate the most expenditure. Australia is tenth in position in the UK's overseas market and yet ranks sixth in terms of expenditure. This is important as high-spending tourists are more valuable to the UK.
- Most of the top five are the UK's neighbours. It is easier and more convenient for them to travel to the UK than for other nations.

- The Irish Republic ranks high as there is a strong VFR (visiting friends and relatives) market between the Republic of Ireland and the UK.

Theory into practice

When you read this you will have access to more recent statistics, find out who are the current top five overseas markets and compare these with the 2005 figures. Comment on any changes and reasons for them.

Volume and value of inbound and domestic tourism

Day visits represent the largest segment of domestic tourism with 60 per cent of expenditure. Remember that these figures are recorded separately in the Leisure Visits Survey. Between 1996 and 2002, domestic tourism expenditure in England increased by 14 per cent. The most popular and fastest growing sector is the leisure breaks sector.

Domestic tourism expenditure includes expenditure as a result of resident visitors travelling within their country and occurs en route, at the place visited and in advance on spending for the trip.

The UK Tourism Survey is very detailed and shows information such as number of tourist trips, number of tourist nights, spending, breakdown between England, Scotland and Wales and purpose of trip. You can find the survey data at Star UK (www.staruk.com).

In 2005, UK residents took:

- 59.3 million holidays of one night or more spending £11.5 billion
- 22.5 million overnight business trips spending £5.3 billion
- 52.7 million overnight trips to friends and relatives spending £5.4 billion.

In 2005, there was a record high of 30 million incoming tourism visits. The value of this business to the economy is £14 billion.

Meanwhile in the same period, UK outbound tourist visits also rose to 63.5 million visits. The number of visits to western Europe hardly changed but visits to North America rose by 15 per cent, possibly reflecting the strength of the pound against the dollar.

Assessment practice

1. Why do you think visitors from Pakistan and India have the longest average stay?

2. The average stay for visitors from New Zealand is 16 days. Why do you think this is?

3. Tourists from Spain and the Czech Republic only stay for an average of 9 days. Why do you think this is?

Taking it further

What factors would encourage Spanish and Czech tourists to stay longer in the UK?

Rank	Country	Average length of stay (days)
1	Pakistan	46
2	India	29
3	Iran	28
4	Nigeria	23
5	Poland	20
6	Saudi Arabia	18
7	Egypt	18
8	Brazil	17
9	China	17
10	Thailand	17
11	Taiwan	17
12	New Zealand	16
13	South Africa	16
14	Australia	14
15	United Arab Emirates	13
16	Hong Kong	13
17	Argentina	12
18	Japan	11
19	Turkey	11
20	Canada	11
21	Russia	11
22	Mexico	10
23	Hungary	10
24	Singapore	10
25	Malaysia	10
26	Portugal	10
27	Spain	9
28	Czech Republic	9
29	Israel	9
30	South Korea	8
	Total world	8

(Source: International Passenger Survey, Office for National Statistics)

Table 3.4 Overseas visitors to the UK 2005 average length of stay

Activity

Match up these terms and their definitions.

Term	Definition
Incoming tourists	People travelling in their own country for tourism purposes
Domestic tourists	A country from where tourists originate
Inbound tourists	The amount of money tourists spend on tourism in a country
Day visitors	A country that is a destination for tourists
Tourism generator	The number of tourists coming to a country
Receipts	People who visit a country which is not their country of residence for the purposes of tourism
Visitor flow	People going on an excursion and not staying overnight
Arrivals	Tourists leaving their country of residence to visit another country
Tourism receiver	Tourists travelling for the purpose of business
Outbound tourists	People who visit a country which is not their country of residence for the purposes of tourism
Business tourists	Tourists going on a holiday
Leisure tourists	Tourists travelling to visit a friend or relative
VFR	The number of tourists coming in and going out of a country

■ Frequency of visits

According to the International Passenger Survey, in 2004 77 per cent of overseas visitors had visited the UK previously (in the last 10 years), compared with 79 per cent in 2001. The larger proportion of first-time visitors in 2004 was explained by an increase in the number of visitors coming from emerging markets such as China and the Czech Republic. Repeat visitors are most likely to come from the Irish Republic (93 per cent repeaters) and least likely from South Korea (only 30 per cent repeaters). Repeat holiday visitors are bigger spenders. In 2004, average spend per visit was around £80 higher than first-timers.

Consider this

How do you think we know how many visitors come to the UK? The data are collected in the International Passenger Survey for the Office of National Statistics. A sample of people are questioned at airports and seaports. People travelling outbound are also questioned. Around 250,000 interviews are carried out per year representing 0.2 per cent of all travellers.

Factors affecting the tourist market

Factors internal to the UK

■ Health, safety and security within the UK

The UK has stringent health and safety legislation so tourists can expect to be as safe or safer than they would be in their own countries. This applies to security also. However, people tend to behave differently when they are on holiday and may not be as aware as they normally are of difficult situations. People who are unfamiliar with their surroundings and the culture are more vulnerable to crime than others. Domestic tourists may also be more vulnerable when visiting a part of the country they are not used to. The Metropolitan Police have issued advice for tourists visiting London and an extract is shown here. You will note that much of the advice relates to common-sense precautions for any large city.

- *Keep your bag or camera where you can see them by wearing them in front of you, not over your shoulder.*

This is especially important if you are in a crowded area such as on a bus or an underground train.

- When in restaurants, bars, theatres or cinemas never leave your bag on the floor or over the back of your chair. Keep it where you can see it.
- Only buy theatre or concert tickets from reliable sources and not from 'touts' in the street.
- If you're out and about at night on foot try to keep to busy, well-lit areas.
- When travelling by bus or train try to avoid using stations in isolated places. When possible sit near the driver on buses, and on trains try to make sure you sit in a compartment where there are other people.
- Always use licensed mini cabs or black cabs. Mini cabs should always be booked in advance. Unlicensed cabs and rogue drivers may compromise your safety. To find licensed mini cab firms in your area, call Transport for London on 020 7222 1234 or visit www.tfl.gov.uk.
- Be particularly vigilant when using ATM cash point machines. Be aware of anyone behind you and if the machine appears to have been tampered with in any way do not use it and report it to the police or bank immediately.
- Take extra care when crossing the road. Always remember to look both ways as traffic may be coming from a different direction than you are expecting.

(Source: http://www.met.police.uk; © Metropolitan Police Service)

Strength of the pound sterling

When the UK economy is doing well, the pound is strong. However, a strong pound actually deters tourists from overseas because when they exchange their own currency for sterling they get fewer pounds for their money, so visiting the UK becomes more expensive. Exchange rates change every day and you can find them reported in banks and in the newspapers.

Accessibility

Many new low-cost airlines are starting up business, bringing increased services between eastern Europe and the UK. In addition, established low-cost airlines are adding new services to Europe, allowing tourists to travel cheaply to the UK. Such services also increase outbound travel.

Accession to the EU has added to the appeal of the UK for new member states. Low-cost air travel, including low transatlantic fares, makes the UK more accessible to all. Emerging markets such as China and India will generate more visitors as air travel agreements between those countries and the UK come into play.

Marketing campaigns

Enjoy England – part of VisitBritain – is responsible for marketing England, both to domestic tourists and to inbound tourists. Here is an example of a marketing campaign in 2006.

£12.9 million invested in persuading the British to Enjoy England

Enjoy England Domestic Opportunities 2006/7

Our plans for 2006/7 include the £2.75 m Enjoy England marketing programme with an à la carte menu of partnerships opportunities to meet all objectives from increasing awareness of your brand to generating response and making sales. This programme is underpinned by a series of lifestyle campaigns focused on particular product themes identified through research. The 2006/7 lifestyle campaigns are Taste England, Outdoor England, City Culture and Just Relax. We are also running a series of tactical campaigns, with a heavy emphasis on PR and promotion. These include: Family Fun, Storybook England and Rock and Pop.

(Source: http://www.tourismtrade.org.uk/
englanddomesticalandinternational/EnglandMarketingLandingPage.asp)

Availability of products and services

Tourism in the UK is subject to seasonal trends and prices fluctuate with seasons. Hotel and transport prices are at their most expensive in peak times such as summer holiday and Christmas periods. Rooms are less likely to be available at such times. Restaurants are quickly booked too. The key for tourists is to plan well ahead if they want to holiday at peak times. Inbound tourists need information about opening hours of bars, restaurants and shops as they may differ from their home country.

Quality of goods and services

Consumers are becoming more discerning and the UK tourist market is responding with help from marketing agencies such as VisitBritain. Since January 2006, VisitBritain has only promoted quality assessed accommodation. Those who do not meet the criteria will not be promoted. In general, the UK has a reputation for good quality and high standards of customer service. VisitBritain also carries out research into visitor perceptions of the UK. The results of this kind of research help to improve quality standards.

Factors external to the UK

■ Exchange rate

The exchange rate continues to exert an influence on visitor numbers. Rates to watch are sterling/euro and sterling/dollar. An improvement in the strength of the dollar could bring a greater rise in visitors from the USA.

■ Travel restrictions

Travel restrictions may impact heavily on the numbers of inbound tourists. Restrictions fall into the following categories.

1 Security-related restrictions

In August 2006, British Intelligence claimed to discover a terrorist plot to blow up aircraft in mid-air. Very stringent hand baggage rules were put in place – this was temporary but caused chaos at British airports and confusion amongst travellers. The extra inconvenience and fear of terrorism could deter people from coming to the UK. The immediate restrictions were:

- If you are travelling within the UK, you will have to check in all your belongings. Wallets, IDs and necessary medications are the exceptions, and must be carried in a plastic bag (clear bags are recommended).
- Laptops, mobile phones and iPods are among the electronic items banned in carry-on luggage on British flights.
- Liquids, gels and pastes are no longer permitted in carry-on luggage on board any aircraft within the USA and UK. (This includes toothpaste, sunblock and perfume.)

2 Customs and excise restrictions

These relate to alcohol, tobacco and gifts. Leaflets are available explaining the restrictions to tourists. These are unlikely to affect large numbers of tourists.

3 Immigration restrictions

EU membership changed dramatically in 2005 when many new countries joined. This is discussed in Unit 7. Residents of member states are free to travel without restriction throughout Europe so the UK has seen a huge increase in inbound tourism from Europe.

Some visitors require visas to enter the UK. There was a large rise in visa prices in 2006, which could deter visitors from India and China.

Theory into practice

Visit the customs and excise website (http://customs.hmrc.gov.uk) and find out what the current allowances for alcohol, tobacco and gifts are for visitors to the UK from within Europe and from outside.

Emergence of new markets

There are several emerging markets that can be targeted to increase incoming tourism. These include the EU new member states already mentioned and increasing numbers of visitors from the rest of eastern Europe. Visits from Poland increased by 478 per cent from 2000 to 2005.

VisitBritain also predicts that visitor numbers from Asia will grow. China is a good example of an emerging market as in January 2005 the UK joined several other European countries and was granted 'approved destination status'.

It is estimated that there are about 25 million Chinese people with enough money to travel abroad. The UK currently has only 0.6 per cent of this market, whereas Germany and France each have acquired more than 1 per cent. VisitBritain has representatives in Beijing and Shanghai and they work with the Chinese press and travel trade to promote the UK as a destination.

The target for the UK is to attract one per cent of the Chinese market. This would generate an estimated £1 billion and create 25,000 extra jobs in tourism.

Activity

1 Find out how many Chinese people are currently visiting Britain.

2 Find an example of an attraction, an airline or a tour operator that has special facilities or services for Chinese visitors.

3 Write up your findings as a newspaper article.

Key term

Approved destination status – this is granted by the Chinese authorities to countries the Chinese people may visit as groups. Travel agents in China are authorised to deal with designated agents in the host country. Apart from making it much easier for Chinese citizens to travel to these countries, this status also has the advantage of allowing destination countries to open offices in China to promote travel to their country.

Theory into practice

Find an example of a marketing initiative from VisitBritain or VisitEngland to promote incoming tourism. Report back on the campaign to your group. Draw up ideas for a campaign to promote your own area to domestic tourists from other parts of the country. **P5**

Competition from other destinations

The UK has to be more appealing than other destinations in order to win tourists. There are many factors, as we have seen, which affect a visitor's decision on where to travel. Table 3.5 shows how the UK compares with other destinations worldwide in attracting tourists.

Activity

Study Table 3.5.

1 Why do you think the USA ranks first as a destination?

2 Why has China risen in popularity as a destination?

3 In 2006, tourists in Turkey were subject to bombings. Find out how this has impacted on Turkey's popularity.

Taking it further

Prepare some presentation notes explaining why tourists should visit the UK rather than the top five destinations.

Evaluate the future of UK inbound and domestic markets, taking into account factors considered in this unit. **D2**

Rank	Receipts			Rank	Arrivals		
	2004 US$bn	2005 US$bn	% change 2005/4		2004 m	2005 m	% change 2005/4
1 United States	74.5	81.7	9.6	1 France	75.1	76.0	1.2
2 Spain	45.2	47.9	5.8	2 Spain	52.4	55.6	6.0
3 France	40.8	42.3	3.5	3 United States	46.1	49.4	7.2
4 Italy	35.7	35.4	-0.7	4 China	41.8	46.8	12.1
5 United Kingdom	28.2	30.4	7.6	5 Italy	37.1	36.5	-1.5
6 China	25.7	29.3	13.8	6 United Kingdom	27.8	30.0	8.0
7 Germany	27.7	29.2	5.6	7 Mexico	20.6	21.9	6.3
8 Turkey	15.9	18.2	14.2	8 Germany	20.1	21.5	6.8
9 Austria	15.3	15.5	0.9	9 Turkey	16.8	20.3	20.5
10 Australia	13.6	14.9	9.5	10 Austria	19.4	20.0	3.0

Table 3.5 International travel: leading destination countries 2004 and 2005

(Source: © World Tourism Organisation)

Economic recession in tourist-generating regions

Economic success depends on the tourists who visit the UK spending their money when they get here. That is why receipts are measured and not just arrivals. Some visitors tend to spend a lot more money than others.

Visitors from Australia and visitors from the Far East are known to be good spenders in the UK and therefore are an aid to our economy. A few years ago a severe recession in the Far East meant that many Asian tourists could not afford to travel to the UK and their absence had an impact on tourism spend in the UK.

Knowledge check

1 Why are day visitors important to the economy?

2 Give two examples of modern attractions.

3 Explain why most domestic tourists travel by car.

4 Which cities in the UK attract most tourists?

5 How is the International Passenger Survey carried out?

6 Why do France, Germany and the Irish Republic generate large numbers of incoming tourists to the UK?

7 Explain why China is an emerging market.

8 What is the difference between arrivals and receipts?

9 Which two countries generate most visitors to the UK?

10 What travel restrictions might deter tourists from visiting the UK?

11 Give four examples of islands lying close to the UK.

12 Give three examples of types of domestic tourist.

13 Explain what a National Park is.

14 Name three National Parks.

15 What is the role of UNESCO?

Preparation for assessment

DCMS has a new Minister for Tourism. You and your colleagues at VisitBritain are surprised at the appointment as the Minister has no experience of the tourism industry and does not appear to be very knowledgeable about it. At a preliminary meeting with the Chairman of VisitBritain, the Chairman tried to explain all the various research reports, marketing campaigns and organisational structures that VisitBritain is involved in to boost tourism but the Minister was very slow to understand and short of time. It was decided that a clear presentation should be prepared covering all the issues essential for a grounding in the work of attracting incoming and domestic tourists and that an afternoon should be set aside for the Minister to listen to this presentation.

The Chairman has asked you to prepare all the materials for the presentation. Remember to keep records of all your reference sources and how you used them in case the Minister wants to return to them. **P1**

1 Produce a map or series of maps which show the Minister where our important gateways, tourist destinations and geographical features are. **P2**

You must include:
- all capital cities
- six coastal resorts
- six historical or cultural cities or towns
- six islands
- six lakes
- six National Parks
- six rivers
- six mountain ranges or upland areas
- six major airports
- six seaports.

2 The Minister should be informed about the features of at least three UK destinations that attract tourists. Prepare a general presentation describing them, giving several examples. **P3**

Grading tip

Make sure your three destinations are from different categories, for example one city, one coastal resort and one cultural destination.

3 Analyse the appeal of the destinations given in your presentation by giving detail on accessibility by transport links, what attractions are available and numbers and types of visitors. Add this information to your presentation. **M1**

Grading tip

To reach Merit level, make sure you give facts and figures from a wide range of reference sources.

4   The Minister needs information on the needs of domestic and inbound tourists. Describe the needs of two types of domestic tourists, e.g. families and business travellers and two types of inbound tourists, for example American and Polish. **P4**

5   Explain how four UK destinations meet the needs the two types of inbound and two types of domestic tourists you chose in task 4. **M2**

6   Evaluate the attraction of the UK for domestic and inbound tourists, making recommendations about how appeal can be increased. **D1**

Grading tip

To reach Distinction level, use the four destinations chosen in task 5 as examples and analyse any new initiatives in those destinations that make the destination more appealing to tourists. Think of things you have read about elsewhere and say how these destinations could implement them.

7   Although the Minister understands the workings of the DCMS as it is the government department he is assigned to, he has not researched key trends in tourism. You need to help him with this too. Prepare a PowerPoint presentation which clearly analyses the external and internal factors influencing recent key trends in the UK inbound and domestic markets. **P5 M3**

Evaluate the likely impact of external and internal factors on the future of the UK and inbound domestic markets. **D2**

Grading tips

To reach Pass level, you must use at least three sets of data for domestic and inbound tourism. You must interpret the trends from the data and describe the factors which have led to those trends.

To reach Merit level, you must analyse rather than describe – this means stating how the factors have influenced key trends. For example, a trend you might introduce, supported by statistics, could be the increase in visitors from Poland. This has been caused by several factors including:

- accession by Poland to the EU so that it is easier for Poles to visit the UK
- increase in provision of low-cost flights between Poland and the UK
- introduction of flights to Poland from regional airports, e.g. Doncaster.

To reach Merit and Distinction levels you must include a minimum of three external factors and three internal factors to the UK.

To reach Distinction level, you must try and assess what the future impact of trends will be.

Grading criteria

To achieve a pass grade the evidence must show that the learner is able to:	To achieve a merit grade the evidence must show that, in addition to the pass criteria, the learner is able to:	To achieve a distinction grade the evidence must show that, in addition to the pass and merit criteria, the learner is able to:
P1 use appropriate reference materials to provide information on UK destinations **Assessment practice page 75**	**M1** analyse the appeal of destinations to domestic and inbound tourists **Case study page 88**	**D1** evaluate the attraction of the UK for domestic and inbound visitors, making recommendations about how appeal to domestic and inbound tourism can be increased **Theory into practice page 83**
P2 locate gateways, tourist destinations and geographical features of the UK **Assessment practice page 76**	**M2** explain how four specific UK destination can meet the needs of domestic and inbound tourist markets **Assessment practice page 94**	**D2** evaluate the likely impacts of external and internal factors on the future of the UK inbound and domestic markets **Taking it further page 103**
P3 describe the features that attract tourists to three UK destinations **Assessment practice page 79**	**M3** analyse external and internal factors influencing recent key trends in the UK inbound and domestic markets **Taking it further page 99**	
P4 describe the needs of the UK domestic and inbound tourism markets **Theory into practice page 83**		
P5 describe external and internal factors influencing recent key trends in the UK inbound and domestic market **Assessment practice page 98**		

Customer service in travel and tourism

Introduction

Customer Service in Travel and Tourism is a core unit for the qualification and an important skill for everyone working in the industry. It is essential to travel and tourism organisations that their staff provide excellent customer service. Many organisations provide similar products and services, and it may be that the level of customer service provided will determine with whom potential customers decide to book. This unit will develop your understanding of why customer service is so important to travel and tourism organisations, and give you the opportunity to develop skills so that you can deliver excellent customer service.

We will first examine the benefits of excellent service to organisations and the real problems that can occur when customer service falls short of the mark. Organisations have an obligation to their customers and many aspects are also covered by legislation. But not all customers want the same: motivations differ and we will be examing why and how.

Your own skills need to be of the highest standard to work in the travel and tourism industry. This section will help you develop skills so that you can communciate effectively with your customers.

Finally, we will be looking at the stages of selling and giving you the opportunity to develop skills which will maximise your ability to make a decent living!

After completing this unit you should be able to achieve the following outcomes:

1 Know the principles and benefits of good customer service in travel and tourism organisations

2 Understand how travel and tourism organisations adapt customer service to meet differing customer motivations

3 Be able to demonstrate customer service skills in travel and tourism situations

4 Be able to demonstrate selling skills appropriate to the travel and tourism industry.

Thinking points

1 When did you last go shopping? Where did you go? Was it enjoyable? If so, why? If not, why not? Make a list of the things that made it a positive or negative experience (e.g. the sales person helped you; you got the clothes you wanted; they had the size you wanted but not in the right colour; you were kept waiting). Make sure you include as much information as possible. Will you go back? Have you told your friends about the good/poor service and/or what you bought?

2 Have you ever been told 'It's not what you say, it's how you say it'? What is meant by this? Work with a partner. Say 'Yes' in ten different ways! Your partner should then say what they think you actually mean.

3 Have you or someone you know ever bought something that they don't really want? Why did this happen? What did the sales person do or say to ensure they got a sale?

Principles

The objective of travel and tourism organisations is not to meet customer expectations, but to exceed them. After all, many of the flights, holidays and hotels we book are very similar and are often within the same price range. So which company customers choose to book with can be determined by the level of service provided – how friendly the travel consultant was, how quickly a phone call was returned, the personality of the receptionist or the cleanliness of the aircraft. As a travel and tourism employee you will need to be aware of the principles of customer service to ensure that customers book with you rather than your competitors.

First impressions

It takes customers just 10 seconds to form their first impressions. First impressions count!

These first impressions could be formed by seeing:

- a queue of customers – or being served immediately
- staff talking to each other and ignoring their customers – or being greeted with a smile
- scruffy staff who are chewing gum – or well-dressed staff with a professional appearance
- staff slouching over desks – or positive behaviour and body language
- eating in the office – or clear, tidy desks.

Once a negative first impression is formed, it is very difficult to change.

Consider this

Research shows that it costs five times as much to attract a new customer as to retain an existing one.

Organisations need to ensure that they retain their customers. It is essential that everyone working in travel and tourism is aware of the importance of first impressions and ensures that they contribute towards making it positive. Personal presentation and non-verbal communication are important elements of a first impression and we will be looking at this later in this unit.

Company image

The images customers have of companies will influence which one they choose to buy their products and services from. An image is personal and depends on your own experiences, expectations, things you may have read and word of mouth. For example, the image that your family hold of your school or college may be very different from your own. Your own image of a summer sun holiday in Ibiza will almost certainly be different from your parents'. All organisations are trying to develop positive images of themselves. They do this through mission statements, websites, logos and ensuring they present an air of efficiency. The appearance and location of premises are also important for many organisations. For example, the location of a hotel or travel agency is vital to ensure 'passing trade'. Similarly, the appearance of their premises is an important part of determing customers' images. By contrast, a tour operator or call centre of an airline can be (and often is) located anywhere.

Key term

Mission statement – a concise statement about an organisation's purpose. Mission statements vary but usually contain information about products, services, beliefs and values.

Logo – a symbol used by an organisation (for example, the tick is the logo of Nike and the happy face the logo of TUI).

Theory into practice

Work with a partner. Think about your images of the following organisations and destinations. What has formed your images?

- Virgin
- Ryanair
- MyTravel
- Paris
- Ayia Napa (Cyprus)
- Australia
- A local hotel
- A local travel agency.

Taking it further

Choose two travel and tourism organisations. Using the internet, find out what their mission statements are. What images are they trying to create through their mission statements and logos?

Speed and accuracy of service

One of the key trends in customer service is the expectation that it will be fast. No one wants to be kept waiting. Customers expect to be greeted straight away, telephones to be answered within three rings and e-mails to be responded to within 24 hours.

In order to be able to provide information quickly and efficiently, several skills are needed. First, you must be organised. You will not be able to know everything – but you must know where to find out about everything! If a customer wants to book a long haul holiday bird-watching in Madagascar, you should know where to find information about such specialist holidays.

Second, you need product knowledge, that is, ideally you will know where Madagascar is. However, if you don't it is important that you can quickly look it up on the internet, bespoke software or in the World Travel Guide (www.worldtravelguide.net/) and establish that it is an island in the Indian Ocean, off the coast of Mozambique.

Product knowledge also includes information about your organisation – what it sells, who to refer complaints to, opening times, and how to use the computer and telephone systems effectively. All of these will help you to provide a speedy and accurate service.

Third, your expertise in using the available technology will determine whether you provide an efficient service. If you lose people when transferring them on the phone, use the incorrect airport code on the computer reservation system or lose an unsaved document you have just produced, you will not be able to give a good service to your internal or external customers.

Everyone working in travel needs to know the phonetic alphabet and the 24-hour clock. They will help you provide an error-free service. Make sure you learn them.

A	Alpha	B	Bravo	C	Charlie
D	Delta	E	Echo	F	Foxtrot
G	Golf	H	Hotel	I	India
J	Juliet	K	Kilo	L	Lima
M	Mike	N	November	O	Oscar
P	Papa	Q	Quebec	R	Romeo
S	Sierra	T	Tango	U	Uniform
V	Victor	W	Whiskey	X	X-ray
Y	Yankee	Z	Zulu		

Table 4.1 The phonetic alphabet

The phonetic alphabet is used for clarity in various forms of communication. For example, pilots use it on radios and a tour operator may use it on the telephone.

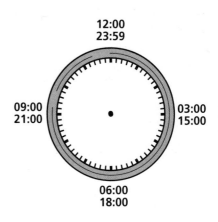

▲ **Figure 4.1 The 24-hour clock**

The 24-hour clock is used by the travel industry worldwide to avoid mistakes and confusion between am and pm when reading timetables.

The day starts at 1 minute past midnight (0001) and the following 12 hours follow the normal system; 1 pm becomes 1300 hours, 2 pm is 1400 hours and so on until midnight. In the travel industry, midnight is not represented as 2400 hours but as 2359 hours in order to make it clear which day is being referred to. The next day is 0001 hours.

Products and services offered

All travel and tourism organisations have to ensure that they are providing products and services that meet cutomers' needs. As customers become more demanding, so products and services have to be more sophisticated. Organisations have to continuously assess whether products and services are meeting their customers' needs. Does the hotel restaurant offer sufficient variety, are there adequate reception staff on duty at all times of the day, should the lifeguard hours be extended and are the evening entertainments suitable?

Customer service policies

A customer service policy is a document written by an organisation to tell customers about the minimum levels of service they can expect from the organisation. It acts as a guarantee of service to the customer but can also be used as a guide to staff. It may include, for example, how quickly a complaint will be dealt with, when tickets will be received and how customers will be compensated in the event of cancellation or delay. Sometimes this information is included in the booking conditions or in a customer charter.

Assessment practice

Research the customer policies of two similar travel and tourism organisations. List ten different aspects of service that are discussed. **P1 M1 D1**

Explain how the needs of different customer types are met in the two organisations.

Teamwork

Teamwork can be wonderful – and it can also be very difficult. You will be able to recall projects where friction has arisen with colleagues because someone has not done their fair share of the work.

All work in the travel industry involves teamwork at some stage. If a team works well, it is more likely to provide an excellent service. Imagine arriving in your holiday resort and finding that someone in the resort team had not told the transfer rep that the flight was going to be early!

A good team will:

- want to achieve the same goals
- have a leader
- involve everyone in the team
- be confident and have self-esteem
- communicate well with each other
- make clear decisions
- pay attention to detail
- respect and trust each other
- have clear roles and responsibilities
- support each other
- have a 'can do' approach.

You will look at teamwork in more detail in Unit 6. The case study opposite shows an extract from Thomson Holidays' Children's Representatives Programme.

All travel and tourism organisations will try to ensure that their staff are working well as a team. As well as contributing to a positive image of the company, a happy staff team is more likely to be efficient. Companies spend huge amounts of money on staff training to help teams work well together.

Case study: Resort teams

Teams in resorts are large and you will be working with many people, not just Thomson staff but hoteliers and officials to name but two. There should always be an attitude of open co-operation within teams, an ideal of working towards the same goal. Although this is sometimes difficult it is essential to focus on what is really important – the customers and their holiday. It is easy to get carried away with personal thoughts and feelings when working in a team but everyone should have their focus on the customer; they pay the wages at the end of the day.

The start of the season is the ideal opportunity to set up your working standards with everyone you are likely to work with. There will probably be one or two people who would not be the colleagues you would choose; your challenge will be to work well with these people despite your personal feelings. If you do that, then the customers will benefit and so will you. There is much more achievement in working well for a full season with someone you don't really like, than there is in moaning and feeling sorry for yourself all summer. Who knows, with your efforts, you may even end up good friends (it often happens!).

Many problems occur in teams because members don't know or understand each other well enough, so make sure you try hard. Talk to your colleagues and really listen to them. Other issues come up because of misunderstandings, which usually occur because of a lack of agreement about standards you will work to, who will do what, etc. It is important that you get the team together and discuss the problems.

It is sometimes difficult to talk to a colleague about something you are unhappy with – but you are much more likely to get it sorted if you do talk!

(Source: Children's Representatives Programme, Thomson Holidays)

1 **Why do problems occur in teams?**

2 **How can they be prevented?**

3 **What are the potential benefits of working in a team?**

4 **Evaluate your last teamworking experience!**

▲ Figure 4.2 Holiday representative helping with children

Effective communication

A vast range of communication methods are used within the travel and tourism industry, all of which contribute towards customer service levels and the image a customer will have of the organisation. In some jobs most of the communication will be face-to-face (e.g. a resort rep), in others it could be exclusively on the telephone (e.g. a home worker employed by a travel agency) while in other roles customer contact is mainly in written form (e.g. a marketing assistant).

All communication contributes towards the overall image the customer will have of a company. The design of the website may attract customers to investigate it further or cause them to look elsewhere for a holiday. If an e-mail has spelling errors, customers will certainly have an impression of poor service levels. Similarly, the way a telephone is answered or a customer greeted will determine customers' first impressions.

Meeting customers' needs

The aim is not to meet customers' needs, but to exceed them. By providing the right products and services and presenting these to the customer using excellent customer service skills this can be achieved.

Customers buy products or services because they believe they need them, for example a drink, a car or a holiday. Expectations refer to what the customer expects from the product or service. A drink may satisfy a need (thirst) but not meet expectations if it does not taste as good as the customer thought it would. If a customer enters a travel agency looking for a summer holiday for a family of four, they may also have certain expectations about the costs, ideal locations and activities available. You could meet the need (by selling a holiday for the family) but to exceed expectations you will also have to provide details of, for example, excursion possibilities, airport transfers, free child places and car hire.

Case study: Cook's call centre is 'the best in Britain'

Thomas Cook's call centre is rated the best, but travel firms in general are not handling calls well.

Robin Searle reports

Thomas Cook has bucked a disappointing travel trend to top a table of best call centre performances.

Many of the 20 travel companies surveyed for *Call Centre Focus* magazine were found wanting, with some criticised for failing to build a rapport with potential customers.

The companies, which included Thomson, Trailfinders, Opodo and British Airways, achieved an average score of just 28 per cent in the 'rapport building' section of the survey.

Sales centres director Nicola Yeomans said the secret of the company's success was good skills and product training, coaching and targeted recruitment. 'We look for enthusiastic individuals with a passion for travel and a natural talent for rapport-building,' she said.

Despite Cook's strong performance, many travel companies failed to develop a relationship with callers, the survey found. It claimed agents were 'no longer using open questions to open up conversations and build rapport'.

The report said the impact of the internet meant that travel had become seen as a 'self-serve' environment where the agent regarded themselves as the last step in a transaction. It concluded: 'The challenge for the travel and leisure agent is to work effectively with the internet, not for it.'

The survey divided customer experience into four sections – welcome, find out, show how and close – to reflect how callers' needs were assessed and the companies' products were showcased.

On average, the 20 travel companies surveyed scored 58 per cent for welcome, 50 per cent for find out, 57 per cent for show how and 56 per cent for close.

Maia managing director David Payne said: 'Many agents were perfectly civil but didn't take the opportunity to engage the customer or differentiate their brand.'

(Source: *Travel Trade Gazette*, 8 September 2006)

1   What is your own experience of call centres?

2   What are the factors that have contributed to Thomas Cook's success?

3   Write a set of 'top tips' for those call centres who need to improve their customer service.

Methods to monitor and evaluate service standards

The world of travel and tourism is constantly changing: customers' needs change, new products develop, competitors emerge. It is therefore essential that organisations continuously monitor and evaluate the service they are providing in order to maintain high levels of customer satisfaction – how else will an organisation know whether their customers still like their products or that their levels of service remain excellent?

We will now examine some of the methods used by travel and tourism organisations to monitor and measure customer satisfaction levels.

Mystery shoppers

Mystery shopping is used by many companies to assess the performance of their staff. People are employed to visit shops or make telephone sales enquires, pretending to want to purchase the products and services. Mystery shopping can involve face-to-face customer contact, for example visiting a travel agent, but a mystery shopper could also use the website of a tour operator or telephone an airline call centre to assess customer service levels. They assess the performance of staff and submit detailed evaluations of their experience using written reports or questionnaires. A mystery shopper can provide organisations with a fair, unbiased opinion regarding levels of customer service experienced. This method of evaluation is commonly used by call centres, travel agency chains and some tour operators.

Although there are now organisations that provide mystery shoppers to assess customer service levels, many large travel companies simply use staff from other parts of the organisation. For example, a ferry company may offer a member of staff from the call centre a free ferry crossing on the basis they complete a mystery shopping questionnaire. Or a travel agent from one part of the country may be asked to mystery shop in another town. Mystery shopping is used by VisitBritain when assessing accommodation standards for its star ratings. The case study below shows how mystery shopping is part of the tourist board assessment for accommodation.

Case study: Mystery shopper (pre-accommodation visit)

Our assessors will research the accommodation from a customer's perspective prior to visiting. We are looking for effective communication and service to customers, response times of call answering and that responses to requests (e.g. for brochures) are dealt with promptly and professionally. We will be looking for staff knowledge of the properties and their location, help, friendliness and advice, together with an explanation of any restrictions and terms and conditions that may apply.

This exercise will involve looking at the web site for ease of use (how easy to navigate, find items and understand), making an enquiry online (booking online and the overall aesthetics of the website), accuracy of property descriptions and photos will be assessed. We may also make enquiries by e-mail, phone, post and out-of-office hours to assess staff knowledge, response times and customer service. We could be asking about procedures for booking, confirming and searching for a property, testing an offer to send a brochure, provide details of local amenities and area of a property, and general enquiries about the accommodation.

(Source: Quality Accredited Agency Standard Information, published by VisitBritain)

List what the mystery shoppers are using to assess the accommodation providers, for example friendliness, staff knowledge. (These are called quality criteria and we will be looking at these in more detail later in this section.)

Theory into practice

Mystery shopping for the TTG

Every week a mystery shopper visits four travel agencies in a town in the UK. Their findings are reported in the *Travel Trade Gazette* (TTG). Research several of these mystery shopping articles. Devise a checklist that the mystery shopper could use to gather their information and 'score' the travel agencies.

Key term

Questionnaire – a form containing a series of questions. Questionnaires are the most common method used in the travel and tourism industry to gain feedback from customers.

Questionnaires are the most common method used for monitoring and evaluating customer service levels. They are a formal method of gathering information and provide organisations with data which they can analyse. While some questionnaires ask open questions and make general comments (see the Norchester Airport questionnaire below), most ask for specific information and require only

a tick response. This has two advantages. First, the customer can quickly and easily complete the questionnaire and therefore they are more likely to do so. Secondly, the data become quantitive and so easier to analyse.

Key terms

Qualitative data – will tell you about people's feelings and perceptions. They are usually gathered by asking open questions (in a questionnaire) or through other research methods (e.g. interviews). They can be difficult to analyse.

Quantitive data – will give specific information. They are usually gathered by asking closed questions, for example 'Did you enjoy your holiday?' (Answer 'Yes' or 'No'.) They are easy to measure, for example '86 per cent of people asked stated that they enjoyed their holiday'.

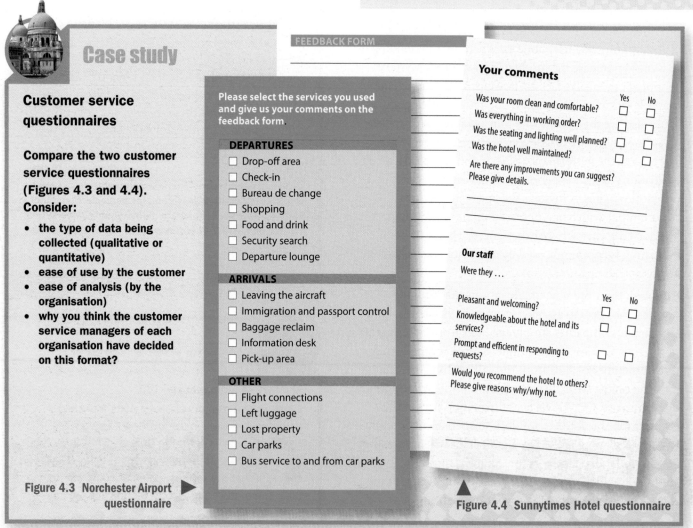

Case study

Customer service questionnaires

Compare the two customer service questionnaires (Figures 4.3 and 4.4). Consider:

- the type of data being collected (qualitative or quantitative)
- ease of use by the customer
- ease of analysis (by the organisation)
- why you think the customer service managers of each organisation have decided on this format?

FEEDBACK FORM

Please select the services you used and give us your comments on the feedback form.

DEPARTURES
- ☐ Drop-off area
- ☐ Check-in
- ☐ Bureau de change
- ☐ Shopping
- ☐ Food and drink
- ☐ Security search
- ☐ Departure lounge

ARRIVALS
- ☐ Leaving the aircraft
- ☐ Immigration and passport control
- ☐ Baggage reclaim
- ☐ Information desk
- ☐ Pick-up area

OTHER
- ☐ Flight connections
- ☐ Left luggage
- ☐ Lost property
- ☐ Car parks
- ☐ Bus service to and from car parks

Figure 4.3 Norchester Airport questionnaire ▶

Your comments

	Yes	No
Was your room clean and comfortable?	☐	☐
Was everything in working order?	☐	☐
Was the seating and lighting well planned?	☐	☐
Was the hotel well maintained?	☐	☐

Are there any improvements you can suggest? Please give details.

_____
_____

Our staff

Were they ...

	Yes	No
Pleasant and welcoming?	☐	☐
Knowledgeable about the hotel and its services?	☐	☐
Prompt and efficient in responding to requests?	☐	☐

Would you recommend the hotel to others? Please give reasons why/why not.

_____
_____

▲

Figure 4.4 Sunnytimes Hotel questionnaire

Case study: assessing the service provided on a European tour

Genine works as a Tour Manager for Cusmar Tours, taking coach parties around Europe. Cusmar offers a bonus to its Tour Managers at the end of every season. To get it the Tour Managers need good tour reports. The Operations Manager at Cusmar knows that Tour Managers often throw away reports if they are not complimentary. So the bonus is calculated on the number of reports returned to him, as well as what they say about the Tour Managers. The reports are simple tick box questionnaires. They are designed so that the customers can quickly and easily fill them in and Head Office can easily analyse them. There is space for brief comments too so that customers can complain or compliment – useful information for Cusmar.

Genine has found that the way to get the most reports back is to hand them out on the last morning of the tour and collect them as clients leave the coach. This way she usually gets 100 per cent returns. As soon as all the clients have left the coach, Genine flicks through the reports. She usually gets excellent grades for her customer service skills, but there is often someone who only ticks 'satisfactory' about her guiding skills. She knows she needs to give more information but it is difficult to know about so many places.

It is part of her job to report informally to the suppliers the feedback from customers. Comments about the coach drivers are usually excellent and she is able to tell the driver there and then what the passengers have said. For each hotel she will pass on the comments on the next tour. If there are any serious complaints she has to call her manager.

At Head Office the operations manager completes a statistical analysis of all the aspects of the reports. If there are any immediate problems with a hotel or coach company he will change them immediately. The analyses are used at the end of the season when each tour is evaluated by the Product Managers. Examples of the sort of information that the reports provide include:

- hotels – levels of service, quality of food, service in restaurants, facilities
- excursions – enjoyable, guides, routes, timing
- Tour Managers – service given, information provided, friendliness and approachability, appearance
- coach – facilities, driver, helpfulness, knowledge, did he get lost?
- overall enjoyment of the tour.

The Operations Manager has a benchmark for the quality criteria assessed. Anything falling below the benchmark is reviewed and action taken before the next season. In some cases this means changing hotels, sacking Tour Managers and changing coach companies.

It is only by continually evaluating and improving its products that Cusmar Tours is able to remain the market leader.

1   **What are the advantages of simple tick box questionnaires?**

2   **Why does Genine give information to the suppliers about the customers' responses?**

3   **Why are the reports analysed at Head Office?**

Theory into practice

Draft a questionnaire (tour report) that Genine could use on a European coach tour.

▲ **Figure 4.5 Representative helping passengers on a coach tour**

Observation

Observing customers and their behaviour may provide information about their levels of satisfaction. At a theme park managers will want to observe queues for rides to establish waiting times at different times of the day. A travel agency manager will be able to tell by a customer's body language whether they are satisfied with the level of service they are getting.

Observation of staff as well as customers can provide valuable information about customer service levels. A good manager will be continuously observing staff on an informal basis. They will note their appearance, attitude to clients and whether their desks are suitably neat and tidy. Some managers may also carry out formal observations as part of an ongoing assessment of customer service levels. For example, a resort manager may be required to observe occasional welcome meetings to ensure all staff are carrying our procedures and maximising their opportunities for sales.

Mystery shopping, questionnaires and observation will all provide organisations with information to evaluate, which will enable them to measure and monitor service delivery. However, feedback from customers will also be received by e-mail, by letter and informally though conversations. Increasingly websites provide online forms to allow customers to give feedback easily.

Quality criteria

All organisations need to determine which quality criteria they are going to assess. Although the context will differ for each organisation, most will need to assess customer satisfaction levels against value for money, reliability, staffing levels and health and safety standards. Other quality criteria could include speed and availability of service, products and services offered, and whether customer information and other needs were met.

■ Value for money

Customers are increasingly demanding. They demand value for money (VFM). If an organisation does not provide it, they will simply buy elsewhere. After all, most travel and tourism products and services are similar, so

if an organisation can't provide VFM they will simply use a competitor. Monitoring customers' perceptions of VFM is vital.

■ Reliability

Offering a reliable and consistent service to customers is all part of excellent service delivery. Organisations need to know whether their customers think this has been provided. Did they get what was promised, did their tickets turn up on time, did the coach have all the facilites advertised, did all excursions take place and was the evening entertainment porgramme exactly as advertised?

■ Staffing levels

The number of staff available to serve customers will determine the level of service received. Did customers have to queue in the Tourist Information Centre; were there sufficient waiting staff present in the restaurant; was the phone at the call centre answered within three rings? All will determine a customer's perception of service levels.

■ Health and safety

Health and safety is a legal obligation. However, to provide excellent service organisations will go beyond the legal requirements. For example, it is not a legal requirement that the cleanliness of toilet facilities is checked regularly but many visitor attractions will do so to ensure they are hygienic for their customers. Many will not allow dogs, to prevent dog fouling and ensure a clean and safe environment for all. All aircraft are cleaned during 'turnaround' as such high standards of cleanliness and hygiene are expected by customers. It is imperative that all customer areas are spotlessly clean ensuring a safe environment.

It is a legal requirement that all places of work meet health and safety legislation. The main piece of legislation is the Health and Safety at Work Act 1974, which requires all employers and employees to have 'a duty of care'. Other legislation exists to ensure the safety of employees and members of the public. Examples of legal requirements that ensure the safety of the travelling public include:

- the provision of safety equipment (e.g. life jackets, oxygen masks and emergency chutes) for all air passengers
- restrictions to prevent passengers getting too close to the jets (engines) when boarding
- tachographs in all coaches – these measure drivers' hours and ensure adequate rest periods are taken
- emergency exists and first aid equipment in all coaches
- signs to indicate when floor surfaces are wet
- adequate fire escapes in all accommodation
- use of signs to indicate exits
- signs to indicate swimming pool depth (and 'no diving' signs if it is too shallow).

Monitoring methods

We have established that mystery shopping, questionnaires and observations are all used by travel and tourism organisations to measure their customer service levels. Data are gathered about a range of quality criteria. But what is done with these data? How can they be used?

The aim of gathering the data is to use them to continuously improve customer service levels. But this can only be done if data are monitored, that is, this year's data need to be compared with last year's, and the customer satisfaction levels in, for example, Marbella need to be compared with those in Kos. A benchmark is often used to monitor customer service levels. This means that a standard is set against which all results can be compared.

Key term

Benchmark – this is anything that can be used as a standard or point of reference. For example, a tour operator might decide that all hotels must be scored 'good' or 'excellent' by 75 per cent of customers for them to be used in subsequent years.

■ Survey results analysis

The results from questionnaires (surveys) are analysed to produce information for management. As we saw in the case study on Cusmar Tours the data produced by questionnaires can result in Tour Managers being sacked, hotels being changed and tour itineraries being adapted. Although qualitatitve data can be analysed this is complex (and subjective!).

Quantitive data are more easily collected and analysed. Questions that produce quantitative data are usually predominant in questionnaires. For example, Yes/No answers (see the Sunnytimes Hotel questionnaire) will provide data that can be easily analysed, although limited information will be obtained. The most common method used within the travel and tourism industry includes systems whereby respondents use tick boxes or a scale to rate services received (see Table 4.2).

Please rate the hotel in which you stayed under the following headings on a scale of 1–7.

	1	2	3	4	5	6	7	
Comfortable bedroom								Uncomfortable bedroom
Extremely clean room								Dirty room
Excellent quality of food								Poor quality of food
Pleasant hotel staff								Rude hotel staff
Excellent hotel facilities								Poor hotel facilities
Very suitable for families								Totally unsuitable for families

Table 4.2 Hotel guest questionnaire on services received

It would be easy for a tour operator using this system to compare the scores received for one hotel with other hotels used. They would be able to advise the hotel which attributes of the hotel were well received and which needed improving, that is, to what extent the product they were offering met expectations. If required they could then make changes for future years.

■ Appraisals

In some job roles, feedback about staff obtained from questionnaires can be reported to the staff at their appraisals. For example, resort representatives will receive direct feedback about their performances on the customer questionnaires. This will be reviewed by the line manager who will discuss it with them. The feedback may result in a promotion or not being recruited for the following season! Similarly, the customer service levels provided by a receptionist in a hotel will often be monitored and reviewed at their appraisal. Customer-facing staff play such a vital role in the delivery of customer service that unless they can provide it to a very high standard they are unsuitable for their job.

Key term

Appraisal – a meeting (which usually takes place once a year with a line manager) at which a member of staff's performance is reviewed. Targets for the following year may also be set. It is also an opportunity for staff to discuss their aspirations with their manager and maybe comment on their manager's performance too!

Providing excellent service, and as a result dealing with satisfied customers, is very rewarding for employees. It is satisfying to be thanked for kindness, efficiency, solving a problem or providing advice. Positive feedback from customers provides job satisfaction and a feeling of well-being. This can contribute towards a good working environment in which everyone is working as a team and supporting each other. For some individuals this may lead to promotion – perhaps with a pay increase or bonus (incentive). The overall result of excellent service and satisfied customers is a staff team that is productive and positive.

Further benefits to staff may include job security. If an employee has a good sales record, with positive customer feedback and customers who return, it is more likely their position in the organisation will be secure. This may enhance their prospects for training and promotion and may give them a sense of personal satisfaction as well as financial security.

Benefits to the employer

All businesses are dependent upon their customers. Whether public, private or voluntary, all organisations aim to provide a high level of customer satisfaction, so that the customers return (bringing repeat business) and ensure the continuation of the organisation. Increased sales and profits may result from repeat business or the fact that the satisfied customers tell other people who then wish to purchase the same product or service. All this results in further increased sales and profits for the organisation.

Benefits of good service

It is recognised that the provision of excellent customer service is essential to a travel and tourism organisation, with benefits for both the employees and the customers.

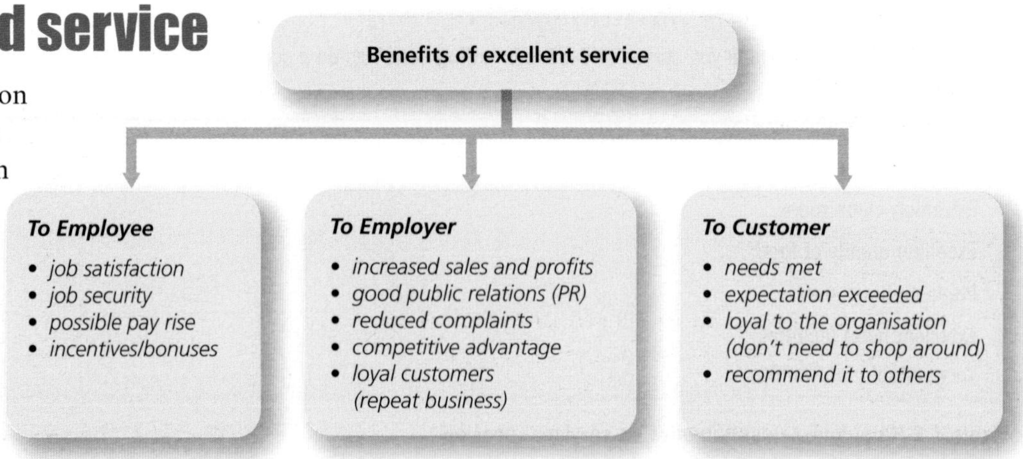

Benefits of excellent service

To Employee
- job satisfaction
- job security
- possible pay rise
- incentives/bonuses

To Employer
- increased sales and profits
- good public relations (PR)
- reduced complaints
- competitive advantage
- loyal customers (repeat business)

To Customer
- needs met
- expectation exceeded
- loyal to the organisation (don't need to shop around)
- recommend it to others

Figure 4.6 The benefits of good service ▶

Competitive advantage and good public relations (PR) also result from high levels of service. PR will be influenced by the reputation of the company, the service people receive from sales consultants, experience of the product or service and after-sales service. All of these will encourage customers to choose products and services from the company rather than a competitor.

Key terms

Competitive advantage – an organisation strives to be better than (have an advantage over) its competitors. This could be through better pricing or a more attractive product. It could also be through a higher level of customer service.

Public relations – the attempts made by an organisation to have a good image and maintain goodwill with the general public.

Consider this

Front-line staff, that is those dealing directly with customers, may be the only people from the organisation that customers meet. Examples include cabin crew, check-in staff and resort representatives. These staff have a key role in determining customer satisfaction levels.

Key term

Customer loyalty – if customers receive consistently good service from an organisation they will want to use it again. They become loyal to that particular organisation because they can rely on its products and services.

Customer benefits

If the principles of good customer service are followed, satisfied customers will feel they have been greeted warmly, dealt with by friendly and efficient staff, and received the goods or services they want. They will go away having had their needs met and expectations exceeded – they will have purchased the ideal holiday, found the perfect hotel or eaten the best food!

Over the long term, customer loyalty will develop so that a customer would not dream of going elsewhere. They will recommend the products and services to their friends too. Such recommendations are a great way to get repeat business – after all it is free marketing!

Theory into practice

Recall a situation when you received excellent customer service. Work in pairs and describe the incident to your partner. What aspects of the service made it excellent? How did it make you feel? Have you ever used a particular organisation or bought a product simply because it was recommended to you?

Consequences of poor service

We have already established the principles of good customer service and why the provision of excellent service is important to organisations and their staff, as well as to the customers themselves. To ensure excellent service is maintained staff training is required, products have to be up to date, the company's premises must be well maintained and levels of service regularly

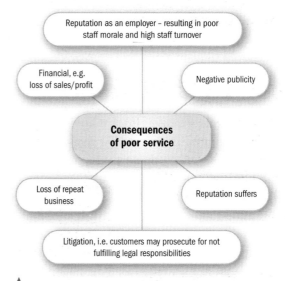

▲ Figure 4.7 The consequences of poor service

Assessment practice

Select two organisations with which you are familiar and list the costs associated with providing excellent service. Then list all the possible consequences of poor service. Present your information in a table like the one below. In this example the organisation selected is a travel agent.

P2

Costs of providing excellent customer service	Costs of providing ineffective customer service
Sufficient numbers of staff, all of whom are well trained, to deal with customer queries	If insufficient staff are available, customers may go elsewhere and so sales will be lost. If staff are not trained they will not be able to sell suitable holidays – customer needs will not be met.
For a clean office cleaners are required	Staff will not feel valued if the office is not clean. Customers will receive a poor first impression.
Up-to-date software ...	

monitored and evaluated. It is clear that the provision of excellent customer service is costly. However, the consequences of poor service are even more costly.

Clearly, the costs of poor service are the opposite of the benefits. The first will be financial: customers will stop coming, with resulting decrease in sales and profits. If an organisation develops a reputation as a poor employer the best staff will start to leave, taking their experience with them. A high staff turnover will impact on customer service levels as new staff will take time to train. Staff morale will be poor and it is very difficult to be cheerful to customers when the office environment is a bit flat! Repeat business will begin to fall as an organisation's reputation suffers. In extreme situations adverse publicity may result which can have disastrous results for the reputation of the company. If customer service levels slip so badly that organisations don't fulfil their legal obligations, litigation can follow. Travel companies have commitments to their customers, not just to satisfy their needs, but also in law. The following Acts of Parliament have relevance to many travel and tourism organisations.

■ Data Protection Act 1998

This Act affects all organisations that hold personal details on customers. There are eight general principles to this Act. Key points are that organisations are not allowed to pass on information about their customers or sell information in mailing lists. They can keep only relevant information and must destroy it once it has served its purpose. For example, Tourist Information Centres cannot ask visitors to enter a prize draw and then use their names and addresses for a mailing unless the customers give permission for them to do so.

■ Disability Discrimination Act 1995

This Act introduced new laws aimed at ending the discrimination some customers faced. The law requires service providers to make 'reasonable adjustments' to ensure their premises are accessible to those with a sensory, physical or mental disability which seriously affects their day-to-day activities.

The Act covers building design and construction, building approaches and exits, as well as public places such as footpaths and parks. Printed material, such as brochures or menus, may also need to be available in braille or audio formats, and websites should be suitable for disabled users.

Consider this

Around 8.6 million people, or 1 in 7 of the UK population, have a sensory, physical or mental disability which seriously effects their day-to-day activities.

■ Trade Descriptions Act 1968

The key point from this Act is that products and services must be correctly described. Hotel descriptions must be accurate, and brochures must contain full and fair information. As brochures are put together a long time before customers go on holiday, the resort representatives have an important role in updating head office staff, who in turn must advise customers of relevant changes, for example that the swimming pool has closed or water sports are no longer available.

■ Health and safety

Other legislation with which travel companies need to be familiar includes health and safety legislation. Coach companies and their drivers need to keep up to date with the regulations that affect the numbers of hours a coach driver can drive without a break. Airlines need to be aware of the Joint Aviation Requirements (JARs). Managers of an office environment (e.g. a travel agency or call centre) need to ensure they keep up to date with health and safety legislation. Examples of their obligations include allowing regular breaks for staff working at VDU screens, monitoring office temperatures, ensuring a trained first aider is on the staff team and keeping an accident record book.

■ EC Directive on Package Travel 1992

Tour operating staff also need to be aware of their responsibilities under the EC Directives. These European regulations caused a storm when introduced to the travel industry over a decade ago. They gave customers

> Imagine you work for a hotel. List the ways in which excellent customer service impacts on customers, staff and the organisation. **P1 P2**

increased protection, and it became the responsibility of any organisation packaging a holiday (selling transport, accommodation and ancillary services as one product) to provide financial security (a bond) in case its business collapsed. Tour operators became accountable for their suppliers, so that if, for example, a coach company was negligent and caused injury to a client, the tour operator became liable.

There are also requirements to ensure brochures are 'legible, comprehensible and accurate'. Precise details of the package have to be included in the contract, including excursions, itinerary, price and payment schedule. Complaints have to be answered within a specific time frame. All aspects of this directive ensure customers needs are protected.

Case study: Travel legislation

Jo works occasional weekends as a tour manager for a company taking weekend tours to Paris.

When doing her training course in Manchester she was surprised by the amount of legislation that now affects tour operators. The trainer made it very clear that Jo's role is really important and her actions and reports could affect the company if it was ever sued. On every tour Jo is required to do the following:

- Check that the hotels used and facilities available are as described in the brochure. Because the brochure is printed about 18 months before the holidays take place, some things may become inaccurate. For example, one week the lift was not working (and this was significant as many clients were elderly). Jo rang head office straight away and clients booked on the following week's holiday were told immediately (and many were offered ground floor rooms).
- Keep accurate records of delays and keep passengers informed. If there are long delays Jo has to inform the duty officer, who may authorise refreshments.
- Ensure all the services booked by clients are provided. For example, one week a special champagne breakfast

had been booked by a group but it had not been provided. Jo spoke to the hotel manager and her own boss and it was provided the following day. Jo was aware that under European Directives, the tour operator was liable for any deficiencies of the supplier (the hotel).

Passengers often complain and for every complaint Jo writes a duty report. She returns this to head office as soon as the tour is over (under the Package Travel Directive, her boss has 28 days in which to respond to the complaint). When completing the report she is careful to be factual and not show any bias – she knows that if the complaint goes to court or arbitration, copies of her report will be seen by many people.

1 **Name four pieces of legislation that affect a tour operator.**

2 **What are the risks associated with a brochure being published up to 18 months before the customer goes on holiday?**

3 **What does 'liable for any deficiencies of the supplier' mean?**

4 **Why must Jo's records be accurate and factual?**

Customer types

We have already seen that the objective of customer service is to meet customer needs and exceed expectations. In order to do this it is first necessary to understand customers' needs – but this is easier said than done. After all, there are many different types of customers all of whom have different needs.

To be able to provide excellent customer service, organisations must understand their customers, recognise their differing needs and provide products and services that meet their requirements. For example, a tour operator will provide a different holiday and range of excursions for a single person than for a group of young people wanting to go clubbing or a couple wanting to escape the British winter. Similarly, on a day trip to a theme park a young couple will have different needs from a family with two children.

Internal and external customers

Before looking at different customer types it is important to differentiate between internal and external customers. Colleagues are known as internal customers, while people outside the organisation are known as external customers.

It is perhaps more obvious why caring for external customers is so important as an organisation is dependent upon them to buy products and services. Without external customers, organisations don't exist – they need sales to make profits and pay wages.

Internal customer service is also important to an organisation. How you deal with colleagues, how you behave in the office and your level of efficiency will all affect your working relationships. This can impact upon how well a team works together, relationships with managers and overall productivity. All of these can also have an effect on job satisfaction and staff morale which in turn can influence the customer service provided.

We will now examine some of the different types of external customers and how their needs may differ.

Key terms

Internal customers – colleagues and other members of staff who work within the same organisation to provide products and services. Internal customers can also include suppliers who contribute towards the products or services.

External customers – people from outside the organisation who buy the products and services.

Individuals

People travel alone for many different reasons. They may be travelling on business. However, leisure travellers also travel alone as they may want to participate in a specialist activity or hope to meet a partner. Some may choose to travel alone, while others may do so reluctantly. Some single travellers are young (18–30) while many are over 50 and some over 70. They will all have differing needs and these needs must be provided for by airlines, tour operators, airports, hotels and their staff.

Groups

Groups include school groups, special interest groups and friendship groups.

Some groups may all know each other and have similar needs (such as a group of young men wishing to go on a day trip white-water rafting). They may be happy to be treated as a single entity for the purpose of their day trip. However, a coach party of Americans who have booked a Blue Badge Guide for their tour of Cambridge may all have differing needs. Some will want to visit the colleges, others may wish to go shopping and others may want to enjoy an afternoon's punting on the river.

For those dealing with groups, it is important to remember that the group is actually made up of many individuals – and to consider their individual needs. This can be very demanding.

Customers with specific needs

Some customers may have specific needs, which may require additional and sensitive customer service. This may be because they have:

- special dietary needs
- mobility problems (e.g. wheelchair users)
- a hearing impairment
- a visual impairment
- speech difficulties
- a medical condition, for example a heart complaint which means a ground floor room is required.

It is clear that all customers with specific needs must be treated individually. Many people are unsure how to deal with specific needs and this can result in customers feeling insulted or patronised.

Read the following extract from *Welcome to Excellence*, customer service training for the tourism industry. It explains how to provide a high level of service to people with a visual impairment.

Assisting customers with a visual impairment

Look out for visual signs, such as a white stick or guide dog

When meeting a visually impaired customer, introduce yourself

Remember that you cannot rely on your body language to communicate a message

Make sure that you say when you are leaving

Be prepared to read information out

Offer to guide the customer to their destination

Provide information in large print, in Braille or on audio cassette

Use spoken announcements

Be prepared to welcome guide dogs

(Source: *Welcome to Excellence: Assisting Customers*, Regional Tourist Board Partnerships Limited)

There are a number of important reasons why it matters to you and your organisation to provide an accessible environment and a high standard of service to disabled customers:

- There are an estimated 8.6 million pople with a disability in the UK and they should not be excluded from accessing the same facilities and services as everyone else
- You have a legal responsibility under the Disability Discrimination Act 1995
- There is a strong business case for attracting disabled customers
- The reputation of your organisation is based on the service standards that you offer all your customers.

Customers with cultural and language needs

There will be many situations in the travel industry where you will have to deal with people who do not speak English and people from other cultures. Your excellent customer service skills must be maintained. Such customers may include:

- UK residents from a variety of cutural and ethnic backgrounds. They may not speak English as their first language.
- The many international visitors to the UK from different cultural backgrounds. While many of these visitors will speak English it will not be their first language and misunderstandings can easily occur.

Customer needs

Products and services

Travel and tourism organisations provide products and services to meet customers' needs. Products and services provided by a travel agency might include:

- a week's summer sun holiday for a family of three
- a cruise for a recently bereaved single woman
- a first-class flight for a business person who needs to attend a meeting in Prague
- a cultural holiday in Cuba for a group of women in their thirties
- day excursions
- insurance
- overnight hotel accommodation at the airport
- car parking
- advice about currency and temperatures.

Case study: doing business in China

Figure 4.8 Business meeting in China

- When doing business in China, punctuality is considered extremely important. Your Chinese counterparts will not keep you waiting; being on time is essential.
- People will enter the meeting room in hierarchical order, as the Chinese are very status conscious. Senior members generally lead the negotiations and will direct the discussion.
- The exchanging of business cards is customary in Chinese business culture. One side should be printed in English and one in Chinese. You should present your card with both hands and the Chinese side facing up. When accepting your colleague's card study it carefully before placing it on the table, never in the back pocket, as this is extremely disrespectful.
- During negotiations, humbleness and patience are the key to success. The Chinese sense of time means that they use it knowingly and there is always enough.

- An important element before commencing a business meeting in China is to engage in small talk. Be prepared, as this may include quite personal questions.

Chinese business etiquette (Do's and Don'ts)

- Do maintain eye contact; avoiding eye contact is considered untrustworthy.
- Do address your Chinese counterparts with a title and their last name. If the person does not have a title, use 'Mr' or 'Madam'.
- Do wait for your Chinese counterpart to initiate formal greetings. Handshakes are the most popular gesture.
- Don't assume that a nod is a sign of agreement. More often than not, it signifies that the person is simply listening.
- Don't show excessive emotion whilst conducting business, as it may seem unfriendly.
- Don't use direct negative replies, as they are considered impolite. Instead of saying 'no', answer 'maybe' or 'I'll think about it'.

Chinese culture quiz – True or False

1 When a Chinese friend says to you 'Have you eaten yet?' he wants to invite you out for dinner.
2 When eating a Chinese meal it is customary to place your chopsticks standing up in the rice before starting.
3 In China white is the colour associated with death.
4 The word for clock in Chinese sounds similar to the expression 'the end of life', so a clock should never be given as a gift.
5 At the end of a meeting, you are expected to leave after your Chinese counterparts.

Answers

1 False. He is simply asking how you are and enquiring after your health.
2 False. This is a symbol of death used at funerals and should never be done.
3 True.
4 True.
5 False. You are expected to leave before them.

Assessment practice

Investigate a large hotel, an airport, an airline or a mass-market tour operator. What particular products or services does this organisation provide to meet the needs of different customers? You may wish to consider the needs of single women travellers, business customers, children travelling alone (airlines only), people of different ethnic origins, group bookings, people of different religions, disabled travellers. Table 4.3 summarises some hints for coping with different customer types. **P3**

Groups	A group is a collection of individuals, each with differing needs. Make sure you treat people as individuals.
	Try to ascertain who is the group leader/organiser before you commence.
	If speaking to a group, gather them into an enclosed space. Make sure everyone can hear you.
People of different ages	People's needs vary with age – a couple in their twenties will have different needs from those in their fifties and again in their seventies.
	Don't be ageist.
	Do not presume! Not all older people want culture and younger people beaches – ask open questions to establish their needs.
Business customers	Business customers are usually under pressure, want an excellent service and are prepared to pay for it.
	Time is important and they may need to work on journeys so consider offering additional products and services, for example express check-in, quiet coach on a train journey.
	Business travel may not be considered to be a perk of the job – many people would prefer to be at home rather than spending three days sorting out problems in an industrial city where no one speaks English. Think how you can make life easier for them, for example an early morning flight rather than travelling the night before.
Those with specific needs	Specific needs can apply to a range of people. Examples of specific needs include: • dietary, e.g. vegan passenger on a plane • physical, e.g. child in a wheelchair visiting a theme park • sensory – a hearing or visual impairment • anyone needing assistance, e.g. minors travelling alone, adults travelling with children, elderly passengers.
	Ask open questions to establish needs.
	Be sensitive but do not be afraid of giving offence – many complaints arise simply because the right questions are not asked.
Language differences	Don't shout!
	Be patient – how many languages do you speak?
Cultural differences	Be sensitive.
	Educate yourself – make sure you have a basic awareness of the beliefs of key religions and also what causes offence.

Table 4.3 Key points about different customer types and how their needs vary

Theory into practice

Work in small groups. List the products and services provided by a Tourist Information Centre, a hotel and an airport.

Key term

Culture – people's beliefs and values.

Ideally a customer will tell you what product or services they want, that is, they will state their needs. However, sometimes key information remains unstated. Often customers simply imply what they want. The customer who says 'Spain was a bit too hot last year!' is really meaning that they would like somewhere cooler this year. Occasionally you will need to anticipate customer requirements! To establish unstated, implied or anticipated needs requires careful questioning!

Key terms

Stated needs – needs the client tells you about, for example 'I would like to book a single room for tomorrow night'.

Implied needs – needs the client may hint at, but does not tell you about, for example a tight budget.

Unstated needs – needs that will affect the client's choice of product, but which he or she does not tell you about, for example they do not say 'We went to Majorca last year and don't want to go there again'.

Anticipated needs – those products or services that you think the customer might need, for example airport parking.

■ Stated needs

You know that in order to provide excellent customer service you must meet customers' needs. Clearly you have to establish what these needs are before you can respond to them. In the ideal situation the customer responds to the simple question 'How may I help you?' with a statement about their needs, for example 'Please could you book me on a train to Edinburgh?' Stated needs are those that the customer clearly tells you about. They are the easiest to deal with.

■ Implied needs

Some customers may not tell you directly about their needs – however, these may be implied. For example, the client who says: 'I wonder if you can find a holiday for me and my three children. I know we are not supposed to go in term-time but I may have to this year. Can you see if there is anything available the week after half-term? We can camp if we have to although a mobile

home would be better for me…' is clearly implying that she is on a tight budget. You will need to ask suitable questions to establish if this is the case.

■ Unstated needs

You may think that simple open questions, such as 'When do you want to travel?', 'Where would you like to go?', will establish customers' needs. However, there may be some things that clients don't tell you, either because they don't think it's important, or because they're embarrassed – or even because they don't realise it themselves. For example, some clients my simply forget to ask about airport parking, regional departures, facilities for children.

■ Anticipated needs

Good customer service involves trying to anticipate some of your customers' needs. The single mum who has implied that she is on a tight budget may want lots of free activities for her children. The business person booking into a hotel for one night may want to make use of the express checkout facility. Similarly, good customer service means offering kids' clubs for family holidays or regional departures for local people – even though these have not been asked for.

Theory into practice

Work in pairs. Role play the following scenarios to the rest of your group. The group must identify (a) the stated needs of the customer, (b) the implied needs and (c) other needs which might be anticipated by the person providing customer service.

- You work in a travel agency. A father and child come in looking for a week's holiday in the sun.
- You are an event organiser. You have been asked to co-ordinate an international conference for 20 delegates representing their countries. They want two overnight stays and a day's conference facilities.
- You are on work experience at your local Tourist Information Centre. Three young men come in. They are in town for 24 hours and want information and recommendations. **P3**

Buyer behaviour

We are now going to look at a variety of factors that influence a buyer. We need to consider what it is that motivates people to travel.

Key terms

Travel motivators – factors that make a person want to take a particular holiday.

Push and pull factors – this term distinguishes between what motivates individuals (push factors) and the pull of a destination. When people are making decisions about where to go on holiday both push and pull factors are at work. There are factors that push them towards a destination (travel motivators), for example the need to get away or desire for sun. At the same time there will be aspects of each possible destination that will attract them (that is, pull them towards it). Examples include the great beaches, nightlife, cheap flights and good food.

Travel motivators

Travel motivators are those factors that make people want to take a particular holiday. There are many theories about travel motivation and marketeers spend a lot of time working out what it is that will make someone buy their particular products.

Travel motivators include:

- **Class/social status:** some people go to specific destinations to enhance their social status. They may be trying to 'keep up with the Joneses' and are looking for attention from other people. Exclusive destinations try to appeal to such people.
- **Purpose of travel:** some people go on holiday to meet new people or they may need to go to visit some of their friends or their relatives (VFR). Many go on business.
- **Media:** what is being written in the media will influence the choice of destination.
- **Relaxation:** many people may go on holiday because they want to have a break. They need to rest, have a change from their working routine and come back refreshed. They may be motivated by the desire to 'get some sun'. People who are motivated by the need for relaxation may simply book a spa holiday; others will spend a couple of weeks on a beach.

Theory into practice

List suitable destinations or holidays for people who are motivated by each of the above categories.

Consider this

Different customers can be motivated by different factors but may purchase the same product (for example, a weekend in New York may be a well-deserved break for one customer, a chance to see some art galleries for another or simply the opportunity to see a friend for another).

Push and pull factors

We have just looked at motivators. These can also be thought of as factors that push a customer towards a destination. For example, the fact that they want to learn about traditional dance may push them toward salsa in Cuba, the desire to learn French may mean they want to go on a course in France or the need for relaxation may mean they are considering going to a spa for a week.

Consider this

The lack of sunny weather in the UK is one of the strongest push factors for those booking European summer sun holidays. There is often a boom in domestic tourism the summer following a heatwave.

Pull factors are those aspects of the destination that make it appeal. Examples of pull factors include climate, culture, nighlife, restaurants, quality of hotels, proximity of airport to resorts, regularity of flights, costs and friendliness of local population. They are the features of a destination that make it popular. Pull factors clearly vary from destination to destination and are different for each individual.

Theory into practice

Name two destinations with which you are familiar. List their potential pull factors for four customer types.

4.3 Be able to demonstrate customer service skills in travel and tourism situations

So far this unit has discussed the principles and benefits of customer service, and how organisations adapt their services to meet differing customer needs.

We are now going to examine the skills you, as an employee in the travel and tourism industry, will need to provide excellent service and ensure repeat business. Some people are naturally good at providing excellent service. They have an outgoing personality, appear to be always positive and are not intimidated by difficult situations. Other people have to learn these skills.

Whatever form of communication you have with customers (whether on the telephone, face-to-face or in writing), the aim is to exceed customers' expectations and send them away satisfied. In a face-to-face meeting with a customer, the sequence of events shown in Figure 4.9 is likely to happen.

We are now going to look at this sequence of events in more detail.

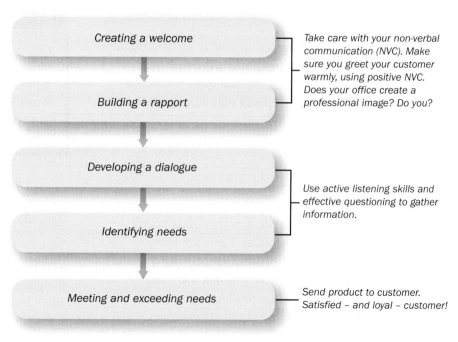

▲ Figure 4.9 The stages of customer service

Creating a welcome

There are many aspects to creating a welcome. It is more than just smiling and saying 'How can I help you?' The environment should be clean, tidy and inviting. Staff need to be displaying positive body language and there should be an atmosphere of quiet efficiency.

Customers will judge you (and the organisation you work for) on:

- your appearance – what you are wearing, whether it is neat and tidy or in need of ironing
- how you care for yourself – is your hair neat, jewellery discreet and nails clean?

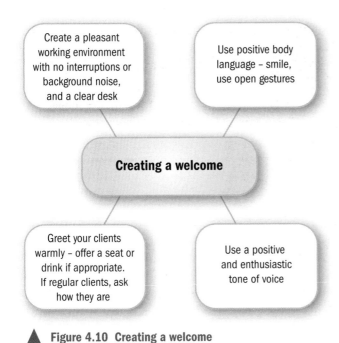

Figure 4.10 Creating a welcome

- your body language – how you express yourself through your behaviour
- how you greet your customer – are you enthusiastic and smiling?
- how organised you are – is your desk neat and the filing system organised, enabling you to find information quickly and easily?

Building rapport and developing dialogue

Key terms

Rapport – relationship. You need to build a positive rapport with your client that is based on trust and confidence.

Dialogue – conversation. An easy, flowing conversation in which you are asking open and relevant questions will help you establish customers' needs whilst also building rapport.

A warm welcome is the first stage of building a good rapport (a positive relationship with your customer). You will then need to use effective questioning and listening skills to develop a dialogue with them.

Both skills will help you to establish customer needs. Throughout all of this you continue to build a relationship with your client – getting to know them and their requirements. We will be examining this in more detail later in the chapter when we consider selling skills.

Effective listening

How good are you at listening? Do you interrupt when your friends are talking, look away or think about something else?

Activity

Complete the following questionnaire to assess your listening skills. Do you:

1	face the speaker?	
2	keep focused on the speaker, maintaining eye contact?	
3	nod and smile when appropriate?	
4	think about other things?	
5	look for body language and listen to the tone of voice (to give you more understanding)?	
6	think about your answer while the speaker is still talking?	
7	interrupt before the speaker has finished?	
8	'tune out' or get bored?	

Consider points 1–8. Which ones indicate that you are listening? Use these (and any others you can think of) to produce some guidelines called 'Improve your listening skills'.

Key term

Active listening – demonstrating through words and actions (body language) that you understand what is being said to you. For example, you can make appropriate responses ('Wow', 'Oh dear') or ask questions ('So are you saying that he shouted at you?'). Body language that demonstrates active listening includes nodding, maintaining eye contact, smiling or looking concerned as appropriate.

Activity

Non-verbal behaviour is an important aspect of listening. Carry out this activity to assess its impact.

Work in pairs. Each of you should choose a topic to talk about (make sure it is something you know a lot about and can talk on for a few minutes). Each speaker should talk on their topic twice. The first time, the listener will practise active listening (nodding, smiling, maintaining eye contact). The second time the listener will demonstrate (through behaviour) that they are not listening. This could include looking away, tapping a pencil or yawning. Remember the listener is practising non-verbal behaviour, so must not speak.

1 What impact does active listening have on the speaker?

2 What impact does it have on the speaker when it is clear that they are not being listened to?

Questioning

Asking the right questions is an important aspect of customer service skills. Whatever your future role in travel you will be asking questions of colleagues and customers. In some situations the type of question you ask is as important as the words used. This is especially so when selling products and services or dealing with a difficult situation.

There are four types of question: closed, open, reflective and leading. These are identified in Table 4.4, together with examples and the limitation of each type of question.

In most situations you will need to be asking open questions, for example when establishing a customer's needs. In some cases reflective questions may be useful, for example when dealing with a complaint or making a sale.

Type of question		Example	Use	Limitation
Closed	One that can be answered only by 'yes' or 'no'.	Have you sent in your booking form? Will you be staying for dinner? Have you received your tickets?	To clarify facts. Should not be used if trying to gather details.	Closed questions will not provide further information for discussion.
Open	One that cannot be answered by a 'yes' or 'no'. They start with words like what, when, how, who, why, where or which.	What did you enjoy most about your holiday? Why are you upset? How can I help you solve this problem? Where have you been on holiday before?	To start a discussion or conversation, to gather information.	A talkative person may answer at length and take up a lot of your time!
Reflective	One that checks understanding and gives a person the chance to think about what has been said.	So you feel the hotel staff were unfriendly? So you want somewhere sunny, but you are not looking for a beach holiday?	Allows you to check understanding and for the customer to add to what has been said.	Takes time. You may lose the thread of the previous discussion.
Leading	One that suggests what the answer should be, or leads the person into answering in a certain way.	So you feel that if the flight had not been delayed you would have had a nice holiday?	Try to avoid using.	Indicates what you are thinking and is unlikely to obtain a full or true answer.

Table 4.4 Question types

Key terms

Open questions – help you to gather information.

Closed questions – may produce only a 'yes' or 'no' response.

Don't use	Do use
Did you enjoy your holiday?	How was your holiday? Tell me what you enjoyed about your holiday.
Did you learn a lot at the welcome meeting?	What sort of things did the resort representative tell you at the welcome meeting?
Do you want to go to Ibiza because of the nightlife?	What is it that makes you want to go to Ibiza?
You've been to Spain a lot, haven't you?	What destinations have you been to before?

Theory into practice

Change the following closed questions into open questions:

- Can I help you?
- Are you OK today?
- Do you like the view from your balcony?
- Would you like to go to Greece again this year?

Change the following closed questions into reflective questions:

- Is your budget £400 per person?
- You don't want to go to Spain?
- Was it the airline's fault?

Non-verbal communication

Non-verbal communication is the main way in which we communicate to others how we feel, although we may not be aware that we are doing so! It is estimated that we convey more messages by the way we stand, use eye contact, hold our heads, gesticulate and use facial expressions (that is, use our body language) than we do with words. It is essential that you are aware of your body language in order to convey a positive message (build rapport) with your customers.

Key term

Non-verbal communication (NVC) – communicating without saying anything. The most common type of NVC is body language – how we use our hands, facial expressions and gestures to convey our feelings.

Theory into practice

Work in pairs. Take it in turns to choose one of the feelings listed below and act it out. Use facial expressions, gesticulate, etc. but don't speak! How successful is your partner at interpreting your body language?

- Angry
- Exhausted
- Confused
- Excited
- Upset
- Cheerful/happy
- Bored

Similarly, our tone of voice can indicate how we are really feeling. We can use the same words in two different situations but our tone of voice may make the words carry an opposite meaning. It's not what we say but how we say it that makes the difference.

Your body language and tone of voice will determine whether the word 'hello' is meant as a cheery sign that you recognise someone, a threat, a put down or an ecstatic greeting. A good actor will be able to convey at least a dozen different meanings with the word 'No'.

An important aspect of providing good customer service is recognising customers' feelings. Watching body language and listening to the tone of voice are the best ways of working out what your customer is really feeling.

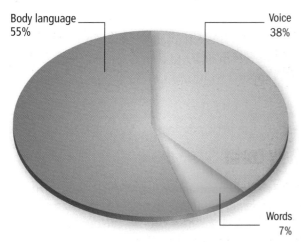

Body language
55%

Voice
38%

Words
7%

▲ Figure 4.11 How we understand messages

Theory into practice

Work in pairs. Imagine you have just been asked to a party. Say 'Thanks, I would love to come' (or a similar positive phrase indicating you wish to go). Say the phrase in as many different tones as you can. You partner must interpret what you really mean – some tones may indicate that you do not want to go at all! You must use the same words each time and change only your tone of voice to indicate a different meaning.

▲ Figure 4. 12 How are these people feeling?

Case study: the role of a crew member for Virgin Atlantic

The primary reason for having cabin crew on board an aircraft is for passenger safety. It is, however, no good being a role model in safety aspects, if levels of customer service are inadequate. The ongoing success of Virgin Atlantic depends on the service we offer and the care and concern we extend to our customers. They will judge us in the first ten seconds of boarding the aircraft. Have they been acknowledged? Have they received a genuine smile? Are the crew giving out positive body language? Has sufficient eye contact been used? Has a friendly and approachable stance been intimated? Is the appearance and grooming of the crew perfect? All these things from you, in addition to the appearance of the aircraft and cabin!

It is imperative that a good impression is created from the outset. You will not get a second chance to make a first impression. You are 'the company' from the customers' viewpoint.

After the first impression has been created, it is important that consistency is maintained throughout the flight.

Our objective must be that our customer service always exceeds passenger expectations and that there is no doubt that they will travel with Virgin Atlantic Airways on their next trip.

(Source: Virgin Atlantic Cabin Crew Manual)

1 What does Virgin mean by a 'genuine' smile?
2 Why is eye contact so important?
3 What does a 'friendly and approachable stance' mean?
4 How can you be 'the company' for the customers?
5 Give three examples of how cabin crew can give consistent service.

Personal presentation

Personal presentation is an important element of a first impression. Your personal presentation reveals how you feel about yourself, your customers and your level of professionalism. Travel and tourism is such a 'people' business that you should be aware of the importance of personal presentation and the impact it will have on customers and their confidence in your ability to provide a good service.

In order to encourage good personal presentation, some organisations provide staff with a uniform. This is usual for staff in roles dealing directly with customers such as in a travel agency, as an overseas rep, as a local guide or in a Tourist Information Centre. There are many benefits of staff being in uniform:

- customers immediately know who the staff are – this is particularly important in some roles, for example as an overseas resort representative or a ride attendant at a theme park
- a corporate image is developed
- staff feel they are part of the company – and the team
- the organisation has direct control over what staff wear.

Guidelines regarding the wearing of the uniform, caring for it and other aspects of personal presentation are usually provided. For example, Virgin Atlantic requires its female cabin crew to manicure and varnish their nails.

Consider this

Uniforms are not usually provided for staff who do not deal with customers. Examples include tour operators' head office staff, airline administration staff and back-office staff at tourist attractions. However, many do provide a dress code. Why do you think they consider this necessary?

Communication skills

Your communication skills need to be of the highest standard – this includes both written and oral communication.

Activity

Carry out a self-assessment. Give yourself a score between 1 and 5, where 1 is excellent and 5 is poor, for the following skills. Discuss your self-assessment with a partner. Do they agree with your scores?

	1	2	3	4	5
Spelling					
Handwriting					
Greeting people					
Developing conversations					
Positive body language					
Good tone of voice					
Telephone skills					

Written communication

Although most written communication will be word processed, there are occasions when you will need to hand write information. Examples include completion of an enquiry form, taking a telephone message or leaving a message for a colleague. In some roles, for example when working as a resort representative, weekly reports would also need to be handwritten. Your handwriting needs to legible and your spelling correct. Use of texting spellings is not acceptable.

When filling in any document bear in mind that it could potentially be used in a court of law. Therefore take your time over it, be professional and make sure the information is full, accurate and legible. Times and dates must be included. Give facts, not opinions.

It is important that the correct form of written communication is used. For example, e-mails and faxes are an excellent method of communication if speed is important. However, they are informal and should not be used, for example, to deal with a complaint. Similarly, a memo would be used only for internal customers.

Assessment practice

Work in small groups. Copy and complete the table, then compare your answers with other members of your group.

Remember that written communication is more formal than face-to-face communication. It is therefore sometimes used to confirm decisions that have previously been discussed. In some of the choices in the table, you may decide that face-to-face communication, or a telephone conversation, is needed as well as some form of written confirmation.

Message	Method of written communication to be used
The manager of a travel agency wants to advise a customer of a change of hotel.	
A resort rep wants to let head office know that a customer has made a serious complaint about the hotel. She thinks other customers will also complain.	
Two hotel receptionists have agreed to swap shifts. They want to tell their manager.	
Head office has decided to make 20 airline staff redundant.	
A customer has had a great holiday and decides to tell the travel agent and tour operator.	
A visitor to a museum has been overcharged. He realises this only when he gets home.	
After two weeks of reading about two destinations, Jamal wants to confirm a holiday with the travel agent.	

Taking it further

Role play or produce the documentation for each situation.  P4 P5 M2 D2

Oral communication

Oral communication includes both face-to-face communication and telephone conversation.

Face-to-face communication

We are all used to face-to-face communication. When shopping, getting on a bus, greeting friends and working in a team we all communicate directly with each other face to face. However, it is important to know how to use this form of communication to its full advantage when dealing with a customer. For example, personal presentation is very important – it will give a good or bad first impression. You must also consider your tone of voice and be very aware of your body language – it will communicate more to your customer than the words you say.

The advantage of face-to-face communication is that you can read your customer's body language, use brochures, leaflets and other materials to help you get information across to your customer, and answer any questions as they arise. Face-to-face communication is often on a one-to-one basis. However, it can also involve groups of people, for example at a staff meeting or a welcome party in a resort.

Telephone communication

To be able to communicate well on the telephone you need good listening skills. Remember that you must listen to the tone of voice as well as the words being said. It is particularly important to speak clearly and check understanding when on the phone – as you cannot read the body language or any other non-verbal information such as gestures and facial expressions.

Other techniques for good telephone communication include:

- be clear – use short sentences and phrases
- avoid jargon

- be concise
- pronounce your words clearly
- speak slowly
- make sure there is minimal background noise
- smile!

You should smile when speaking to customers on the phone because it will show in your tone of voice and be reflected in the customer service you provide. Many travel and tourism organisations require all their staff to answer the phone in the same way. For example, 'Good afternoon, Travel First. Harry speaking. How may I help you?' This is to ensure consistently good service and to present a corporate image.

Identifying customer needs

We have already established that a customer's needs may be straightforward and stated (for example, 'Please could I book a single room for tonight'). However, customers may not be clear about their needs and/or may only imply them. Good questioning skills are required to establish what it is a customer really wants.

Meeting customer needs and exceeding expectations

Once you know what a customer really wants you can use your product knowledge to find them the holiday to match their requirements. Of course, you cannot know about every destination so don't be afraid to ask colleagues for their opinions or advice. Most tour operators offer in-house training and educationals and in many travel agencies there will be someone who knows about or has been to a destination. This will help you to find the perfect holiday for your customer.

Assessment practice

Look at the table below. Imagine you are working in a travel agency and a customer has stated some of their needs. Write down some of the questions you could ask to find out more about their needs. The first one has been completed to get you started.

Implied or stated needs	Questions you may need to ask
We are on a tight budget	How much are you planning to spend? Does that include extras such as insurance and transport to the airport?
We will be on our honeymoon and want to make sure we get a double bed	
My husband is 80 next year	
I sometimes use a wheelchair	
It is our first wedding anniversary while we are away	
While we were on holiday last year my partner was very ill	
My son is epileptic	
I really need a break from the kids	
I am pregnant	

Practise asking different kinds of questions with a partner who wants to book a holiday.

Clearly, your aim is to exceed customers' expectations. You may do this by finding a special offer, suggesting a resort they had not thought of or simply by your level of customer service skills and knowledge about the destination. Sometimes you will need to 'go an extra mile' to exceed expectations. You may need to carry out extensive research on their behalf, tailor make an itinerary, phone a tour operator to find out particular details about a hotel or even book a specific room.

Theory into practice

Imagine you work as a resort representative. List things you may need to do in order to exceed expectations ('go the extra mile').

Range of situations

The travel industry is so diverse and customers' needs so varied, you need to develop your customer service skills so that you are able to deal with a variety of situations. You will soon have the skills required to deal with simple requests. Examples might include responding to straightforward enquiries, giving timetable information or taking simple bookings to destinations with which you are familiar. You will need to develop your skills to be able to deal with complex requests as well. Examples for a travel consultant could include dynamic packaging (tailor-making a holiday for a client) or dealing with

problems and complaints. In a resort, representatives sometimes have to deal with serious illnesses (requiring hospitalisation or repatriation) and occasionally deaths.

We will now focus on the most common situations that you will meet within the travel industry.

Requests for information

The ability to provide correct information in a customer-friendly manner is vital to excellent customer service. Customers require some information in almost all encounters with travel and tourism organisations.

Some staff are employed simply to provide information, for example at the Customer Information desk at an airport or a visitor attraction. Similarly, it is the primary role of all staff within a Tourist Information Centre to provide accurate information on such issues as car parking, visitor attractions, transportation and accommodation. Simple queries that may be asked of almost anyone within the industry could include:

- When does your office close?
- May I have a refund?
- How can I make a complaint?
- May I speak with your manager?

Information provided must always be accurate. If you are unsure about anything, you must check – this may mean looking something up or asking a colleague. After all, telling a customer that a beach is ideal for small children when in fact there are dangerous waves, could have disastrous consequences and is sure to result in complaint.

Giving advice

While information is factual, when asked for advice you are expected to give your personal opinion. Examples of advice requested from a travel agent could include: 'Do you think we should go a week later?', 'Would Benidorm be a better destination?', 'Do you think that would suit us?' If you have good product knowledge and have established your customers' needs you should be able to make appropriate recommendations.

Clients may also ask for advice about visa and health requirements. In these cases it is important to follow published advice. The most up-to-date information is available on the Foreign Office website (www.fco.gov.uk).

Complex requests

Some clients may have complex requests. Examples could include a family requiring priority seating or a business person wanting a flight upgrade. In these examples you would simply need to contact the airline and discuss the requirements. Some airlines will want this type of request to be confirmed in writing. Whatever the request it is important to make contact with the supplier to check their procedures as these will vary. For example, if a disabled passenger needs airport assistance this must be requested at the time of booking. Passengers cannot simply turn up at the airport and presume someone will be available to assist them.

Complaints

Unfortunately complaints are common within the travel and tourism industry. Many are justified. Examples may include poor quality accommodation or rude staff. However, some complaints result even though the problem may be outside anyone's contol. Examples are flight delays due to poor weather and holiday cancellations due to a hurricane. It is widely recognised that we live in a 'compensation culture' where people will complain in the hope of gaining a refund! Such situations will certainly stretch your customer service skills. We will be looking at how to handle complaints later in this section.

Business skills

Completion of documentation

Keeping appropriate records and documents is an important aspect of providing excellent customer service. You will need to record information in the following situations:

- taking an enquiry for a holiday (establishing customers' needs)
- dealing with a complaint
- taking payment
- booking an excursion
- taking a telephone message
- dealing with a problem (with a colleague, customer or your manager).

In many situations pro formas (that is, a form to fill in) are provided. One example is an enquiry form which prompts the travel consultant to ask specific questions such as dates of travel, number of adults and children, preferred resort, preferred departure airport, length of stay. Another example is a customer report form used in resorts. A resort representative will need to use this to write a factual report if a complaint is received. The report will then be sent to their head office.

General guidelines for all paperwork:

- Write in block capitals in black ink
- Make sure all copies are clear and can be read easily
- Fill in all sections – if they are not applicable write 'n/a', don't leave them blank
- Don't use jargon or foreign words (or your own abbreviations)
- Check the form once it is complete
- Make sure you are using the correct form – if unsure ask
- State facts not opinions.

Use of ICT

Using ICT is an integral part of most people's working lives. This is no different in the travel and tourism industry. For most roles in the industry you will need generic IT skills (such as word processing, use of databases, spreadsheets and e-mail systems) as well as skills specific to a role. For example, people working in an airline reservation team will receive training on the use of computer reservation systems such as Galileo or Amadeus. In a Tourist Information Centre you would need to be able to access the sites and use the software that provide timetables and local information. In most job roles you will have access to the internet and will need to be able to use it effectively.

Theory into practice

Many of the large travel agency chains always use standard letters and all use pro formas to gather information from customers. What are the advantages and disadvantages of this?

Case study: using the internet

Customers can get a lot of what they want from the internet so travel agents must offer service and expertise to attract customers.

The impact of the internet on agents is clear. Customers have become more demanding. They expect greater flexibility and choice, internet pricing in shops, as well as personal recommendations and experienced sales people with the insiders' touch. The internet continues to improve and travel websites get better every month. Search engines can now integrate dynamic packaging products (that is, can put the separate parts of a holiday together). Customer reviews are now often added to information about holidays and hotels, giving customers the confidence to make the right choice.

But agents can still add significant value. They must use their product knowledge to focus on high-value complex journeys. For short breaks they must ensure that their technology is at least as good as that on the internet. Their expert knowledge must justify an extra fee from the customer.

The added challenge to agents is to ensure that they have access to an extensive product range, as well as the technology to meet customer demand as quickly a possible. Can you satisfy the customer who wants to book a break within three hours to a sunny destination for under £200 per person? Somewhere with great beaches, suitable for kids and with a bit of culture thrown in? Can you show them agent and customer reviews of the hotel? Beyond the basics, can you add to the package by saving them money on car hire and transfers, as well as offering them deals on restaurants and on the attractions or concerts that are on during their stay?

It is service that is the key – it enables the agent to add value in many different ways. This will lead to true customer loyalty.

(Source: Adapted from article by Brent Hoberman, chief executive of lastminute.com, *Travel Trade Gazette*, 10 June 2005)

1 **What has been the impact of the internet on travel agents? Do you think travel agents will survive?**

2 **How is the internet changing?**

3 **What must agents do to compete with the internet? (List at least five ways.)**

4 **What can travel consultants and their managers do to improve product knowledge within the agency?**

Key term

Dynamic packaging – tailor-making a package holiday for a customer.

Complaint handling

Dealing with problems and complaints

Working in an environment with such a high level of person-to-person contact means that problems and complaints are inevitable. Problems such as lost luggage, delays or stolen goods do not initially reflect badly on the company. Indeed, some of the problems may in fact be the customer's own fault. Examples of problems include the customer who has:

- lost their passport
- forgotten their ticket
- left a case at the airport
- broken a leg
- had a heart attack.

It is important to be aware that if a problem is not handled quickly and efficiently, it can often result in a complaint. You will deal with a problem in the same way as a complaint (Figure 4.13). However, the customer is less likely to be angry and therefore the situation may be easier for you to handle.

Consider this

Seven out of ten customers will do business with you again if you resolve the complaint in their favour.

| Listening | Use active listening so that the customer knows you are taking the complaint seriously. Take notes if you need to. |

| Questioning | Ask probing questions, but don't interrupt. You will need to use a mixture of open, closed and reflective questions. Gather as much information as you can. |

| Empathising | Try to see the situation form the customer's point of view. Use phrases such as 'I understand why you are so upset', 'That must have been really frightening' to reassure the customer that you do understand. |

| Understanding the problem | You may understand the problem once you have listened to the customer. You may, however, have to go and investigate. This may be a simple check to see if tickets are in the file or it may be more complex – you may have to write to an airline or a supplier. In this case you must tell the customer what you need to do. |
| | Before you are able to offer solutions you need to be sure that you have understood the whole problem. |

| Taking control of the situation | You may have to take control of the situation if it is in danger of escalating. For example, an angry customer at a hotel reception should be taken into a manager's office, a doctor may have to be called for a sick child, police may have to be contacted if a hotel guest is threatening other residents. |

| Agreeing solutions | If you are able to agree a solution, do so. But make sure you know your responsibility limits. If unsure, involve your manager. |

| Follow up | Whatever the agreed solution, do it! Make it a priority. This is your chance to turn a complaint into a repeat booking by being efficient. |
| | Make sure you follow company procedure regarding dealing with complaints. Fill in the appropriate forms/reports and send them to the right people. |

▲ **Figure 4.13 Dealing with complaints**

Even the most successful travel companies receive complaints. Sometimes these may be justified and sometimes not. Whichever the case, knowledge of procedures will help you to deal with the situation calmly without taking the complaint personally. It is important to view a complaint as an opportunity to 'turn a customer around', that is, to change a complaining customer into a satisfied customer. This is challenging but it will ensure repeat business and customer loyalty as well as giving you job satisfaction.

Examples of complaints a tour operator might receive include:
- flight delays
- inaccuracy of information on the website
- call centres not answering phones quickly enough
- poor excursions
- resort representative being late for an excursion
- lack of cleanliness at hotel
- excursion prices.

Selling is just one of the many customer service situations that you may be involved in when working in the travel and tourism industry. It may be an important part of your job, or just a small aspect of it. For most travel and tourism organisations, sales are a fundamental activity as the number of sales determines profit levels and the ultimate success of the organisation.

Much selling still takes place in a face-to-face situation, such as in a travel agency. However, there is a growth in telephone sales as a result of the growth in call centres. The internet is also a key sales tool for many tour operators and airlines. These sales are achieved through written communication, that is web pages and e-mails.

Whether you are selling face-to-face, on the phone, by letter or e-mail, the same skills are needed and the same process is followed.

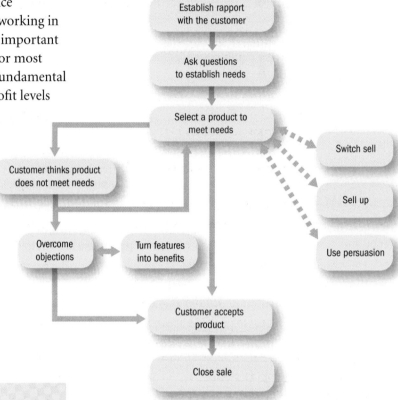

▲ Figure 4.14 The stages of selling

Key term

Commission levels – these are usually given as a percentage. Travel agencies traditionally earn a commission of approximately 10 per cent for each package holiday they sell and 7 per cent for each scheduled airline ticket. In some agencies, staff are also given commissions – they earn more the more they sell. In resorts the representatives earn commission for all the excursions they sell. This is an important part of their income.

Building rapport

The first stage of the sales process is to build a good rapport (a positive relationship) with the customer. Customers must feel positive and relaxed and under no pressure to buy. They must trust the salesperson and be confident in their ability to find the right product to meet their needs. The environment in which you are working,

your tone of voice, body language and what you say to your customer will all contribute towards the rapport.

The environment (office and desk) is important. For example, if purchasing a holiday in a travel agency, customers would expect:

- the office to be clean
- staff to be seated at their desks
- no eating or drinking at desks
- clear, neat desks
- telephones to be answered quickly
- no radios or loud background noise
- staff who are not serving to be working (not gossiping with each other).

As a salesperson you will also establish rapport by:

- first impressions – smiling and greeting your customer warmly
- your appearance – clean, tidy, neat hair and minimal jewellery

- offering customers a seat
- making good eye contact
- positive body language
- not being distracted by other people or the telephone.

Establishing needs and expectations

Once rapport is established, you will need to find out the customers' needs and expectations. This is perhaps the most difficult part of the sales process, as customers may not know what they need themselves. Through careful questioning and listening you will have to work out what it is they really want. You have already seen that there is a huge range of customers, all of whom have different needs. Remember that your clients may also have unstated needs which they do not tell you about.

The first stage is to ask questions to establish factual information, gather information about the stated needs and try and pick up on any implied needs. For example, if selling a holiday you can ask questions to establish how many people are going, when they want to go and for how long. Clients may also be able to tell you what type of accommodation they would like and their preferred destination. Other clients may need you to guide them. Some clients will know only that they want a holiday and expect you to find the perfect holiday to meet their requirements. Careful questioning will be required!

You will have to ask open questions to make sure you get all the information you need. Open questions begin with what, why, who, how, when, which or where. They will perhaps give you more information than you require, but this may help you discover the underlying expecations and guide a customer to a particular type of holiday.

You will also need to practise active listening. This will help to maintain the rapport that you have established and encourage your clients to give you further information. You should take notes, write down key points, nod or say encouraging things ('I know what you mean', 'I see'). If you are working in a travel agency you will be required to complete a customer enquiry form.

To establish customer needs you must:
- ask open questions
- listen actively

- use reflective questions to check understanding – 'So you think Greece was too hot for you in August last year?'
- maintain a positive rapport through good eye contact and positive body language
- keep asking questions and discussing options until you have established customer needs.

Selecting the products to meet requirements

Once you know the customer's needs, you must find a holiday to match them. If the enquiry is straightforward – the customer knows exactly what they want – this can be done through a simple search on the computer reservation system. However, if customer needs are less clear, it is your product knowledge that may determine whether you can meet them. Do you know the different resorts, are you familiar with the brochures, do you know which operators offer particular holiday types?

For example, a couple may ask about going to Spain for a romantic beach holiday, but you may be able to recommend a Greek island which you know is very popular with young couples. This is called 'switch selling'. You may also be able to 'sell up', which means selling something more or of higher quality than the customer originally intended.

Key terms

Switch selling – the process of selling the client something different from what they thought they needed. For example, a group of young people could come into your travel agency saying they want a clubbing holiday in Ayia Napa (Cyprus). However, you know that Ayia Napa is now much more a family resort than it was three years ago and you 'switch sell' them to Palma, Mallorca.

Selling up – selling something of greater value than was asked for. For example, you might sell a client a holiday in the Caribbean when they came into your agency asking for a week in Tenerife, or you might encourage a client to travel first class. Selling up means the agency (and possibly the travel consultant) earns extra commission.

Feature of holiday	Your benefit statement
The hotel has a large swimming pool and a children's pool	'This hotel has a really large pool. There will be plenty of room for you to swim and you won't be disturbed by children's games.'
The hotel is isolated	'It is a wonderfully quiet location – no neighbouring hotels to share the beach with. You will also have great views from all rooms.'
The hotel is in the middle of a town	'You will be right in the middle of things. You can stroll out each evening and really get involved in local life.'
Excursions included	'You have two excursions included in the price, both of which are guided, so you will certainly get a lot of local information.'
Representative available	'A representative will be on hand if you have any queries while you are in the resort. They will be able to advise you where to go and can arange local excursions and car hire if you decide to explore while on holiday.'

Table 4.5 Examples of benefit statements

Features and benefits

When presenting the product it is important that you identify the three or four things that are most important to the client and describe how this product matches these needs – that is, you will introduce the features of the holiday and turn them into the benefits for the customer. For example, 'I have just found this holiday in The Gambia, it is available for when you want to travel. I know you want some sun and the temperatures there will be high at that time of year. There is five-star accommodation available and it has a pool, which you particularly requested.'

Key terms

Features – particular aspect of a holiday, for example location of hotel, excursions included, local pick-up.

Benefit – what the customer gains from a feature.

Theory into practice

Work in pairs. Use brochures to select a holiday destination. Write down ten possible features of the destination. Take it in turns to convert your partner's features into benefits. **P6**

Overcoming objections

You will also need to overcome objections. Customers may not agree with you that the holiday you have selected for them matches their requirements. This may be because you have misunderstood their needs, or simply have not asked enough questions (and so you don't know their underlying needs). If this is the case you must ask probing questions to re-establish their requirements and select a different product.

However, it may be that the customer requires more reassurance. They may be hesitating and unsure what to do. You should establish what it is they are unsure about. For example:

You: 'What is it about the holiday you are unsure of?'

Your customer: 'The hotel isn't very close to the beach.'

You: 'That's true. But it's only five minutes' walk and you are right in the middle of town, so it will be great for the nightlife you wanted.'

Overcoming objections is really like turning features into benefits. You need to first establish what the objection (feature) is and then turn it into something that the customer can view as a benefit. You are persuading the customer that this holiday really does meet their requirements.

Theory into practice

In pairs, each write down five objections that a customer might make when buying a holiday. Take it in turns to listen to each other's statements, and reply in a way that attempts to overcome the objection. **P6**

Closing the sale

Once you have overcome objections you must look out for buying signals. These may be things that are said (verbal signals) or simply body language (visual signals). Examples include a customer:

- nodding to their partner
- looking in their bag for their cheque book or cards
- asking you to reconfirm the total price
- checking flight details again.

It is important that you never rush a customer. Some people are happy to make quick decisions, while many are indecisive. You must look out for these verbal and visual signals. If they are strong and it is clear the customer wants to book, then you could say 'Would you like me to book this for you, before it goes?' Other customers will clearly ask you to book it, for example saying 'Let's get it booked, then!' In these cases, the sale is closed and you need to reconfirm holiday and payment details with the client, complete the paperwork and take payment.

However, there will always be some customers who remain unsure. You may have overcome half a dozen objections, turned all features into benefits and been extremely persuasive, but they may need time to think or discuss the decision with their family. Offering to 'hold' a holiday or reassuring the customer that there is plenty of availability is all part of excellent service. Make sure customers know your name, how to contact you and when you are available. Hard selling often turns people off – you are more likely to end up with a satisfied customer if you pick up on their signals and don't pressurise them.

Case study: Thomson rolls out screensaver

Agency chain shows holiday videos on its 6000 computer screens when idle in a bid to boost agents' knowledge and sales.

Chris Gray reports

Thomson has turned the screensavers on each of the 6000 terminals in its shops into a selling and training tool.

The screensavers display videos of Thomson's specialised products to staff and customers on a 20-minute loop.

They are also used to carry training information, and to generate income from travel industry suppliers who pay to be featured.

Thomson plans to extend the content within months to include products linked to travel, such as cosmetics from Boots and books from Waterstones.

The screensavers have been introduced in all Thomson's 750 shops after a six-month trial in 150 outlets showed an increase in sales for six of the seven holidays featured. Two increased by more than 100 per cent.

The screensavers are changed each month but Thomson ultimately hopes to be able to update them instantly to display last-minute bargains, or to respond to rivals – by matching their foreign exchange rates, for example.

Doug Glenwright, Thomson customer experience marketing manager, said the screensavers had encouraged customers to try new types of holidays. They had also helped staff get more of a feel for what they were selling.

(Source: *Travel Trade Gazette*, 3 March 2006)

1　**What are the benefits of these new screensavers to customers?**

2　**How do the staff benefit?**

3　**How will Thomson's revenue increase?**

Completing documentation

Documention varies from organisation to organisation. However, some documentation will have to be done after every sale. Most of this will be done electronically. The sales consultant in a travel agency will need to collect a deposit, issue a receipt and diary the next payment. A resort rep completing a sale for an excursion will need to take passenger names, collect monies and issue a receipt.

After-sales service

Customer service does not end with the close of the sale. To ensure repeat business you must also offer an excellent after-sales service. Some of this takes place before your customers go on holiday (pre-departure). There is also after-sales service when your customer comes back from holiday (post departure). Both will help to ensure repeat business.

Pre-departure

You may have closed the sale but have you offered all the 'extras' available? How is your customer getting to the airport? Would they like you to book airport parking for them? Or maybe overnight accommodation near the airport so they don't have to leave home so early? Furthermore, your customer isn't actually going on holiday until next summer. During that time they may

pop into the travel agency to make changes to their bookings. They may even have to cancel due to family problems or other unexpected circumstances. Dealing with these issues in a positve and professional manner is all part of the sales process.

Post departure

How you deal with a customer on their return may determine whether or not you get their repeat business. This part of after-sales service is therefore an important element of customer service. On their return you may telephone your customer to check if they have had a good time. This is an opportunity for you to find out more about the resort they went to and improve your product knowledge. It is also an opportunity to ask them where they want to go to next year and see if you can get another sale! Sometimes you will also have to deal with problems that have occurred on holiday. There may have been delays or luggage could have been lost. In either case you will need to provide details of carriers to contact (or you may do this on your customer's behalf). You may also need to advise how to make an insurance claim – in case the lost luggage does not turn up.

Situations

Many jobs in travel and tourism involve selling. Staff working in a travel agency or call centre will constantly be booking holidays, making accommodation reservations and flight bookings. Those employed in Tourist Information Centres, booking agents or simply at a desk within a visitor attraction may be selling tickets for excursions, guided tours or events. In resorts, the representives earn commission from excursion sales. This is a great incentive to develop good sales skills!

Knowledge check

1 How much does it cost to attract a new customer (compared to retaining an existing one)?

2 What are the benefits of uniforms to organisations?

3 What is meant by body language?

4 How can you demonstrate to someone that you are listening?

5 What is meant by 'rapport'?

6 How does product knowledge help you to provide excellent customer service?

7 Write out the phonetic alphabet.

8 How do you write midnight using the 24-hour clock?

9 What are the benefits of teamwork?

10 What is a customer policy?

11 List the benefits of excellent customer service to the customer.

12 List the benefits of excellent customer service to staff.

13 Describe what is meant by the following terms: competitive advantage; public relations; customer loyalty.

14 Describe a situation when you would use a memo rather than a letter.

15 Give five words which are used to begin open questions.

16 What does 'commission' mean?

17 What is the difference between a feature and a benefit?

18 Give four examples of things you can do to ensure that you give a positive first impression.

Preparation for assessment

You have just gained a work experience placement with an independent travel agency in your home town. The manager, Shena Bajart, calls you into her office on the first day of your work experience to discuss what you will be doing. The agency is doing quite well, but Shena is concerned that a competitor is setting up at the other end of the high street. She wants to improve the customer service her staff give to customers to ensure competitive advantage.

As you have just completed the customer services unit on your travel and tourism course, Shena asks you to carry out the following tasks.

1 a) Research how customer service is provided in two travel and tourism organisations. Shena would like you to use this information to write a report in which you do the following:
- Describe how the principles of customer service and the methods used to evaluate it are applied in the two organisations. **P1**
- Describe the benefits of good quality customer service and the consequences of poor service to the two organisations. **P2**
- Describe how differing buyer behaviour and motivations can influence the service provided by two travel and tourism organisations. **P1**

b) Now you will be able to compare the service provided by the two organisations, explaining how it will meet the needs of different customer types. **M1**

c) Finally, you must evaluate the customer service provisions in the two organisations and make recommendations as to how improvements could be made to meet the needs of a wider range of customers. (You must also justify your recommendations.) **D1**

2 All staff need to improve both their customer service and selling skills in order to ensure that they do not lose business to their new competitor. Shena asks you to demonstrate good practice to them. Work with a colleague and write a total of five scenarios. You will role-play these to staff to demonstrate good practice.
- Provide a service to customers in two different travel and tourism situations. **P3**
- Deal with two complaints (one of which must be in writing). **P5**
(If you work independently and your customer service skills please both your customers and your company these tasks may also provide evidence for M2.)
- Demonstrate selling skills in a travel and tourism situation. **P6**
(If your selling skills are effective and meet the needs of differing customer types in differing situations this may also provide evidence for M3.)

Grading tip

To reach Distinction level in task 2 you will need to demonstrate excellent customer service skills – you will:

- be consistent
- be confident
- show a thorough understanding of customer types, their needs and wants in different situations.

Grading criteria

To achieve a pass grade the evidence must show that the learner is able to:	To achieve a merit grade the evidence must show that, in addition to the pass criteria, the learner is able to:	To achieve a distinction grade the evidence must show that, in addition to the pass and merit criteria, the learner is able to:
P1 describe how the principles of customer service and methods used to evaluate it, are applied in tow different travel and tourism organisations **Assessment practice page 112**	**M1** compare the service provided by two travel and tourism organisations explaining how it meets the needs of different customer types **Assessment practice page 112**	**D1** evaluate the customer service provision in two organisations and make justified recommendations as to how improvements could be made to meet the needs of a wider range of customers **Assessment practice page 112**
P2 describe the benefits of good quality customer service, and the consequences of poor service, to two different travel and tourism organisations **Assessment practice page 122**	**M2** independently demonstrate skills in handling customer service situations effectively and dealing with complaints to the satisfaction of both the customer and the company **Assessment practice page 136**	**D2** consistently and confidently handle customer service situations (including a complaint and a sale) showing a thorough understanding of customer types, needs and wants in different situations **Assessment practice page 136**
P3 describe how differing buyer behaviour and motivations can influence the service provided by two travel and tourism organisations **Assessment practice page 127**	**M3** demonstrate effective selling skills to meet differing customer needs in different situations **Assessment practice page 146**	
P4 use customer-service skills to provide service to customers in two different travel and tourism situations **Assessment practice page 136**		
P5 deal with two complaints (one of which must be in writing) **Assessment practice page 136**		
P6 demonstrate selling skills in a travel and tourism situation **Theory into practice page 144**		

Marketing travel and tourism products and services

Introduction

This unit introduces you to marketing in the context of the travel and tourism industry. You will learn about the marketing mix and apply it to organisations in travel and tourism. You will examine the factors which affect marketing in travel and tourism and the constraints that apply.

You will consider different methods of market research, and how they are used in travel and tourism. You will demonstrate practical skills in marketing by carrying out a marketing research activity and organising a promotional campaign.

After completing this unit you should be able to achieve the following outcomes:

1 Understand the factors affecting marketing in travel and tourism

2 Know the marketing mix (the four Ps) of a travel and tourism organisation

3 Be able to conduct a marketing research activity for a travel and tourism organisation

4 Be able to organise a promotional campaign for a travel and tourism organisation.

Thinking points

Before you try to understand the principles of marketing and how it is practised, you need to understand what is meant by the concept of marketing. If you ask people what they understand by marketing, they often mention advertising or selling; these things are not marketing, but they are a part of it. Marketing embraces all business decisions that are made in order to get a product or service to the right customer or consumer.

A company which has adopted the core philosophies of marketing puts the customer at the heart of its business. Every product made has a customer who needs or wants that product, even if they don't quite know it yet. For every service that is offered, the company has established that there are customers who would like to use that service. Of course, this doesn't always work out in practice. If it did, no companies would fail. But companies that are successful in the long term are those which are carefully providing for the needs of their customers.

An organisation that aims to practise successful marketing tries to have excellent customer knowledge and to anticipate customers' needs. Most travel and tourism companies understand that putting the customer first is crucial to success in business.

Definitions

Marketing

This is how the Chartered Institute of Marketing (CIM) (www.cim.co.uk) defines marketing:

The management process responsible for identifying, anticipating and satisfying customer requirements profitably.

There is an argument that 'profitably' is not an essential word in the definition – not all organisations aim to make a profit. Charities give all the money they make to the cause they work for. They have to market themselves to raise that money. Public organisations such as tourist boards provide services to consumers, but don't usually make a profit. They still use marketing principles to ensure that the services they provide are right for their customers.

Here is another definition, provided by a famous marketing expert called Philip Kotler:

The marketing concept holds that the key to achieving organisational goals lies in determining the needs and wants of target markets and delivering the desired satisfaction more efficiently and effectively than the competition.

(Source: *Marketing Management, Analysis, Planning, Implementation and Control*, Prentice-Hall, 6th edition, 1988)

Again the importance of the customer is emphasised, but now there is also mention of the competition. Travel and tourism is a very competitive industry. Consider how many holiday companies there are to choose from when you book a holiday. So to be successful, a company not only has to provide what the customer wants but must do it better than competitors.

It is difficult to think of travel and tourism companies that have reached the stage where customers flock to them because the product or service is exactly right. But this is certainly something to aim for.

Theory into practice

Ask ten people what they understand by marketing. Write down what they say and bring your notes for discussion with your colleagues. How many people are close to the definitions given?

Customer service

As part of your course you are also studying customer service. You may be wondering how customer service and marketing differ from each other. Good customer service is part of the marketing process; it is concerned with how the product or service is presented to the customer, how the company is presented to the customer and how the customer is dealt with. Good customer service involves developing personal service skills. The function of marketing, however, is to encompass the whole process of deciding which products and services the customer will want and how they will be delivered to the customer.

Principles of marketing

The principles of marketing are to:

- find out about customer needs
- produce products and services that meet those needs
- know the market – including competitors
- make sure the whole organisation is marketing orientated
- find and communicate with customers
- manage any threats that affect the marketing process.

In the UK, marketing has been a high-profile aspect of business since the 1970s, and today it would be difficult to find travel and tourism companies that do not acknowledge its importance. Most will have a marketing department or marketing manager.

Company ethos

Moral issues for travel and tourism include matters relating to social responsibility and ethics. For example, the tourism industry depends heavily on the natural environment and therefore has a moral obligation to protect that environment. Green tourism, otherwise known as sustainable tourism or responsible tourism, is of increasing importance because of the enormous growth in travel. However, some of the biggest tour operators have been accused of paying lip service to responsible tourism and not having real policies to safeguard the environment.

An organisation called Responsible Travel organised a petition to lobby three tour operators on their environmental policies, and invited members of the public to send in stories about environmental degradation. The company's website encouraged people to sign and return the petition.

Of course, there are significant marketing advantages to going green. A recent MORI poll showed that

61 per cent of consumers believe that environmental issues are important when choosing a holiday. As this is a topical subject, green marketing campaigns also attract positive publicity from the media.

Consumer protection

Travel and tourism companies are subject to many regulations and pieces of legislation. Adherence to these impacts on their marketing activities.

Legislation

The Consumer Protection Act 1987 makes it an offence to give customers a misleading price indication about goods and services. It lays down rules about the use of terms such as 'reduced' and 'bargain'. Price indications given verbally are also covered. In travel and tourism, this legislation has most relevance to brochures and advertising.

Case study

Look at www.responsibletravel.com for the latest news on this campaign. Discuss your findings with your group and decide whether the campaign was justified.

(Source: http://www.responsibletravel.com)

Please sign our petition …

Dear Thomson Holidays, Thomas Cook and MyTravel,
I've had enough of the way mass tourism often tramples over local people and cultures, and damages the environment.

In the interests of local people, the environment and those of us who want more enjoyable and authentic holidays, I request that you publish policies for responsible travel in your brochures and on your websites.

Yours sincerely

Name …

E-mail …

Send us your stories

We want to hear your stories of mass tourism holidays and evidence of environmental degradation and of negative impacts on local people and culture.

Figure 5.1 Organisation of a marketing company

The Trade Descriptions Act 1968 is one of the most important pieces of consumer legislation, and section 14 is its most relevant part for travel and tourism. This section deals with the supply of goods and services. It states that it is an offence to make a statement that is known to be false or to recklessly make a statement which is false. This applies to the provision of services, facilities and accommodation and the location of amenities for any accommodation. An offence can be committed even when there is no intention to deceive the customer.

The Unfair Terms in Consumer Contracts Regulations 1999 apply to all contracts. When you book a holiday, a hotel room or a flight you enter into a contract with the seller. The seller will publish terms and conditions associated with that contract – you can read these in any holiday brochure.

These regulations protect consumers against unfair terms in contracts. Sometimes attempts are made to introduce terms and conditions that may reduce the consumer's statutory rights or may impose unfair burdens on the consumer over and above the obligations of the ordinary rules of law.

The Data Protection Act 1998 provides rights for those who have information held about them in 'relevant filing systems'. This may be on computer or in paper files.

The act also requires those who record and use personal information to follow sound practice.

An individual can have access to information held about them and, if necessary, have it corrected or deleted. People must have the opportunity to consent to the collection and processing of their data. Personal data must be kept secure, up to date and not for longer than necessary.

The Information Commissioner's Office (ICO) administers this act. If you want to have access to information about yourself, you must make a written request to the holder of the information. Travel and tourism companies hold a lot of customer information, which must be revealed if a customer asks for it.

Codes of practice

The British Code of Advertising, Sales Promotion and Direct Marketing has the following main general principles.

- All advertisements should be legal, decent, honest and truthful.
- All advertisements should be prepared with a sense of responsibility to consumers and society.
- All advertisements should respect the principles of fair competition generally accepted in business.

- No advertisements should bring advertising into disrepute.
- Marketing communications must conform with the code. Primary responsibility for observing the code falls on marketers. Others involved in preparing and publishing marketing communications such as agencies, publishers and other service suppliers also accept an obligation to abide by the code.
- Any unreasonable delay in responding to the Advertising Standards Authority's enquiries may be considered a breach of the code.

The Advertising Standards Authority (ASA) is an independent body set up by the advertising industry to police the rules for advertising, sales promotion and direct marketing. The system is one of self-regulation aiming to protect consumers and maintain the integrity of marketing communications. The ASA continually checks a sample of advertisements, but also relies on the public to complain about advertisements which do not comply with the code. The ASA can ask for an offending advertisement to be withdrawn or changed. Of course, some complaints are judged to be unfounded. Travel and tourism organisations are subject to legislation. However, these laws differ internationally. Tour operators in particular have an obligation to ensure the health and safety of their customers on holiday and should have extensive procedures in place for this.

In some countries, such as the UK, access for people with disabilities is taken very seriously and legislation is in place under the Disability Discrimination Act 1995 (amended 2005) to ensure accessibility. For example, all new buildings must be accessible to people in wheelchairs.

Tour operators may find that other countries do not have such policies and that access is restricted, particularly at historic sites. Again, tour operators need to make checks and advise customers in their marketing literature.

Consider this

Not all buildings are easily accessible to people with disabilities. Think about what provisions there are for the disabled in your local cinema or theatre.

External constraints

Travel and tourism companies need to be aware of the external factors that affect the operation of their businesses. An analysis of these factors is described as a PEST analysis, because the factors involved are categorised as:

- Political
- Economic
- Social
- Technological.

A PEST analysis should take place at regular intervals as part of a review of marketing activities. Management should be constantly aware of topical issues which may impact on business, even when a formal analysis is not taking place.

Companies also need to undertake a thorough analysis of internal factors affecting operations. This is known as a SWOT analysis, looking at the company's:

- Strengths
- Weaknesses
- Opportunities
- Threats.

You need to know how to carry out these types of analyses and use the information gathered.

Key term

PEST – a PEST analysis helps an organisation to take stock of the external factors affecting its business, identifying political, economic, social and technological factors. The PEST analysis helps with the SWOT analysis as it can point to opportunities and threats.

The following are some of the external (PEST) factors which currently affect travel and tourism companies.

Political factors

These often relate to changes in legislation introduced by government. A recent example of legislation affecting the travel and tourism industry is the Denied Boarding, Cancellation and Delay EU Regulation, which was accepted in 2004 and became operational in 2005. This regulation gives passengers much greater compensation when flights are delayed or cancelled. Airlines are generally unhappy about these new regulations and believe that they will have to pay out a lot in compensation. Airlines' associations are presenting a legal challenge to the regulations, claiming that they will lead to higher fares and less choice for consumers.

Theory into practice

Find out what EU regulations promise to consumers in cases of flight delay or cancellation. What do you think of the regulations? Carry out a debate, with half the group representing the airlines and the other half representing a consumer group. **P1 M2**

When regulations are proposed, various groups campaign to or 'lobby' Parliament to get their views heard and try to make sure that legislation represents their interests. The airline associations lobby on behalf of airlines and the Association of British Travel Agents (ABTA) lobbies for travel agents. ABTA and similar organisations help their members to keep up to date with industry changes, as it is sometimes difficult to monitor new developments.

Tour operators have to be aware of the political situation in the destinations they offer. Some places can become very dangerous to visit. Situations might change rapidly, but tourists will avoid places where there have recently been serious incidences of unrest or terrorism. For example, the Bali bombing deterred tourists for some time, and currently it is not advisable to visit many parts of the Middle East because of terrorist activity.

Such occurrences cause problems to tour operators as they are unexpected and cannot be planned for. If the situation in a country becomes dangerous tour operators may have to repatriate holidaymakers and switch destinations for those who have booked to go there. The Foreign Office website (www.fco.gov.uk) gives the current situation on safety in countries all over the world. Tour operators have to try to reassure holidaymakers through their marketing that they will be safe in the destinations they use and that if an incident occurs the tour operator will be able to get them home safely.

Changes in taxes affect tourism as they raise costs. Passengers on airlines have become used to paying air passenger duty, just as they are used to paying road tax. When taxes are raised or newly introduced they become contentious. In the USA a room tax is added to the hotel bill.

Case study: Florida ponders tax on car hire

Visitors to Florida may face a new levy on car hire from November. Three counties covering the Orlando, Miami and Fort Lauderdale areas may vote for a proposal to add a $2-per-day tax to car hire rates to fund road upkeep. The levy would add about £15 to a typical fortnight's car hire.

The fee will be in addition to a $2-a-day car rental levy used to fund Visit Florida's activities, which is included in headline prices when bookings are made in the UK.

Florida governor Jeb Bush is unlikely to use his powers to veto the proposal as it will mainly affect tourists, especially repeat visitors – many of whom opt for fly-drives.

Opponents of the tax believe it will prevent Florida from expanding its market share. The area's visitor numbers from the UK have remained static this year.

Dollar Thrifty Europe managing director Tom Knopek said: 'Local government is looking to tax international visitors to help maintain the highways.

'That is not a good way to encourage tourism from a state already under pressure to maintain tourism at previous levels.'

It is unclear how the tax would be collected.

(Source: *Travel Trade Gazette*, 12 May 2006)

1 **What do you think about the tax? Is it a good thing or not? Give the arguments for and against.**
2 **How could the tax be collected?**

Taking it further

Find out about some other tourist taxes by carrying out research on the internet.

Another important economic factor is interest rates. If rates rise it can affect a business's ability to repay loans.

The exchange rate can also dramatically affect a company's costs. For example, a tour operator with contracted accommodation in Spain will pay in euros. A weak pound will buy fewer euros and will bring increased costs to the tour operator. Eleven European countries have adopted the euro, and although the UK has retained sterling and is not a member of the euro zone, travel and tourism businesses in the UK are still affected by the euro. Customers who come from the continent may expect to use euros in the UK and in fact some hotels and shops will accept them, giving change in sterling.

Rises in fuel prices also affect the economic health of airlines and tour operators, as the case study below shows. Read it carefully and answer the questions.

Travel and tourism businesses operate in a rapidly changing market. It is important that marketers take notice of social changes affecting their customers.

People in the UK today generally live longer and are healthier. They have more money to spend than previous generations, and time to spend it. Older people make up a vital market for travel and tourism operators, who have lost no time in creating holidays specifically for them in off-peak periods. This market is known as the 'grey' market.

Tastes change from season to season. Tourists want to visit new destinations, and as travel costs are comparatively cheaper than a few years ago, much of the world is easily accessible. People are taking short breaks as well as the traditional summer holiday. More people are wanting

Case study: EasyJet fears oil hike

EasyJet has warned its full-year profits will be hit to the tune of £4 million if oil prices continue to ride high.

The no-frills airline said profits could slip to about £52 million if oil prices stay at more than $40 a barrel. The airline has hedged 55 per cent of its fuel to the end of September.

However, it ruled out adding a surcharge to its tickets as airlines such as British Airways, Virgin Atlantic and Singapore Airlines have done.

EasyJet piled further pressure on its share price – which plummeted by 21 per cent on Monday to 158p – when it warned of a tougher trading environment later this year.

Chief executive Ray Webster said: 'We indicated in our interim announcement that we were seeing unprofitable and unrealistic pricing by airlines across all sectors of the European industry.

'We expect this to continue during the rest of the year. While demand for low-cost travel remains strong, the forward pricing environment is exceptionally competitive.'

His words echo those of Ryanair chief executive Michael O'Leary, who warned of a fares 'bloodbath' this winter.

Revenue climbed by almost a quarter year-on-year to hit £1.015 billion in the 12 months to May.

This outstripped Ryanair's annual revenue which also climbed, by 28 per cent, to about £671 million.

But the Irish airline's profit is more than double easyJet's at about £128 million.

Passenger figures rose by 23 per cent to 22 million in the year to May. But load factors dipped by two percentage points to 81 per cent.

(Source: *Travel Trade Gazette*, 11 June 2004)

1 **Investigate and explain these terms:**
   - **no-frills**
   - **hedging**
   - **surcharge**
   - **forward pricing environment.**
   - **revenue**
   - **profit**
   - **load factor**

2 **Explain how a rise in fuel prices affects an airline's profits.** P1 M2

3 **What measures could an airline take to avoid the risk to profits?** D1

◀ **Figure 5.2 New Zealand**

The internet has revolutionised the way we book our holidays and travel. Online booking systems are common for all modes of transport and for many holidays. Hotel bookings can also be made online, showing a view of the room and the facilities.

Travel agents are under great threat from the internet. Their commissions have been slashed as operators cut costs and encourage internet bookings. If tourists can do their research on the web, 'see' their destinations and book easily, why use a travel agent? Those agencies that survive will be the ones that adapt their role so that they offer a specialist service and excellent advice, rather than just a booking service. In fact, those that survive will be those that practise the best marketing.

to stay in mobile homes rather than tents, and so tour operators are providing them. Sunbathing is not so popular now, as the public is increasingly aware of the risks of skin cancer.

To meet the changes, tour operators need to provide different types of holidays. There are city breaks, adventure holidays and spa holidays, all providing the tourist with a variety of things to do. 'Cultural tourism' is the term coined for holidays which include excursions to sites of interest, museums and galleries.

The media has a great influence on our culture. Films make us aware of places and inspire us to visit them. Tourism to New Zealand has increased since the release of the *Lord of the Rings* trilogy of films which was made there. Tourism New Zealand research shows that 10 per cent of foreigners visiting are at least partly motivated by the chance to tour sites shown in the films.

Technological factors

Technology is probably the area of greatest change with rapid developments in many areas. The building of the Channel Tunnel opened up the UK to its neighbours and allowed more options for outbound travel. Aircraft are being developed that will hold many hundreds of passengers, and airport runways are being expanded to accommodate them. Self check-in is becoming more common at airports, including passengers checking in their own baggage. It is now possible to hire a car without any personal contact, collecting keys and making payment via a vending machine.

Assessment practice

You have read many examples of PEST factors that may influence marketing in travel and tourism. Remember that these influences can occur on a local, national or international level.

1 Work with a partner and choose a tourist facility in your area. This could be a tourist attraction, a tourist office or a hotel. Describe the facility and its location. What is its target market?

2 Identify all the political, economic, social and technological factors that will impact on its future planning. You may need to do some research to find out what is going on in your local area, for example new housing developments that will bring new customers. Look at what is happening nationally as well. Present your findings to your group and discuss the variations that occur. Are any of the factors you have identified opportunities or threats? **P1** **M1**

3 Explain how these factors will affect the application of marketing principles by your chosen tourist facility. **D1**

Marketing mix

The marketing mix describes the key elements that an organisation uses to achieve its objectives and meet the needs of its customers. These elements are commonly known as the four Ps: product, price, place and promotion. The four Ps give us the core of a company's marketing strategy.

Before any travel and tourism organisation can determine its marketing mix it needs to plan. Plans may be short term, perhaps for a year, or longer term, up to five years and beyond. The organisation must have an idea or vision of where it wants to be in its market in the future. It may even plan to enter a different market.

Marketing planning

A marketing audit is first carried out, including a PEST analysis and sometimes a SWOT analysis.

The organisation should then be in a position to set its objectives. Objectives are goals, and set out what the company is trying to achieve. They focus on where the company is heading and clarify what the business aims to do. For example, a hotel is not just in the business of providing a bed for a night, but offers a host of other services that affect the consumer's choice.

■ Mission statements

Goals can be summarised in a mission statement. This is a short statement, consisting of a few lines, which states what the company aims to do. Mission statements are usually published in company literature, on websites and in the reception areas of company offices. The mission statement is useful to customers as it tells them what to expect in terms of product or service. It is also useful to employees as it gives them a focus for what the company wants to achieve.

It would be surprising to find a mission statement that says the company wants to make a lot of money, even if we think companies do. It is likely that the emphasis will be on service. Here are some examples of mission statements from travel and tourism organisations.

Holidaybreak plc mission statement:

Holidaybreak is the European specialist holiday group. Group companies retain a distinctive identity whilst sharing expertise and exploiting opportunities in areas of common interest.

Our aim is to achieve continuing profitable growth by developing our existing businesses and market leading brands in the UK and European holiday markets and through acquisitions within the travel sector.

(Source: http://www.holidaybreak.co.uk)

This statement manages to tell us a lot about the company in those few lines. It tells us who Holidaybreak is, and that there are different companies under the Holidaybreak umbrella. We know it is already profitable as it talks about 'continuing profitable growth' and we know that the company wants to acquire more travel businesses.

EasyJet mission statement:

To provide our customers with safe, good value, point-to-point air services. To effect and to offer a consistent and reliable product and fares appealing to leisure and business markets on a range of European routes. To achieve this we will develop our people and establish lasting relationships with our suppliers.

(Source: http://www.easyjet.com)

Some organisations write a 'vision statement' as well. This summarises the goals that the company hopes to achieve in the long term, recognising that these goals are not likely to be achieved in the short term but do show the direction the company is working in.

Hilton's vision statement:

Our company vision for the UK and Ireland is: 'To be the first choice of the world's travelers'.

(Source: http://www.hilton.co.uk)

Theory into practice

Find three examples of vision or mission statements for travel and tourism organisations. For each example try to identify at least three facts about that company from the statement. List the facts and discuss them with your group.

Figure 5.3 Strategic objectives

■ Objectives

Objectives should reflect the mission statement but will be very specific. The objectives may be strategic (general) or operational (broken down into specific targets).

Examples of strategic objectives are shown in Figure 5.3.

The SMART approach is often used to help set objectives. This means that objectives should be:

- Specific – it is evident what has to be achieved
- Measurable – there will be evidence as to whether the target has been achieved
- Achievable – it is possible that this can be done
- Realistic/Relevant – moving the company towards longer-term goals
- Timed – there must be a time limit on when this is to be achieved.

Operational objectives are more specific and allow the organisation to achieve its strategic aims or objectives.

The four Ps

The four Ps are the tools that allow the organisation to meet its strategic objectives. We will study each of the four Ps in turn, but always remember that they are interdependent.

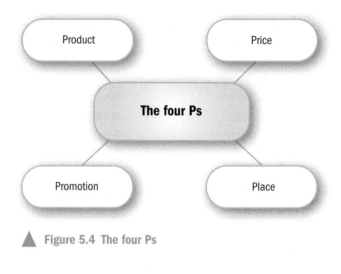

Figure 5.4 The four Ps

Product

According to Philip Kotler and Gary Armstrong:

A product is anything that can be offered to a market for attention, acquisition, use or consumption that might satisfy a want or a need. It includes physical objects, services, persons, places, organisations and ideas.

(Source: *Principles of Marketing*, Prentice-Hall, 11th edition, 2006)

This definition shows that a service is also considered to be a product, and in travel and tourism, businesses are predominantly concerned with the marketing of services.

The marketing for services may be different from that for a physical product as it is highly dependent on the people delivering the service.

A fifth P, people, is often added to the marketing mix for services.

■ Nature of the product

1 Intangible

When you buy a product, it is usually tangible – you can touch it. Buying a travel and tourism service is not like that, because travel and tourism products are rarely tangible. They are intangible. This means that you can't see them or touch them before you buy. You may be able to see pictures and brochure descriptions but you can't try out the real thing.

2 Perishable

Travel and tourism products and services are often perishable (like food going off in a supermarket). Once a flight has left the airport it is too late to sell any more seats. They have perished. Airlines have to make sure their flights are as full as possible to make a profit.

3 Service related

Another challenge for marketers is that the service is inseparable from the person providing it. In a restaurant, the food may be of a consistent quality because of the use of high-quality produce and standard recipes. However, the diner's experience will still be ruined if the waiter is having a bad day. Hence the reason for the importance of the fifth P, people.

Theory into practice

1 Look at a holiday brochure. Choose a holiday and write down everything that is included in the price. You can include items for which you must pay a supplement if you wish.

2 Try to decide which aspects are tangible products and which are services. Make a table of your findings and compare it with a colleague's. For example, a free T-shirt is tangible. The services of the rep are intangible.

■ Characteristics

Another way of looking at products is to examine their features and benefits. The product features represent the core value of the product. For example, the features or core of a package holiday are the accommodation and transport. There will be a whole range of added features, depending on the holiday chosen. These might include food, sports facilities and entertainment.

The features convert into benefits for the consumer, such as relaxation, the opportunity to go sightseeing or to learn a new skill, such as windsurfing.

Companies are always looking for new features to add to their products and services. They want to give further benefits to the customer and maintain competitive advantage. Theme parks introduce new rides each

season to attract customers. Cinemas sell a wider range of foods and drinks and offer plusher seats and more leg room.

The product must have some quality that sets it apart from the competition – this is known as the Unique Selling Proposition (USP). Every product aims to have a USP even if it is just the packaging or the colour.

■ Branding

The brand is the name and image that go with the product, and it aims to suggest something about the product itself. Some brand names such as Thomson or Thomas Cook are well established and have built up a good reputation. Under these 'family' brand names the company owns other familiar brands. For example, Portland is part of the Thomson group. Thomson itself is part of the TUI group. TUI is not as well known as Thomson in the UK, so when TUI acquired Thomson it wisely decided to retain the original brand names.

Consider this

How many holiday brands can you think of? Do the brand names suggest anything about the companies? What kind of image does each brand try to project?

Branding can be expensive as companies spend a lot of money on research trying to find exactly the right name, logo and image. It is particularly important when the brand has to work in several countries and languages. Finding a name often starts with a brainstorm activity where people are asked for their ideas, a shortlist is made and more research carried out with consumers before a name is selected.

Branding is used as part of differentiation. This is where an organisation tries to ensure that its product or service is different from that of the competition. It is promoted in terms of its differences, usually claiming to be of better quality.

If a brand is successful, it can build up brand loyalty among consumers, where they begin to prefer it over its competitors.

Niche products

Throughout the 1990s and at the beginning of the twenty-first century much of the UK holiday market has been characterised by mass-market tour operators. There has, however, always been room for niche operators, which are usually smaller, highly specialised companies. They may specialise in a particular type of product, for example diving holidays, or a particular area, say Madeira. Or they may market to a particular group of people – perhaps the over-fifties like the travel company Saga. This is called niche marketing.

Product life cycle

The concept of product life cycle is used to show how a product moves through different stages in its life, until it becomes obsolete. It is a useful concept in marketing as it impacts on how the product is marketed depending on what stage the product is at.

It is also important that a company has products in each stage of the life cycle. If all the products were in the decline stage, the company would soon be heading for bankruptcy.

- **Introduction:** The launch of a new product is a very exciting, but tense, period. A lot of the marketing budget is assigned to advertising and letting customers know it exists. Developing the product will have cost both time and money, so little or no profit is expected in the introduction stage. If the product is accepted by the market then some contribution to costs will be made. The people most likely to buy the new product or try out a new service are known as 'innovators'. They are the kind of people who like to be the first to try something new. The price charged at this stage is often high – this appeals to innovators, who do not mind paying for exclusivity – and it helps to repay costs. Some products never go beyond this stage. Recently, an airline failed before it had flown a single plane, because its finance deal broke down.

- **Growth:** This is the most profitable stage in the product's life cycle and companies are eager to gain these profits while they can. Word-of-mouth promotion is important at this stage, as consumers hear about the new product and want to try it. Competitors will rapidly enter the market, bringing

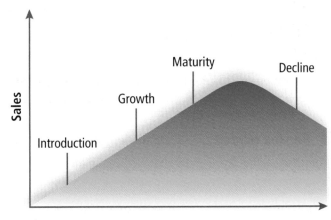

▲ Figure 5.5 The product life cycle

out their own versions of the new idea. Because of this increased competition, it is important for companies to try to build up some brand loyalty. The promotional budget is usually devoted to stressing the product's benefits over competitive products (differentiation).

- **Maturity:** Competition is at its most intense at this stage. Weaker competition will be squeezed out of the market by aggressive marketing strategies. Marketing efforts focus on being competitive, often by promoting low prices. The low-cost airlines are currently in maturity, having had years of unprecedented growth. In spite of this, newcomers are still entering the market, although new entrants are not usually successful at this stage. Maturity is the longest stage of the life cycle.

- **Decline:** Sales and profits start to fall at this point. Marketers must recognise when products are likely to move into this stage, as they must decide whether it is worth staying in the market. An organisation should be diversifying into other markets or products at the beginning of the decline stage (at the latest) to ensure survival. But there are examples of companies who have managed to stay profitable because they are the only player in a market that everyone else has abandoned – in effect they become niche marketers.

Successful companies have products at each stage of the life cycle. It is difficult to predict how long each stage will last, as many external factors affect the product's life. In travel and tourism, the product life cycle can be applied to products, services and destinations.

Theory into practice

For this exercise you will need to draw a template of the product life cycle. If you do this on an overhead transparency you will be able to overlay your work onto it and show your findings to the group.

Study the list of destinations below and discuss with your colleagues where the destinations are geographically and what they have to offer. Then decide where you think they are in terms of the product life cycle. Put them onto your template.

- Costa Brava
- Costa de la Luz
- Bali
- Kenya
- Prague
- Paris
- Bulgaria
- Barbados
- Haiti.

Repeat the exercise, this time with these travel products and services:

- free meals on flights
- leisure centres in hotels
- internet booking for holidays
- Channel ferries
- spa holidays
- self check-in
- A380 aircraft
- super ships.

Be prepared to justify your decisions and discuss them with your group.

▲ Figure 5.6 A safari park in Kenya is a popular long haul destination

Price

The second element of the marketing mix is price. Travel and tourism organisations must use pricing as a means of achieving their objectives. If the company doesn't get the price right it will not make a profit.

The simplest approach to pricing is the 'cost plus' method. For this the organisation calculates the cost of producing the product and then adds a percentage to give the return it wants as profit. Although it is simple, it is not the most effective approach to pricing. If sales targets are not met, there won't be a profit. Also, this approach ignores the basic premise of marketing, about identifying customer needs. Every approach to pricing should start with the principle of asking 'What is our customer prepared to pay? Are all the customers going to pay the same price?'

There are many different pricing strategies. A company will determine the strategy to be adopted by considering the stage the product has reached in its life cycle, competitors' activity and the prices of other products offered by the company.

■ Market skimming

This pricing strategy normally applies to a new product, particularly anything that involves new technology. When the product is launched costs are high and the company needs to recover the costs as quickly as possible. The new product appeals to innovators who can afford to pay a premium price for it. This introductory high price gives the product an air of exclusivity, which may appeal to certain consumers, but may be lowered as the product enters the growth stage of the life cycle, in order to attract new customers.

■ Market penetration

This is another common strategy for the introduction of new products. In this case, a very low price is set. The idea is that the low price attracts customers and builds market share quickly. The most common use for this type of pricing is with fast-moving consumer goods such as household products and groceries. It is a useful short-term strategy, but problems may arise in trying to hold onto customers when the price rises to a more realistic level.

■ Competitive analysis

This is used in highly competitive markets where companies keenly watch the prices of their competitors and react quickly to any lowering of prices by reducing their own. This happens constantly in airline and tour operation businesses. It also relies on a lack of brand loyalty among customers, as they must be prepared to switch brands to get the best price. It can be a dangerous strategy if prices drop so low that weak companies fail and others lose money.

■ Odd pricing

This simple approach to pricing can be used in conjunction with any of the others. It assumes that customers will feel that the price is cheaper because it is an odd number rather than the next-highest round number, say £499 rather than £500 – the idea is that psychologically this seems significantly less than £500. Although it is common practice no one knows whether it works. What do you think?

■ Promotional pricing

With this approach the price is linked to a special promotion for a limited period of time. Sometimes the customer has to collect tokens to be eligible for the special price. This draws attention to the product and gains publicity, so it especially useful for new products. Tourist attractions often use this method of pricing.

■ Differential pricing

With this method, different prices are charged for different groups of people. For example, in museums and cinemas, senior citizens and students can expect to pay reduced prices. On trains, the purchase of a Railcard (family or young person's) gives the holder access to discounted fares.

■ Discounting

As above, some people receive a discount because they belong to a certain group, for example students. Discounts may be given to avoid losing a sale. For example, although hotels have set rates they are usually flexible. If you are looking for a hotel room and you book on the day, always ask for their 'best rate'. You are sure to get a discounted price because remember, the hotel room is perishable. If no one takes it, it hasn't made any money.

■ Seasonal pricing

This is particularly important in the tourism industry. The whole season is divided into three – peak, shoulder and off-peak. Peak season always coincides with school holidays and is when prices are at their highest. This causes problems for parents, who have to pay the highest prices. Some parents take their children out of school to avoid peak-season holidays, but now that they can be fined £100 for doing so, this is likely to be a less popular option.

It is not just tour operators who charge higher prices at times of high demand. Airlines charge more on Friday afternoons and at the end of weekends, and rail fares cost more during rush hours.

This is the element of the marketing mix that considers how to get the product or service to the customer. The means of getting the product to the customer is known as the channel or chain of distribution. In the travel and tourism industry, the channel is complicated by the fact that there is often no tangible product to pass from one to another through the channel.

■ Types of distribution channel

The traditional channel of distribution in travel and tourism is set out in Figure 5.7.

As we saw in Unit 1, there are many variations on this traditional channel, including use of the internet, telephone call centres, etc.

Case study: seasonal holiday prices

There have been complaints about 'unfair and unjustified' travel and holiday prices during school holidays. Executives from Britain's biggest tour operators have been asked to explain why prices go up so much at the end of term.

Groups such as Working Families have pushed for an enquiry. A representative said, 'I do think parents are between a rock and a hard place. On the one hand, most do not like taking their children out of school in term time but, unfortunately, once it gets to holiday time, prices do shoot up.'

This enquiry is well timed. Parents now face fines of £100 for taking their children out of school during term time. But July and August are the most expensive times to go away, with prices rising by almost £1000 on a fortnight's holiday in Spain for a family of four.

A spokesman for the Association of British Travel Agents said, 'If you look at the big travel companies' financial results, you will see that they make a loss or only a tiny profit out of season. If they did not charge the higher prices during the peak they would soon be out of business.'

1　What do you think about the high prices? Are they justified?

2　Look at some brochures and compare prices from season to season. Work out the percentage increases.

3　What extra costs do you think tour operators have in the peak season?

4　Make notes on your answers and discuss them with your group.

The internet has considerably reduced distribution costs for airlines. Some low-cost airlines take more than 80 per cent of bookings via the internet. This is good news for the airlines and for consumers, but it is not so good for travel agents. Travel agents work on a commission basis. They take a small commission from the principal for every product sold. However, airlines have drastically cut travel agents' commissions and in some cases do not use agents at all. If this trend follows with tour operators, then travel agents will be in a very vulnerable position.

Another development in distribution is for tour operators to have sales channels on television. For example, TUI launched the Thomson TV Channel which sells holidays, not only from Thomson but from other suppliers too. This means of distribution has been so successful that annual holiday sales through television channels have soared.

However, travel agents still offer a valuable service, particularly for tour operators, some of whom have acquired chains of travel agents (vertical integration) in order to better control their representation to the public. Going Places is owned by MyTravel and Thomson (TUI) owns its own travel agencies. Thomas Cook has both a tour operation and a travel agency operation.

Figure 5.8 shows the advantages to the tour operator of selling through travel agents.

Producer (hotelier, airline, transport company)

↓

Tour operator

↓

Travel agent

↓

Consumers

▲ Figure 5.7 Traditional channel of distribution

The tour operator's products are on display to the public

Travel agents are in every town

The travel agent can give personal advice on the products

Customers have easy access

Many customers still prefer to buy from travel agents

Figure 5.8 Travel agents offer a valuable service

Some of the disadvantages to tour operators of selling through travel agents are that:

- commission must be paid
- the agent decides how to rack the brochures and may not give prominence to a tour operator's product
- tour operators have little control over the quality or method of selling
- travel agents take add-on sales, for example car hire and insurance.

Some of the advantages of direct selling are having:

- control over how the product is sold
- commission-free products
- control over brochure racking.

Some of the disadvantages of direct selling are that:

- there is no high street presence
- there are high advertising costs to reach potential customers
- there is a need to have call-centre operations, even if only to back up the internet.

■ Global Distribution Systems

Several companies provide electronic distribution services through computerised reservation systems and internet-based systems. You may have heard of Galileo,

Amadeus, Sabre or Worldspan, all of whom offer Global Distribution Systems.

The major low-cost airlines do not use Global Distribution Systems because of the commission payable, although this situation may change as these companies negotiate to attract low-cost airline business.

■ Physical location and accessibility

Some travel and tourism organisations, such as visitor attractions, have different considerations in terms of the 'place' mix. Customers have to travel to them in order to enjoy what they have to offer. This means the location of the attraction is important, as it must be accessible to customers. Purpose-built attractions such as Disneyland Paris are located near to major road networks. Hotels and ample parking are provided in the vicinity to ease access for visitors and to encourage them to stay longer.

Promotion

In order to achieve their marketing objectives, travel and tourism companies must make both consumers and trade customers aware of their products and services.

The tools they use to do this are collectively known as promotion and form part of the marketing mix.

The authors Sally Dibb, Lyndon Simkin, William Pride and O.C. Ferrell provide a definition of promotion:

> *The role of promotion in a company is to communicate with individuals, groups or organisations with the aim of directly or indirectly facilitating exchanges by informing and persuading one or more of the audiences to accept the firm's products.*

(Source: *Marketing: Concepts and Strategies*, Houghton Mifflin, 3rd edition, 1997)

Communication has an important role to play here, and this branch of marketing is often described as 'marketing communications'. The individuals, groups or organisations for whom the promotion is targeted are known as the 'target audience'.

■ Promotional methods

1 Advertising

The Advertising Association describes advertising as 'messages paid for by those who send them, intended to inform or influence people who receive them'.

Advertising is paid for and is placed in the media. The media is the collective term for television, newspapers, radio, magazines, directories, outdoor sites and advertising on transport. It also includes the internet, although this still tends to be described as 'new media'. New media also includes new forms of advertising such as text messaging.

2 Television

The British Broadcasting Corporation (BBC), which does not carry advertising and is funded by payment

	1996	1997	1998	1999	2000	2001	2002	2003	2004	2005
National newspapers	1510	1650	1824	1991	2252	2062	1930	1902	1974	1919
Regional newspapers	2061	2238	2390	2483	2762	2834	2878	2962	3132	2994
Consumer magazines	583	660	709	727	750	779	785	784	819	827
Business and professional	1018	1106	1209	1195	1270	1202	1088	1048	1082	1064
Directories	692	737	780	831	868	959	990	1029	1075	1131
Press production costs	550	577	620	650	702	669	643	634	660	653
TOTAL PRESS	6413	6967	7531	7877	8604	8504	8314	8359	8742	8589
Television	3379	3704	4029	4321	4646	4147	4341	4378	4653	4820
Direct mail	1404	1635	1666	1876	2049	2228	2378	2467	2469	2371
Outdoor and transport	466	545	613	649	810	788	816	914	986	1043
Radio	344	393	460	516	593	541	547	584	606	579
Cinema	73	88	97	123	128	164	180	180	192	188
Internet	-	8	19	51	153	166	197	465	825	1366
TOTAL	12,080	13,340	14,415	15,412	16,984	16,537	16,772	17,348	18,472	18,956

Table 5.1 Total advertising expenditure by media sector (£ million)

(Source: Advertising Association, *Advertising Statistics Yearbook 2006*, World Advertising Research Center (http://www.warc.com) reprinted with permission of World Advertising)

of a licence fee, is probably the most easily recognised organisation in British television. Most channels are commercial channels, that is, they are funded by the sale of advertising or sponsorship and they do not receive any of the licence fee. Examples include all ITV channels.

Ofcom is the regulator for all UK communications industries, not just television. It also covers radio, telecommunications and wireless communications.

Under the Communications Act 2003:

3(1) It shall be the principal duty of Ofcom, in carrying out their functions;
(a) to further the interests of citizens in relation to communications matters; and
(b) to further the interests of consumers in relevant markets, where appropriate by promoting competition.

Ofcom publishes codes about how much television advertising is allowed and when it can be shown. Here are a few examples:

- No more than 12 minutes per hour of advertising is allowed.
- It must be evident what is a programme and what is an advertisement, so there must be obvious breaks in between.
- Some programmes must not be interrupted by advertising, for example news or children's programmes of less than 30 minutes.

The codes are very detailed. You can find out more about them and the role of Ofcom by visiting the Ofcom website (www.ofcom.org.uk) and the ASA website (www.asa.org.uk).

Advertisers wishing to use television have dozens of commercial channels to choose from with the advent of cable and satellite services. Advertising is sold in 'spots'. One spot is usually 30 seconds long. There is no fixed rate for a spot, as the price varies according to time of day – peak time is 5.30–10.30 pm when most people are watching. Premium rates will be charged if a particularly popular programme such as an important football match is being shown.

Advertisers buy a package of spots. If you watch television for any length of time you will note that the same advertisements are repeated often. This is to ensure that the message reaches as many people as possible.

The number of people viewing an advertisement is called the 'reach'. The final episode of *Friends* was broadcast in May 2004 in the USA. It attracted over 50 million viewers and advertisers paid over £1 million for 30-second spots. All the spots were sold by January 2004. Television advertising expenditure reached £4740 million in total in 2004.

There are many advantages to television advertising (Figure 5.9).

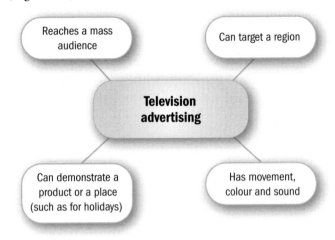

▲ Figure 5.9 Advantages of television advertising

It is, however, very expensive. Not only are spots expensive but there are also the production costs of the advertisement to cover.

Another form of advertising on television is sponsorship. Sponsors pay to be associated with a programme and their logo and product shots appear at the beginning, end and at either side of each commercial break.

Television advertisements to focus on quality of service

PROMOTION

A TELEVISION advertising campaign is being planned for next year to promote the Travel Counsellors brand among consumers.

The adverts are still in the planning process, but will focus on the agents' specialist service and are likely to appear in January 2007.

'We have done some short tie-ups with suppliers on adverts in the past but this will be our first real venture into consumer television advertising,' said managing director Steve Byrne.

'We need to make customers aware that they can use their own travel counsellor to buy their holidays and the service is free.'

Chairman David Speakman added: 'It is going to be about the service we provide because that is what we are.'

(Source: *Travel Trade Gazette*, 26 May 2006)

Theory into practice

Find some examples of television sponsorship. For each example, think about why the sponsor wants to be linked with that programme. Look at travel programmes – are they linked with travel and tourism companies? Discuss your findings with your group.

3 Radio

As with television, it is the commercial sector of radio that carries advertising. BBC radio stations are funded by the same licence fee as television. There are many local commercial stations and you should note the ones in your locality. There are also some national commercial stations, for example Virgin Radio.

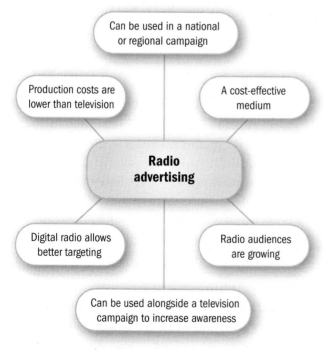

▲ **Figure 5.10 Advantages of radio advertising**

You can find out about radio stations by visiting the Radio Advertising Bureau (RAB) website at www.rab.co.uk. This is an independent body that gives information on advertising issues to industry members, but also to the public.

Spots are sold on radio in the same way as on television, with peak times attracting greater revenue. In 2005, commercial radio advertising revenue was £614 million in the UK, according to the RAB.

Radio advertising is becoming more popular. One of the reasons is the advent of digital radio, which allows greater targeting. Advertisers who wish to reach 15- to 24-year-olds often use radio as they represent a large part of radio audiences. RAB reported that total commercial reach was 62.6 per cent of adults in 2005. This meant that 62.6 per cent of adults in the UK listened to commercial radio.

Audience research for radio – including the BBC – is carried out by Radio Joint Audience Research (Rajar). Ofcom is the regulatory body.

4 Press media

The term 'press' refers to newspapers, magazines and directories.

The National Readership Survey is a non-profit-making body that provides estimates of the number and type of people who read the UK's newspapers and magazines. The survey covers about 250 publications. The reader

▲ **Figure 5.11 Advantages of national newspaper advertising**

profiles are broken down by age, sex, region and other demographic and lifestyle characteristics. Publishers of press media use these profiles to sell advertising space, and advertisers use them to target the correct audience through appropriate media.

For national newspapers, the UK has twelve daily newspapers and eleven Sunday newspapers. The *Sun* has the biggest circulation of all the national dailies and the *News of the World* is the most popular Sunday newspaper. Between them they attracted an advertising spend of £1919 million in 2005.

Advertising is sold by the page, half-page or column. Prices vary according to the position of the advert. The front and back pages are most expensive, as they are most prominent. The newspapers with the highest circulation command the highest rates; therefore the *Sun* is the most expensive.

Theory into practice

Find out the latest circulation figures for the UK's newspapers. You can do this by looking at a newspaper's website; looking at the National Readership Survey website (www.nrs.co.uk/) or by studying a publication called BRAD in a library. Draw up a bar chart comparing the figures.

There are also hundreds of regional newspapers, some of which are free. Some are very highly regarded, such as the *London Evening Standard* and the *Yorkshire Post*. Circulations vary and some circulations are very small, but for a company that wants to advertise its services in a particular locality, they are useful and inexpensive. Regional newspapers attracted a spend of £2994 million in 2005, even greater than the national newspapers. Much of this goes on classified advertising, which is more likely to be read in a regional paper than in a national one.

Magazines come in different categories:

- consumer magazines
- business and professional journals.

There are over 3000 titles of consumer magazines in the UK, so the advertiser can be very precise about target audience.

Figure 5.12 Advantages of magazine advertising

One of the biggest sellers is the *Radio Times*, which has a circulation of over 1 million. Some hobby magazines sell only a few thousand copies.

There are several travel magazines aimed at consumers, and many aimed at buyers or owners of property abroad. These can be useful media for transport companies. Women's magazines are also an important category of consumer magazines.

Business and professional publications are aimed at people within particular industries. There are two important ones for travel and tourism, with which you should be familiar. These are *Travel Weekly* and *Travel and Tourism Gazette*.

A disadvantage of magazine advertising is that the copy must be ready to go to press quite a while before publication, so it is not as flexible as newspaper advertising. It is not suitable for the last-minute discounted offers which are popular in the tourism market.

An advertorial is a promotion that is written in the style of a feature. It looks like the editorial pages but is promoting a company or a product. Readers will probably assume that it is a feature unless they look closely at the small print, which will state 'advertising feature'.

5 Cinema

As with any media, marketers look at the audience profile before deciding on a campaign. For cinema, Cinema and Video Audience Research (CAVIAR) provides this information. Advertisers aiming to reach 15- to 24-year-olds may well choose cinema advertising as cinema-going is the number one leisure activity for this group.

▲ Figure 5.14 Billboards are strategically placed for maximum impact

▲ Figure 5.13 Advantages of cinema advertising

Cinema advertising

- The audience is seated and highly receptive
- Can be targeted regionally
- Good for reaching 15- to 24-year-olds
- Still advertisements are cheap to produce for small local businesses

Theory into practice

Next time you go to the cinema, take a notebook with you. List all the advertisements you see including any 'still' advertisements at the beginning. Try to decide who the target audience is. Is it always 15- to 24-year-olds? Are the advertisements linked to the film in any way? Are any travel and tourism organisations showing advertisements?

Discuss your findings with your group.

Overall, 86 per cent of the population say they go to the cinema. However, the current annual average is only three visits per person. There is also a seasonal pattern to cinema-going. In 2006, the busiest months were August, October and December, school holiday periods and not surprisingly, the biggest box office takings were for *Pirates of the Caribbean 2*.

Total advertising spend on cinema in 2005 was £188 million, much less than any other form of media.

However, the production costs of full advertisements are high and the advertisement will not have the same reach as television.

6 Outdoor and transport

Outdoor media usually means advertising billboards. These are placed all over the country in strategic sites, usually on roadsides. Companies which specialise in outdoor advertising sell the space to advertisers. Advertisements can also be placed on taxis, buses, in the London Underground, at railway stations and at bus stops. Large, colourful posters are excellent for the travel and tourism industry, reminding commuters that they can get away to sunnier places.

7 Internet

As soon as you connect to the internet you will find advertising messages. These can be linked to searches, so that if you search for low airfares, for example, you will find pop-ups for travel sites such as ebookers.com. The internet advertising spend is growing year on year as it becomes more widely used.

Advertisers choose sites which they think their potential customers will visit. They can buy banner advertisements or pop-up advertisements on the host site. These not only advertise but link to the advertiser's own website. It is even cheaper to buy a text-only link.

8 Brochures and leaflets

These are essential promotional tools for tour operators. They are costly to produce, but provide a showcase for the company's products and services.

Getting the brochure out on time is important, because if it is not available when the booking of main holidays begins, sales will be lost. This means that the information in the brochure has to be collated and prices fixed a long time before the season in question. This can cause major headaches for tour operators and may lead to extensive discounting during the season.

Other organisations in the travel and tourism industry produce leaflets but these are usually smaller and less costly, so it is easier to change them more regularly.

Public relations

Public relations is a major part of the promotional mix and very important to those travel and tourism companies that have small marketing budgets. This is because public relations activities are much cheaper than other forms of promotion. Public relations may be carried out in-house or contracted out to a specialist PR agency.

The responsibilities of the public relations department may include the following:

- generating press releases
- media liaison
- organising events
- organising exhibitions
- publication of newsletters
- organising receptions.

■ Press releases

Press releases are used to place favourable reports about a company in the media or to inform them about a new product. They are extremely cheap to produce and can result in a lot of free publicity.

A good press release should have the following features:

- it should be targeted at the right audience, via appropriate media
- it should be presented in such a way that it can be inserted into a news page or feature with little alteration – this saves work for the receiving editor
- there should be an attention-grabbing headline
- the press release should be dated and show the corporate logo and address
- if an event is being publicised, the venue, date and time must be given
- a photo can be included
- contact details for further information must be given.

Sales promotion

Sales promotion includes all those activities which aim to bring about an early or extra purchase of a product, and they are found extensively in the travel and tourism industry. A sales promotion is very useful for boosting sales in the short term but will run for only a few weeks, otherwise the impact is lost.

Examples of sales promotions are money-off coupons, competitions, buy-one-get-one-free offers and loyalty schemes. Most hotel chains offer incentives such as free nights to regular guests through loyalty schemes. Airlines also operate loyalty schemes, the most famous of which is the AirMiles scheme. This has even been extended to some shops.

Trade promotions are very common in travel and tourism, where call centres and travel agents receive financial or other incentives for sales.

Direct marketing

Direct marketing, as its name suggests, deals directly with the consumer, and can take several forms.

Case study: using a press release

Brentwood College of Travel and Tourism Studies

Trenton Park Brentwood BD5 6AG

Press Release

21 May 2007

Second-year travel and tourism students at Brentwood College are racing to Paris!

As part of their course they are required to arrange a residential study. The students decided to make their trip as challenging as possible and to race each other! Their trip takes place in the first week in October and lasts for four days.

The fourteen students will be travelling by various routes including Eurostar, air from Gatwick, and car and ferry. They will carry out an evaluation of each route in terms of speed, cost, convenience and service.

Their tutor, Billie Myson says: 'This will be the hardest assignment the students have ever attempted. They have arranged every detail of the trip by themselves. I am very proud of them and look forward to the trip and to hearing their final reports.'

For further information please contact Billie Myson on 0146 777565 or Joanna Smith on 07789 567432.

1 **Compare the press release with the criteria shown above. Does it match them all?**

2 **The press release concerns students on a travel and tourism course.**

   • **What is the purpose of the press release?**
   • **What media are likely to be approached?**
   • **Why would these media be chosen?**

■ Direct mail

Direct mail is a form of direct marketing where advertising is sent in the post to the customer, personally addressed. It is sometimes referred to as junk mail – but by consumers, not advertisers! This is because we receive a lot – 5418 million items were sent in 2004 – and throw a lot of it away. The response rate is about 11 per cent, but it is still a popular promotional tool in travel and tourism. For every £1 spent on direct mail about £14 is generated according to the Direct Mail Information Service.

■ Direct response

Direct response is a form of direct marketing that does not depend on the mail, so it can be used in all the same media as advertising. The difference is that a response is solicited. The reader might be invited to send for a brochure or send an e-mail asking for information. The value of direct-response marketing is that it is easier to monitor than advertising. You are able to measure the response rate, and with every response you gather more customer information.

■ Telemarketing

Telemarketing is similar to direct mail except that the telephone is used. Cold calling, that is making unsolicited calls, is very unpopular with consumers and is not often used in travel and tourism. However, telemarketing is important in selling holidays and travel to callers who are responding to advertising or other forms of promotion, and there are many call centres in travel and tourism businesses.

How do promotional methods work?

According to AIDA theory, the aim of promotional activities is to take the consumer through four key stages that lead to the adoption of a product, service or idea.

AIDA stands for:

- Attention – the promotion attracts the attention of the customer
- Interest – having spotted the promotion, the customer is sufficiently interested to want to know more
- Desire – the customer decides that they want it! The information about the product has stimulated the customer's desire for it
- Action – the final stage, the customer knows what action to take to complete the purchase.

5.3 Be able to conduct a marketing research activity for a travel and tourism organisation

Marketing research is imperative in the marketing process, especially in travel and tourism where not enough is known about why consumers behave as they do. Marketing research enables an organisation to find out about the market, the competition and what consumers want.

Many different methods are used to carry out research, depending on the purpose of the specific research project. Research may be carried out on behalf of a company by a specialist research agency, or it may be done by the company itself, in-house.

the users or potential users for that product. Therefore, in market research, a company would like to find out who these people are, how many of them there are, what they are like, where they are, and so on.

It will also want to know who else provides products or services in this market and how many sales (or how much market share) they have. Market share can also be measured in financial terms. If a competitor is performing better than the company is, it will need to find out why. It should find out what the sales are worth for the whole market and whether the sales trend is up or down.

Areas of research

Research may be related to any area of the marketing mix or to the market overall. The most complex area of marketing research relates to consumer behaviour. These areas of research will be covered in more detail before studying the methods of marketing research.

Market research

Market research is a category of marketing research that involves finding out about the market for a product or service. Remember that the market for a product is all

Product research

For a physical product such as a new type of aircraft, a long period of research and development is needed, including testing the product to make sure it works and is safe. At the same time, the developer must find out about the market for the product. Who wants this aircraft? What features do they want incorporated?

Tour operators research destinations to add to their product portfolio. Again, they need to find out whether there is a need for the product – are many people likely to go to this destination? These questions take the marketer from product research into market research.

Figure 5.15 Paris café scene: the price of a service must represent good value to the customer

Price research

The price charged for a product must represent good value to the consumer. This does not mean the product has to be cheap. The most expensive cocktail in the world is over £200 and available in a bar in Paris. It is made with a very rare brandy and some people are prepared to buy it. Research that concerns price might involve finding out what competitors charge for similar products, or asking consumers what they would be prepared to pay.

Promotion research

This might include looking for new methods of promoting the product or the company, assessing competitors' promotional activity, or trying to evaluate the success of a promotional campaign. It is difficult to determine whether promotions work. Even if there is an increase in sales, we can never be absolutely sure whether it is due to the promotion or to some other factor, like the weather.

Place research

This area of research means finding out whether the distribution methods being used are the most suitable to reach the consumer, and finding new ways of reaching the customer.

Consumer research

Consumer behaviour research is very difficult to conduct, as consumers themselves often cannot explain why they act as they do. Although challenging, this area of research is possibly the most useful as it can lead to an understanding of consumer needs, and their attitudes to a product, and help a company to determine which products or services will fulfil consumer needs.

Market segmentation – classifying consumers

In order to market their products effectively, travel and tourism companies must segment the market. The market is divided into groups of people with similar characteristics, each group making up one segment. The segments at which the company directs its marketing activity are the target markets.

Market segmentation can be done in various ways. Most companies choose to use not just one but a combination of methods.

Key term

Market segmentation – identifying different groups of customers for a product. The members of each group will share similar characteristics.

Demographic segmentation

Demographics is the study of the make-up of the population. Demographic trends illustrate how the population is changing. Factors that affect the make-up of the population are the birth rate and life expectancy.

Currently in the UK there is an ageing population as people live longer and the proportion in the older age group increases. This is, of course, of interest to marketers, who have termed older people the 'grey market'. The birth rate is low at the moment but in the years immediately following the Second World War there was a rapid rise in the birth rate as families were reunited and looked to the future. These babies are now in their fifties and, due to their sheer numbers, they have been an influential and important market all their lives. They are known in marketing as the 'baby boomers'.

When demographic segmentation is used, consumers are grouped according to:

- age
- sex
- ethnic grouping
- family life cycle.

The family life cycle is a useful, if old-fashioned, method of segmentation. The stages of the life cycle are as follows:

- young singles
- young marrieds
- full nest 1 (youngest child under 6)
- full nest 2 (youngest child 6 or over)
- full nest 3 (older, but still dependent children)
- empty nest 1 (children gone)
- empty nest 2 (children gone, parents retired)
- solitary survivor.

These life stages do not relate to age, but to family development. The idea is that needs and wants change according to where we are in this cycle. Families with young children expect hotels to provide appropriate services for them and look for family holidays, whereas an empty-nest couple is looking for different services and may have a greater disposable income.

Socio-economic segmentation

In this method of segmentation the population is divided according to socio-economic grouping. These groupings are based on occupation, not income. The classifications are used extensively by advertising media to describe their readership.

A	Upper middle class	Higher managerial, administrative or professional
B	Middle class	Intermediate managerial, administrative or professional
C1	Lower middle class	Supervisory or clerical, and junior managerial, administrative or professional
C2	Skilled working class	Skilled manual workers
D	Working class	Semi-skilled and unskilled manual workers
E	Those at lowest level of subsistence	State pensioners, casual or lowest-grade workers

Table 5.2 Socio-economic segmentation

Geographic segmentation

The marketing data company CACI has produced a classification called ACORN (A Classification of Residential Neighbourhoods) based on postcodes. Every street in the UK is included and categorised into 54 typical neighbourhood categories. Streets which have broadly similar residents are categorised together. The classification is arrived at using information drawn from the census and from market research data.

Travel and tourism companies can easily find out the geographic location of their customers as they usually have access to addresses on their databases. The geographic area from which the customers are drawn is known as the 'catchment area'. The catchment area

Theory into practice

Go to the website www.upmystreet.co.uk. Enter your postcode and then click on ACORN profile. Find out what your profile is. You can get a detailed profile if you wish.

is very important for tourist attractions as they need to draw customers from as wide an area as possible. Organisations such as VisitBritain need to know from which countries incoming tourists originate in order to target their marketing activities.

Psychographic segmentation

With this type of segmentation, consumers are categorised according to personality types, lifestyle and motivation. When it is done well, it is very effective in determining targets, but it is difficult to do accurately.

It is very relevant to travel and tourism. For example, environmentally aware people will be interested in sustainable tourism products.

Marketing research plan

Identifying objectives

There must be a reason for the research – a set of objectives. What does the organisation want to know? It could be that an organisation wants to know:

- who is buying the products
- why sales are going up
- why sales are going down
- what people think of the organisation's image
- what new destinations should be introduced.

The range of possibilities for research is endless, but a single piece of research should not try to cover too much ground.

Case study: English Tourism Council

Researchers sometimes come up with their own psychographic categories. In 2001, the English Tourism Council did some research about reviving the UK's coastal resorts. It came up with the following groups:

- Conformists – this is the largest group – they desire sameness and familiarity. They like a comfortable environment, chatty atmospheres and scenic fresh air. They want to be surrounded by people like them.
- Sentimentals – this group does not respond to any trends. Any change or drop in standards can alienate them.
- Seekers – these people are image-driven and like to see themselves as trendy. They like to be in the right place with the right people. They like to have fun but often have responsibilities and are constrained by budget.
- Radicals – free spirits and frequent travellers. They work hard and play hard and like to discover a destination before other people. They want distinctive restaurants, pubs, bars, clubs and nightlife.
- Independents – seek out different cultural experiences

away from the crowd. Upmarket restaurants, sports, heritage, accommodation and beaches are important to them.
- Pragmatists – highly cultured and artisan people. They enjoy peace and quiet and go to places where they can enjoy the outdoors and fresh air. They are the least willing to spend money and 20 per cent of them never take a holiday.

(Source: English Tourism Council Report 'Sea Changes' 2001)

1 In 2003, the English Tourism Council became part of the new organisation VisitBritain. How do you think this study helped VisitBritain promote coastal areas in the UK?

2 Decide what media you might use to reach each of these groups. (Read through the section on promotion to help you do this.)

3 Which of the English Tourism Council's groups do you think you belong to?

Planning the research methods

Once organisations know what they are trying to find out, they can consider the methodology necessary to find the information.

- Who do they want to ask?
- How will they sample?
- How will they reach consumers/what method of data collection should they use?
- Where will they do the research?
- Who will do the research?
- When will they do the research?

Target group – sampling

It's not usually possible to ask everyone who might be relevant to take part in research. If, for example, every single holiday maker completes a questionnaire, this is called a census. A census covers the whole population where the population is all the possible respondents for that survey.

It is more usual to interview a sample of customers, as it is very expensive to carry out a census. The sample should be representative of the whole body of customers, otherwise the results will be biased.

With *random probability sampling*, every member of the population has an equal chance of being selected. The company could use its own database as the source of respondents, and a percentage of these could be selected at random. When a national survey is undertaken, the electoral register can be used as the source of respondents.

Quota sampling is a method where not everyone has an equal chance of being selected. The choice of respondents is up to the interviewer, but they have a quota to fulfil based on factors such as age, gender and socio-economic group.

With *stratified sampling* the population is divided into groups or strata, according to common characteristics. Then, a random sample is taken from each group.

Collection of data

At this stage the research is carried out and the data are captured either on paper or electronically. Personal interviewers are usually issued with lap-top computers to make the whole process much easier.

Analysis of data

It is possible to analyse data by hand, but it is time-consuming and laborious. Computer analysis is the most common technique, and ensures cross-tabulation of data. It is more difficult to analyse qualitative data electronically, because of the diversity of responses.

Evaluation of data

Once the data have been produced and analysed they must be interpreted and conclusions must be drawn from them. Recommendations will be made so that the findings can be acted on. The data, the conclusions and the recommendations should be presented in a report.

Choosing methods and designing research documentation

Types of data

Data are often divided into the categories quantitative and qualitative.

Quantitative data consists of facts and figures, for example the number of people admitted to a museum in one day. Qualitative data are more difficult to collect and to analyse as they are about why people behave as they do and what they think. Sometimes consumers themselves have trouble knowing why they choose to buy certain things.

Data can also be primary or secondary.

Primary data

These are data that have been collected for the first time – they didn't already exist somewhere. Collecting these data is sometimes called field research. Researchers do this type of research only when they are sure that the information they require has not been collected elsewhere.

Methods of collecting primary data include the following types of surveys:

- questionnaires
- observation
- focus groups
- feedback cards.

Surveys are often interviews carried out with consumers. They may be completed by mail, telephone, personal interview or through an internet site. They are usually based on a questionnaire rather than free discussion.

■ Questionnaires

It has become common practice for tour operators to give their customers questionnaires to complete at the end of their holiday. The response rates are usually good for these types of surveys, particularly if the holiday makers are travelling by plane. They are a captive

audience and air crew can easily collect the completed questionnaires. The results of these surveys help with planning for the next season and show up faults which the company can then investigate.

When designing a questionnaire, remember the following points.

- Before you write any questions, make a list of what you want to find out.
- Go through the list and discard anything that is not absolutely essential.

Key terms

Respondent – the person who is answering the questions.

Filter question – one that allows the respondent to omit certain questions which may not be applicable. For example, 'If you answer no to question 5, go to question 11'.

Classification data – the age, sex and occupation of the respondent. This is used to group respondents into categories.

Quota – the number of people in different age or socio-economic groups to be questioned.

Method	Advantages	Disadvantages
Personal interview	Interviewer can explain	May introduce bias questions to respondent
	Response rate is good	Very expensive to administer because of interviewer's time
	Can use 'prompts' to aid recall	Difficult to recruit trained interviewers
Telephone interview	Easy to carry out	People find telephone calls intrusive
	Many calls can be carried out in a short time	No visual prompts
	Response rate is fairly good	
	Personal contact with respondent	
Mail questionnaire	Cheap to administer	Very low response rate
	Few staff needed	Needs an appropriate list of addresses
		No explanation of questions to respondents
Internet questionnaire	Easy to administer	Limited to respondents who access that website, therefore biased
	Instant response	No explanation of questions to respondents

Table 5.3 Advantages and disadvantages of some different survey methods

Case study:
a holiday questionnaire

Look at the Happiness Holidays questionnaire and answer the following quesions.

1 **Which questions are examples of open questions?**

2 **Why is a free holiday on offer?**

3 **Why does Happiness Holidays ask which newspapers are read by the respondent?**

4 **Which classification data are asked for?**

5 **Where could this questionnaire be distributed?**

6 **What is your opinion of the questionnaire?**

Happiness Holidays Questionnaire

Help us and you could win a FREE holiday worth up to £1000!

At Happiness Holidays, we are committed to making sure that you have the best holiday possible. To help us achieve this, we would like to ask for your help. By providing your views and comments in this questionnaire, you can tell us what you think about your holiday and where you feel there is room for improvement. As a way of saying thank you, you will be entered into our FREE PRIZE DRAW to a win a holiday – so don't forget to include your contact details.

SECTION 1 Your holiday booking

1   Please state your holiday start date: Day............Month............Year............

2   At which resort are you staying? ....

3   When did you book your holiday? Month............Year............

4   Is this your first holiday with Happiness Holidays? Yes............No............
    If no, when was the last occasion? Year............Which resort? ....
    How many Happiness Holidays have you taken in the past five years? ....

5   How did you hear about Happiness Holidays?
    Television ad ❏ National newspaper ad ❏ Magazine ad ❏ Internet banner ad ❏
    Friend's recommendation ❏ Newspaper/magazine article ❏
    Internet search engine ❏ Travel agent ❏

6   How did you book your holiday?
    Direct ❏ Through travel agent ❏

7   Did you use a brochure or the Happiness website to obtain holiday information?
    Brochure ❏ Website ❏ Both ❏

SECTION 2   Your holiday satisfaction

8   How do you rate your holiday overall?
    Better than expected ❏ As good as expected ❏ Worse than expected ❏
    If worse, please state why: ....
    ....

9   Was there anything you particularly liked about your Happiness holiday? If so, what?
    ....

10 How do you rate the value for money of your holiday?
    Excellent ❏ Very good ❏ Satisfactory ❏ Less than satisfactory ❏

11 How likely are you to book another holiday or short break with us?
    Already booked ❏ Very likely ❏ Quite likely ❏ Not likely ❏

SECTION 3 About you

12 Please state the age and gender of the person who made the booking.
    Male............Female ....
    18–24 ❏ 25–34 ❏ 35–44 ❏ 45–54 ❏ 55–64 ❏ 65+ ❏

13 Please describe the occupation of the principal wage earner in your household
    Unskilled worker ❏ Skilled worker ❏ Lower management ❏
    Middle management ❏ Senior management ❏
    Director ❏ Self-employed ❏ Part-time worker ❏
    Homemaker ❏ Retired ❏ Student ❏ Unemployed ❏

14 Which daily newspapers do you regularly read?
    The Sun ❏ The Star ❏ Daily Mirror ❏ Daily Mail ❏ Daily Express ❏
    The Times ❏ Daily Telegraph ❏ The Guardian ❏ The Independent ❏
    The Financial Times ❏

15 Would you be interested in receiving future holiday news and special offers from Happiness Holidays?
    Yes ❏ No ❏

- Go through the list again and try to order the information you require in a logical way.
- Write the questionnaire asking general questions first and then more specific questions. Never ask more than one thing in a question.
- Avoid bias in a question.
- Try to use closed questions – the answers are easier to analyse.
- Use a limited number of open questions if you want to find out the respondent's opinion.
- Use a filter question if the respondent does not need to answer every question.
- Always put classification data at the end. It is not a good idea to start off by asking respondents how old they are and what they do for a living. The exception to this rule is when you need to establish whether the respondent fits a quota.

Theory into practice

1 Using the guidelines given above, design a short questionnaire to be given to your colleagues or friends and family. It could be about where they are going for holidays, or plans for future travel. Make sure it has no more than ten questions and limit the open questions to one. Don't forget to ask for classification data.

2 Ask at least ten people to answer your questions and then try to analyse the data according to age/gender groups.

3 Explain what kind of travel and tourism organisation would find your questionnaire useful, and how it would produce it. **P4 M3**

■ Observation

Observation is a very simple and yet effective research method. There are several ways of doing this; in its simplest form, observers can watch consumers, for example at airports, and report on how they behave. Cameras can be used instead of live observers, and the tapes can be analysed at a later date. The observer will use a checklist or take notes to aid later recall.

Mystery shoppers can be used in any sector; for example, staff pose as customers and report on the performance of a travel agency. Journalists in travel and tourism often use this technique, as shown in the extract below from *Travel Trade Gazette*.

Going Places

High Street

This agency created a strong first impression with a colourful, smart and eye-catching window display. This was matched by an impressive interior and the smartly dressed staff.

I was approached by a friendly consultant. Her welcome was very warm and she asked what kind of holiday I had in mind.

The consultant hand-picked three brochures and asked if I had time to spare so that she could check the system for prices and availability. She invited me to take a seat and then asked me further questions about my needs.

Her customer service was most professional and she made eye contact at all times. She spoke clearly and made me feel comfortable.

The agent consulted her computer and brochures to find a suitable holiday. She eventually found two holidays to match my requirements.

Even though she did not know very much about one of these destinations, she sensibly asked other members of staff, who were able to give me more information. The consultant also checked on the internet for further information on the resort and accommodation.

We discussed insurance requirements and she gave me a print-out and the appropriate brochures to browse through, along with her contact details.

I would definitely consider booking a holiday here. I felt I received excellent service within a pleasant atmosphere, and not once did I have to prompt for any information.

(Source: *Travel Trade Gazette*, 12 May 2006)

Undercover journalists often use the participant observation method of research. It involves full participation, so if you were researching a travel agency, you would get a job and become a travel agent in order to observe the others.

Observation is not cheap as you need observers or cameras, and it is time consuming. The observer can also bias the results unless they are completely unobtrusive. The results are also subject to analysis by an observer – who may not be completely objective.

■ Focus groups

This method of research involves inviting a group of people to participate in a group discussion in someone's home, a hotel or an office. They may be offered an incentive to attend, such as a flight voucher. The objective of the discussion is to find out people's attitudes to a product or service. A group leader, often a psychologist, leads the discussion.

■ Feedback cards

These are used in retail travel agents quite often and are simply a means of collecting immediate customer feedback. Sometimes they ask for a name and address. If this is the case, the customer will be added to a mailing list.

Secondary data

Secondary research is sometimes called desk research as it can be done at a desk, computer or in a library. It collects data that already exist and are available to researchers. These data sometimes have to be paid for and may be internal or external to the organisation. Secondary research is done first – it may lead to primary research if you do not find everything you need to know.

Sources of secondary data that are internal to an organisation include:

- company sales records
- customer database
- costs
- profits
- load factors (airlines)
- productivity.

External sources of secondary data include:

- World Tourism Organisation (WTO) – statistics on worldwide tourism

- tourist board websites
- VisitBritain and Star UK websites
- UK International Passenger Survey – statistics on inbound and outbound tourism
- *Social Trends* and *Cultural Trends* (Her Majesty's Stationery Office publications)
- Keynotes and Mintel reports – regular reports on everything you can think of; available only to subscribers, but libraries often subscribe
- National Readership Survey figures for newspapers
- Department for Culture, Media and Sport statistics
- travel trade reports
- newspaper surveys and reports.

Theory into practice

Visit www.vts.rdn.ac.uk and find the travel and tourism tutorial. Take a tour and find out where you can gather travel and tourism information on the web. Remember these are secondary data.

Assessment practice

A local branch of Trailfinders wants to find out what kind of travel opportunities students would like in a gap year. They will use the information to source flights and accommodation in various destinations. They have asked you to arrange a focus group with at least six young people who might be taking a gap year and planning to travel. Prepare a plan for organising the focus group, including details of:

- target group
- when
- where
- who
- means of reporting.   **P3**

Carry out the focus group and produce a report for Trailfinders.   **P4** **M3**

Recommend how Trailfinders could use the results of the market research activity.   **D2**

Devising a promotional plan

A promotional plan forms part of a promotional campaign. It is the detailed schedule of promotional activities that are to be undertaken, where and when they are to be undertaken and the cost.

If this is carried out by an expert, in an advertising agency, for example, then the expert is known as a media planner. A media planner has detailed knowledge of all the different media and their costs and will place the bookings to secure advertisements. They are not responsible for actually creating the promotional materials.

A good promotional plan will give:

- coverage – it will reach a good proportion of the target market
- frequency – there will be opportunities for the message to be repeated throughout the campaign
- good value for the given budget.

Key term

Promotional plan – the detailed schedule of activities that are to be undertaken, where and when they are to be undertaken and the cost.

Objectives of promotion

Remember that promotion is being used with the other elements of the mix to help the organisation achieve its marketing objectives.

The objective may be to:

- inform the public about a new product or service
- inform the public about a change to the product or company
- increase sales
- increase market share
- give reassurance to existing customers

- respond to competitors' promotions
- remind consumers that the company is there
- reinforce the corporate image.

These objectives will be achieved only if the company chooses the right promotional mix – the right medium must be chosen to reach the consumer, and the timing must be right.

Promotional methods

A method or combination of methods appropriate to reach the target group must be chosen.

■ Timing

The right time for promotion is when the purchaser is at the stage of deciding what to buy.

- Hotels will advertise their services when there is a special event in their vicinity, such as a sporting event.
- Theatres send out programme guides at the beginning of each season so that people can book ahead and plan their theatre trips.
- Holiday companies traditionally start their major campaigns just after Christmas. Once the festivities are over, people start to think about their holidays.

Timing is not just about the right time of year; marketers must also consider what day and what time to place advertisements. These decisions will be constrained by their budget.

■ Budget

Promotional budgets can run into millions. It is easy to see why when you consider that a 30-second spot on national television can cost as much as £25,000. Companies can spend only what they can afford, and it is possible to have a good campaign on a very tight budget by using regional media or by devoting the budget to cheaper public relations activities.

A company will use past experience to set budgets for new campaigns and may set a budget as a percentage of estimated sales to be derived from the campaign.

■ Target group

The entire budget is wasted if the promotional campaign does not reach its intended audience. If advertising needs to be aimed at a mass audience, then television is often the best medium. In the average home in the UK the television is on for more than five hours a day. Of course, that doesn't mean the viewer is watching the advertisement or even that there is a viewer!

Usually the advertiser wishes to reach a particular group of people and will choose a medium where the profile of the audience matches the profile of the intended customer. All the media publish profiles of their audiences, that is, their genders, age groups and socio-economic groups. These profiles help advertisers to select appropriate media. There are several companies that carry out audience research to produce these profiles. One example is the National Readership Survey, which identifies who reads which newspaper. Another example is the Broadcasters' Audience Research Board (BARB), which collects information every week about the number of people watching television.

Theory into practice

Try this puzzle: match up the products and services on the left with the appropriate choice of promotion media.

Duty-free perfume	Business travel magazines
Palm-top computer	Local newspapers
A cruise	National quality newspapers
Travel insurance	Women's magazines
Union Jack beach towels	Local radio
Spa holidays	*Sun*
Cinema listings	Airline magazines
New travel agency opening	Saga magazine

Procedures for monitoring and evaluating

The process for monitoring a campaign involves evaluating the following.

- Does the campaign reach the target market?
- Have appropriate media been used?
- Does the campaign meet the company objectives?

How is this done?

- All comments/reviews of the campaign are collected.
- Sales are carefully monitored to assess impact, if any.
- Post campaign surveys are carried out to assess recall of the campaign.

Theory into practice

Choose a current promotional campaign for a travel and tourism company. You can choose a trade or consumer campaign. Collect materials from the campaign or make detailed notes on the campaign materials and media schedules. Evaluate the campaign by trying to decide what the original objectives were and whether you think it meets them. Write a report on your findings suggesting recommendations for improvements. **P5 M4**

Research tip

Marketing, *Marketing Week* and *Campaign* magazines often carry reviews of advertising campaigns.

Case study: Kuoni UK

The Kuoni UK brand has always been about offering inspirational travel experiences and personalised holidays whilst appealing to many different segments of customers. 'Dream holiday, think Kuoni', the instantly recognisable Kuoni globe and the strapline 'World of Difference', all represent the attributes that are associated with the brands equity and attention to detail.

Kuoni uses a number of different media to market its products and marketing efforts are split into targeting both the consumer and trade. Typical marketing activities include newspapers, magazines, radio and direct mail (the latter using the company's specialised database).

Details of Kuoni's promotional activities to both the trade and the consumer are given below.

Consumer	Trade
Kuoni Traveller – monthly e-mail newsletter	Advertising in the trade press, e.g. *Travel Weekly*, *Travel Trade Gazette*. *Kuoni News* – full page in *Travel Weekly* appears each week and updates agents on the latest product news from Kuoni
Classified and display adverts in national newspapers	
Direct mail – customer loyalty magazine, 16-page newsletter, bespoke items	Overseas agent educationals and seminars
Competitions/promotions	UK regional training days
Adverts in consumer magazines	Brochure Launch Roadshow
Window displays in the two Kuoni retail shops	Travel agents' website

(Source: Extracted from http://www.kuoni.co.uk (student pack))

Consumer promotions

1 **Who would you expect to be targeted by the e-mail newsletter?**

2 **Which magazines would be appropriate for Kuoni advertisements and why?**

3 **Find an example of a classified or display advertisement for Kuoni in a national newspaper. Discuss the effectiveness of the advertisement including choice of media.**

4 **Suggest a competition that could be used to promote Kuoni.**

Trade promotions

1 **Who are regional training days and educationals aimed at?**

2 **What is the purpose of an educational?**

Assessment practice

Prepare an item of promotional material for Kuoni, suitable for inclusion in a trade magazine, so that it attracts agents to Kuoni products.

P6

Knowledge check

1 Give a definition of marketing.

2 Explain the following terms as they are used in travel and tourism marketing – 'service related', 'tangible' and 'perishable'.

3 What is meant by social responsibility in marketing?

4 What kind of research methodology does mystery shopping fall into?

5 What are the four elements of the marketing mix?

6 Why is the Trade Descriptions Act 1968 important in marketing travel and tourism?

7 What is a PEST analysis?

8 What is a SWOT analysis?

9 What is the function of the ASA?

10 Explain the different methods of segmenting the market.

11 What is the difference between qualitative and quantitative data?

12 Explain the advantages and disadvantages of different survey methods.

13 What is the difference between primary and secondary research?

14 Describe some different methods of sampling.

15 What is a mission statement?

16 What is niche marketing?

17 Describe the stages of the product life cycle.

18 Explain two pricing strategies.

19 What are the different types of press media?

20 What are the differences between public relations and advertising?

Preparation for assessment

Flybe

Flybe is an Exeter-based low-cost airline, owned by the Walker Trust. It is one of Europe's largest low-cost airlines. It has a unique low-fare airline business model designed to be very different from Ryanair and other low-cost airlines.

Flybe was launched on 18 July 2002. It grew out of an airline that started life in 1979 as Jersey European. Exeter became the company's headquarters in 1985 and was also a base for technical services. Jersey European gained its first London route in 1991 from Guernsey to London Gatwick and shortly afterwards the Jersey–London route came into operation.

Also in the 1990s, routes were introduced from Belfast City to London, and Belfast City to Birmingham. Business class service was launched, making Jersey European the first domestic airline to offer two classes of service. Jersey European won the 'Best UK Regional Airline' award in 1993 and in 1994.

Jet maintenance was brought to Exeter in 1994, which expanded the scope for third-party services. In 1995, the fleet consisted of seven jets. Three new business lounges were opened at Belfast City, Jersey and Guernsey and the Ticket to Freedom frequent-flyer loyalty scheme was launched.

In 1996, the first franchise routes in conjunction with Air France began offering flights from London Heathrow to Toulouse and Lyon. This partnership continued to expand in 1997 to include Birmingham International to Paris Charles de Gaulle and Glasgow.

In 1999, expansion continued with the acquisition of eleven Bombardier Dash 8s and four Canadair Regional Jets. A major new base at London City was introduced, with services to Dublin and Edinburgh. The brand was changed to British European and then to Flybe.

In 2001, after the terrorist attacks in September of that year, the airline found itself with problems and losses. The situation was critical and a transformation plan was required, with the following objectives.

1   Traditional distribution channels are expensive. Flybe aimed to get 80 per cent of sales through the internet. Travel agent commission was reduced from 7 per cent to 1 per cent and the lowest fares were available only on the internet.

2   It was decided to re-align pricing, product and terms and conditions to reduce costs and increase ancillary revenues. This means charging for catering and excess baggage. Prices were to be transparent, with no hidden extras and no refunds offered. The target was to achieve £25 million per annum of ancillary revenue.

3   The route network was to be rationalised to create profitable routes and defendable bases. The strategy to achieve this was to continue the 'Backbone Britain' policy, to pick up routes in continental Europe and to open new bases in Birmingham, Bristol and Exeter. It was also decided to develop volume routes in Germany, Italy, France and the Nordic countries. The market split was 65 per cent leisure and 35 per cent business.

4   The aim was to consistently reduce costs but exceed customer expectations. A customer satisfaction survey was undertaken, with good results.

5   People matter – staff and customers were to be involved in the transformation. A policy of 'open channel' communications was adopted, alongside a no-blame culture, allowing staff to report incidents without fear of reprisal or blame.

In 2003, Flybe was voted the 'Most recommended UK Low Fares Airline' by *Holiday Which* magazine. In 2004, record half-year profits of £14 million were announced.

In 2005, services were launched from John Lennon airport and from Norwich.

Flybe also has an aviation services division employing 350 people in engineering at Exeter. Support was given from the Regional Development Agency.

Flybe runs aggressive newspaper advertising campaigns and also undertakes local sponsorship of football teams.

Flybe concentrates approximately 80 per cent of its seat capacity on serving UK domestic routes, 10 per cent to regional France and a further 10 per cent serving sun and ski destinations.

Flybe offers different classes of travel including business and economy plus.

(Source: Compiled from http://www.flybe.com)

1 Carry out research into the aviation sector and explain the factors affecting marketing in the sector. Give examples from different organisations in the sector. **P1**

2 Analyse how constraints affect marketing at Flybe. **M1**

3 Recommend how Flybe could adapt its marketing strategy to deal with the constraints. **D1**

Grading tip

To reach Pass level, you need only complete task 1. To reach Merit or Distinction level you need also to focus closely on Flybe's activities. Carrying out a PEST and SWOT analysis will help you.

4 Describe the marketing mix at Flybe. **P2**

5 Explain how the four Ps work together as a marketing mix at Flybe. **M2**

Grading tip

To reach Merit level you need to show how the four Ps are interdependent, for example price is always emphasised in a promotion. You can find examples of this in the press.

6 Prepare a plan and documentation for a marketing research activity at Flybe. **P3**

7 Explain how your plan and documentation will meet your market research objectives. **M3**

8 Conduct the market research activity. **P4**

9 Recommend how Flybe could use the results of your market research activity. **D2**

Grading tip

Ensure you choose an activity that is feasible for you to carry out. For example, you could test the effectiveness of Flybe's advertising on your colleagues or you could find out how aware your fellow students are of Flybe's services. If you are near to one of the airline's bases you may be able to carry out research with friends and family who have flown with Flybe. Don't forget to analyse your findings.

10 Plan a promotional campaign for Flybe, giving specific objectives for the campaign. **P5**

11 Prepare an item of promotional material for use in the campaign, stating the target audince for the material. **P6**

12 Explain how the planned campaign would meet the objectives set. **M4**

Grading tip

To reach Merit level, say how your chosen times and media would reach the target audience and how your promotional material would appeal to the target audience.

Don't forget to visit www.flybe.com for more information.

Grading criteria

To achieve a pass grade the evidence must show that the learner is able to:	To achieve a merit grade the evidence must show that, in addition to the pass criteria, the learner is able to:	To achieve a distinction grade the evidence must show that, in addition to the pass and merit criteria, the learner is able to:
P1 explain the factors affecting marketing using examples from different travel and tourism organisations **Theory into practice page 156**	**M1** analyse the constraints of marketing in relation to a selected travel and tourism organisation **Assessment practice page 158**	**D1** recommend how the selected travel and tourism organisation could adapt to the constraints of marketing **Case study page 157**
P2 describe the marketing mix of a selected travel and tourism organisation **Assessment practice page 174**	**M2** explain how the 4 Ps work together as a marketing mix in a specific travel and tourism organisation **Theory into practice page 156**	**D2** recommend how the organisation can use the results of their market research activity **Assessment practice page 182**
P3 prepare a plan and documentation for a market research activity in a travel and tourism organisation **Assessment practice page 182**	**M3** explain how their plan and documentation will meet their market research objectives **Theory into practice page 181**	
P4 conduct a market research activity for a travel and tourism organisation **Theory into practice page 181**	**M4** explain how the planned campaign would enable the objectives to be met **Theory into practice page 184**	
P5 plan a promotional campaign for a selected travel and tourism organisation to achieve staged marketing objectives **Theory into practice page 184**		
P6 prepare an item of promotional material as part of a planned promotional campaign for a target market **Assessment practice page 185**		

Preparing for employment in the travel and tourism industry

Introduction

This unit will provide you with the opportunity to explore all aspects of working in the travel and tourism industry. You will already have had experience of observing some of the career opportunities and job roles in travel and tourism when you have been on holiday or visited tourist attractions. In this unit you will investigate those roles, but also be introduced to other 'behind-the-scenes' opportunities. You will find out about the different entry requirements, progression routes and training opportunities. You will undertake a personal review focusing on skills, attributes, experience, qualifications and achievements.

The process of recruitment and selection will be examined, and you will develop the personal skills that will prepare you for employment. You will learn how to put together your curriculum vitae (CV), a letter of application and personal statement in order to apply for jobs.

To help you prepare for the workplace, we will examine working practices, so that you appreciate the factors which help motivate employees and contribute to an effective workplace. These include working relationships, performance management, teamwork and training and development.

After completing this unit you should be able to achieve the following outcomes:

1 Know about career opportunities in the travel and tourism industry
2 Know the procedures for recruitment and selection in travel and tourism
3 Be able to apply for employment in travel and tourism
4 Understand the factors that contribute to an effective workplace.

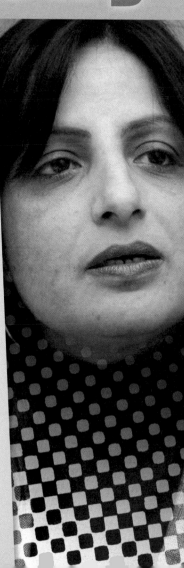

Thinking points

Globally, the travel and tourism industry is a major employer, with about 2 million new jobs being created each year, according to the World Travel and Tourism Council (WTTC) (www.wttc.org). These jobs total almost 3 per cent of world employment. If tourism-related jobs were included, it is expected that the total would reach over 8 per cent of world employment.

When you are thinking about which sector of travel and tourism you want to work in, bear in mind the global nature of the industry and think about opportunities which could take you abroad to travel and experience different cultures.

Why do you think employment in travel and tourism is increasing?

What do you think is meant by 'tourism related'?

Give some examples of small firms in travel and tourism.

Based on what you have already learned about the travel and tourism industry, which sector of the industry would you be interested in working in?

This unit will examine the following sectors and look at the types of careers, entry requirements and progression opportunities they offer:

- accommodation
- transport provision
- attractions
- tour operations
- travel agents
- tourism development and promotion
- trade associations and regulatory bodies
- ancillary services.

In each sector we will look at examples of types of jobs and the roles and responsibilities attributed to them. In addition we will look at the entry requirements.

Accommodation

To work in the accommodation sector you need to be able to work in a team, work unsocial hours and have initiative. Many students look for work in hotels when they complete their BTEC awards because there are opportunities to work both at home and away, and there is a variety of jobs to choose from. Some students who are not ready to leave home may look for employment in local hotels. For others finding a job in a hotel in another area of the country provides an opportunity to move away from home.

There are jobs in hotels which do not need qualifications, for example working in the kitchen or in housekeeping. These jobs can be done part time while studying and give you good experience of the hospitality industry. Other jobs in a hotel might need specialist qualifications, such as catering or accountancy.

Hard workers are soon rewarded. You may start as a receptionist but can quickly move into reservations, managing housekeeping, or managing events or business activities. For those people prepared to travel, the opportunities are even greater as many hotels are part of international chains. You can find out about jobs in this sector by researching on the websites of leading hotel chains and the website www.catereronline.com.

If you want to work in a hotel as soon as you finish your BTEC course, you can combine your career with study for a degree. One example of the kind of opportunity available is given in the case study opposite.

Transport provision

Airlines and airports

Airlines employ a variety of personnel such as air crew/flight crew and maintenance staff. Some airlines contract out the maintenance and engineering to specialist companies. Most airlines also contract out services like baggage handling and check-in. Companies based in airports handle these services – examples are Aviance, Groundstar and Servisair.

Many airports in the UK are expanding and that means there are more jobs available. The types of job vary a great deal. There are many unskilled and relatively poorly paid jobs, such as baggage handlers and catering staff who prepare in-flight catering and bar carts. There are also highly-skilled jobs such as air traffic control (based in air traffic control centres such as Swanwick) and operations management. Some jobs require very few qualifications if any, and others are open only to graduates. At Manchester Airport 19,000 people are employed across 250 companies, illustrating the variety of jobs available.

Remember that public services such as immigration control, customs, police and fire services are all provided at airports and each of these has its own career structure. Connexions (an organisation that offers advice on education, careers, housing, money, health and relationships for 13- to 19-year-olds in the UK) produces a booklet called *Working in Airports* which includes interviews with staff in airports and gives the entry criteria for their jobs. Visit the website for Manchester Airport (www.manchesterairport.co.uk), and find the education section. Here you can read or download the Connexions booklet.

Case study: Paramount group of hotels

Management Trainee Opportunities and get a Foundation Degree at the same time!

Want a recognised qualification combined with two years' great work experience? Want a formal qualification in a lively industry? Want to start earning right now, rather than be laden with student debt? Want a qualification with the guarantee of a permanent job and a career at the end? Then look no further!

So how does the programme work?

Paramount group of hotels is one of the UK's fastest growing and most successful hotel groups. We've teamed up with the University of Gloucestershire and developed our unique 2 year programme to give you a fantastic start in our industry. We've created a programme that combines hands on work experience with formal study.

Throughout the 2 years you'll spend time in different departments throughout the hotel, and these will include Reception, Housekeeping, Kitchen, Accounts and many more! As well as being able to put theory into practice, you'll really be able to decide which area you want to specialise in when you finish your course, as you will have tried them all!

You'll also be studying for a Foundation Degree in Hospitality and Tourism Management, with the University of Gloucestershire. A Foundation Degree is a recently introduced qualification, worth 240 credits, the same as a Higher National Diploma (HND). You'll meet up with the other trainees within the group for a series of residential blocks throughout the year, some of these will be at one of our hotels, and you'll also spend time at the university campus. You'll also be working on assignments when you are back at your own hotel. When you've successfully completed the 2 year programme, then we'll guarantee you a permanent position with us.

What's stopping you?

We'll pay you a salary of £10,500 each year, and we'll also pay your tuition fees, accommodation and travel costs when you're away on your residential studies.

So is it for you?

If you don't fancy studying full time and you can't wait to get started in your career then this is for you! Remember that you'll be juggling full-time work with your studies so it won't be easy – you'll be on a fast-track programme and that means hard work and commitment.

However, if you're up to the challenge, in just 2 years you'll be well on your way in a fantastic industry!

Apply right now!

We have a management trainee place available at each one of our hotels, with the next course starting in September, so apply right now!

You'll need at least one A level (grade C or above), a BTEC Certificate or Diploma, or (G)NVQ Level 3. OR if you're over 21 we're willing to consider relevant work experience. If you already work for Paramount, and want to be considered for the programme, then talk to your Personnel and Training Manager.

You need to be eighteen or over by September 2006 to apply, and you must already be eligible to live and work in the EU.

Remember that we won't consider graduates for this programme, it has been created to be an alternative to university, by combining study with practical work experience. If you've already completed a university course, then check out our graduate section for opportunities!

How do I apply?

We have a trainee place available at each one of our hotels, and you need to decide which hotel you want to apply for. Remember that we do not usually offer live-in accommodation, so you really need to live locally to the hotel of your choice.

Who do I apply to?

You need to apply direct to the Personnel and Training Manager at the hotel of your choice. You will find full location details of our management trainee vacancies, along with contact details for applications within the vacancies section of the website.

What happens next?

We will only contact you if we are going to call you to attend for interview. Interviews will be held at the hotel that you have applied for. If you are shortlisted for the trainee programme, you will need to attend our 2 day assessment centre.

(Source: http://www.paramount-careers.co.uk)

1 **Do you measure up? Look at the entry criteria and see whether you could apply.** P1 M1

2 **Search some other hotel websites and see what their management trainee schemes are like. Try the websites of hotel chains represented in your area.**

3 **Produce a comparative table of your findings.**

Taking it further

Review your personal skills audit and evaluate your skills in relation to those required for this type of programme. Produce a brief report on your findings.

▲ **Figure 6.1 Cabin crew at work**

Here is an example of the kind of entry criteria used for cabin crew:

- Minimum age of 19 years
- Physically fit to undertake flying duties
- Height between 1.60 and 1.89 metres
- A visual acuity of 6/9 with or without glasses
- Educated to at least GCSE standard or equivalent
- Fluent in spoken and written English
- Successful experience within a customer service environment
- An EU country passport and the unrestricted right to live and work in the UK and unrestricted entry into other countries.

Theory into practice

Think about the nature of cabin crew work – it has a glamorous image, but is it really glamorous? Think about when you have flown. What were the cabin crew's activities on the flight? What is the effect on their bodies of constant flying? What impact would this lifestyle have on their personal lives?

Travel and tourism students often express a desire to be air cabin crew, but remember that there are many behind-the-scenes jobs at an airline. There are opportunities for call centre staff dealing with reservations or customer enquiries. As in any company there are positions in finance, accounts, marketing, human resources and customer relations. In addition, there is usually a yield management department which constantly monitors sales and adjusts pricing according to demand. The operations department looks at routes and determines where new routes should be developed.

The role and responsibilities of air cabin crew are primarily to take care of health and safety. This means if there is an incident on board they have to deal with it in a calm and efficient manner, be able to keep passengers calm and be able to evacuate the aircraft if necessary.

When you travel on an aeroplane, you will see cabin crew giving information, selling goods and serving passengers. Although these tasks form part of the job description, they are not as important as health and safety. Next time you have the opportunity to fly, note how the crew pay attention to health and safety in sometimes small ways: making sure a passenger has their seat belt fastened; telling everyone to be seated in areas of turbulence; checking doors are properly closed.

Assessment practice

Visit the Virgin website (www.virginatlantic.com) and find the page on cabin crew recruitment by going to 'Careers', and then 'Cabin Crew'.

1 In the section 'The Recruitment Process' on the cabin crew page, you can see that applicants are assessed in a group interview on teamwork, customer relationships and attention to detail. Think of two examples for each of these skills where you can show how you have demonstrated these competencies in your past work or study. Describe these examples to a colleague. Ask for constructive feedback on how convincing your examples are. **P2**

2 Do you meet the minimum requirements listed for Virgin cabin crew? If not, will you be able to meet them in the future? Write notes on how you meet or could meet the requirements, and share your findings with a colleague. **D1**

Cruising

Cruising is a wonderful way to travel: it is a chance to see the world and get paid for it! There are many different jobs on offer on a cruise ship. Figure 6.2 shows some examples.

When a ship comes into port most of the passengers go ashore, so the crew are allowed time off to go ashore themselves. If you have a long-term contract on a ship you will visit the same ports several times, so you will have a chance to get to know the ports well.

To apply for a cruise ship job:

- apply directly to individual cruise lines
- research the products and services offered by the line
- be specific about the jobs you are interested in
- describe your training, experience, talents and skills.

When applying for a cruise ship job it is best for to apply directly to the cruise ship company.

▲ Figure 6.3 Staff at work on a cruise ship

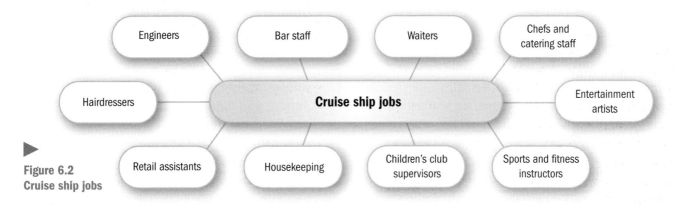

► Figure 6.2 Cruise ship jobs

Engineers · Bar staff · Waiters · Chefs and catering staff · Hairdressers · **Cruise ship jobs** · Entertainment artists · Retail assistants · Housekeeping · Children's club supervisors · Sports and fitness instructors

Attractions

As in every other sector of the travel industry, visitor attractions require marketing, human resources, accounting staff, etc. These jobs are vital to run any business.

Other jobs available at an attraction will vary according to the type of attraction. For example, at theme parks, engineers are needed to design and build the rides. At stately homes, guides are needed with a detailed knowledge of the history of the house and grounds. Restorers are also needed to work on the fabric of the buildings or on the tapestries and paintings. If an historic property requires a manager they will be looking for someone interested in heritage or conservation work who is able to manage a team of people. Similar categories of

jobs are available in other organisations. For example, Disneyland Resort Paris employees are called 'Cast Members'. They do a wide range of jobs, from dancing in the daily parades to welcoming guests on attractions or even taking calls at the central reservations centre. This is the role of a marketing representative:

You take part in setting up the marketing operations for which your manager is responsible. You are in charge of developing product strategy in order to increase sales and you coordinate the process in order to facilitate implementation of the strategy.

Education: High School Diploma or equivalent + 5 years' business or marketing school.

(Source: http://www.disneylandparis-casting.com)

Tour operations

This is one of the most exciting sectors in which to work as it offers a wide range of opportunities. Unlike travel agencies, tour operators are not represented in every town. Tour operator jobs are either at head office or in a resort, often overseas. There is a career structure in each:

- head office roles
- reservations/sales
- marketing
- accounts
- customer relations
- contracting.

If you want to work in tour operations in a head office role you will have to move to the head office location if you don't live within commutable distance.

Resort representatives

Many students say being a resort representative is their chosen career, and this is not surprising as it gives an opportunity to meet new people of a similar age and to live in a resort. Some resort representatives are employed all year round, but there are many more positions available in the summer high season. This means there are jobs for students during their holidays. If you do get a permanent job you should expect to move resorts between winter and summer seasons.

The pay is often low, but accommodation is included and it is possible to earn commission and tips.

Resort representative duties are described by MyTravel as:

- *holding regular welcome events*
- *carrying out airport duties and coach transfer for arriving and departing passengers*
- *handling complaints and solving problems*
- *ensuring noticeboards are up to date and professionally displayed*
- *selling excursions and additional services in resort*
- *guiding excursions*
- *working with hoteliers to ensure company procedures are followed*
- *monitoring health and safety in the properties you are responsible for*
- *ensuring paperwork and accounts are completed neatly and accurately and to specified deadlines*
- *undertaking hospital and police station visits as required.*

(Source: www.mytravelcareers.co.uk; © MyTravel)

MyTravel recruits representatives to work for all of its different brands. The job can vary according to brand. For example, the Escapades brand is aimed at the 18–35 age group and needs representatives who want to have a good time like their customers. They need to know all about local nightlife as well as the usual holiday information. They also need lots of stamina to cope with the long hours.

No formal qualifications are needed for this role but applicants need the right skills and personal attributes. These are described as follows by MyTravel:

> *If you are interested in becoming a representative for children's holidays or clubs you will probably*

need a childcare qualification and you will also have to undergo a check with the Criminal Records Bureau. This is common practice for anyone working with children and involves completing a form which is then processed to disclose any convictions. If you have got convictions it does not mean you will not be able to work with children – it depends what the conviction is for.

(Source: www.mytravelcareers.co.uk; © MyTravel)

Theory into practice

Research another tour operator. Find its internet site and find out about the resort representative jobs it offers. Describe the jobs and the qualities and skills needed. Comment on how they are similar to or different from the MyTravel requirements. **P1** **M1**

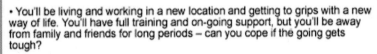

Welcome to MyTravel Careers Website

Airline   Overseas Opportunities   Retail Opportunities   Home | MyTravel

> Overseas Home
> Positions Available
> What's In It For You?
▫ Have You Got What It Takes?
> Apply For A Job

Overseas Opportunities

TELL A FRIEND !

Click here to send these exciting opportunities to a friend

Be honest with yourself!

Working overseas does sound like a dream job. BUT, do ask yourself a few questions about how it could work for you – make sure you answer these questions honestly! Here's some food for thought:

• You'll be living and working in a new location and getting to grips with a new way of life. You'll have full training and on-going support, but you'll be away from family and friends for long periods – can you cope if the going gets tough?

• You won't be working traditional 9 to 5 hours – and, whatever the time, you'll need to be fresh, professional and outgoing to handle whatever comes your way.

• You'll face all sorts of challenges – from being an entertainer, to a sales person to a diplomat, and even a shoulder to cry on….when you're on duty, it's non-stop. Can you take the pace?

• You'll need the flexibility to tailor your approach to a diverse range of customers. So can you build immediate rapport and deliver exceptional service to ensure customer loyalty and repeat business?

• As well as having a friendly, motivated personality, are you reliable, responsible and resilient?

• Are you a planner and organiser? Do you have a pro-active approach to meet sales targets, and are you confident enough to problem-solve and make decisions quickly?

• Above all, if you're having a great time, so will our customers! Think you can do it?

© MyTravel Group plc 2005   Legal Notice | Privacy Policy | Contact Us

▲ **Figure 6.4 MyTravel web page**

(Source: http://www.mytravelcareers.co.uk/overseas/whatittakes.asp; © MyTravel)

Graduate jobs

Some tour operator positions are open only to graduates. If you are thinking of studying for a degree in the future you might be interested in joining a graduate trainee scheme.

Travel agents

Many recruits to travel agencies are college leavers. They have acquired a good background knowledge of the travel and tourism industry and are usually enthusiastic and willing to learn the essential travel agency skills.

Case study: Thomas Cook graduate programme

You'll be doing a real job
From the moment you start with us you'll have day-to-day responsibilities, working alongside some of the best professionals in the industry. The programme allows you to learn and develop in a live work environment, with a mentor who's also an experienced, supportive manager.

You'll learn transferable skills
Courses such as Project Management, Presentation Skills, People Management and Decision Making are useful throughout your life and your career.

The opportunities are ongoing
Your placements will be tailored to your development needs, as well as your job role. You could be working for our airline, spending time overseas in resorts, learning the ropes in one of our retail shops, or understanding how the package holiday is constructed by working with our tour operators.

If you're flexible about where you work and up for trying different things, you can really make the most of your career.

Retail
Join any of our 600 retail branches and you'll learn how to manage a team, inspire people to do a good job and exceed their targets, and, of course, explore your own potential too.

Multi media
Multi media includes direct sales, travel clubs and dotcom; which is our fastest growing sales channel.

Tour operations
Working with our award-winning Tour Operators, you'll learn how to put together and deliver the holiday experience, occasionally travelling abroad to negotiate deals. You might be part of a Purchasing, Commercial or Customer Delivery team, and based in Peterborough or Bradford, but in any case you'll have to be fired up to succeed.

Airline
Thomas Cook Airlines is one of the largest charter airlines in the world, with a fleet of 24 A320, A330 and 757 aircraft travelling to around 60 worldwide destinations. If you're based in either Manchester or Gatwick, you'll have the opportunity to get an all-round view of our operation.

(Source: http://www.thomascookjobs.co.uk/USER/graduates/programme.htm; Thomas Cook Jobs website 2006)

Imagine that you want to apply for this graduate scheme or a similar one in a few years' time.

1   **Produce an audit of the personal skills you have that would be appropriate for this job.**   **P2**

2   **Compare the entry levels and opportunities for promotion at Thomas Cook with those for another job. Explain why you think you are suitable for one of the jobs. Think about the further education, skills and qualities you would need to develop for the job, and list all your training and development needs.**   **M1**

3   **Think about how you will achieve these attributes. Where will you study? What will you study? What work experience will you need? Produce a detailed action plan for the next five years, showing how you might meet your training and development needs.**   **D1**

Research tip

Go to www.thomascookjobs.com to find out more about careers at Thomas Cook. Also useful for graduate opportunities is www.prospects.ac.uk.

If you choose to work in a travel agency you can work in retail travel or in business travel. Retail travel agents deal with leisure travel, which usually means holidays, whereas business travel agents organise transport and accommodation for business clients. There are many similarities in the work, but also some important differences. Business clients are usually more concerned about reliability and convenience than cost.

Leisure clients may be booking a long time ahead, whereas business clients may be booking a few days ahead. Business travel agents may hold accounts for large companies and cater for all those companies' travel needs.

If you work in a travel agency your prime responsibility is to sell but you will also have to look after filing systems, take payments and be adept at finding and giving information.

Role and responsibilites of a travel agent

- Find out customer needs and select products.
- Calculate costs for customers including add-ons.
- Make bookings using IT systems and telephone.
- Plan itineraries for customers.
- Collect payment from customers.
- Keep records of transactions.

There are opportunities for progression in both types of agencies. With chains you can progress to area and then to national management. In independents you can reach management level and may then choose to move to a larger company.

Theory into practice

Study the two job advertisements, one for a business travel agent and one for retail. Comment on their differences and similarities. Decide which one you would prefer, and why.

BUSINESS TRAVEL CONSULTANT

Travel Professionals Consultancy is looking for an experienced travel consultant to work in a small, specialised business travel team. We specialise in group travel such as product launches and sales conferences.

A minimum of two years' travel experience working in a business travel environment, together with knowledge of a CRS, preferably Galileo, is essential.

The salary package includes pension, private medical insurance and health club membership.

Apply with your CV to Samuel Okobo at Travel Professionals Consultancy, e-mail sam.okobo@travprof.co.uk.

Figure 6.5 Advertisement for business travel agent job

Sales consultants required

Snow.com is a leading internet-based retailer specialising in the sale of ski and snowboarding holidays. Due to expansion, we have some exciting new opportunities available in our London office for

SKI SALES CONSULTANTS

You will be responsible for booking ski holidays to the European and North American ski resorts.

The ideal candidate will be computer literate, have excellent organisations skills, an eye for detail and preferably telesales experience. You will also be friendly and self-motivated, able to work in a pressurised environment, and have a good knowledge of appropriate destinations.

If you want to join a fast-moving, dynamic company and have a genuine passion to deliver the best, we want to hear from you! In return we offer a competitive salary, a free winter holiday, uncapped commission and excellent career prospects.

Please e-mail your CV with covering letter detailing your experience to recruitment@snow.com.

Figure 6.6 Advertisement for retail travel agent job

Tourism development and promotion

You may decide to work in local government – most local councils now have a tourism department. You would expect to enter as an assistant tourism officer and work your way up to more senior positions, such as tourism development officer.

Tourism officers spend most of their time in offices within the local authority. The activities of a tourism officer are described in this extract from www.lgcareers.com:

- *promoting existing attractions; working with press and public relations people, designers and photographers to advertise local features. Where there is little history of tourism, the job also involves research into local history and developing potential attractions;*
- *engineering newsworthy events in order to generate publicity in the local, national and trade media;*
- *organising exhibition stands at conferences and at exhibitions both nationally and overseas to promote the area;*
- *assessing the impact that any planned developments may have upon the local environment weighed against of course the potential benefits;*
- *working very closely with businesses in attracting holidaymakers, tour operators, restaurants and guest-houses, to build a picture of how effective existing policies are and what may need addressing in the future. An important part of the work is seeking to attract exhibitions and conferences to the area;*
- *overseeing the council's tourist information offices;*
- *operating their marketing and development activities within a set budget. (This financial aspect may also include the need to look for outside assistance – advertising or sponsorship support, for example.)*

Theory into practice

What do you think the entry requirements are for this kind of post? Describe the skills and knowledge that you would expect from a potential candidate for the post of tourism officer. Compare your ideas with those of your group.

After your BTEC course you should be eligible for a position with a Tourist Information Centre. Becca Hammond tells us about working in her local TIC.

After finishing college, I wanted a year out before I went to university, so I decided to stay at my Saturday job, which is at the Cambridge Tourist Office. As I know the job quite well I didn't really need help in settling in and getting some training.

When I started back it was August so it was a busy time for Cambridge and for us at the Tourist Office. Working in a tourist office brings you new things to do each day. No day is the same! Because there are various different things to do in the office we do shifts of one hour in the gift shop and in our call centre. Then we have periods of time on the front desk dealing with enquiries face-to-face with the public. We also have an accommodation desk at the front which isn't staffed, but if people want to book accommodation we help them.

The past few months I've been asked to do what's called advance accommodation bookings, which are done over the phone. It is a different perspective on the way in which customers approach you. Personally I have benefited from it a great deal.

At times in the job there is pressure, e.g. visitor numbers, getting them through the door, giving out the correct information. There is another different pressure when working on the advance booking desk. It's trying your best to get the right accommodation for the customer, and when really busy it's getting all the paperwork right, sent out to the customer and to the establishment as well as getting our own paperwork all correct.

Working full time in the tourist office has given me a great deal of experience for working in the tourism industry and the working world! So I'm off to university to study travel and tourism. I'm going to Buxton in Derbyshire for three years. The course is a Foundation Degree in Travel and Tourism Management. Obviously I hope to work in the tourism side of the industry and maybe work for a big company like the National Trust.

Trade associations and regulatory bodies

Organisations such as the Association of British Travel Agents (ABTA), the Civil Aviation Authority and the Federation of Tour Operators plus the many other organisations which supply supporting services in travel and tourism also require staff and there may be some interesting opportunities for you in these companies. If you are passionate about a cause, such as responsible tourism or alleviating poverty, then contact organisations like Tourism Concern to investigate opportunities. Many of the posts will be administrative but there may be opportunities in public relations and marketing. Remember too that there are opportunities to work in car hire or insurance services.

This advertisement from Responsible Travel is an opportunity for a bright travel and tourism student to get valuable experience whilst studying.

Interns – responsibletravel.com – A minimum of 2 days per week with a commitment for at least 3 months

We require the help of some bright and enthusiastic people who want to gain an insight into responsible tourism, and have a high degree of accuracy, on an ongoing basis to help maintain and build pages on the website and communicate with our members. You'll either be based in Brighton or have your own computer to be able to work from home.

Longer internships are also available where you can get involved in other special projects. Previous interns have worked on The Responsible Tourism Awards which were launched in association with the Times *at the World Travel Market in London, November 2005, creating a product database and developing our 'weather to go' information. The position is unpaid but travelling expenses will be covered.*

Skills required

- *Knowledge and interest in responsible tourism*
- *Good working knowledge of major computer packages (knowledge of web design packages not essential)*
- *Excellent communication skills*
- *Ability to work independently*

(Source: http://www.responsibletravel.com/Copy/Copy101751.htm)

Factors to consider when working in travel and tourism

As we have seen, travel and tourism careers vary from sector to sector and even within different sectors. It is therefore necessary to look at the types of employment in the different sectors. There are some general points to be made about working in travel and tourism:

- The work is often seasonal as it varies with demand from tourists
- Shift work is often required
- A lot of the work involves direct contact with customers
- The work is very varied
- Travel is not always involved
- Some sectors are low paid
- Contracts are often temporary or fixed term so that there is little job security
- There are many perks such as cheap travel, seeing new places and, of course, dealing with people.

Training and continuing education in travel and tourism

You are undertaking education at the moment, as you are studying for a BTEC qualification. It is most likely that you will want to continue with education or training in the future, and you need to be aware of the opportunities available to you. There are many different kinds of qualifications and courses, but you will first have to determine where you want to do your studying or training. There are three basic paths:

- full-time education
- full-time work with on-the-job/off-the-job training
- full-time work with college provision.

Full-time education

Travel and tourism courses are available from foundation level to postgraduate degree level in further and higher education. You may already have completed a BTEC First in Leisure and Tourism before starting your current course. After completion of the BTEC programme you have several options.

BTEC National Award (6 units)	
BTEC National Certificate (12 units)	BTEC National Diploma (18 units)
HND, e.g. Travel and Tourism	Degree, e.g. Travel and Tourism
Top up to degree	
Postgraduate qualification, e.g. MSc in Tourism Management	

Table 6.1 The BTEC programme

As Table 6.1 indicates, you are unlikely to be offered a university place without at least a 12-unit (BTEC National Certificate) qualification unless you also have 'A' levels. A 12-unit qualification at Pass level would allow you to be accepted onto an HND programme, and if you had good grades you might get onto a degree programme. Points are awarded for your grades and each university sets its own entry criteria. If you start with an HND programme (2 years) you can convert it to a degree by studying for a third year.

There are other examining boards offering equivalent qualifications to BTEC, such as OCR and AQA, and these programmes are equally acceptable for university entrance.

There are hundreds of travel and tourism courses available at universities. Of course, you do not have to study travel and tourism at all – you may choose to study a different subject. Suitable courses include business studies, marketing and event management. All the details of courses are available on university websites, and it is worth spending time researching courses as each travel and tourism course differs from the others.

You should begin by looking at the UCAS website. This offers you various search options, by subject, university or geographic location. Once you have found courses that interest you, you can go to the relevant university websites for more information.

Some students don't like the idea of going on to higher education straight after their BTEC course. This may be for many reasons: the cost, a desire to get straight

into work or having had enough of study. However, you should be aware that many people, after experiencing the realities of working life, decide to go to university a year or two later. You can go to university at any time, but only if you have the entry qualifications – so get them now!

Theory into practice

Visit www.ucas.co.uk and find six degree or HND programmes that interest you. List them and write down the reasons for your choices.

Full-time work with on- or off-the-job training

Much of this unit concerns jobs and how to get one, but even when you are employed you will be expected to carry on learning and undergo training. There will be plenty of opportunities open to you. In some sectors training is desirable and in others it is essential – for example, if you work as air crew you must attend fire training annually.

Accredited Travel Professional Qualification is a new qualification for travel agents. Agents accrue points towards the qualification by completing distance-learning modules and attending conferences. The purpose is to ensure that travel agents have the necessary expertise to cater for complex customer demands and offer an excellent service. There are three proposed levels:

- Bronze – minimum National Vocational Qualification (NVQ) Level 2 or equivalent plus 2 years' industry experience
- Silver – minimum NVQ Level 3 or equivalent plus 4 years' industry experience
- Gold – minimum NVQ Level 3 or equivalent plus 7 years' industry experience.

The levels have to be renewed annually with re-accreditation requiring proof of continuous professional development.

One possibility for gaining points for accreditation is attending an educational travel event. These events are provided in resorts by tour operators for agents to learn about the destination and the tour operator's products.

Leisure travel agents who want to learn about business travel can complete a 'Passport to Business Travel' course. These are run by the travel management company Carlson Wagonlit Travel.

A useful aspect of continuing training for travel agents is destination training. Many tourist boards and companies now offer destination training online, and some of it is free. Examples of destinations agents can learn about online include Canada, Thailand, Australia and Malta, and more destinations are coming onstream all the time.

The travel agents benefit because they can carry out the training at home if they wish, or at work in quiet periods. The training increases their knowledge and therefore boosts their confidence and helps them sell. There is no pressure – the training is done at your own pace. The tourist board or company promoting the training benefits as it makes agents more aware of its products and better equipped to sell them. The programme on Malta has prizes for agents who achieve more than 85 per cent in their online exam. If you want to try this training, you will be able to do so if you have work experience or a job at a travel agent. You need the ABTA number to register online, but some programmes allow students to sign up.

Cosmos has a similar programme to help agents sell many Cosmos products – not just one destination.

Travel agents have other qualifications available to them. The Certificate in Travel (Travel Agency) is the standard examination-based qualification for travel agents, accepted by large organisations and independents. The course is available at Levels 2 and 3.

A similar qualification is available for tour operators, the Certificate in Travel (Tour Operators).

A two-level, self-study training course on travel insurance is available from ABTA for travel companies, travel training organisations and any company that sells travel insurance.

For employees of airlines, a 'Passport to Air' qualification is available. Ticketing qualifications are useful for employees in airlines or in travel agents. These

Case study: Aussie Specialist Programme

The Aussie Specialist Programme has been designed by Tourism Australia specifically for the retail travel trade. Who better to provide you with the most up-to-date information on every aspect of tourism to and around Australia?

The online format of the Aussie Specialist Programme was created to equip you with the knowledge and skills you need to sell Australia effectively. The online learning environment also allows you complete flexibility throughout the course – learn in your own time and at your own pace. But remember – don't take too long. The sooner you qualify, the sooner you will reap the rewards of being a certified Aussie Specialist.

The structure of the programme is simple and straightforward. There are four modules to complete, each with a short exam which needs to be passed with a score of at least 85 per cent before you can move on to the next module. Once you've completed all four modules, the final exam will test your knowledge

– successfully complete this, and you qualify.

Each module covers various aspects of Australia:

- introduction to Australia
- features and attractions of each state and territory
- building effective itineraries.

Your membership lasts for 12 months from the date you register, and to remain on the programme, all you need to do is complete our renewal quiz. The renewal quiz is designed to ensure that you are kept up to date with developments in the Australian tourism industry.

(Source: http://www.specialist.australia.com)

1 **Go to the site for the Aussie Specialist Programme, www.specialist.australia.com, and find out what the benefits to the travel agency are of putting staff through the training programme.**

2 **Carry out a search on the internet and make a list of other destination training that is available.**

are accredited by the International Air Transport Association (IATA) and are exam based.

Specialist qualifications are available from BTEC and NCFE for those who choose to be resort representatives.

If you are working in a Tourist Information Centre or for a tourist board you will probably train in the 'Welcome Host' and 'Welcome Host Plus' programme. Welcome Host is the official qualification for the tourism industry and it is designed specifically for the service sector (hospitality, retail, transport, library boards, leisure, etc.). Welcome Host is designed to enhance fundamental standards of service by all staff.

Many of these specialist courses can be added on to full-time college programmes or done in the workplace.

Full-time work with college provision

■ Foundation degrees

There are other ways of doing a degree besides full-time education. They are available through open learning, and a new proposal is the foundation degree. This has been designed for employees at supervisory level who want a qualification in higher education. Once the foundation degree is completed you can progress to a full degree. It can be undertaken at a college of further education on a flexible basis, taking your work commitments into account.

■ Modern apprenticeships

These are available only to young people between the ages of 16 and 24. Under this scheme you work full time and study for an NVQ at the same time. The most appropriate NVQ is Travel Services.

Modern Apprenticeships are available at foundation or advanced level. This scheme might be of interest to you if you leave college with a BTEC First or lesser qualification, but otherwise you should be aware that an Advanced

Modern Apprenticeship is a Level 3 qualification and you will already have one if you complete your BTEC National programme.

Thomson is an example of a company with a good Modern Apprenticeship scheme. PGL, a company which offers activity holidays for young people, is another company that offers a Modern Apprenticeship scheme.

Changing direction

Some students change direction completely after studying travel and tourism, but still find the training useful. Here is Lisa telling us about what she is doing.

I work for a music magazine called Sound On Sound. *I am an administration assistant so I do reception duties, e.g. answering the phone and sending out the mail. We also have a mail order department where customers can buy magazines and merchandise directly from our shop, and I am in charge of this. I take the payments and send out the goods that have been ordered.*

I also help in two other departments. I help the subscription manager by sending out renewal forms and I help in the credit control department by typing up and sending out the invoices. I send out the magazine to our advertisers every month.

Even though I have not gone into the industry, I am glad I did the travel and tourism course. I found it very interesting, especially as when I started the course I wanted to live in Spain! I really benefited from doing the course as I became much more confident and my social skills improved immensely. My favourite part of the course was organising our residential study visit. I loved the fact that we did it ourselves and worked together to organise a trip abroad. It was a very successful trip and great fun to do.

Human resources departments usually handle the recruitment and selection process for organisations. It is vital to the success of any organisation that the best staff available are employed in the right positions. A system is needed so that recruitment and selection are carried out properly and the employment of staff is not left to chance. The procedure varies from organisation to organisation, depending on the size and nature of the business, but it is possible to identify the essential stages.

In this section we will study how Canvas Holidays, a tour operator specialising in camping holidays, carries out recruitment and selection procedures. You can look at its current vacancies by going to www.canvasholidays.co.uk, going to the 'Contact us' section and finding the recruitment pages. Take a look at the interviews with the operations team – note how many of them started their careers as couriers and enjoyed the company so much they never left.

Organisation

Identifying company needs

There should be a staffing plan for any company. This gives ideal numbers of staff in each capacity within the organisation. When a vacancy arises for whatever reason, the impact of the vacancy should be considered against the staffing plan. It may be possible that the post is no longer required, or that the nature of the post should change. There may be an opportunity to move staff into different positions better suited to company needs.

Sometimes, major restructuring takes place without a vacancy having arisen, due to changes in the business or economic circumstances of the company, for example a takeover of another company or a major economic downturn.

Canvas Holidays looks at courier staffing numbers every year and sets a courier/unit ratio of about 1:10 (a unit is a mobile home or tent). This can vary according to the site and whether it is used as a long stay or overnight stop. Once numbers are established, a staffing budget can be decided for the year. The courier service is deemed to be really important as it directly impacts on the customer's enjoyment of the holiday.

■ Job descriptions

A job description is a general statement explaining the purpose, duties and responsibilities of a job. It should include the following information:

- job title and department
- job purpose – the main duties of the role
- responsibilities – to whom the job holder is responsible, and all the responsibilities of the post
- physical conditions – where the work is performed, the hours, any hazards or special conditions
- social conditions – in teams, with clients or alone
- economic conditions – salary range, commissions, bonuses, pension, sick pay
- prospects for promotion and training.

Figures 6.7 and 6.8 show two edited examples of job descriptions from Canvas Holidays.

■ Person specifications

A person specification is used to match the right person to the job. It describes the desirable personal attributes of the job holder. It is usually based on a seven-point plan which includes:

- physical make-up – does the job require any special physical characteristics such as strength, good eyesight or height?
- attainments – what type of education is needed? What special occupational experience or training is required?
- intelligence – how much general intelligence should be evident?
- special aptitudes – is a skill in writing or drawing needed? Does the applicant need to be a car driver or speak a second language?
- disposition – what type of personality is desirable? Does the applicant need to be reliable or hard working?
- circumstances – does the applicant need to be mobile? Does he or she have to travel away from home?
- interests.

JOB DESCRIPTION

Job title: Campsite Courier

Reports to: Area Manager, Site Manager, Site Supervisor, Senior Courier

Liaises with: Camp Proprietors, Specialist Couriers, Warehouse Personnel, Operations Department

General function

To ensure that every aspect of our customers' holiday is of the highest standard possible by participating in montage, providing excellent Customer Service during the season and by participating in demontage. This will be measured through feedback from Customer Questionnaires and Area Managers.

Duties and responsibilities

- Participate in montage and demontage as and when required.
- Montage, clean and prepare units, prior to customer arrival.
- Cultivate and maintain good working relationships with the camp proprietor and campsite staff.
- Clean and maintain all units on site throughout the season, ensuring that they are clean and tidy at all times.
- Reflect appropriate Company Image at all times, as per the Overseas Staff Handbook, ensuring correct uniform is worn at correct times and that guidelines regarding corporate identity, dress and alcohol code are rigorously upheld.
- Where applicable, organise and supervise a programme of events for children, aged 4–11 years, at least twice per week.
- Ensure that local information in Information Book and on notice board is kept up to date and that information is added, where possible, to enhance the level of customer service.
- Provide each customer with a personal welcome on arrival.
- Monitor the quality of campsite facilities, as laid out in Health and Safety Guidelines.
- Ensure that campsite Health and Safety Audits are completed accurately and on time and that they are submitted to your Area Manager by the deadline set by him/her.
- Complete all necessary paperwork promptly and accurately.
- Work in a flexible manner in order to achieve the overall objectives of the Company.

▲ **Figure 6.7 Job description for a Campsite Courier**

(Source: http://www.canvasholidays.co.uk)

JOB DESCRIPTION

Job title: Area Manager

Reports to: Recruitment and Training Manager

Liaises with: Operations Department, Campsite Owners and Staff, Warehouse Personnel

General function

Be responsible for overseas staff welfare and overall running of a designated geographical area ensuring the best possible standards of customer care at all times, thereby achieving the customer satisfaction levels detailed in the Area Manager Handbook and the Operations Departmental Aim.

Duties and responsibilities

- Co-ordinate and supervise the complete montage and demontage of all accommodation, storage and specialist units in designated area following procedures laid down at training and in Area Manager Handbook.
- Take responsibility for the welfare and performance of all staff ensuring that they are appropriately trained and developed throughout the season and by carrying out regular performance monitoring as outlined at training and detailed in Area Manager Handbook.
- Ensure that staff maintain all units (customer and courier) to a high standard throughout the season thereby upholding the correct Company Image in the field, following procedures laid down at training and in Area Manager Handbook.
- Cultivate and maintain good working relationships with all Camp Proprietors and campsite staff thus ensuring the smooth running of the Canvas operation on site. Regular communication must be maintained throughout the season with staff, campsite owners and the Operations Department.
- Ensure that all administration tasks (e.g. Health and Safety Audits, Emplacement Assessment Forms, Site Visit Forms, Staff Assessments and Appraisals, Demo paperwork) are completed accurately and on time by following the procedures detailed in the Overseas Staff and Area Manager Handbooks.
- With the aid of Health and Safety Audits and Defect Forms, monitor the quality of campsite facilities, identifying any problem areas and immediately reporting them to the appropriate personnel.
- Ensure appropriate Company Image is being reflected at all times, ensuring correct uniform is worn by all Canvas staff on site at correct times and that, as per the Overseas Staff Handbook, guidelines regarding corporate identity, dress code and alcohol code are rigorously upheld.
- Ensure care and upkeep of all company vehicles, reporting any incidents immediately to the Logistics Manager, as per procedures laid down at training and in Area Manager Handbook.
- Carry out contracting responsibilities including camp hunting, emplacement selection and contract negotiation as required.
- Monitor quality of Canvas product on site, ensuring customers receive the best quality equipment available within budgetary and logistical constraints.
- Monitor all expenditure within a certain geographical area, ensuring it is accounted for by means of appropriate receipts, reports and accounts, which are submitted weekly to the Operations Department.
- Work in a flexible manner at all times in order to achieve the overall aims of the Company.

▲ **Figure 6.8 Job description for an Area Manager**   (Source: http://www.canvasholidays.co.uk)

The job description and person specification are kept on record together and are used to help the recruitment team find the right person for the job.

Theory into practice

Study the Canvas job descriptions carefully. Using the seven-point plan, draw up a person specification for each of the jobs. Compare your person specification with that of another member of the group.

Advertising

Advertising is used to find suitable candidates. There are many possible locations for placing advertising. The most important consideration is reaching the right people, but cost must also be taken into account. The following could be used.

- Recruitment agencies – general or specialist. There are specialist travel and tourism agencies. To fill a permanent position, the agency charges a percentage of the annual salary for the post, so they are expensive.
- Job centre – usually used to recruit unskilled or semi-skilled staff. As the Department for Education and Skills provides the service, it is free. Job centres will also pre-interview for the company.
- Press – local press is ideal for local companies.
- Radio – frequently used for recruitment; more suitable for local jobs.
- 'Milk round' – companies visit universities searching for suitable graduate applicants.
- Internet – on their own websites or through specialist recruitment sites.

Canvas Holidays advertises in national newspapers such as the *Daily Mail* and the *Guardian*. An advertising schedule is prepared and shows all the publications that are to be used, along with dates and costs. The extract in the following case study shows the publications and websites that Canvas Holidays decided to use in 2006.

Case study: Canvas Holidays – advertising list

Papers and magazines
Guardian – Monday and Saturday
Daily Mail – Thursday
Travel Weekly (Area Manager advertisement)
The Lady magazine (Hoopi advertisement)
TNT magazine (Hoopi advertisement)
TTG (Area Manager advertisement)

Internet
Countryside Jobs Service
Net Recruit
Hot Recruit
Summer Jobs Abroad
Season Workers
Job Opportunities
Anywork Anywhere
Gaptastic
British Sports Trust
Nanny Jobs
Jobs Abroad Bulletin
Vacation Work Publications

Other
Job Centre advertisements – Children's Courier, Montage Assistant and Warehouse Assistants
Colleges and universities – Leeds, Sheffield Hallam, Thames Valley, Greenwich, Hull, Liverpool, Napier, Robert Gordon, Southampton
iStage – Dutch placement company

(Source: Canvas Holidays)

Study the list of publications and websites used for advertising by Canvas Holidays and answer the following questions.

1 **Why are particular days specified for the *Daily Mail* and the *Guardian*?**

2 **Why was the *Travel Trade Gazette* (TTG) chosen for the Area Manager position?**

3 **What kind of people do you think Canvas is trying to attract by advertising in the publications listed?**

4 **Why do you think universities are included in the schedule?**

Consider this

What do you think happens to an application that has spelling mistakes, crossings out or is badly presented?

Roadshows

When companies send their recruitment teams to venues in major cities to undertake a recruitment drive it is often called a roadshow. They advertise their presence locally, and potential applicants turn up and find out about career opportunities with that company. 'The milk round' is a particular type of roadshow when companies travel to universities in an attempt to recruit students who are about to graduate.

Recruitment agencies

These are organisations who earn their income by charging a fee to companies for undertaking their recruitment for them. Some are specialist companies. An example of a recruitment agency specialising in travel and tourism is Holiday Resort Jobs, an online resort jobs directory.

Short-listing applications

The initial methods of selection involve comparing applications to the job specification and person specification. A list of essential criteria may be used, and this will result in many applications being rejected.

At Canvas Holidays an interview checklist is used to help decide who should be shortlisted. Essential requirements include availability, a bank account, experience of working with the public, experience of overseas travel or camping. Desirable requirements include a language and experience of working with children.

Interviewing

An interview is a two-way process and can be described as a problem-solving activity to decide whether the interviewee is right for the job and whether the job is right for the interviewee. The interviewer has to direct and control the discussion in order to make an objective decision. Interviews may be carried out individually, in groups or by telephone.

Successful interviewers prepare well by:

- reading carefully through applications
- deciding on questions
- considering seating and room layout for the interview.

To establish rapport with the interviewee, they:

- smile and maintain good body language
- welcome the candidate
- start by confirming the information in the application.

When questioning, an effective interviewer will:

- start with simple open questions about what the candidate has done
- continue with more difficult, probing questions
- practise active listening
- repeat questions or reword them if necessary
- avoid leading questions
- avoid answering the question for the interviewee
- write notes afterwards, not during the interview
- ask all candidates the same questions to be fair
- encourage each interviewee to talk
- ask if the candidate has any questions
- end on a positive note
- tell candidates what will happen next, for example 'We will write to you next week'.

Key terms

Leading questions – those which lead candidates to a specific answer rather than one they have considered themselves, for example: 'We really frown on lateness here. How is your punctuality?'

Active listening – the process of demonstrating to a speaker both verbally and non-verbally that you are listening and that the information is being received. It is done by maintaining eye contact, nodding and expressing agreement in appropriate places.

Theory into practice

1. Next time you are on the phone, think about how you know the other person is listening. You can't see them, so how do they show verbally that they are listening?
2. Talk to a colleague face-to-face. How do you know they are listening to you? Make a few notes after the conversation and then compare your findings with your group.

At Canvas Holidays, one-to-one interviews are the preferred procedure. Interviews are held at head office in Dunfermline as well as in hotels in major cities such as Manchester, London and Bristol. Interviews follow the same format, and interviewers receive both in-house and external training (see Figure 6.9).

Psychometric tests

These are used to test ability or personality. They usually take the form of fairly lengthy questionnaires and the respondent is judged as suitable for a position or not depending on the responses given. The tests are used to support other selection methods rather than as a selection tool that stands alone.

Theory into practice

If you want to try out a psychometric test you can find some on the internet. Carry out a search for 'free psychometric tests online'. Be aware that they are usually quite long!

Offers of employment

If you are successful at interview you can expect to receive a letter which constitutes an offer of employment (Figure 6.10).

This is followed by a contract which lays out the terms and conditions of employment. It will include details such as:

- hours of work
- location
- start and finsh times/shift times
- holiday entitlement
- rate of pay.

This is quite a lengthy document. You will be required to sign and return the contract but you will be given a copy to keep for reference.

Applicant

Job applicants also have procedures to follow when looking for work. These procedures include:

- researching opportunities
- producing CVs
- speculative enquiries
- responding to advertisements
- preparing for inteviews
- attending interviews
- responding to job offers
- references.

We will look at these procedures in detail in the next section.

INTERVIEW ASSESSMENT FORM – Courier   Result: ......

Name:	Date:	Place:
Exact dates:	Position: Courier	Interviewers:

First impressions/ Reasons for applying	
Job awareness CLEANING!!	
Relevant work experience	
Customer expectations & customer service	
Problems (real or theoretical)	
Ideas for Hoopi (children's club)?	
Language skills	
Hobbies	
Montage/demontage	
Driving	
Camping/travel	
What do they hope to gain from a summer with Canvas?	
What would they do 'to make a difference'?	

Preferred area & why:	Single or team:	Suggested site:

Any additional comments:

Figure 6.9 Interview assessment form   (Source: Canvas Holidays)

SEA BREAKS

7 February 2006

Stuart Brown
12 Gladstone Park
Cambridge CB14 3RQ

Dear Stuart

Offer of employment

I am pleased to advise you that you have been successful in attaining the position of Lifeguard for the coming season. You will be based at La Rochelle (France), commencing employment on 27 June 2006 and finishing on 31 August 2006. You will be required to travel to site two to three days prior to your start date.

This offer of employment is subject to the receipt of satisfactory references.

There will be a trial period of two weeks, during which time either the employee or employer can give notice to terminate employment.

Your salary will be 1500 euros per month, with deductions for tax and accommodation.

If you wish to take up the offer of employment please return the enclosed form confirming your acceptance and availability within seven days. If you are unable to accept the offer please indicate this on the form and return it. Please note, if we have not received your written acceptance within seven working days we reserve the right to withdraw this offer.

Prior to your departure you will receive a starter pack, containing your travel details and essential packing guide.

Yours sincerely

John Blake

John Blake
Recruitment Team

▲ **Figure 6.10 Offer of employment**

Assessment practice

1 Arrange to do some practice interviews within your group. Carry out the following activities to prepare:

- choose one of the two Canvas Holidays jobs described in this unit
- complete an application form, which you can download from the Canvas Holidays website
- the interviewer should prepare questions and the interviewee should prepare to be interviewed. **P4**

(Alternatively you could download job descriptions and applications forms from the internet sites of other companies that interest you.)

Take it in turns to play the role of:

- the interviewee
- the interviewer
- the observer.

2 Describe the stages of the recruitment and selection process. **P3**

3 Produce guidelines for success in completing the application form, preparing for interview and the interview itself. Use the guidelines to evaluate your own performance in the recruitment process. **M2**

Grading tip

Use an assessment form like the one shown in Figure 6.9 when it is your turn to act as interviewer. It is a good idea to videotape the interviews so that you can discuss them in your group.

6.3 Be able to apply for employment in travel and tourism

Personal skills audit

You must be realistic about your capabilities, and therefore your options – there is no point in applying for a job for which you have no qualifications. If you are lacking in one or two points only, decide how important they are and whether you should try anyway. Remember that all the things you do in your spare time help develop your personal skills so include membership of clubs, achievements in sports, etc.

It might be useful to carry out an audit of your skills, attributes, experience, qualifications and achievements. This will help you complete a training and development plan as well.

Activity

Complete the following skills audit. Do this with a partner and discuss how you can each improve on your skills and qualifications.

Skill area	Aspect	Good?	Improvement needed?	Qualification held
Communication	Taking notes			
	Spelling			
	Writing letters			
	Writing reports			
	Oral presentation			
	Interviewing			
Numeracy	Calculating			
	Interpreting statistics			
	Presenting graphs and tables			
IT	Word			
	Access			
	Excel			
	Internet			
	E-mail			
Working with others	Contributing to a team			
	Assertiveness			
	Listening			
Improving own learning	Time management and performance			
	Action planning			
	Organisational skills			
Vocational skills in travel and tourism				
Languages				

Here are examples of audit methods you can use to help set, plan and achieve your targets for the development of your personal skills and qualifications.

1 Setting targets

Target	When?
Find an interesting and challenging job	
Gain BTEC qualification with good grades	
Complete final assessments	
Update CV	
Contact tutor about possible jobs	
Carry out research for assessments, prepare CV and covering letter	
Interview practice with tutor, regular reviews of progress with tutor	

2 Development plan

Target	How?	When?	Resources needed
Apply to university	Research courses	Summer holidays	UCAS website, prospectuses, friends at university
	Prepare personal statement	By beginning of October	UCAS instructions
	Complete application online	By October	Tutors or careers advisers
	Prepare for interviews	By December	
Improve knowledge of travel and tourism current affairs	Read the travel press regularly – keep a cuttings file	From now	Newspapers, trade press, websites
Improve language skills	Evening class	September	Local college information on language classes
Pass course	Keep to deadlines, prepare timetable of work	By June	Tutors, parents, library and internet

Design a similar target-setting form or development plan and complete it for yourself. You can keep it confidential if you prefer, or you can discuss it with your tutor. If you use the form to show how you will meet your training and development needs, you can use it for your assessment. **D1**

Applying for work

Research

Before you apply for work you will have to carry out research to find suitable jobs to apply for. Some relevant sources of information are given throughout this unit but you will need to find other sources which are appropriate for the type of work you hope to do. These will include:

- newspapers – national and local
- trade magazines such as *Travel Trade Gazette, Travel Weekly, Leisure Opportunities* and *Caterer Online*
- careers specialists
- recruitment agencies
- company websites.

Preparing a curriculum vitae (CV)

Curriculum vitae literally means an account of your life – it is a summary of your work experience, education and skills. The purpose of your CV is to bring you to the attention of an employer and get you to the interview stage.

Your CV should be constantly updated, and although you will keep a basic CV on file you should adapt it to fit the particular requirements of each job you apply for. Of course, this doesn't mean changing the facts – it means altering the emphasis of the CV to make the relevant points stand out.

Your CV should include:

- personal information
- work history
- education
- skills
- references.

■ Personal information

Give your name, address, telephone numbers and e-mail address. There is no need to give your gender, marital status or number of children, if any. Age need not be mentioned either, but if you are young it is a good idea to put your date of birth as there may be jobs you are not eligible for because of your age.

■ Work history

This is where you list all your employment, starting with your current or latest job. If you have never had a job, include any periods of work experience or voluntary work you have done. For each job give the job title, the name of the company and what it does, if it is not well known. Add a list of your responsibilities in that position. If you can think of particular achievements in that position, list them too.

■ Education

List your qualifications. As with work history, start with your most recent qualification or course. Include schools from secondary onwards. Do not include GCSEs below 'C' grade. Write the name of the college/school and against it the qualifications you achieved there.

■ Skills

List any other skills you have. Examples include languages, with an indication of your level, driving licence, first-aid certificate or lifeguard qualifications. Include your key skill and IT qualifications here too. For IT, say which software packages you can use.

■ References

It is usual to include the names and addresses of two referees. One must be an employer or tutor. Alternatively, you can state that referees are available on request – this gives you time to ask referees for permission to give their contact details.

■ Profile

Some people choose to start their CV with a brief personal profile. It sums up your skills and experience and gives the employer an instant idea of whether you are suitable for the post. It can easily be adapted to fit a particular post.

CV writing tips

- Keep it brief – two sides of A4 is the maximum.
- Don't try to be funny.
- Don't include visuals, special designs, etc.
- Don't add a passport photo unless specifically asked to do so.

- Tailor the CV to the job in question.
- Don't include anything negative.
- Print it on good-quality paper.
- Ask referees for permission before mentioning them.
- Ask someone to check the grammar and spelling.
- Keep a copy of your CV on disk.

An example of a CV is shown in Figure 6.11.

Charlie Richardson
15 St John's Street
Oldham
Lancs OL7 5DH
0161 886 2121
C.Richardson@aol.com

Enthusiastic college leaver with Distinction in BTEC National in Travel and Tourism seeks challenging post in tour operation

Work history
June 2003 – present

Information assistant
Oldham Tourist Information Centre

Responsibilities include responding to general enquiries, ordering promotional literature, making theatre and accommodation bookings

Offered this post following work experience.

Education
Sept 2002 to June 2004
Oldham College

BTEC National in Travel and Tourism
Distinction

Sept 2001 to June 2002
Oldham College

GNVQ Intermediate Leisure and Tourism
Distinction

Sept 1996 to June 2001
St Giles High School, Oldham

GCSEs:
Maths   C
French   C

Skills

Full, clean driving licence
First aid certificate
Basic Spanish
IT Key Skill level 3

References

Available on request

▲ **Figure 6.11 Curriculum vitae**

Theory into practice

Follow all the guidelines and the example given above and produce your own CV. Make this a basic CV which can then be adapted to fit a particular job application.

Case study: matching a CV to a job advertisement

> ### FRIENDLY TRAVEL
>
> Friendly Travel has been in business successfully for 25 years and has become one of the UK's leading independent travel companies. We pride ourselves on the range of products and the outstanding level of customer service we provide for our clients.
>
> #### Customer Relations Executive
>
> We are looking for a well-organised, customer-focused person to be responsible for logging in-coming correspondence, acknowledging customer complaints and liaising with other departments to ensure customer complaints are resolved. The post is suitable for a new entrant into the travel trade and training will be given. As much of the correspondence is written, applicants will need excellent letter-writing skills and must also be confident in verbal communication. A knowledge of tour operators and their regulatory practices would be beneficial.
>
> Please forward your CV and letter of application to …

Read the job advertisement above.

1 **Adapt Charlie's CV so that it is suitable for this position.**

   - **List the Customer Service and Tour Operations units under the BTEC National qualification.**
   - **In the profile add 'well organised'.**
   - **Under TIC responsibilities add 'dealing with customer complaints'.**
   - **Make any other changes that you think are appropriate.**

2 **Now adapt your own CV, drawing on your own experience and skills so that your CV is suitable for this position. If you prefer, you can choose another job advertisement for this task.** **P4**

Application forms

Application forms are usually sent out to applicants in hard copy from a company. Some companies prefer application forms to CVs as they then have information in the same format from all candidates and can more easily match it to their criteria. There are some companies who allow online applications, however they often use the online form as an initial screening and require a written application from those who manage to get through the screening. You should bear in mind that you should never apply for a job by e-mail unless expressly invited to do so.

When completing an application form remember to:

- photocopy the form and practise first on the copy so there are no errors on the submitted form
- write clearly – black ink is often preferred as it photocopies better
- answer all questions
- try to give original answers to open-ended questions on customer service, leadership, etc.
- get someone to proof-read the form for you
- ask permission from referees before you include them.

Letters of application

You should never send your CV without a covering letter. Remember your CV is up to two pages long, and the purpose of your letter is to focus on why you are suitable for the job.

If the letter is poorly presented you will not be selected, so make sure you have studied the section in this unit on writing a business letter.

■ Speculative enquiries

Letters of application may be speculative – this means a letter is sent even if you don't know whether a job vacancy exists.

Responding to advertisements

If you are writing in response to a job advertisement, make sure you say which advertisement and give examples of the skills and qualities you have that match the job advertised.

Theory into practice

Write a letter of application for Charlie for the job at Friendly Travel. Use the letter-writing guidance given here and Charlie's CV to help you.

chosen course of study. Detailed guidance on what should be included in a personal statement is provided along with the UCAS application form. Make sure you read it carefully and practise writing your statement before you complete the final copy or online submission. Don't forget to ask a tutor to check the personal statement with you.

■ Writing a business letter

A business letter is a formal letter. It is often on headed paper, and it is always word-processed. The most common format of a business letter is fully blocked format. This means that everything is aligned to the left.

You should:

- include the name of the recipient if you can, otherwise write to 'Dear Sir/Madam'; never assume a particular gender
- use an ordinary font such as Times New Roman, size 12
- begin a new paragraph for each new point
- if you are responding to a job advertisement, include a reference to the advertisement
- end with 'Yours faithfully' if you started with 'Dear Sir/Madam'
- end with Yours sincerely' if you started with 'Dear [name]'
- print on good white paper
- check everything and then ask someone else to check it again.

Figure 6.12 provides an example for you to follow.

If you are applying for university, you will have to write a personal statement. This is possibly the most important part of your university application as it is your opportunity to explain what is special about you and why the university should choose you for your

15 Somerset Gardens ← *Your address*
Hereford
HG6 4WA

Ms J Atherton   ← *Recipient's name and address*
Fanfare Travel
Woodcroft Way
Hemel Hempstead
HP0 1WW

2 May 2006

Dear Ms Atherton

Vacancy for Travel Assistant ← *Reference to advertisement*

I am writing with reference to the above vacancy which was advertised in *Travel Weekly* on 27 April 2006.

I am about to complete my BTEC National Diploma in Travel and Tourism at Hereford College and I would like the opportunity of working in a busy travel agency.

I have undertaken work experience in a travel agency in Hereford. They were very pleased with my performance and I was offered a full-time job, but I wish to work in Hemel Hempstead and I know your agency has a good reputation.

I have been working part-time at the local library during my studies. This has given me excellent experience of customer service and improved my administrative skills as I had to use the library database. ← *Note new point in each paragraph*

I am sure I have the necessary skills and experience to succeed in the advertised post. I have pleasure in enclosing my CV and look forward to hearing from you.

 Reference to enclosed CV

Yours sincerely

Sanjit Atwal

▲ **Figure 6.12 Writing a business letter**

Interview skills

Advance preparation

This includes deciding what is appropriate to wear, making sure you know the location of the company, how to get there and how long the journey will take.

■ Company knowledge

Make sure you have carried out research into the company and its products and services. You might be asked about your opinions of the company; if you don't know anything about it you will look foolish. For example, an interviewee may be asked what they thought about the company's new holiday programme for Asia. It would not look good if they replied that they didn't know the company sold holidays to Asia.

Telephone screening

Telephone interviews are quite common when there are a lot of applicants for a job. It can be more stressful for the applicant than a face-to-face interview as the interviewer cannot see your expression or your body language.

A telephone call can be very important; you create an impression even though you cannot be seen. You should prepare for your telephone call just as you would for a face-to-face meeting.

Make a few notes about what you want to say or ask – but don't write a script and read it out, or you will sound very unnatural.

During the call:

- stand up – good body language will affect your voice
- use an appropriate greeting
- introduce yourself – for example, 'Good morning, this is Katy Johnson'
- end the call properly – say thank you and goodbye.

When you are speaking:

- use your voice to make a good impression; vary the pitch, be clear and not too quiet or too loud
- don't ramble, but make your points succinct.

Theory into practice

Practise making telephone calls. Ask your teacher or tutor for a telephone set. Set up a situation with one of your colleagues and ask them to practise with you. Listen and give constructive criticism on each other's performance.

Here are some ideas for tasks:

- Leave an answerphone message for Ms Hendry saying you have to change your interview date.
- Telephone and find out the name of the manager at a travel agency.
- Ring and ask for an application form for an advertised post.

Attending interviews

Personal presentation

In the travel and tourism industry, staff often have direct contact with the public, so dress code is important. Employers have the right to control their business image, especially when employees are in direct contact with customers, and most travel and tourism companies require their staff to wear a uniform or obey strict dress codes.

Most airlines do not allow visible piercings (except for simple earrings) or tattoos. Thomas Cook does not allow facial studs, body piercings or visible tattoos.

In a resort, employees sometimes wear shorts and T-shirts depending on their role. This would be suitable for campsite couriers, for example. They are still part of a uniform provided by the company.

If you are preparing for an interview you should dress in a conservative way. This means wearing formal business dress, unless you are specifically told otherwise.

Make sure every item you wear is clean and free from creases, and make sure you too are clean and sweet-smelling. If you smoke, do not do so just before you enter an interview – it will not give a good impression. Remember to smile!

Men	Women
Suit – if you don't have one, wear a plain shirt, tie and smart trousers. No T-shirts	Suit or smart trousers/skirt and top – no mini-skirts. No low-cut tops or thin straps
Polished dark shoes – no trainers	Polished dark shoes – no trainers, and heels should not be too high
Hair – freshly washed and tied back if long	Hair – freshly washed
	Wear tights with skirts – no bare legs

Table 6.2 Dress for an interview

Projecting a positive image and attitude

If you look the part and have done enough preparation you will feel more confident. Paying attention to your body language will also help project a positive image. Smile and shake hands when you are introduced to the interviewer (or panel). Do not sit down until you are invited to. If you cannot answer a question, take a few moments to think before giving an answer, don't leap in. Show a positive attitude by listening attentively, showing interest in the information you are being given and asking relevant questions.

Body language

Pay attention to your body language during the interview – try to appear relaxed and open, even if you are feeling nervous. Leaning forward slightly shows you are alert and interested, and maintaining eye contact (without staring) shows you are confident and are engaging with the interviewer.

Responding to and asking questions

Questions are often asked about instances where you have been able to demonstrate your skills. Prepare examples of situations where you have demonstrated particular skills. You should be able to guess the skills that would be appropriate from the job description. For example, think of situations where you had to solve a problem, where you demonstrated leadership or where you showed good customer service skills.

You might be asked:

- Give me an example of when you gave excellent customer service.
- Give me an example of how you handled a difficult customer.
- How have you shown leadership?
- How have you demonstrated initiative?

Take some care in responding to questions, for example avoid giving Yes/No answers, counter negative suggestions, etc.

At all interviews an opportunity is given for the interviewee to ask questions. Make sure you have some ready. Don't ask about the pay and holidays – you can find out about these later if they haven't already told you. Ask about training and promotion prospects. If interviewers want to give you a hard time they will start by asking for your questions. Don't be intimidated, take out your pad of prepared questions and fire away!

Time management

Being late does not give a good impression! Plan to arrive 10 minutes before your interview appointment, so that you feel calm and prepared. If possible, do a practice run of the journey to time it – preferably at the same time of day to allow for traffic conditions.

Evaluation

You may not always be successful in the recruitment process. In fact, you may have to apply for many jobs before you receive an offer of employment. Some companies will offer you feedback. If this is the case, listen to the feedback and use the experience to help you positively in your next application or interview. Take this as an opportunity to evaluate your strengths and weaknesses and determine areas for improvement.

Responding to job offers

If you are offered a job, and you wish to accept it, you may receive and accept the offer by telephone but make sure you formally accept it in writing. You may be offered a job that you don't want. In this case, write a polite letter refusing the offer.

Working environment

Location

In travel and tourism, you may be lucky and work at a resort. The holiday atmosphere contributes to a sense of well-being. The sun shines, customers are happy to be on holiday and it is relatively easy to have a positive attitude to work. Contrast this with working in a call centre where you are office bound and have to spend most of the day on the telephone. The organisation has to consider how this poorer environment can be improved so that staff remain motivated.

Hours of work

Hours of work vary tremendously throughout the industry – some people are happy to work unsocial hours because it fits in with their lifestyle or they wish to have time off when everyone else is working. However, the overall number of hours per week should not exceed 40.

Health and safety

Safety and security factors must be considered in the workplace, and legislation such as the Health and Safety at Work Act 1974 must be adhered to. Specific regulations also apply where food is served or where there are chemical hazards, for example in a swimming pool. All these requirements are important.

For some organisations a lapse in safety procedures can mean the collapse of the business and even a prosecution. Companies that organise activity holidays for children, for example, must make health and safety a priority. Health and safety is important for both customers and employees. Employees need to know that they can go about their work in a safe environment and work together to ensure their customers are safe.

Equipment and resources

State-of-the-art equipment and a pleasant environment are important to motivate staff.

Theory into practice

Think about the resources you would like to work with if you have a part-time job. Can you think of areas for improvement that would make your job easier?

Social events

Most companies have a Christmas party or social outings for staff. These are useful events to create a camaraderie amongst staff and build teams.

Theories of motivation

The motivation and commitment of employees is key to the success of a team and therefore to the company.

Theory into practice

What factors motivate you to go to your job or your course? Think about a member of your family or someone you know who has a good job. What motivates them? Is this motivation different from yours?

Several theorists have come up with models of motivation. We will look at two here, Maslow and Herzberg.

■ Maslow

Abraham Maslow was an American who in the 1940s developed a theory of motivation. The theory is valid still for understanding how people are motivated in the workplace. Employers can use it to provide conditions that fulfil people's needs at the different levels.

The web page shown in Figure 6.13 describes what is on offer if you work overseas for MyTravel.

Welcome to
MyTravel Careers Website

Airline   Overseas Opportunities   Retail Opportunities   Home | MyTravel

> Overseas Home
> Positions Available
☐ What's In It For You?
> Have You Got
  What It Takes?
> Apply For A Job

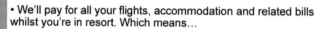

Overseas
Opportunities

We'll provide more than the flip-flops!

So you want even MORE than just the chance to experience a whole new way of life. You want to enjoy fun times and make friends with a whole gang of people as energetic and enthusiastic as you are!
Here's what you can expect from us:

• We'll pay for all your flights, accommodation and related bills whilst you're in resort. Which means…

• You can choose to spend or save your competitive salary – paid into your UK Bank Account every month – as you wish!

• In some roles, you'll also be able to earn extra commission in resort.

• We'll provide full medical and personal insurance to keep you covered for any eventuality. And a uniform to keep you covered!

• You'll also get 4 weeks' paid holiday per year – the perfect chance to take advantage of our generous holiday discounts.

• Whilst we're currently recruiting for the 2007 Summer season only and we'll offer you an initial contract for the 6 month season, there are opportunities, however in our Winter resorts, Sun Ski, head office or retail stores in UK. So, you may have the opportunity to work through Winter.

• We do our best to keep our talent within the MyTravel Group, so whether you're looking to potentially run your own resort one day or would prefer to climb the ladder at Head Office, we can help turn your passion for travel into a rewarding career.

TELL A FRIEND !

*Click here
to send
these exciting
opportunities
to a friend*

© MyTravel Group plc 2005   Legal Notice | Privacy Policy | Contact Us

 Figure 6.13 MyTravel web page   (Source: http://www.mytravelcareers.co.uk/overseas/whatsinit.asp; © MyTravel)

Explain how the factors described motivate staff.

Figure 6.14 Maslow's hierarchy of needs

Maslow's theory is displayed as a pyramid because employees can only move up the levels once the lower levels are fulfilled. So, an employee cannot achieve at work (level 4) if they are having problems in their personal life or with work colleagues (level 3). Similarly, if they have just been made homeless (level 1) their concern will be finding shelter not performing at work.

Consider this

Do you agree with Maslow's hierarchy of needs? Can you think of examples from your own experience?

■ Herzberg

Herzberg's theory is also known as the 'Hygiene' theory. Herzberg identified characteristics which make people satisfied with their jobs and those which make them dissatisfied: 'satisfiers' and 'dissatisfiers'.

The satisfiers are factors which give people long-term motivation and enable them to enjoy their work:

- the type of work
- promotion prospects
- having responsibility
- sense of achievement

- personal development
- gaining recognition.

The dissatisfiers or hygiene factors need to be operating well in an organisation but according to Herzberg do not ultimately motivate people. However, if they are unsatisfactory then they do demotivate people. These are:

- salary
- working conditions
- relationships with others – colleagues and managers
- company policy.

Consider this

What are the factors that motivate you to do your course or your part-time job?

Working relationships and impact on motivation

Management style

Management is about motivating people to act in certain ways so that the team can achieve its common goal. A good manager must inform, motivate and develop the team.

An autocratic manager

An autocratic manager makes all the decisions and announces them to the team. This person is the boss and so has full control. The main advantage of this kind of leadership is that decisions are made quickly, as no consultation is involved. Its other advantages include:

- where there is a need for urgent action the autocrat will take control
- some team members gain security from being told what to do.

The disadvantages are:

- team members may become frustrated at their lack of control
- there may not be room for the team to express creativity
- there may be over-dependence on the leader.

Autocratic management belongs in a traditional hierarchical structure.

Consultative management

With consultative management, the leader still makes the decisions but discusses them with the team. The advantages include:

- the team is informed of what is going on
- open discussion is encouraged
- the manager spends time with the team.

The disadvantages are that the team may feel involved but frustrated by having no real power.

Democratic management

With democratic management, the decision-making is shared among the team. The advantages include:

- ideas are encouraged from everyone
- there is greater involvement and commitment from team members
- the team is likely to be supportive of the leader
- the team is fully informed.

The disadvantages include:

- some team members may not be able to cope with being involved in decision-making
- the democratic process can take too long
- the leader may not agree with the decisions of the team
- powerful team members may take over.

Laissez-faire management

With laissez-faire management the team is left to sort itself out and get on with its work. The manager does not get involved and therefore is not leading the team.

The advantages include:

- highly motivated and skilled people are able to get on with their tasks
- the team is empowered.

The disadvantages include:

- new team members will be uninformed
- the team may be left with little or no direction.

Teamwork

Teamwork skills are essential in the workplace. You must be able to work with other people in a team even if you don't happen to like them.

A team is a group of people who are working together to achieve common objectives. Even when you are not physically with other members of your team, you can work together by contributing to a sequence of activities with a common aim. If you were working as a resort representative in Spain, you would still be working in a team with colleagues in head office in the UK. In this part of the unit we will consider the factors that contribute to effective teamwork.

Team roles

Good teams achieve synergy; that is, together they can achieve more than the members could individually. More ideas, energy and resources are generated as a group because:

- the team solves problems and makes decisions together
- the team focuses on priorities, with everyone working towards the same aim
- the team provides a sense of belonging and a sense of status
- the team provides a support network.

Not everyone in a team is the same – each person has their own strengths and weaknesses. If each person had the same weaknesses, the team could not work; there needs to be a balance of skills. A method of recognising individuals' strengths and weaknesses is needed in order to build an effective team.

The management expert R. Meredith Belbin has outlined nine team roles necessary for a successful team. One person can represent more than one role, as most people have strengths in more than one area.

Belbin's roles:

1 **Chairperson/co-ordinator** – the group leader, likely to be relaxed and extrovert, also likely to be a good communicator. They will build on the strengths of team members and give them encouragement.

2 **Plant** – the ideas person in the team, a person who is creative in looking for solutions to problems, but not always good at details, and so may make careless mistakes.

3 **Shaper** – the task leader, who unites ideas and effort. Needs to be dominant and extrovert in order to make things happen.

4 **Monitor/evaluator** – the team analyst, who is not so good at ideas but pays attention to detail, thus keeping the team directed towards its target.

5 **Implementer** – the organiser of the team, who is able to take the ideas of the plant and shaper and turn them into manageable and realistic tasks. A practical, stable and disciplined person.

6 **Resource investigator** – the person who is outgoing and will explore and report on ideas and developments outside the group; this person always has a solution to problems, is sociable and enthusiastic, and good under pressure.

7 **Team worker** – a very people-oriented person, sensitive to others' needs. The team worker has good communication skills and will be good at motivating others. A natural mediator, who will deal with any conflict within the team, this person is very good to have around in a crisis.

8 **Finisher** – a person who sticks to deadlines and likes to get on with things. Will probably be irritated by the more relaxed members of the team.

9 **Specialist** – this person is single-minded and a self-starter, and provides knowledge and skills in specialist areas.

Each of Belbin's roles acquires a different level of importance according to the objectives of the team and the stage in the team's life.

Theory into practice

Which of Belbin's roles do you think you fit? Visit the website www.belbin.com to find out more about Belbin roles. You will find a self-perception questionnaire that is used to analyse roles. You are able to complete it, but the analysis itself has to be paid for.

Team development

Formal teams are part of the structure of an organisation and are planned in order to meet that organisation's objectives. The formal team will follow rules and regulations and may meet on a pre-arranged schedule and complete administrative procedures. Examples in travel and tourism include sales teams and marketing teams.

Informal teams work within or outside formal teams. They are sometimes based on personal relationships between members rather than on work roles. When you complete group work for assignments, you often choose the colleagues you wish to work with. You choose to work with people you like and ones you know will be as committed as you are to the work. This is an informal team.

There are several theories of team structure and development, which will help you to understand the effectiveness of teams. Bruce Tuckman (1965) identified four main stages of team development:

1 **Forming** – at this stage, team members form their first impressions of each other and establish identities. They are sounding each other out and finding out what is expected of them.

2 **Storming** – the team members have, by now, become more used to each other. Members are prepared to put forward their ideas forcibly and openly; they are also prepared to disagree and so there may be some conflict and hostility.

3   **Norming** – the team now begins to establish co-operation. Conflict is controlled, views are exchanged and new standards introduced.

4   **Performing** – the team is now working together; it begins to arrive at solutions and achieve objectives.

There can also be a fifth stage, called 'adjourning' or 'mourning', where the team has disbanded and the members miss being part of the team.

Job roles and lines of responsibility

An organisation chart shows the structure of the company and how the work is divided into different areas. It also shows the lines of responsibility between staff, so that it is apparent who is responsible to whom. An employee studying a chart will find the possible promotion routes.

The chart may show a hierarchical structure or line relationship. This is a very traditional structure and shows a chain of command with each person responsible to the person above them. It is sometimes referred to as a pyramid structure.

Many organisations today would be depicted in a chart with a flatter structure. There are fewer layers of management, and each manager has a broader span of control. Restructuring of organisations often involves getting rid of middle managers, hence the flattened structure.

▲ **Figure 6.15 Pyramid structure**

Channels of communication

Open communication must be encouraged and ideas should be freely expressed in the workplace. There should be trust and support between team members. An effective leader can encourage good communication and shape the way the team works.

Verbal

Verbal communication can be as informal and as simple as members of staff discussing a problem with each other, or a manager giving information or instructions. Staff enjoy socialising at break times and will discuss their work. This is the most common way of communicating within an organisation.

Verbal communication can take place more formally at meetings. Meetings may be scheduled or ad hoc, that is, held as they become necessary. In one low-cost airline the management team meets for the first hour of each day to discuss developments and determine strategy.

Meetings are more formal than conversations. In a business meeting there is usually an agenda, or list of items to be discussed, and minutes are taken to record what has been agreed. In a more informal meeting there may not be an agenda and minutes, but there is the risk that decisions will not be actioned in these circumstances.

The telephone is also a means of verbal communication within an organisation. It is easy for staff members to call each other and internal networks can be set up even where staff are in different locations.

In international operations it is cheaper to set up a telephone conference than for personnel to travel for a meeting. However, as you cannot see body language during a telephone conference some nuances of conversation may be missed. To solve this problem, video-conferencing became very popular in the 1990s, but it is less so now. It works via interactive two-way video.

Consider this

What do you think are the advantages of travelling to meet someone face-to-face rather than talking by telephone or by video-conference?

Written

Written communications within an organisation include minutes of meetings. These record decisions made and who is to action them, and they are distributed to all relevant staff.

Notice boards are also used to give staff news items about company developments or forthcoming events. The notice board is a one-way communication system and therefore can be a cause of conflict if it is used to inform staff of unpopular decisions, as staff cannot easily communicate their concerns.

Memos have become far less common as a means of written communication with the advent of e-mail, but they are still used in some organisations. A memo is a brief informal document which is used to pass on information within a company.

Letters are rarely used as a form of internal communication except in formal situations involving warnings, redundancy or dismissal. Of course, they may also bring news of pay rises or promotion.

Large companies often have an in-house magazine or newsletter. This helps staff in different locations to be aware of company developments, and can also serve as a morale booster as it reports on successes within teams.

Here are some examples of how the Co-op Travel Group and Thomas Cook keep in touch within their organisations.

Travelcare
part of the Co-operative Group

UNITED CO-OP hosts a staff forum called Reform Councils. It is open to more than 900 members of staff within the retail division, plus the Apollo and Barrow Travel call centres.

Forty-nine trained staff are responsible for gathering information and feedback for the regular council meetings, which occur about four times a year. Topics can range from pay and conditions to uniforms and sales development.

'Training takes time and commitment but it is well worthwhile – everyone knows what is expected of them. The feedback has been excellent,' says Jane Webb, group human resources manager.

The council representatives are of all ages and experience, and include branch managers, travel advisers, foreign exchange staff and apprentices. Some are also members of the shop workers' union, and there are even shop stewards and full-time union officials on the councils.

'The union people can really help us because they have ideas from other companies,' says Webb.

'We have a good relationship and have the same objectives. It also benefits them as they understand the company's issues and financial performance, so are more realistic.'

Thomas Cook

THOMAS COOK has an intranet 'Get in Touch' facility, to which all staff have access. There is also a dedicated e-mail address for staff to send feedback direct to UK chief executive Manny Fontenla-Novoa. A spokeswoman added: 'We issue an annual staff questionnaire to gain a temperature check on morale and motivation within the company.'

Cook also runs panel sessions – made up of a cross-section of the business – which are held regularly to provide feedback on new ideas and marketing initiatives. Other internal forms of communication include a quarterly magazine and monthly videos for stores.

(Source: *Travel Trade Gazette*, 30 July 2004)

Electronic

Electronic communications for internal use include e-mail, which is a popular way for staff to communicate with one another, and intranets.

An intranet is a website that has restricted access, usually for employees only. It may hold information that a company wishes to share internally but not externally.

Equal opportunities and legislative requirements

Legislation exists to ensure that personnel receive equal opportunities and that there is no discrimination. The acts of parliament that you should be aware of are explained below.

Race Relations Act 1976

This Act makes discrimination on racial grounds unlawful in employment, training, education and the provision of goods, facilities and services. The Act defines two main types of discrimination:

- direct discrimination, which occurs when someone is treated less favourably because of their colour, nationality, citizenship or national origin
- indirect discrimination, which occurs when rules which apply to everyone and appear to be fair, put a particular racial group at a disadvantage in practice.

Sex Discrimination Act 1975

This Act makes it unlawful to discriminate against someone on the grounds of gender, marital status, gender reassignment or sexual orientation.

The Act was updated in 1986 to remove restrictions on women's hours of work – it allows women to take jobs with flexible hours. The Act not only covers discrimination in the workplace but in job advertisements and interviews.

Disability Discrimination Act 1995

A person with a disability is anyone who has a physical or mental impairment which has a substantial or long-term adverse effect on their ability to carry on normal day-to-day activities.

This Act makes discrimination against people with disabilities unlawful in respect of employment, education and access to goods, facilities, services and premises.

Employers are required to make reasonable adjustments to accommodate people with disabilities. Examples include providing specially adapted keyboards for arthritis

Case study: employment rights

Alison is the manager of a retail travel agency. She went on maternity leave and had a baby, Marcus. When she went back to work, she realised that she didn't want to work full time any more; she wanted to work part time and have some time with her baby son. Her employer said she could not work part time and had to work full time or not at all.

Alison was going to resign, but got in touch with her union, the Transport Salaried Staffs' Association (TSSA) and explained the situation. An employment rights adviser discussed with her the idea of finding a job-share partner, instead of resigning without trying to find a solution. Alison did manage to find someone who wanted to job share, and the TSSA helped them put together a proposal which was accepted by the employer.

1 **Find out what the TSSA is and what it does.**

2 **Was there discrimination in this case, and if so, why?**

sufferers, facilitating wheelchair access and relocating people with limited mobility to the ground floor.

Equal Pay Act 1970

This Act was introduced to address the problem of women being paid less than men for the same work. It allows employees to claim equal pay for work of equal value in terms of demands made on them, such as effort, skills and decisions made. There is also an EU Directive that states that for the same work or work of equal value, sex discrimination must be eliminated in all aspects of pay.

Age discrimination

Legislation prohibiting discrimination on the grounds of age was introduced in the UK in 2006. This is in line with a European Employment Directive. This Directive also added sexual orientation and religion to the cases covered by discrimination laws, and these are already in place. The legislation on age discrimination was delayed until 2006 to give the government time to resolve the complex problems associated with its introduction and to allow employers sufficient time to prepare for the changes.

Travel agencies have already increased the number of older staff working in agencies. A Co-op Travel Group manager was quoted as saying 'Mature staff make our customers more comfortable when booking – they are booking with their peers, as most of our customers are 35 plus'. Thomas Cook has been recognised by the government's Age Positive campaign as an 'employer champion' based on its recruitment of older staff for its shops.

Other forms of discrimination

Discrimination at work is a very serious issue and can result in large amounts of compensation being awarded following successful tribunals, not to mention a lot of bad publicity. Employers need to set up policies to ensure that the workplace is free from discrimination.

Measures to be taken include:

- setting up a comprehensive equal opportunities policy covering all aspects of discrimination
- training staff in discrimination legislation and on how to implement the equal opportunities policy
- setting up complaints procedures for instances of discrimination

- ensuring that discriminatory behaviour is never condoned and that action is taken where necessary.

However, discrimination may sometimes be reasonable and is therefore lawful. For example, at airports female security officers are required to search female passengers.

Theory into practice

Find out about the equal opportunities policy at your place of work or education. Is provision made for all aspects of discrimination? What happens if someone feels they are being discriminated against? What training is given to staff or students in equal opportunities? Make notes on your findings and discuss them with your group.

Employment Rights Act 1996

When you get a job you can expect to receive a contract of employment. This is a legally binding agreement between the employer and the employee. Under the Employment Rights Act, the employer must give the employee a written

Case study: equal opportunities awareness quiz

A holidaymaker, lying on a sunbed, looks up and shouts 'Hey, gorgeous' to a passing lifeguard. The same lifeguard casually mentions this to a senior manager. The manager says 'I'd never do that'. The manager has two grown-up children who are 22 and 30. They get on very well. One is a sergeant in the army, the other is a make-up artist. The manager divorced last year and is currently dating someone.

Complete the table and discuss your results in a group. Are you aware of any stereotyping?

Statements	True	False	Don't know
The holiday maker was lying on a sunbed			
Not every man mentioned would shout 'Hey, gorgeous' to a lifeguard			
The manager is no longer living with his wife			
The manager has a new girlfriend			
The manager's son is in the army			
The younger child is a make-up artist			
At some point a man spoke to a woman			
A woman was shouted at			

document including the following information, in writing, within 2 months of starting work:

- name of employer and employee
- date employment began
- rate of pay and interval of pay
- hours of work
- holiday entitlement and pay
- job title and brief description of duties
- place of work
- notice entitlement and requirements
- sick leave entitlement and sick pay
- pension and pension schemes
- disciplinary procedures and grievance procedures
- date of end of employment if fixed term
- additional details about working abroad if appropriate.

Some terms are 'implied' in a contract of employment, which means they may not be mentioned but they are still legally binding. For example, the employer has a duty to provide safe systems of work, a safe workplace and to employ competent staff who are not a danger to themselves or other staff.

Notice periods

After one month of continuous employment an employee is entitled to one week of notice if the employment ends. After 2 years' employment they are entitled to 2 weeks' notice, after 3 years, 3 weeks' notice and so on. After 12 years the legal maximum of 12 weeks' notice is reached.

A employee must also give notice of leaving to an employer. After one month of continuous employment, an employee must give a minimum of one week's notice.

Employees are entitled to normal pay during notice periods as long as they are working or available for work.

Disciplinary and grievance procedures

These must be included in the employee's written statement or contract, or at least there must be a reference to where they can be found.

Disciplinary procedures deal with such matters as warnings to be given before dismissal. Warnings might arise from the following:

- lack of capability or qualifications – although the employer has a responsibility to give training
- misconduct – which includes habitual lateness
- gross misconduct (for example, assault or theft) leads to instant or summary dismissal.

Grievance procedures deal with complaints by employees who are not satisfied with aspects of their employment. Employees must be given the name of a person to whom a complaint can be made and should be informed of rights of appeal.

Redundancy

Redundancy pay is calculated according to the employee's age, length of service and salary. Employees can claim for unfair dismissal if they suspect:

- there is no real redundancy
- they were unfairly selected for redundancy.

Dismissal is treated as redundancy if the whole business is closing or a particular job disappears or requires fewer employees. An employer may offer alternative employment. If the employee unreasonably refuses it, they are not entitled to redundancy pay.

EU Directives on hours and pay

The European Working Time Directive was enacted in the UK through the Working Time Regulations 1998. This lays down the following:

- a maximum 48-hour week, averaged over 17 weeks
- at least 4 weeks' paid annual leave
- a weekly rest period of at least 24 hours in each 7-day period
- a daily rest period of at least 11 consecutive hours between each working day
- an in-work rest break of 20 minutes for those working 6 hours or more per day.

Some sectors are excluded from the regulations; one of these is transport.

National Minimum Wage Act 1998

This Act provides workers with a minimum hourly rate below which their wages will not fall. Those who work part time benefit most, because they are often badly paid. The Low Pay Commission advises the Secretary of State on the value of the minimum hourly rate. A special lower rate applies to 18- to 21-year-olds.

Maternity and paternity leave

The Employment Relations Act 1999 provides for basic rights for maternity leave. There are three periods of maternity leave. *Ordinary maternity leave* is for a period of 18 weeks which coincides with the period for statutory maternity pay. This applies to all employees. *Compulsory maternity leave* extends to a period of 2 weeks after the birth; the employer must not permit the woman to return to work during this period. *Additional maternity leave* follows immediately after the original 18-week period and must end within 29 weeks of the birth. Employees with at least one year's service with an employer are eligible for the additional maternity leave.

Under the same Act there are provisions to allow parents 3 months' leave in order to care for a child. This is intended to be taken before the child is five. It is intended to be available to men and to women, in addition to maternity leave.

Paternity leave is available to men who:

- have or expect to have responsibility for the child's upbringing
- are the biological father of the child, or the mother's husband or partner
- have worked continuously for their employer for 26 weeks ending with the fifteenth week before the baby is due.

Eligible employees can choose to take either 1 week or 2 consecutive weeks' paternity leave (not odd days).

Statutory Sickness Pay

An employer must pay Statutory Sick Pay to employees who become sick and who normally earn at least £79 per week. After 28 weeks, Incapacity Benefit or Income Support must be claimed instead.

Theory into practice

Find out how employment rights are implemented at your place of work. There should be a staff handbook with details of grievance and disciplinary procedures. You should have a contract of employment.

If you do not have a job ask a relative or friend if you can look at the information received from their place of work. Remember that issues such as pay are confidential. Make detailed notes on the procedures and systems in place. Comment on how they contribute to a more effective workplace.

Investors in People

Investors in People is a UK quality standard developed in 1990. Those companies who gain the award have proved that they invest in the training and development of their staff. This is beneficial to employees and also to customers and suppliers.

The standard for Investors in People is based on four key principles:

1 Commitment from the top to develop all employees
2 Regular review of training and development needs
3 Taking relevant action to meet those needs throughout people's careers
4 Evaluating training and development outcomes for individuals and the organisation in order to continuously improve.

These principles are subdivided into 24 indicators of effective practice, and the organisation provides evidence for assessment against the indicators.

Once the organisation gets the award it is entitled to display the Investors in People logo on company literature.

Theory into practice

What do you think are the benefits to an organisation of gaining the Investors in People Award? Make notes on your ideas. Research a travel and tourism organisation which has been given the award and try to analyse what effect this has had on the organisation.

Mentoring

Mentoring schemes are growing in popularity. They offer employees a one-to-one relationship with a mentor, someone with greater experience and a willingness to listen and advise. The mentor and the mentee meet regularly and discuss aspects of the mentee's job, such as career development.

The mentor does not act as a line manager or superior and is never judgemental, but acts as a sounding board and is able to offer ideas and a different outlook on work issues.

The Hilton hotel chain runs a mentoring scheme for its staff at all levels. Its purpose is to support staff in their career development. Mentors at the Hilton chain are often colleagues of the mentees doing similar jobs, which departs from the traditional model. All of the mentors have had mentoring training. Some companies have similar, but sometimes less formal, schemes where a new member of staff is given a 'buddy' as a source of information and help.

Job security

Many contracts today are fixed term, especially in areas such as visitor attractions. This means that the period of employment is not indefinite but lasts for a period of months or a year or two. The reason for such contracts is flexibility for employers – they can lose staff on fixed contracts at the end of the period without penalty. However, such contracts are demotivating for staff as they worry about their future income and job prospects.

Incentives

Incentives can be used to motivate staff. Here are some examples:

Remuneration

Remuneration means how much you get paid. You would imagine that this is very important as a motivator. In fact, it is an important factor in attracting people to a company but research shows that it is not the most important incentive.

Incentive schemes

An example of an incentive scheme could be a competition that staff are invited to enter. The competitions may be based on generating new ideas within the company, or how to boost sales, customer satisfaction or commissions on sales.

Bonuses

Bonuses are often based on overall profits and awarded to all employees – usually performance related.

Discounts

Discounts may be given on holidays or travel for those working in the industry. Many who work in travel and tourism receive cheap travel, perhaps by going on standby if they work for an airline or by going on factfinding trips to a destination if they work for a travel agent.

Holiday entitlement

In the UK employees can expect around 4 weeks' paid holiday per year. In the public sector more holiday is often given, but this may be balanced against lower pay.

Pension schemes

You are probably too young to be worrying about your pension but a good pension scheme can act as an incentive for many people who are concerned about security in retirement.

Perks

As a perk, employees in the travel and tourism industry are often provided with a uniform. They may get to travel or live abroad and be paid to live there. They may be provided with a company car.

Opportunities for promotion and progression

Many employees need a challenge and if they are in the same position, doing a job they find easy, they may become bored and less efficient. Thus, opportunities to move on and face new challenges are an important incentive. Opportunities may arise within an organisation and good people are quickly promoted. You may wish to let it be known that you are interested in progression and ask to be sent on relevant training courses and conferences.

Training

Those employers who wish to ensure an effective workplace will offer ongoing training and development to staff. There are several benefits to organisations and to their workforces. Training can:

- improve individual performance
- improve team performance
- allow staff to be better informed
- equip staff to deal with change and emergencies
- make for a more flexible workforce
- improve morale
- allow managers more time to manage through delegation of other tasks.

Induction training

Employers have to provide instruction and training to ensure health and safety, and this is usually a part of induction training. The induction is the first stage of training and is given to new employees; it is important as new employees need to be made welcome and become effective in their work as quickly as possible.

Induction covers:

- the nature of the job
- introduction to the workplace and to staff
- the lines of responsibility
- facilities such as toilets, lockers, canteen
- health and safety basics.

Training opportunities

In-house training

Large companies offer their own in-house training and may even write their own materials. These training courses are very beneficial as they are tailor-made to meet the needs of the company.

External courses

Thousands of external courses are available. These may be specific to travel and tourism or other professional qualifications in areas such as marketing or human resource management. They may be offered by colleges, by travel associations or by private companies.

Companies may allow individuals or groups to attend such courses. Some may be long term, leading to advanced qualifications, so a great deal of commitment is required on behalf of the individual. .

Theory into practice

Consider the advantages and disadvantages of in-house training and external training. Draw up a comparative table showing your analysis. Discuss your findings with your group.

Appraisal

A good appraisal scheme can be a motivating factor for employees if they feel involved in the process and are given constructive feedback. Canvas Holidays has a typical appraisal system, described in Figure 6.16.

Canvas Holidays appraisal

i) Pre-interview preparation

Your Area Manager will provide you with your pre-appraisal interview questionnaire and a date and time for your interview 7–10 days in advance. Using the questionnaire you can then prepare for your interview. You do not have to use this form and you do not need to submit it to your Area Manager before the interview: it is entirely for your own benefit.

ii) The appraisal interview

This is the time to discuss and agree on your overall performance, taking into account every aspect of the job and to review performance assessments that have been completed during the season.

iii) The performance appraisal form

The discussion during your interview is recorded on this form and your performance to date is evaluated under the headlines provided. Future job/career aspirations, including future work with Canvas Holidays, should also be discussed at this point.

Once the appraisal has been completed, both parties should sign the appraisal form.

- One copy will be returned to Head Office for your personnel file.

- You will retain one copy.

- Your Area Manager will hold one copy.

▲ **Figure 6.16 Appraisal system**

(Source: Canvas Holidays)

Case study: PGL Travel management systems

PGL Travel provides activity holidays for groups and schools. Established for 50 years, PGL has developed comprehensive, externally verified safety management systems.

This starts with the recruitment procedure. Recruitment officers make an initial selection of applicants based on a detailed four-page application form. Formal written references are obtained from two people who know the applicant in a professional capacity. Qualifications claimed by applicants must be supported by documentary proof in order to be taken into account. Successful candidates are offered contracts of employment subject to vigorous internal vetting and then via the Criminal Records Bureau. They must then successfully complete a probationary period.

All new staff follow a formal induction procedure. Upon successful completion of the induction programme, staff gain a nationally recognised Open College Network qualification. PGL is an approved centre for Edexcel, BTEC and City and Guilds, offering courses such as Modern Apprenticeships at foundation and advanced level. There is a permanent team of qualified staff responsible for delivering in-house training and assessment as well as setting up external courses. Reviews of staff performance take place throughout the period of employment.

(Source: http://www.pgl.co.uk)

Visit www.pgl.co.uk for further information. Look particularly at the section headed 'Company information'.

1 **Describe the factors at PGL that contribute to an effective workplace. Consider:**
   - **the working environment**
   - **working relationships**
   - **incentives**
   - **training.** **P5**

2 **Explain how the factors described motivate staff.** **M3**

Taking it further

Analyse the factors that contribute to an effective workplace.

Give examples of good practice at PGL. Compare them with examples from another travel and tourism organisation.

Grading tip

When you analyse, do not just describe each factor – say why it works. For example, PGL has centres on beach locations in the south of France. Most jobs are available in the summer season so the working conditions are good in terms of weather and environment. Teamwork is important to ensure that health and safety is prioritised for the young customers who are doing water sports. These factors help contribute to an effective workplace because:

- the environment attracts fit and qualifed instructors who want to work outside and respect others with the same attitude to working and playing hard
- close teams are built up not just through working together but through living and socialising together
- people who are there for a second or third season will be given increased responsibility.

Knowledge check

1 What different aspects of travel agency work are available?

2 What does the job role of a resort representative include?

3 Describe the range of jobs in an airport.

4 What kinds of courses can follow a BTEC programme?

5 How would you build up your knowledge of destinations if you worked in a travel agency?

6 What is a Modern Apprenticeship programme?

7 What information would be included in a job description?

8 What is the purpose of a person specification?

9 Summarise Maslow's hierarchy of needs.

10 What should your CV include?

11 Give five tips for writing a CV.

12 Why is good teamwork important?

13 What are Tuckman's stages of team development?

14 Give some examples of methods of motivating staff in the workplace.

15 What is the principle of the 1975 Sex Discrimination Act?

16 What differences will the legislation on age discrimination make to the travel and tourism industry?

17 What legislation covers hours and pay?

18 What is induction training?

Preparation for assessment

This assessment is designed to provide you with a portfolio of work which will help you in the future when you are looking for a job or looking for a change of job or promotion.

You will consider a range of different jobs in the travel and tourism industry and select two of interest for comparison. You will analyse your own skills and attributes and prepare to participate in the recruitment and selection process. You will also consider the factors that contribute to an effective workplace and think about how you can use your own skills to make the workplace more effective.

1 About the jobs

- Describe a range of career opportunities in the travel and tourism industry. Use the information in this unit and your own independent research to find relevant information. You must describe opportunities from a range of at least four different sectors and describe at least six different roles. **P1**

- Choose two job roles in travel and tourism which are of interest to you. Describe each of these roles in detail. You should include: responsibilities; work pattern (for example, seasonal, permanent, full time, shifts); pay and conditions; qualifications required; skills required; personal attributes required; entry levels, for example school leaver/BTEC National/A level/graduate; progression. This information could be presented in a table with detailed notes. **P1**

- Compare two jobs in travel and tourism taking into account the entry levels and opportunities for promotion and progression. **M1**

2 About the workplace

- Describe the stages of the recruitment and selection process in travel and tourism. **P3**

- Produce guidelines for success in the different stages of the recruitment and selection process. **M2**

- Describe the factors that contribute to an effective workplace in travel and tourism organisations. **P5**

- Explain how different travel and tourism organisations motivate staff in the workplace. **M3**

- Analyse the factors that contribute to an effective workplace, with examples of good practice from different travel and tourism organisations. **D2**

Grading tip

When thinking about factors contributing to an effective workplace, discuss the relative importance of each factor and give examples of how organisations counter factors which can be negative, such as working split shifts in a restaurant.

3   About you
- Undertake an audit of your personal skills and attributes in preparation for employment.   **P2**
- Evaluate your suitability for a chosen job and prepare a detailed action plan which shows how your training and development needs could be met.   **M2** **D1** **d**

Grading tip

The difference between reaching a Merit or a Distinction level depends on an ability to identify the gaps in your skills and knowledge – that is, training and development needs (Merit) and preparing a detailed action plan to say how you will meet those needs (Distinction).

- Adapt your CV and prepare a letter of application for one of the jobs in this unit.   **P**₄
- Prepare for an interview for the job. Your interview preparation should cover: company background; prepared responses to questions you could be asked; questions you want to ask about the job.   **P**₄
- Present all your information in a portfolio for submission.

Research tip

Use a variety of sources to find information on jobs in travel and tourism. These might include websites, newspapers and trade magazines. If you are interested in a specific area, for example working in an airport, look at the relevant websites.

Grading criteria

To achieve a pass grade the evidence must show that the learner is able to:	To achieve a merit grade the evidence must show that, in addition to the pass criteria, the learner is able to:	To achieve a distinction grade the evidence must show that, in addition to the pass and merit criteria, the learner is able to:
P1 describe career opportunities in the travel and tourism industry and produce a description of two chosen jobs **Case study page 193**	M1 compare two jobs in the travel and tourism industry taking into account the entry levels and opportunities for promotion and progression **Case study page 193**	D1 evaluate own suitability for a chosen job and prepare an action plan to meet all training and development needs **Assessment practice page 194**
P2 produce a personal skills audit in preparation for employment **Assessment practice page 194**	M2 produce guidelines for success in the different stages of the recruitment and selection progress and use these to evaluate personal performance **Assessment practice page 213**	D2 analyse the factors that contribute to an effective workplace, highlighting good practice from different travel and tourism organisations **Case study page 234**
P3 describe the stages of the recruitment and selection progress **Assessment practice page 213**	M3 explain how different travel and tourism organisations motivate staff in the workplace **Case study page 234**	
P4 demonstrate suitability for employment during different stages of the job selection process **Assessment practice page 213**		
P5 describe the factors that contribute to an effective workplace in travel and tourism organisations **Case study page 234**		

The European travel market

Introduction

This unit will provide you with the opportunity to study the European travel market. Many sectors of travel and tourism require a sound knowledge of tourism in Europe in terms of key destinations and which markets are expanding or declining.

You will locate different countries, gateways and key destinations within Europe. You will find out what factors contribute to the appeal of destinations and appreciate the diversity of tourism products on offer in Europe.

You will find out the types of leisure experience that can be enjoyed in key destinations and what is provided for different types of customers.

Developing and declining destinations will be studied along with the factors that affect development.

After completing this unit you should be able to achieve the following outcomes:

1 Know the key factors of the European travel market

2 Understand the factors determining the appeal of leisure destinations in the European travel market

3 Be able to segment the European travel market by leisure experience

4 Understand the factors affecting the development of the European travel market.

Thinking points

According to figures from the Office of National Statistics, UK residents made 64 million overseas visits in 2004 compared with 18 million in 1980. Although long haul travel is growing, most of the journeys made are to and from countries within Europe. Spain is the most popular destination for UK outbound tourists, with 20 per cent of all journeys, followed by France, the Irish Republic, Germany and Italy. Eastern European destinations are growing in popularity as air routes give easier access from the UK. In 2004, 79 per cent of UK residents' trips abroad were by air, 14 per cent by sea and 7 per cent by the Channel Tunnel.

Where do you think most UK residents travel to?

How do they get there?

What do they do when they are there?

A survey by the European Tour Operators Association investigating the appeal of Europe to tourists found that the criteria that most influenced their decision to visit were scenery, culture and history.

Theory into practice

Take some time to think about any destinations you have already visited in Europe. How easy was it to get there? How did you travel within the destinations? What was it you liked about the places? Was it the scenery or the culture and history? Perhaps it was the nightlife and beaches? How do different destinations appeal to you in different ways?

If you haven't travelled in Europe yet, make a wish list of places you would like to visit and why.

To know the European travel market you need to be able to locate countries, gateways and key leisure destinations within Europe. In this part of the unit we will begin to identify these key locations and you will become familiar with terminology used in defining areas of Europe.

Countries

The map opposite shows all the countries of Europe.

Some of the countries of Europe belong to the European Union (EU). The EU is a partnership between countries who have formed a common market by eliminating trade barriers. It has its own parliament and council of ministers representing the member countries. Over the years membership has gradually grown and there are currently 25 member states. The euro, the EU's currency, was launched in world money markets on 1 January 1999; it was adopted by 11 EU states and began use in 2002. Greece and Slovenia have since adopted the euro.

Key term

European Union (EU) – the European Union is a partnership in which countries work closely together for the benefit of all their citizens. They work together on issues of common interest, where it is considered that collective action is more effective than individual state action.

Countries that have joined the EU are:

Austria	Greece	Poland
Belgium	Hungary	Portugal
Cyprus	Ireland	Slovakia
Czech Republic	Italy	Slovenia
Denmark	Latvia	Spain
Estonia	Lithuania	Sweden
Finland	Luxembourg	United Kingdom
France	Malta	
Germany	Netherlands	

On 1 January 2007, Romania and Bulgaria joined the EU, bringing the total number of members to 27.

Some of these EU countries are part of the Eurozone, which means they have adopted the euro as their currency. In addition, some countries are known as Schengen countries. A total of 15 countries have entered into the Schengen agreement: Austria, Belgium, Denmark, Finland, France, Germany, Greece, Iceland, Italy, Luxembourg, Netherlands, Norway, Portugal, Spain and Sweden. Note that Norway and Iceland are members of the Schengen agreement but not members of the EU. Candidate countries are those countries who have expressed a wish to join the EU but have not yet been accepted.

Theory into practice

Find out the names of the capital cities of the EU countries. Locate them on the map shown in Figure 7.1.

P1

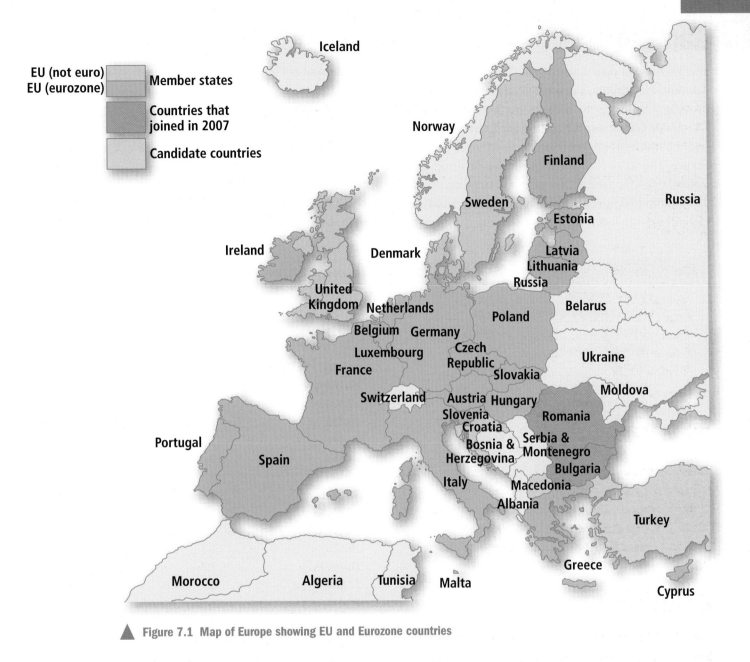

EU (not euro)
EU (eurozone)

Member states

Countries that joined in 2007

Candidate countries

Iceland

Norway

Finland

Sweden

Russia

Estonia

Latvia

Lithuania

Russia

Ireland

Denmark

Belarus

United Kingdom

Netherlands

Poland

Belgium

Germany

Luxembourg

Czech Republic

Ukraine

France

Slovakia

Moldova

Switzerland

Austria

Hungary

Slovenia

Romania

Croatia

Serbia & Montenegro

Portugal

Bosnia & Herzegovina

Bulgaria

Spain

Italy

Macedonia

Albania

Turkey

Greece

Morocco

Algeria

Tunisia

Malta

Cyprus

▲ Figure 7.1 Map of Europe showing EU and Eurozone countries

Key terms

Eurozone – the thirteen countries that have adopted the euro as their common currency.

Schengen – the name Schengen comes from a small town in Luxembourg. In 1985, seven countries decided to remove border controls and checkpoints between their countries. There are now fifteen Schengen countries. The removal of controls means that citizens can pass easily from one country to another to visit or even to work. This has an impact on tourism also as tourists can easily travel from one country to the next without being stopped or having to show documents and answer questions about their movements.

Gateways

You know from your study of UK destinations that a gateway is an airport, a seaport or destination which provides easy access to other destinations. For example, Charles de Gaulle airport in Paris is a gateway to Paris and the transport systems from Paris to other parts of France. The services through the Channel Tunnel, that is Eurostar and the Shuttle, are gateways between the UK and continental Europe. The Eurostar is the passenger rail service which currently has terminals at Waterloo, London and Ashford, Kent. The Shuttle service takes cars by train through the tunnel and is accessed at the terminal at Folkestone.

You need to be able to locate key gateways throughout Europe.

Airports

Europe's 30 largest airports are listed in Table 7.1 with passenger numbers for 2005. Note that London's Heathrow is in first position and London Gatwick is in

Rank	Airport	Country	Passengers ('000s)	Percentage change 2004/5
1	London Heathrow	UK	67,915	0.8
2	Paris Charles de Gaulle	France	53,756	4.9
3	Frankfurt	Germany	52,219	2.2
4	Amsterdam Schiphol	Netherlands	44,163	3.8
5	Madrid	Spain	41,940	8.4
6	London Gatwick	UK	32,784	4.2
7	Rome Fiumicino	Italy	28,620	2.0
8	Munich	Germany	28,619	6.7
9	Barcelona	Spain	27,121	10.5
10	Paris Orly	France	24,857	3.3
11	Manchester	UK	22,730	5.5
12	London Stansted	UK	22,018	5.3
13	Palma de Mallorca	Spain	21,237	4.0
14	Copenhagen	Denmark	19,751	5.0
15	Milan Malpensa	Italy	19,619	5.7
16	Dublin	Ireland	18,450	7.7
17	Zurich	Switzerland	17,850	3.7
18	Stockholm Arlanda	Sweden	17,241	5.4
19	Brussels	Belgium	16,121	3.4
20	Oslo	Norway	15,896	6.9
21	Vienna	Austria	15,859	7.3
22	Düsseldorf	Germany	15,511	1.7
23	Athens	Greece	14,272	4.6
24	Moscow Domodedovo	Russia	13,975	15.6
25	Malaga	Spain	12,649	5.2
26	Berlin Tegel	Germany	11,533	4.4
27	Lisbon	Portugal	11,235	4.0
28	Helsinki	Finland	11,062	3.1
29	Prague	Czech Republic	10,777	11.1
30	Hamburg	Germany	10,676	7.9

Table 7.1 Top 30 ACI airports in Europe by total passenger throughput, 2005*

(Source: © Airports Council International (ACI))

*Total passengers enplaned and deplaned (passengers in transit counted once); data not available for Istanbul (ranked 17 in 2004) and Antalya (ranked 24 in 2004), but Moscow Sheremetyevo has dropped out of the top 30.

sixth place. Prague and Barcelona had large increases in traffic from 2004 due to the increased popularity of these city destinations.

Theory into practice

1 Locate all the airports in Table 7.1 on a map of Europe. Find out their three-letter International Air Transport Association (IATA) codes. An IATA code is assigned so that each airport has a unique code and there can be no confusion about which airport is which. For example, Manchester airport in the UK has the code MAN and Manchester airport in Boston, USA is MHP.

2 Find out which airports these codes refer to: AMS, MAD, TOJ, LBG, CDG, ORY, IBZ, PMI, LMZ. Make some comments about your findings. What kind of work do you think this knowledge is useful for? **P1**

Ports

Although we have many ports in the UK, some of them are trading ports for freight traffic rather than passengers. The ones of interest to tourists are those that give access to ferry services or to cruise ships (see Unit 3).

Leisure destinations

There is a huge variety of leisure desinations in Europe. You need to be able to locate seaside resorts, including winter sun, winter sports, countryside areas, cities and cruise areas. There are many to choose from but you can begin by investigating some tour operators' brochures to find out which destinations are popular with UK outbound tourists.

Summer sun brochures will have details of seaside resorts such as those in Spain, including Marbella, Benidorm and the Almerian coast. In Portugal, the Algarve is a popular coastal area. Turkish beach resorts and Greek islands will be featured too.

Specialist winter sports brochures have maps and details of main resorts such as the French Alps, including Meribel and Courchevel. Kitzbuhel and Mayrhofen are popular in Austria; in Italy, Claviere and La Thuile. Remember that in summer, these are promoted as destinations suitable for walking and enjoying the countryside.

Look at city break brochures to find details of city locations. These are usually capital cities easily accessible by air or train. Cruise areas are usually in the Mediterranean or Scandanavia.

Theory into practice

For each European country identify at least three key destinations and state whether they are seaside resorts, winter sports resorts, countryside areas, cities or cruise areas. Locate the destinations on a map of Europe, using a colour key to identify different destination types. **P1**

We will look at factors which contribute to the appeal of a destination, including:

- accessibility
- geographical features
- attractions
- culture
- economic factors.

Accessibility

Most tourists do not want to travel too far from their country of origin for trips, for reasons of time, cost and convenience.

UK tourists most commonly take city breaks in Europe as they can easily access the destination for a weekend and still put in a full week's work.

Travellers will also take into consideration how much further they have to travel to the destination having arrived at the gateway airport or port.

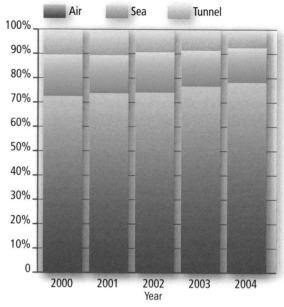

(Source: Travel Trends, 3 November 2004)

▲ Figure 7.2 Visits by mode of transport

Consider this

Skiers, in particular, have to consider carefully access to the resort when deciding how to travel. Even if they fly to a gateway airport such as Geneva or Lyon, they will still be faced with a lengthy drive or rail journey into the mountains.

Theory into practice

Hold a discussion with your colleagues about factors contributing to the trends described above. **P2**

Transport routes

Without effective transport routes, tourists cannot reach their destinations. Indeed, the transport available is usually a factor in choosing a destination. Figure 7.2 shows that the most popular mode of transport by far for UK outbound tourists is air, in fact trips by air increased by 22 per cent between 2000 and 2004. In contrast visits by sea and by the Channel Tunnel both fell, sea trips by 7.2 per cent in the same period and Channel Tunnel visits by an average of 4.6 per cent per year.

■ Road and rail

It is straightforward for tourists travelling between the UK and the rest of Europe to make their journey by road. The Channel ports, both sea and rail, give immediate access to motorway networks in France and the UK. From northern France there are excellent motorways connecting with the rest of Europe. These motorways are less congested than those in the UK, so make for less stressful driving. Major roads have been reclassified throughout Europe with 'E' numbers to clarify route planning for motorists.

Traditionally, campers heading for France and Spain travel by road, and the ferry costs are included in their camping package. Camping operators provide information about driving abroad and route maps. However, with many low-cost flights available, campers are more often choosing to fly to their destinations. The trend is for camping tour operators to provide fixed tents or mobile homes as camping equipment is too heavy for passengers to carry by air.

The main disadvantage of travelling by road is the length of the journeys, particularly in continental Europe where the speed of coaches is restricted below the normal speed limit. Eurolines is a well-known international scheduled service coach operator. A typical service is the trip from Birmingham to Paris at a cost of £49. However, the journey takes 11 hours.

The major Eurostar terminals are located in London Waterloo International, Paris Gare du Nord and Brussels Midi. Eurostar also has intermediate stations in Ashford and Lille. On 14 November 2007, following the opening of High-Speed 1, Eurostar trains will no longer depart from Waterloo International but will instead use the brand new London hub at St Pancras International. Shortly after this date a new station will also open at Ebbsfleet International in Kent. The opening of High-Speed 1 will allow Eurostar trains to travel at 186 mph all the way to the Continent, greatly reducing journey times.

Eurostar also offers passengers connecting tickets to over 100 other destinations in France, Germany and the Netherlands. This service makes travel by rail so much easier for UK-originating passengers, as they can book the whole trip through Eurostar and get all the information they need without contacting the rail networks in the countries they wish to travel to. Some of the destinations served by Eurostar and connecting Continental rail services are shown in Figure 7.3.

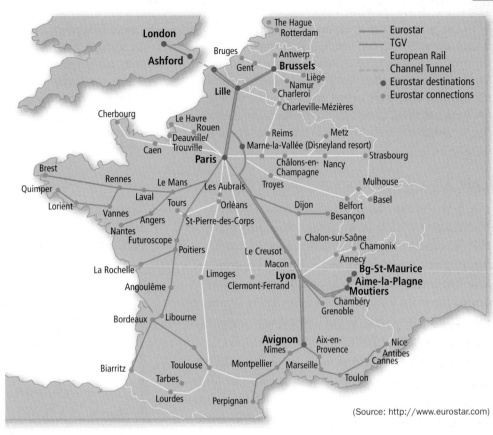

(Source: http://www.eurostar.com)

▲ Figure 7.3 Map showing Eurostar destinations and connecting rail routes

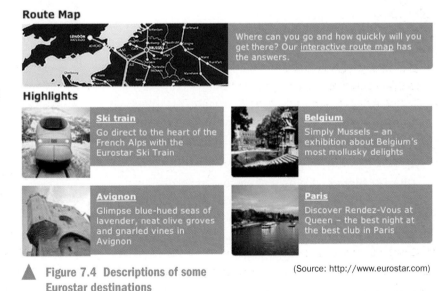

(Source: http://www.eurostar.com)

▲ Figure 7.4 Descriptions of some Eurostar destinations

Activity

When planning a journey to Paris the main considerations are cost, convenience and comfort. How long do you think it would take to drive to Paris from the UK? The train through the Channel Tunnel takes less than half an hour but you need to arrive half an hour before departure. From Calais to Paris takes about 2½ hours and then you need to add on the time it takes to drive from where you live to Folkestone. When you calculate costs remember to add petrol costs and motorway charges (in France) to the cost of crossing the Channel. Find out how much it would cost to go from where you live to Paris by coach. Draw up a chart comparing the two journeys in terms of convenience, cost and comfort. Say which one you would choose and why.

■ Air

As we have seen, air travel is the main form of long-distance travel and the most rapidly expanding transport sector. To cope with increased demand for air travel, many gateway airports have had to expand capacity. For London, Heathrow is building a fifth terminal, and Stansted has plans for a second runway. There are over 50 regional airports in the UK, but distances are not so great as to make air travel a preferred option within the UK.

There are two main categories of air travel: scheduled and charter. Tourists travelling on a package holiday are likely to be travelling on a charter plane, often owned by the tour operator they are travelling with. For example, Thomson is a tour operator and has a sister airline company called Thomsonfly. Charter airlines will sell seat-only deals to fill up their flights and achieve better load factors.

The extract from the easyJet information pack in the following case study gives an explanation of how a low-cost airline achieves its low fares.

Case study: the easyJet service

easyJet offers a simple, no-frills service at rock bottom fares. Fares can be offered at such good value due to the following main reasons:

easyJet IS A TICKETLESS AIRLINE… All you need to fly is your passport and your booking reference. This is less hassle for the customer, who doesn't have to worry about collecting tickets before travelling, and is cost-effective for easyJet.

EFFICIENT USE OF AIRPORTS… easyJet flies to main destination airports throughout Europe, but gains efficiencies through rapid turnaround times, and progressive landing charges agreements with the airports. By reducing turnarounds to 30 minutes and below, easyJet can achieve extra rotations on the high-frequency routes, thereby maximising utilisation rates of its aircraft.

THERE'S NO SUCH THING AS A FREE LUNCH… so easyJet doesn't offer one. Plastic trays of airline food only mean more expensive flights. easyJet passengers are given the choice as to whether they wish to buy themselves drinks or snacks from the in-flight easyKiosk. Our customer feedback illustrates that passengers do not want a meal on board a short haul flight. They prefer to pay less for the flight and have a choice to purchase snacks on board if desired.

(Source: http://www.easyjet.com)

1 Visit the Ryanair website and see if its explanation of low costs is the same.

2 Compare with easyJet and make notes.

3 Discuss your findings with your group.

Key terms

Scheduled flights – flights sold on a seat-only basis and run to a timetable, revised for winter and summer schedules.

Charter flights – flights that operate to holiday destinations and according to holiday demand. They do not operate every day to the same destination.

Hub-and-spoke airlines – offer connecting services between regions and major airports.

Point-to-point services – operate between paired cities or towns.

Low-cost airlines – these have developed over the past few years. They offer very few services, such as catering or allocated seats, but do offer low fares. The low fares are not available at peak times or to late bookers.

Assessment practice

The Kidman family is going to the Vendée in France for a camping holiday. They live in London. They went last year and drove to their campsite, having crossed the Channel using the Shuttle. They are considering flying or rail this year and want to know which route is the best option for them. The family consists of the parents, a ten-year-old boy and an eight-year-old girl. Cost is a consideration, but time and convenience are also important.

1 Draw up a table showing the different routes. (You may first need to locate the Vendée region.)

2 Describe the advantages and disadvantages of the different routes and draw some conclusions about how the features of the routes add to the appeal of the Vendée as a destination. **M1**

The airline industry is very competitive and many low-cost operators have entered the market throughout Europe. Some of the new airlines are operating from eastern Europe as the recent entry into the EU of several eastern European countries has encouraged travel to and from this area. Passengers are not always aware whether they are travelling on a scheduled service, low-cost scheduled service or charter flight, as the distinctions between the different airlines become less obvious.

■ Sea

Ferry services across the English Channel are surviving despite the building of the Channel Tunnel. P&O operates a service from Dover to Calais, as does Sea France.

The journey takes about an hour and a quarter by boat but the loading and unloading of cars adds another hour. However, some people enjoy the crossing and do not mind the extra time.

The UK is linked by ferry to its neighbours in Ireland and also to Holland and Scandinavia. Because of competition from air travel and the Channel Tunnel, operators such as P&O offer many products and services to encourage people to travel by sea. P&O offers shopping cruises, entertainment cruises and city cruises, including two-night cruises from Hull to Holland or Belgium.

Access is not just about transport links. Politics and economics also affect access. Only 15 years ago, eastern Europeans were not free to travel to their relatives and friends in the west, and vice versa. Even when they received their political freedom with the fall of the Berlin Wall and the dissolution of the Soviet Union, the people of eastern Europe could scarcely afford to travel. However, western Europeans benefited from visiting new destinations they could easily afford. Prague is a good example, now in the top ten of city breaks from the UK.

Most eastern European countries have not yet experienced much tourism, so their potential for development is great. There are already some airlines operating between the UK and new member states. Remember that these countries are not yet part of the Eurozone so retain their own currencies.

Assessment practice

Choose one of the countries that entered the EU in 2004 that is increasing in popularity with tourists. Find out what is currently provided for tourists in that country or in one destination within it. Look at transport both to the destination and within it.

1 Describe the accommodation, facilities, attractions and information and identify gaps in provision for tourists. **P2**

2 Explain how the different factors described above influence the appeal of your chosen country for a group of 30 older people (65+) from a University of the Third Age group and for a hen party. **M1**

3 Make recommendations about how the destination could increase its appeal for older people and for hen parties. **D1**

Geographical features

The geographical features of a region can add to its appeal, especially where the geography lends itself to particular activities such as walking, mountaineering or fishing. Particular features of the topography may appeal to different types of visitors.

Coastal areas

Coastal/seaside areas have great appeal to families. The traditional idea of a holiday is 2 weeks by the seaside. For UK tourists this changed in the 1970s, from 2 weeks by the sea in the UK to 2 weeks by the sea in Spain or another Mediterranean resort. The appeal of the seaside is obvious to us all, but the sea can also provide a variety of activities of interest to tourists such as water-skiing, surfing, deep-sea fishing or whale watching.

Tourists from northern European countries such as the UK and Germany tend to travel south to the Mediterranean for a better climate. There is no need to travel long haul for the sun in summer. Other popular coastal areas include the Italian Adriatic resorts of Rimini, Sirmione and Cavtat. Sirmione was once a Roman spa and has a fifteenth-century castle which is an important attraction. Cavtat has beautiful beaches and some very luxurious hotels.

Turkey has the Mediterranean Sea and its inlets of the Aegean Sea in the south and west and the Black Sea in the north. A popular Turkish resort on the Aegean is Bodrum, which has busy nightlife but is also a very pretty resort sitting amongst pine-clad hills. There are a number of beach resorts along this part of the Turkish coast, including Cesme and Altinkum. This part of the coast is known as the Turquoise Coast as the waters are so blue. The Aegean Sea stretches along to mainland Greece and many of the inhabited Greek islands are to be found here east of the Greek mainland and west of the Turkish coast. Examples are Hios, Samos and Lesvos.

The Bulgarian part of the Black Sea coast goes from Cape Kartel on the Romanian border to the Turkish border. Golden Sands is a famous Bulgarian beach resort on this coast. Varna was the first important resort on this coast and has spa centres with mud treatments. Today it is a lively resort with nightlife and casinos.

Spain's resorts attract many package holidaymakers, but change is occurring. Tourists are less likely than before to spend their holidays in areas like the Costa Blanca and are heading for cities like Barcelona, which offers a variety of activities. The Spanish coasts are very popular with the Germans and Dutch as well as the British. Some tour operators such as First Choice think that the Costa Brava has had its day and have dropped it from their programmes.

There are two groups of Spanish islands: the Balearics, located to the east of the mainland in the Mediterranean, and the Canaries, located off the coast of Africa in the Atlantic.

The Balearics consist of Majorca, Minorca, Ibiza and Formentera. Formentera is the least developed of the four and is reached by a 45-minute ferry ride from Ibiza. All are suitable for family holidays, but Majorca (Magaluf) and Ibiza (San Antonio and beyond) have also built up reputations as clubbing destinations for young people.

The Canaries are a group of islands with tourism concentrated on the four largest. These are Tenerife, Gran Canaria, Lanzarote and Fuerteventura. The islands are dry with sparse vegetation, and are mainly volcanic. Fuerteventura has wide, sandy beaches but those on Tenerife are less appealing, consisting of black volcanic sand.

Mountain ranges

Ski resorts are obvious examples of destinations in mountainous areas. France is the UK's favourite ski destination with the highest resorts, examples include Courchevel, Meribel and Belle Plagne. St Moritz is popular in Switzerland. Andorra, sandwiched between France and Spain is a principality with ski resorts. Mountains are suitable for adventure sports such as climbing and abseiling and for other less extreme activities such as hiking and rambling.

Case study: the appeal of Spain

There are both scheduled and chartered flights to Spain from all major airports in the UK and from the rest of western Europe. From the UK there are also ferry services to Bilbao and Santander. The ferry services are useful if travellers are happy with a fairly long sea journey and then a drive to their final destination. There are also good ferry links from Barcelona to the Balearics. Tourists or immigrants from Africa travelling to either Spain or France enter via southern Spanish ports like Algeciras.

Many UK visitors drive through France to reach Spain. Most visitors to the Canaries arrive by air, because of the location of the islands.

On the Spanish mainland transport is easy, with good rail and bus links and easily accessible car hire. Spain is also reasonably cheap compared with many other destinations, which contributes to its accessibility.

In Spain the culture varies enormously from one area or resort to another. In the cities the visitor is more likely to experience authentic Spanish culture with opportunities to see opera, dancing and arts events and try Spanish dishes and tapas. Around Holy Week there are many religious festivals in all areas.

On the Costa del Sol, in most of the Balearics and the Canaries the lifestyle is similar to that in the UK and English is widely spoken. In some purpose-built resorts in the Canaries there are no local people. Those that are Spanish have come from other regions of Spain to find work in the tourist industry.

The sun rather than wanderlust is the main reason for travelling to Spain, with decades of development having taken place to cater for western European sun-worshippers. Those looking for unspoilt Spain will head away from the costas and islands to the interior or northern coastal areas. Those motivated by the love of culture will travel to the cities of Barcelona to view the architecture of Gaudí or Seville to experience the Easter festivities and religious parades.

Spain has a beautiful coastline (stretching for 4964 kilometres), and mountainous areas such as the Pyrenees and the Sierra Nevada where skiing is popular. The climate is generally mild, with up to 10 hours of sun in the summer and with the highest temperatures in the south.

The Canaries enjoy a temperate climate all year round which attracts those looking for winter sun.

Each area of Spain has its particular attractions, for example Granada is famous for its beautiful setting and historical palace and buildings. There are also plenty of attractions offering entertainment for families, such as waterparks and the famous theme park, Portaventura, situated on the east coast near to Barcelona.

1   Mark the following 'costas' on a map of Spain. Identify the gateway airports serving these areas. Find out which are the major resorts in the areas and locate and name them on the map. You can download a map from www.geoexplorer. com or you can use a map from an atlas.
  - Costa Calida
  - Costa del Sol
  - Costa de la Luz
  - Costa Verde
  - Costa Blanca
  - Costa Cantábrica
  - Costa de Almería
  - Costa Dorada
  - Costa Brava.

  P1

2   Answer the following quiz questions on Spain.
  a) In which city is the Prado museum?
  b) Which city is famous for Gaudí's architecture?
  c) Name the islands that make up the Balearic Islands.
  d) Name the islands that make up the Canary Islands.
  e) In which city is the Alhambra Palace?
  f) Which city hosted the 1992 Olympic Games?
  g) Which football team signed David Beckham in 2003?
  h) Which country, also famous for tourism, borders Spain to the west?
  i) Gibraltar is a territory of which country?
  j) What is the native language of Barcelona?

Assessment practice

1 a) Find examples of mountain ranges and ski resorts in Italy, Austria and Scandinavia. For each, locate the area on a map and name the main resorts. **P1**

   b) Choose one area from each country. Use brochures to compare the ski facilities and costs across the three areas. **P3**

2 Recommend a ski resort for a family of four with one grandparent accompanying them, going on their first ever ski holiday. **M2**

Inland waterways

Amsterdam and Venice are both famous for their waterways yet their appeal as city break destinations is quite different. Think of Venice and you think of romance and beautiful palazzos overlooking the Grand Canal, water taxis bustling up and down with sightseers and commuters whilst gondolas float along at a more leisurely pace. In Amsterdam, the city is vibrant with young people sitting in coffee shops, bars or clubs. There are famous museums alongside designer fashion streets.

For those who like leisurely boating trips, inland waterways like those of the Canal du Midi in France and the waterways of Holland provide a relaxing holiday. River cruises are available along the Rhine and the Danube.

Theory into practice

Draw up detailed profiles of typical weekend break visitors to Venice and Amsterdam.

Case study: example of a Danube River Cruise

Itinerary

DAY 1	Depart from London Heathrow to Munich and transfer to your ship in Passau for late afternoon embarkation. Sail at 18.00 h.
DAY 2	Arrive Melk 0.800 h. Melk is set amidst Austria's wine growing region. There is an optional visit to Melk Abbey before the ship sails at 12.00 h.
DAY 3	Arrive Esztergom 07.00 h. Enjoy an optional excursion to Esztergom and the Danube bend before the ship sails at 12.30 h. Arrive Budapest 17.00 h.
DAY 4	Discover Budapest at your leisure or join the optional city tour today viewing the highlights of Hungary's capital including the Fishermen's Bastion. The ship sails at 20.00 h.
DAY 5	Arrive Bratislava, the dynamic capital of Slovakia at 13.00 h. There will be an optional city tour. Depart 23.00 h.
DAY 6	Arrive Vienna 07.00 h. Discover this famous city on today's optional sightseeing tour. The ship departs Vienna at midnight.
DAY 7	Arrive Durnstein 08.00 h. There will be an optional walking tour before the ship sails at 12.30 h.
DAY 8	Arrive Passau 08.00 h. Disembark after breakfast and transfer to Munich Airport for the flight to London Heathrow.

(Source: http://www.cruisingholidays.co.uk)

1 List all the towns visited on the cruise in a table. For each, state which country it is in and what its attractions are.

2 Locate all the towns on a map.

Taking it further

Find a similar cruise on the Rhine and repeat the exercise.

Figure 7.5 The romance of a gondola in Venice is part of its appeal as a destination for a city break

Lakes

Italy is famous for its beautiful lakes including Como, Garda and Maggiore. Visitors to Lake Garda can go on walking tours of the area and take boat trips on the lake. The historic city of Verona is nearby where visitors can attend the opera. In Switzerland the resort of Interlaken allows access to Lakes Thun and Brienz. Bonigen on Lake Brienz is a quiet resort with lakeside walks and pretty chalets.

There are many beautiful countryside areas in eastern Europe with lakes to discover. In Slovenia, Lake Bled is set against a mountain backdrop thick with forests. In Hungary, Lake Balaton is famous for its beauty. The town of Balatonfured is on the north shore, and offers health and spa facilities.

Temperature and precipitation

Northern Europeans tend to head south for a sunnier climate. Poor summer weather in a destination will influence sales for the next season. For example, Brittany in France offers lush countryside and gorgeous beaches. However, it often rains and a rainy summer deters visitors for the next season. Likewise a hot British summer encourages people to stay at home and take domestic holidays the following summer. Ski holidays are dependent on snow and if there are poor snow conditions bookings are seriously affected. In summer months mountain areas attract walkers as the weather is mild and often sunny.

Winter sun holidays are of necessity further afield. Popular destinations in Europe for winter sun are the Canary Islands which, although Spanish, are located near the coast of Africa.

Unexpected climatic conditions can be a disaster for tourism and for the destination. The case study article below illustrates the effect a flood had on Prague's tourist industry in August 2002.

Case study: effects on tourism of worst floods in 200 years

Czech residents were forced out of their homes as central Europe faced the worst floods known for over 200 years. The River Vltava burst its banks, causing death and destruction. Fourteen people died in the Czech Republic alone. Buildings crumbled and great piles of mud were left by the flood waters.

The floods were caused by a period of heavy sustained rainfall over about a week. The water rose up through the sewers, and the basement of the National Theatre was flooded.

Ten thousand Czech soldiers are involved in the clean-up operation, aided by civilians. The EU has pledged $50 million in aid to help the Czech Republic, which hopes to join the EU in 2004.

In neighbouring Slovakia, a state of emergency has been declared as the Danube threatens to flood the capital, Bratislava.

1 Find out about the long-term effects of the floods on tourism in Prague.
2 Has the city recovered?
3 What was the economic effect of the floods?

Taking it further

1 How did the entry of the Czech Republic into the EU affect tourism?
2 Can you find statistics on tourism in the Czech Republic? Try internet searches, newspaper archives and World Tourism Organisation statistics.

Attractions

Natural attractions

Natural attractions include all the geographical features mentioned earlier. Nature has great appeal to tourists who may spend much of their life in urban environments and at work. Holidays give an opportunity to visit lakes, mountains and forests and spend time outdoors.

Built attractions

Built attractions are developed with the intention of appealing to tourists. They include theme parks, museums, galleries, clubs and theatres. There are several theme parks in Europe but the most famous is Disneyland, Paris, now more than 10 years old. Theme parks in the UK mostly appeal to the teenage market but Disneyland has been targeted to appeal to families. This is why there are fewer thrill-seeking rides and more rides that the whole family

Case study: Lofoten Islands

These islands are located north of the Arctic Circle and they are difficult to access. One way of visiting them is to travel first to Norway and then take a 25-minute bumpy flight from the mainland to the town of Svolvaer. Adventure sports on the islands include snow-shoeing, skiing and whale watching, but in the winter it is dark most of the day so you have to make the most of the few hours of daylight. In the summer, you can try kayaking, boating and fishing in the fjords and at this time of year, there is almost constant light.

1   **Locate the Lofoten Islands on a map.**

2   **Find out how you would get there from the UK and find prices.**

3   **Find an example of a tour operator offering trips to these islands.**

4   **See if you can find a local website about Lofoten and note what information it offers.**

5   **What type of tourist would be interested in visiting the Islands?**

▲ Figure 7.6 A mountainous landscape can be explored in the Lofoten Islands

Taking it further

1   Find out about tourism in Norway. What resorts are popular and why?

2   How dependent is Norway on tourism? What other industries help the economy?

3   What is the currency and how do costs relate to those in the UK?

Produce a fact sheet with your findings.

can enjoy together. The Disney theme is followed through into the site's hotels, shops and entertainment.

Museums and galleries in cities are important attractions to visitors. Popular and famous museums include the Uffizi in Florence with paintings by Botticelli, Da Vinci and Michelangelo, the Louvre in Paris where visitors can see the *Mona Lisa* and the Prado in Madrid.

Figure 7.7 Botticelli's *Birth of Venus* is an important attraction at the Uffizi in Florence

Historic buildings

It is well known that Americans love to see the historic buildings of Europe and although the UK has its share of history, UK outbound tourists also find the historic buldings of Europe appealing. Some are well known, like the Eiffel Tower, the Louvre, the Sacré Coeur and Notre Dame in Paris. In Granada the Palace of the Alhambra attracts queues of tourists and Barcelona is famous for its two cathedrals, the Sagrada Família designed by Gaudí and the much older (Gothic) and traditional Santa Eulalia.

The cities of eastern Europe also have many historic buildings and these are being restored as economies develop and funds permit.

Nightlife and entertainment

Most people enjoy some form of nightlife on holiday. It may be music and dancing or a show in a hotel bar or a club or a casino. Many cities or resorts appeal to young people on holiday because of the nightlife they offer. Ibiza, Magaluf and Barcelona are examples of Spanish destinations where clubbing is a prime feature. Berlin has a 24-hour clubbing culture which some tourists like.

Casinos are a form of entertainment directed at older groups. On the French Riviera coast there are at least ten casinos. Bulgaria also has casinos.

Theory into practice

Identify at least five museums in Paris. Name them, say where they are located, whether they are free or paying and what their attraction is to visitors. Display your information in a table like the one below.

Name	Location	Free or paying?	Attraction

Culture

Consider this

Think of somewhere you have been where you felt you were in a different culture from your own. In what ways did it feel different?

Experiencing local culture is about trying the local food and drink, and being observant about local traditions and codes. It is understood that not all hotels offer a full English breakfast or tea with milk, and that shops may close from lunchtime until 4.00 pm. Some tourists love to experience a different culture and lifestyle when on holiday. Some do not! Some hope to find bars and restaurants serving the same food as they get at home and access to their usual daily newspapers. Certain resorts in Spain, for example, Torremolinos and Benidorm, cater so well for British, German and Dutch tourists that the Spanish culture is hidden. In contrast, Barcelona is a typically Spanish city, with authentic restaurants and Spanish culture in evidence.

Trying traditional food and drink is fun for tourists; at restaurants, local wine will be recommended by waiters and local dishes should be on offer. These vary from region to region but there are also some national dishes. For example, in France tourists love to try all the cheeses and wines. Pastis, an aniseed-flavoured drink, is often served as an aperitif. In Greece, a similar tasting drink to pastis is ouzo and moussaka is a national dish.

Consider this

What would you serve visitors to your region as signature food and drink?

Cultural and sporting events attract tourists, for example the World Cup in Germany in 2006. Sometimes tourists need to be made more aware of what to expect from the host country and its culture, so that their behaviour and

Case study: appeal of a European Capital of Culture

Lille is an example of a city destination which is fast rising in popularity. It is situated in northern France near the Belgian border. Two major factors, access and culture, explain its appeal.

For UK tourists, access to Lille is excellent by Eurostar. There are nine trains a day from London Waterloo and the journey time is 1 hour 40 minutes. This is less time than some people spend commuting! There are also three buses a day from London Victoria, operated by Eurolines. Although not so rapid as the train, this is an inexpensive way to travel.

Lille airport is 10 kilometres from the town but there are no direct flights to London. To fly to Lille it would be necessary to fly to another hub in France and out again. There are, however, air links to other European cities such as Barcelona, and to many French airports.

Lille was named European Capital of Culture for 2004. A different city is nominated every year – Cork was the European Capital of Culture for 2005. The European Commission provides funding to:

- promote diverse cultural activities to a range of people
- increase social cohesion
- create a sustainable cultural heritage.

Lille had over 2000 different exhibitions and performances during 2004, attracting many new tourists. Once in the city, tourists found many other features of Lille to enjoy. There is a medieval town centre, Vieux Lille, with cobbled streets and individual shops. The architecture is interesting, with Gothic churches, and there are good restaurants and bars.

1 **Find out which city is currently European Capital of Culture. Describe the following factors and how they contribute to the city's appeal:**
   - **location of the city**
   - **access for UK tourists**
   - **special activities planned for the year**
   - **other tourist attractions in the city.**

2 **Choose two different types of visitor, for example a family and a group of 18 year olds. Say what kind of leisure experiences they might find in Lille that would appeal to them. Compare your findings with a new Capital of Culture in a different European country, using the same customer types. Consider the lifestyle differences between the capital and the UK. P2 P3 M2**

dress are respectful and do not offend. One of the most bizarre and dangerous cultural events occurs annually at the San Fermin Festival in Pamplona, Spain. San Fermin is the patron saint of Pamplona and was martyred in Roman times by being dragged through the streets by bulls. This grisly event is commemorated every year with a week-long festival. Each morning some brave but somewhat foolish people run for their lives through the streets of Pamplona as bulls are released to chase them.

Economic factors

The cost of a holiday is important to its appeal. This does not necessarily mean that the cheapest holiday is most appealing. Tourists need to know what quality they are receiving for their money and what is included. An all-inclusive holiday might appear more expensive to start with, but once meals and drinks outside of those included in half board or bed and breakfast have been considered, the all-inclusive might in the end be better value.

Key term

Package holidays – holidays that include transport, transfer and accommodation with the following variations:

- all-inclusive – also includes all food and local drinks, and sports activities apart from motorised sports
- full board – includes breakfast, lunch and dinner
- half board – includes breakfast and lunch or dinner
- bed and breakfast – includes breakfast
- accommodation only – includes no food.

Availability of low-cost travel

Cheap flights are available for those tourists who book their holidays a long time ahead and take advantage of special offers. Booking at the last minute with low-cost carriers is usually expensive, particularly in peak season. However, the growth of low-cost carriers has opened up routes to several destinations that were previously only served by expensive scheduled flights. For example, Ryanair offers flights to the Italian islands of Sardinia and Sicily: a few years ago these islands were difficult to access cheaply and rather chic. Now, there are daily, low-cost flights from London and twice-weekly ones from Liverpool.

Activity

Carry out the following calculations and see the difference in cost a change in the rate of exchange makes.

1 In Kos:
- a beer costs €3
- a sandwich costs €5
- a meal out for four costs €75
- an hour on a pedalo costs €15
- a room in a hotel costs €5 per night.

2 Calculate all these costs in pounds at an exchange rate of €1.6 to the pound.

3 The exchange rate changes to €1.45 to the pound. Recalculate the prices and show what difference the rate of exchange makes to costs on holiday.

Impact of rate of exchange

Tourists have to consider the price of visiting local attractions, entertainment, car hire and eating out when choosing a destination. Tour operators often provide useful comparisons with the UK to help them. However, these comparisons are made at a particular rate of exchange so that the cost to a UK tourist changes as the rate of exchange goes up or down.

These examples from a travel brochure show approximate costs of a few items in Kos:
- a glass of beer: from £2
- a bottle of house wine: from £6
- a three-course meal: from £10.

Perceived value for money

Some destinations such as those developing in eastern Europe are very cheap. Black Sea coastal resorts are examples of relatively cheap destinations. Some city destinations in eastern Europe are also growing in popularity as they are 'new' destinations for the UK market and cheap to get to and to stay in. Tourists may think that these destinations represent good value for money but may find that this is only a perception and the reality is that high standards of accommodation and food and drink are not yet widely available as they are in western Europe. Where luxury hotels are available they are likely to be as expensive as the rest of Europe.

You were introduced to market segmentation in Unit 5.

Key term

Market segmentation – identifying different groups of customers for a product. The members of each group will share similar characteristics.

In travel and tourism it is important to segment the market so that the right products and services can be targeted at the right people. As we saw in Unit 5 there are many ways of segmenting markets from age and gender to psychographic methods.

It is common for tour operators to segment by destination, that is, to produce brochures for the USA, for Spain, for European beach areas, and so on. However, as tourists become more sophisticated and well travelled they are less likely to choose their holiday on destination alone but also on what kind of holiday they want when they get there. This is what motivates tourists to travel and to choose a particular destination. They are likely to choose their holiday based on the leisure experience they desire, such as a beach holiday in the sun, a skiing holiday, an adventure holiday or a city break looking at culture. A beach holiday gives the opportunity to relax; a cultural holiday offers an opportunity to learn; and an adventure holiday could be motivated by the need for excitement.

Tour operators use this knowledge to advantage and produce more brochures targeting these kinds of leisure experiences.

Table 7.2 shows the type of holiday taken by UK tourists, based on questioning 1690 adults aged 15 or older who had taken a holiday abroad. It helps us understand the types of leisure experiences people like on holiday and what motivates them on holiday.

	Percentage
Beach/resort holiday	47
City-based holiday	16
Visiting friends and/or relatives	16
Lakes and mountains holiday	7
Touring by coach	6
Touring/travelling independently (e.g. Inter-rail, island-hopping, round the world, etc.)	6
Camping holiday	4
Touring with car/caravan	4
Other sports or activity (e.g. golf, cycling, watersports) holiday	4
Other type of trip (incl. stag and hen weekends)	4
Cruise	3
Skiing/snowboarding	3
Themed holiday (e.g. wine tasting, painting)	2
Don't know	3

(Source: © Euromonitor International 2005)

Table 7.2 Type of holiday taken, July 2005

Beach holidays remain by far the most popular type of holiday. City breaks are the second most popular choice, vying with visiting friends and relatives.

Table 7.3 gives a bit more detail about the activities undertaken whilst actually on the holiday, also based on questioning 1690 adults aged 15 or older who had taken a holiday abroad. You can see that eating is the most popular activity, followed by shopping!

Theory into practice

Carry out your own survey into types of holidays taken. Use a table similar to Table 7.2 and ask a cross-section of people what type of holiday they took on their last holiday. Pool your results with those of the rest of your group and discuss whether your findings are the same as the Euromonitor survey.

	Percentage
Ate local food	62
Went shopping	57
Lay on the beach or around the pool	47
Visited museums, churches and old buildings	40
Visited countryside, mountains or parks	39
Experienced the local nightlife (bars, nightclubs)	36
Went on guided tours (incl. hop-on, hop-off buses)	21
Visited friends and family	17
Played watersports, other sports or watched sports	17
Visited cultural events (e.g. carnival in Venice, Gay Pride Parade)	14
Saw music concerts, dance performances or plays	11
Watched satellite television	8
Visited a spa/had a spa treatment	3

(Source: © Euromonitor International 2005)

Table 7.3 Leisure activities undertaken on holiday, July 2005

Consider this

How does it help tour operators to know what kind of activity people like to do on holiday? What other information would help them?

The following information from a Thomson brochure shows that this tour operator is very aware of what people like to do and has provided exactly the information needed. When tourists choose a holiday, they will choose destinations that offer the type of leisure experience they are looking for, whether it be a sun holiday, an active holiday, a cruise or tour or attending a sporting event.

Resort details Tunisia

Beaches
Sousse's long, fine beach of pale sand shelves gently into the sea; watersports in high season include parascending and windsurfing.

Eating out
There are some quality restaurants and simple cafés in Sousse, particularly those serving French-style cuisine.

Various international dishes and local specialities are also on offer to satisfy your taste buds.

Nightlife
Most of the entertainment in Tunisia is hotel-based, although there are a few cafés and bars in Sousse. There is also a smart casino often featuring international shows.

Shopping
There are plenty of shops in the town selling most of the traditional souvenirs, leather, ceramics and carpets. Why not visit some of the local shops and experience the art of bartering?

Local information
Explore the old medina and try out some of the watersports in high summer, including windsurfing and parascending. There are also several tennis courts available if you just can't get enough of the active lifestyle.

Location 23 km from Monastir airport

Transfer time 35–50 minutes

(Source: http://www.thomsonbeach.co.uk/th/beach/viewSelectedResort.do?seasonCode=S2006&resortCode=000433&destinationCode=000431&brochureCode=TH44)

Customer types

Having thought about the types of experience people want on holiday, travel and tourism organisations segment these types even further. For example, backpacking holidays do not just appeal to young single people any more. Older people on a career break may be able to carry out a more luxurious form of backpacking – perhaps with a wheelie case and staying at three-star hotels.

Here is a summary of the main categories of customer that organisations need to consider providing for, but there are a lot of possible variations.

Solo travellers may want to join a group but may prefer the privacy of a single room to sharing, and will want to avoid single supplements. Some tourists take a holiday in order to meet new people. This is especially true of singles holidays or 18–30-type holidays. Some people combine their love of activity holidays with meeting a new group of people, perhaps by joining a walking or cycling tour.

Couples without children may not want to be anywhere near children and may be looking for romantic locations or adventure or sports activities. They may need rest and relaxation having worked hard all year so they may choose a holiday in the sun or a spa holiday where rest and well-being are emphasised. An ABTA survey found that the main reason British people went on holiday was to relax in a sunny environment. Of people surveyed, 74 per cent had taken a summer sun package holiday within the last 12 months, 19 per cent had taken a winter sun holiday.

Older couples may have more time if they are retired and many have money to spend on luxury travel. They are also able to choose when to travel and avoid costly school holiday periods.

Families will need babysitting, children's clubs, etc. They may want less extreme sports that children are able to participate in. They will probably want other children around. Families with babies and toddlers may be looking for childcare and special meal times. Those with older children may hope that activities are provided to keep children happy and occupied.

Some people will be looking for a holiday experience that caters for a **special event** such as a wedding.

In the rest of this section we will look at some examples and try some activities to put this type of segmentation into practice.

Some destinations have so much to offer that they are can provide leisure experiences for all types of people. Paris, one of the top city break destinations, is a good example.

You may wish to choose Paris to research for your assessment, and this activity will help you start it. You will need plenty of information about Paris. Consider using the following:

- atlas/road map
- brochures
- travel guides
- internet sites
- French tourist office or website.

Remember that you should use more than one source of information.

Theory into practice

Study the descriptions of people listed in the left-hand column, and match them with suitable holiday destinations from the right-hand column.

Descriptions	Destinations
Joe and Parminder are about to celebrate their first anniversary – Joe is going to surprise Parminder with a weekend away	Two weeks in Cyprus in Ayia Napa with lots of clubs and bars
Sarah, a tourism lecturer, is arranging a trip for 20 tourism students	A few days in a four-star hotel with all facilities on the seafront in Nice
Paul is very overweight and concerned about his health	Five days on the Costa del Sol, including talks from a holiday representative and clubbing at night
A group of six lads have been friends since school and spend every weekend out on the town – they want to go away for 2 weeks together	A week at a detox and yoga centre in the Algarve
Kelly is exhausted – she has spent the past 6 months looking after her new baby. Her mum is going to babysit for 5 days so Kelly can go away with her husband for a rest	Diving holiday in the Red Sea
Veronica is taking a month out to get some adventure after working in the city for 5 years	A coach tour of European cities
Moassem and Raj are planning a trip to show their elderly relatives from India around Europe	A weekend in Venice including a trip on a gondola
Graham and Martin have a weekend free from their busy air-crew jobs – they can take free flights and they want to visit some galleries and have a couple of special quiet dinners	A couple of days in Florence staying in the city centre

Assessment practice

First, ensure you can locate Paris. Find it on a map and research access from the UK. Start from your home town and find at least two different routes to get there.

Choose two of the travellers mentioned in the table above and research what they could do in Paris and where they could stay. Write up your findings in a brief article suitable for a travel feature. Everything you choose must fit their needs. For example, if you choose a couple looking for romance, you will need to find:

- a charming hotel with character – and perhaps a four-poster in the room
- a quiet restaurant
- a romantic walk along the river
- a boat ride on the river in a bateau mouche. **M2**

Consider this

A trip or holiday may provide more than one leisure experience. Football fans who went to Germany for the World Cup in 2006 might have enjoyed the football and also visited some of the cities and natural attractions.

Assessment practice

You work in a small independent travel agency. Your speciality is matching destinations to clients who are looking for specific leisure experiences. Your portfolio of work this week includes finding holidays for five different sets of customers:

- Sarah and Malik are a couple in their early thirties. They are keen mountaineers and are extremely fit and healthy. They are going to take a 2-week break in early spring to indulge their hobby.
- Nick has just finished his 'A' levels. He and seven friends want to spend a week in a lively city to let off steam. They want it all – nightlife, beaches and even a bit of culture.
- Jonathan is 45 and divorced. He has recently met a wonderful woman whom he has fallen in love with. He knows that she likes to relax on holiday as she works so hard all year. She also likes culture and to be pampered on holiday. He wants to take her away for a week's holiday and show how much he cares for her.
- Bill and Doris are celebrating their fiftieth wedding anniversary. They have never left the UK. In fact they have hardly been out of their home town of Oldham in Lancashire. Their children are paying for a week's trip to somewhere in Europe. The couple need to be well looked after as they are such unsophisticated travellers. They want a relaxing holiday but want to do some sightseeing.

▲ Figure 7.8 Different types of customer

- Suzie has invited six friends to join her on a spa weekend to celebrate her forthcoming wedding. Although it is her hen party, she does not want a raucous wekend but a weekend of spas and relaxation for them all.

1 Recommend at least three different destinations for each of these client groups. Each of the three recommendations must be from a different European country. You must state why each destination is suitable for the customers' needs. You can present your information as a series of information sheets to hand to each set of clients. **P3**

2 Decide which of your three recommendations should be most suitable for each set of clients. Explain why it best meets your customers' needs. Carry out a presentation to your customer with your explanation. Use visual aids. **M2**

Case study: Malta client match

Malta may struggle to shed its image as a package holiday destination for older clientele, but the island has a lot to offer a wide range of customers. **Dave Richardson** looks at the options.

Families

Not all resorts in Malta have sandy beaches, but of those that do, the best can be found in the north-west. Mellieha, Ramla Bay, Golden Bay and Ghajn Tuffieha are the most popular among families with young children, and there are a few hotels actually on the beach, Mellieha Bay (exclusive to Thomson), and Radisson SAS Golden Sands at Golden Bay which opened last summer.

Some five-star hotels in St Julian's, such as the InterContinental, have their own small beaches.

Belleair Holidays agency sales manager Emma Yorke says: 'St Julian's has great facilities, and the hotels are very affordable.'

Families with older children tend to head for the neighbouring island of Gozo, which has a good choice of sandy and shingle beaches.

Large families often rent one of the island's many converted farmhouses.

Couples

Almost any resort is suitable, and the compact size of Malta means that sightseeing around Valletta is accessible from anywhere.

Holly Gilbert, Thomson product manager for Malta, recommends Bugibba. 'It is a developed resort that suits couples of all ages looking for a more lively atmosphere. There is lots on offer in terms of restaurants, bars and nightlife,' she says.

Sunspot Tours managing director Martin Bugeja says a hotel favoured by couples is the Fortina in Sliema. 'The spa packages there are very attractive. All our clients get deluxe rooms, so it has become a big seller,' he explains.

Many couples join together to rent a Gozo farmhouse, as featured by Cosmos. Tracy Young, Cosmos Villas with Pools product manager says: 'For 2006 we have included a range of higher standard villas which our customers are clearly looking for. They see Gozo as a more specialist product for which they are prepared to upgrade.'

Cadogan Holidays marketing manager Jennie Mugridge adds: 'For city-lovers, Valletta is popular. The hotels are generally set in quieter areas but close to the city centre, making it easy to explore and then relax at the end of the day.'

The tiny island of Comino also attracts couples who value seclusion and opportunities to dive and snorkel.

For the over-55s, spring and autumn are key times to visit Malta, but there is also a long-stay market in winter. They tend to avoid the busier resorts and peak summer, but do a lot of sightseeing.

'Sliema is particularly popular with this age group because it has a beautiful promenade and many opportunities for walking,' says Belleair's Emma Yorke. 'There is high repeat business and a lot going on, even in winter.

Party animals

Malta is rarely thought of as a party destination, but the neighbouring resorts of St Julian's and Paceville have developed lively nightlife in recent years without compromising the many luxury hotels nearby.

Sunspot's Martin Bugeja says: 'Paceville has lots of bars and restaurants, and clubs stay open until four in the morning. Malta may still have a crusty image but this area is amazing, without being vulgar.'

Belleair's Emma Yorke agrees that St Julian's is the big draw for clubbers, and says many of them can afford five-star hotels.

Activity lovers

Watersports in general and diving in particular are popular on the islands, and due to their compact size most resorts make good bases.

Main dive sites include Marsamxett Harbour, where World War II wrecks HMS *Maori* and *Carolita Barge* lie; and Dwejra, in Gozo, with the Inland Sea underwater tunnel and Blue Hole.

Thomson's Holly Gilbert says: 'For summer 2007 we're looking to promote Gozo as a location for active holidays, due to the quality diving, cliff walks and unspoilt landscapes.'

(Source: *Trade Travel Gazette*, 24 March 2006)

The article on Malta demonstrates how a destination can provide different holiday experiencees for different types of people. Read it carefully and then write a similar article for a European destination of your choice. Choose four types of customers to consider when matching features of the destination to needs. You could include illustrations and make your article large enough to display alongside those of others in your group. **P3** **M2**

Having looked at the appeal of destinations for tourists and at tourist motivation, it should be obvious that destinations have to change over time to accommodate the changing motivation and needs of tourists. Developments in transport and access open up new areas of the world and allow them to be developed for tourism. Governments and representatives from interested private sector companies have to work together to plan and develop areas so that tourism is sustainable and evolves without detriment to the interests of local people.

Destination life cycle

Study of the destination life cycle developed by R. W. Butler in 1980 helps us to understand how tourist areas develop and evolve. It cannot be strictly applied to all destinations, but is a useful planning guide and shows how destinations can be viewed as resources which have a finite life. Some communities become dependent on tourism and if a destination goes into decline their livelihood is at risk, as are the resources and infrastructure invested in tourism.

Figure 7.9 depicts the destination life cycle. You will note the resemblance to the product life cycle (see Unit 5).

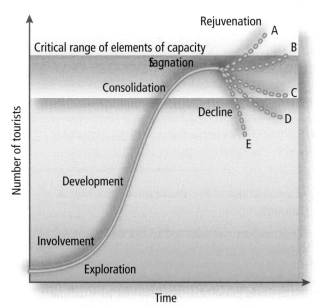

Figure 7.9 The destination life cycle

(Source: R.W. Butler, 'The concept of a tourist area', *Canadian Geographer*, vol. 24, no. 1 (1980), pp. 5–12)

Stage 1 Exploration

At this stage there are few tourists. Awareness of the destination is very limited. In fact, the few tourists are more likely to be termed 'travellers', as they are the type of people who are looking for adventure and new experiences. They will have found their own independent transport to the destination as the area will have poor access. There are few facilities and basic infrastructure. Nothing has been put in place for tourism and as there are so few tourists their impact is negligible. The local culture remains intact and the natural attractions undisturbed, adding to the attraction for the independent traveller.

Stage 2 Involvement

The destination begins to develop, travel companies start to organise transport links and there is an increase in tourist numbers. Local people may start to take advantage of the new opportunities opening up to them and build facilities such as restaurants and offer accommodation in their homes. The public sector starts to investigate how tourism can be developed and to invest in facilities and infrastructure. There may be some advertising of the destination.

Stage 3 Development

The early 'explorers' will no longer visit this destination. Instead the tourists are more institutionalised and likely to arrive on organised tours. There is a rapid growth in the number of tourists. The local people start to lose control of development as private companies move in and take control. There will be marked changes in infrastructure and in the appearance of the destination. There may be massive building projects for accommodation and also of attractions. The public sector's role is very important at this stage if the resident population's interests are to be protected and if tourism is to be sustainable. A tourist season will have emerged and there is heavy advertising to market the destination.

Stage 4 Consolidation

Tourist numbers are still growing but not so rapidly. The host population has become resentful of the tourists rather than expressing an interest in the visitors. There is extensive marketing to try to extend the season and attract yet more visitors.

Stage 5 Stagnation

This is the stage of mass tourism. Peak numbers have been reached and the types of tourists are those who are looking for much the same experience as at home, possibly with a better climate. The natural environment may have been spoilt or hidden by the man-made attractions and infrastructure in place. The problems and negative impacts of tourism are most evident. The destination is over-commercialised and overcrowded.

Stage 6 Decline

Some of the tourist facilities are closed or fall into disrepair as tourist numbers decline and the tourists go elsewhere. The destination may lose tourism altogether.

Stage 7 Rejuvenation

If action is taken, destination managers can avoid the decline and the resort can be rejuvenated. This involves sometimes drastic action and redevelopment and the injection of capital.

A destination with tourism potential will be located at the start of the destination life cycle in 'exploration' or 'involvement'.

Growth of leisure travel

Holidays

■ Short break holidays

The short breaks leisure market continues to grow. There are several reasons for this:

- availability of low-cost flights
- increased disposable income
- more choice of destinations
- trend to independent travel and booking
- desire to try new activities.

Case study: destination life cycle – Faliraki

Once a tiny fishing village, you would be hard put to find a fisherman here now. Dubbed 'lively' in the brochures it is, in fact, little more than a noisy teenage play pen. Jet skiing, go-karting, even bungy jumping are on offer to the daily influx of frolicky young visitors whose idea of fun appears to be getting drunk on fizzy beer and making as much noise as they possibly can. And noise there is, brain-addling at night as the bars and clubs wind up to full power. The din is in evidence several kilometres away. Drinks cost up to six times supermarket prices and street touts for the clubs and bars can be persistent and aggressive. Beaches are a grey, gritty sand and packed with holidaymakers from dawn to well after dusk. Food here is as plastic as you would expect and the only good meal to be had is snapped up by millions of mosquitoes homing in from the nearby lowland to

gorge on the bare teenage flesh. Perversely, recent hotel complexes have adopted a Cycladic village theme for those wishing to enjoy the 'Greek experience'. If you have a two-watt bulb for a brain and an ever-open wallet you will feel very much at home with the majority of visitors in this Greek version of the Spanish costas.

(Source: http://www.greekisland.co.uk)

1   **At what stage of the destination life cycle is Faliraki?**

2   **What factors contributed to the development of Faliraki as a tourist destination?**   **P4** **M3**

3   **In your opinion does it have any future tourism potential? Consider what measures can be taken to attract tourists to Faliraki. Make some notes and discuss your ideas with your group.**   **D2**

According to ABTA the most popular destinations in Europe for short breaks in 2005 were, in order, Paris, Prague, Barcelona, Tenerife, Rome, Edinburgh, Berlin and Amsterdam.

■ Activity holidays

These are a growing market sector as tourists look for holidays where they can indulge in a hobby or learn a new skill. The range is varied, with holidays available to learn languages, do painting or cooking or learn how to dance.

Most activity holidays are provided by small companies who specialise in particular activities, especially in the UK market. However, many large tour operators have acquired specialist tour operators in order to gain representation in a growing market for activity holidays, particularly overseas holidays.

New products and services

■ Low-cost airlines

The UK has the largest number of low-cost airlines and this means that the markets for European travel by UK outbound tourists will continue to increase. The increase is particularly marked in the short breaks market.

■ New destinations

The development of new destinations in Europe is linked to the provision of low-cost flights. In 2006, direct scheduled flights started up to Bulgaria's Black Sea Coast and Croatia is becoming very popular. Economic factors are also an influence as these eastern European countries are much cheaper than the UK. Ryanair launched flights to Lake Balaton in Hungary in 2006, which means that resorts in Hungary outside Budapest are now easily accessible. The UK is the most important source of tourism to the Czech Republic, with more than 7 per cent of total arrivals.

Political factors

Accession into the EU of ten new member states in 2005 meant that travel between these countries was no longer subject to restriction. (Refer to page 242 to remind yourself who they were.) In order to attract tourists, individual state governments must invest in the infrastructure, buildings and facilities to develop tourism. They can fund such developments through taxation or by applying for EU funds. In addition the country needs to adopt legislation and set up a public sector structure to support the development of tourism. Such a structure is very well developed in the UK and you should be familiar with it from Unit 1. Marketing is also a factor and the developing country will need representation at events such as the World Travel Market in London.

Economic factors

The UK economy is one of the strongest in Europe, levels of disposable income are rising and expenditure on leisure is growing. The introduction of the euro made a great impact on tourism within Eurozone countries as tourists are able to travel without changing currency and can expect less variation in prices as they travel. Even for UK outbound tourists there are advantages. Although you have to change pounds into euros you do not need a whole collection of currencies if you intend to travel throughout Europe.

Key term

Disposable income – the income left after tax, national insurance and pension contributions are deducted from pay.

We have high expectations in terms of travel and tourism and it is an important item of expenditure. Most people have travelled abroad, in contrast with previous generations.

Holiday homes

As more people can afford a second home, many choose to buy in Europe. There are many British people with holiday homes in Spain and France and now Croatia has a growing property market. Homeowners need different products from holidaymakers: they do not use hotels but they do need regular flight and car hire facilities.

Knowledge check

1 Name five of the countries which joined the EU in 2005.

2 What is the Schengen agreement?

3 What is Eurostar?

4 What is the appeal of road travel?

5 What is the appeal of air travel?

6 What is the common feature of Venice and Amsterdam?

7 Where are the Loften Islands located?

8 Which Spanish resorts offer nightlife to young people?

9 What are the three most popular leisure activities on holidays according to research?

10 What are the stages of the destination life cycle?

11 Define disposable income.

Preparation for assessment

You and your colleagues at your college or school are planning to welcome a group of exchange students from the Czech Republic. They are studying travel and tourism too and you are looking forward to sharing experiences, skills and knowledge related to the European travel market.

You have decided to have a workshop day where you will present information in various forms themed around European travel outbound from the UK.

The Czech students will benefit from an increased knowledge of the UK outbound market and develop their map skills and knowledge of European destinations.

A room has been set aside for you to prepare for the visit. You will need the following:

- PCs with internet access
- a full range of holiday brochures featuring European destinations
- atlases
- European travel guides
- travel and tourism textbooks
- OAG gazeteer.

1   Prepare a series of maps for the walls. You should be able to complete the maps without reference materials. **P1**

Map 1: On a blank map of Europe locate all the countries, indicating with a key which ones are in the EU and which ones are Schengen countries.

Map 2: On a blank map of Europe locate the main receiving areas of: France, Spain, Italy, Austria, Greece, Portugal, Turkey, Switzerland, Croatia, Ireland, Bulgaria, Serbia, Cyprus, Malta, Norway and Estonia.

For each country mark:
- three key air/road gateways
- three key passenger ports
- Eurostar terminals where appropriate
- at least three key destinations for winter sun, summer sun, lakes and mountains, city and cruise port for each country as applicable.

Prepare a table or chart listing the identified air gateways along with their IATA codes.

2   Prepare a series of posters illustrating the factors that contribute to the appeal of leisure destinations within the European travel market. **P2**

Grading tip

To reach Pass level you must prepare posters on destinations in Europe representing three of the following themes:
- summer sun
- winter sun
- lakes and mountains (summer and winter)
- cities
- cruise areas.

Your posters should have information and explanatory notes on:
- accessibility
- geographical features
- attractions
- cultural factors
- economic factors.

3   Prepare for an oral presentation for the exchange students, giving an explanation of how factors in each of your chosen destinations (in task 2) influence the appeal to different types of customers. **M1**

Grading tip

Choose the customer types from those mentioned in the text, for example families or solo travellers.

NB This task uses scenarios which you can role-play with your exchange students or use to prepare written notes.

4 You must recommend three different destinations to meet customer needs for specific leisure experiences using the following scenarios: **P3** **M2**

a) Raoul and Sarah want to go on a week's beach holiday in the summer. They will spend their nights clubbing.

Recommend three different destinations for Raoul and Sarah saying why they would appeal.

b) Peter and Dorothy are 'empty nesters', so they are able to take a holiday without any children. They enjoy good wine and are interested in a wine-tasting week. They will take their own car to Europe.

Recommend three different destinations for Peter and Dorothy saying why they would appeal.

c) A group of 18- to 19-year-old girls are are looking for a 3- or 4-day holiday in a city destination. They want to stay in a budget hotel and spend most of their time shopping, spending the cash they have earned over the summer.

Recommend three different destinations for the girls saying why they would appeal.

d) The Reichrath family from Cheshire consists of the parents and their three children, aged 10, 11 and 12. They are going to take a winter holiday, probably in February, and want to go to a skiing resort that is suitable for beginners. None of them has skied before and they will require lessons.

Recommend three different destinations for the Reichrath family saying why they would appeal.

e) Jonathan who is 25, works in the city for a leading bank. He and three friends want to take a 4-day break to relax from city life. However, they want to participate in some kind of extreme adventure sport or activity on their break. They are all extremely fit.

Recommend three different destinations for Jonathan and his friends saying why they would appeal.

Grading tip

Choose different destination examples from those in tasks 2 and 3.

To reach Merit level, you must say which destination would best meet their needs and why.

5 Choose one of the leisure experiences mentioned in the previous task, for example skiing or city shopping breaks. Assess the current provision in Europe for this type of leisure experience. **D1**

Grading tip

Make sure you discuss the countries and regions which provide this type of experience and give examples of specific destinations. Make sure your information is up to date and comes from a variety of sources.

6 Prepare four information sheets for the Czech students. These sheets must describe the development of destinations in Europe and identify the factors which have contributed to development. **P4** **M3** **D2**

Two sheets must be about a developing European destination.

Two sheets must be about a declining European destination.

Grading tip

To reach Pass level, in your information sheet describe:
- the features of development or decline (e.g. you know it is declining as tourist arrival numbers are going down)
- why it is developing or declining (e.g. money has been spent on refurbishment or there have been terrorist attacks)
- position in Butler's cycle.

To reach Merit level you need also to:
- show analysis of both key trends that are shaping the development of one of your destinations, for example a low-cost airline has started a route to the destination so this will mean increased numbers of tourists, and key trends that are shaping the decline of another of your destinations.

To reach Distinction level you need also to:
- assess current trends and say how they might affect the development of destinations in general in the future, for example further terrorist activity in Turkey will deter tourists from visiting tourist resorts.

Grading criteria

To achieve a pass grade the evidence must show that the learner is able to:	To achieve a merit grade the evidence must show that, in addition to the pass criteria, the learner is able to:	To achieve a distinction grade the evidence must show that, in addition to the pass and merit criteria, the learner is able to:
P1 identify and locate countries, gateways and key leisure destinations within the European travel market **Theory into practice page 242**	**M1** explain how different factors influence the appeal of specific leisure destinations for different types of customer **Assessment practice page 249**	**D1** recommend how a European destination could increase its appeal for different types of customers **Assessment practice page 249**
P2 describe factors that contribute to the appeal of leisure destinations within the European travel market **Theory into practice page 246**	**M2** explain how specific European destinations meet the needs of different customer types **Assessment practice page 252**	**D2** evaluate the effects of current factors on the European travel market in the future **Case study page 264**
P3 describe, with examples of destinations, European leisure experiences and their appeal to customer types **Assessment practice page 252**	**M3** analyse factors that shape development of the European travel market. **Case study page 264**	
P4 describe the development of the European travel market and identify factors that have contributed to this **Case study page 264**		

Long haul travel destinations

Introduction

This unit focuses on long haul destinations. There has been an increase in popularity of long haul travel with UK outbound tourists in recent years.

To be successful in many sectors of travel and tourism, a knowledge of long haul destinations is desirable. You need to know what types of destinations are available – from cities to beaches and from areas with natural appeal to those with cultural appeal.

You will use different reference sources to help you locate destinations and gateways. You will explore the effect of factors such as health restrictions, travelling times and international conflicts on the long haul market.

You will examine the features of different destinations in relation to the types of visitors they attract.

You will develop your practical skills by learning how to put together an itinerary for a multi-centre tour.

After completing this unit you should be able to achieve the following outcomes:

1 Be able to locate major long haul destinations of the world

2 Understand the nature of long haul travel and the factors which affect customer choices

3 Understand the features which make long haul destinations appealing to different customer types

4 Be able to plan a long haul tour.

Thinking points

Long haul travel up by 15 per cent

Britons are going on a record number of long haul trips, according to latest government figures.

The number of visits by Britons to areas outside western Europe and North America jumped 15 per cent to 11.7 million in the year to February, according to the Office for National Statistics.

Visits to North America fell 5 per cent to 4.7 million during the same period, while those to western Europe increased by 2 per cent to 50.2 million.

Inbound arrivals grew by 6 per cent for the same period, despite fears that the July terror attacks would dampen demand. There was, however, a 4 per cent fall in North American visitors to 4.2 million.

(Source: *Travel Trade Gazette*, 14 April 2006)

Reference sources

You will need to become proficient in using a range of reference material to investigate destinations.

Atlases

You should have become used to using a good atlas when studying the other destination units. You will need it again to practise locating long haul destinations.

Country guides, area guides, resort and city guides

These are extensively available in bookshops and libraries. They are constantly updated, so do check the dates of library editions as many libraries cannot afford to update their whole collection of travel guides regularly.

Some of these guides are very well produced and include maps, hotel and restaurant recommendations, and plenty of information on what to see and do. They are ideal for tourists but not so useful for students, who may need to research facts and figures on tourism and trends.

The *World Travel Guide* is probably the best-known directory for the travel trade. It contains factual information on every country including transport, accommodation, visa requirements, health and a social profile.

Manuals

OAG produces a comprehensive series of guides for air and rail. The travel trade commonly uses these. Some of them are quite complex to follow, and demand a knowledge of time zones and airline codes.

Timetables

Timetables are published by all transport carriers and are readily available in published form and on the internet. Airports amalgamate the timetables of their carriers and post them on their websites.

Brochures

Most tour operators produce specialist long haul brochures and it will be useful for you to collect a selection of these as you work through this unit. Remember that some tour operators now produce electronic brochures which you can download from their websites.

The internet

You have already been using the internet for your research but now you need to look at specific long haul destination websites. Useful examples are:

- www.geographia.com – destination information
- www.worldatlas.com – maps and country information, and it has some map tests.

You will also find tour operator websites and websites from the tourist boards of countries which interest you.

Many travel guides are available online. Examples include www.fodors.com and www.lonelyplanet.com.

The World Tourism Organisation (WTO) is a useful source of statistics on visitor numbers to destinations. You might find the printed version in your library, but it is also available online at www.world-tourism.org. You will find some excellent information freely available on this site but detailed reports are available only to subscribers.

Travel trade journals

Your library should have copies of travel trade journals, which give up-to-date features on the industry and on specific destinations. If you wish you can subscribe to these publications with a student subscription. The national and regional press also carry regular travel pages, which are full of informative features and advertising.

Assessment practice

Go to the website www.world-tourism.org.

1 Find WTO's 'Tourism 2020 Vision' in the statistics section:
   - Where are the top three receiving regions expected to be?
   - What will world international arrivals be?

2 Download the report 'Tourism Highlights':
   - Find out the latest figure for world international tourism arrivals.
   - What was the 1990 figure?

- What is the percentage change?
- Find the same figures for receipts.
- What is the difference between receipts and arrivals (latest figures)? What does this mean?
- Why are receipts shown in US dollars?
- Find the top ten world tourism destinations (arrivals and receipts). Are they the same? Explain any differences. **P1**

Ask your teacher or tutor to check your work.

Key terms

Tourism receiver – a country that tourists choose to visit. France is a major receiver.

Tourism generator – a country where tourists originate. The UK is a major tourism generator.

Tourist arrivals – numbers of tourists visiting a country expressed in numbers of visits.

Tourist receipts – the amount of money spent in a country by tourists.

Destination range

A long haul destination is one with a flight time from the UK of over 6 hours. All European countries, north African countries and Asian countries bordering the Mediterranean are therefore excluded.

A destination can be a town or city, coastal area, tourist island or island group, countryside (natural) area or purpose-built resort area. Examples of destinations include New York, the Gold Coast in Australia, Hong Kong, the Maldives, the Canadian Rockies, Walt Disney World.

The range of long haul destinations available to UK outbound travellers has increased dramatically in recent years. We can visit cities such as New York and Sydney and experience their unique culture. Destinations like Florida offer beaches and exciting visitor attractions that suit all members of the family. Far-flung countries like Vietnam, Cambodia and China are now accessible. Knowing about these long haul destinations is important for working effectively in travel and tourism and in this unit you will be able to develop these skills.

You need to know the location of major long haul tourist destinations, particularly those which are most popular and those which you choose to study in depth. The following activity is designed to revise or kickstart your geographical knowledge.

Major tourist receiving areas

Some of the areas you have located are known as 'major tourist receiving areas'. This means they attract tourists in great numbers and usually from many areas of the world. You will have found that these areas include the Caribbean islands, popular for island holidays and cruising, and south-east Asia.

There are other areas that you should be able to locate which are diverse in appeal, some well known and others less so.

Assessment practice

For this activity you will need a world map. You can download a map from www.geoexplorer.co.uk or you can use an outline map from your world atlas.

1 Locate and name the following on the map:
   - the equator
   - the northern hemisphere
   - the southern hemisphere
   - the continents of Asia, North America, South America, Africa, Australasia, Europe
   - the Atlantic, Pacific and Indian oceans.

Use an atlas to help you complete your map and ask your teacher or tutor to check your work.

2 Study Figure 8.1 and then locate the regions on a world map. For each region identify five main tourist destinations and locate them on your map. Decide what type of destinations they are, for example city or coastal, and use a key to identify the type. **P1**

3 In an earlier activity you looked at the World Tourism website and found out which countries had the most

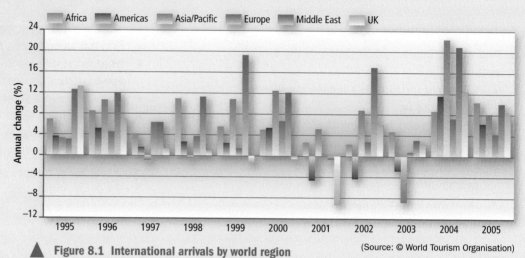

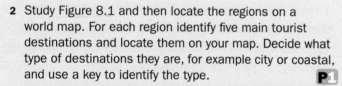

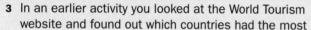

▲ Figure 8.1 International arrivals by world region

(Source: © World Tourism Organisation)

tourism arrivals. Locate these countries on the world map. Find out the name of the capital city for each country and locate these also. **P1**

4 The statistics for regions and countries you have looked at so far have come from international statistics – so they tell us which regions and countries are most popular with all tourists not just British tourists. Look at Table 8.1 to see where British tourists choose as long haul destinations.

5 Locate all the destinations in Table 8.1 on a world map. Remember that this information represents Kuoni bookings only. **P1**

	2000	2001	2002	2003	2004	2005 (up to June)
Thailand	1	1	1	2	2	2
Maldives	2	2	2	1	1	3
USA	3	4	6	5		
Sri Lanka	4	3	3	3	8	13
Egypt	5	5	4	4	4	4
Hong Kong	6	6	8	17		
Dubai	7	9	5	6	3	1
Singapore	8	7	10	15		
Malaysia	9	10	9	12	5	5
Kenya	10	8	7	11	20	17
Indonesia	11	11	16	–	19	9
Seychelles	–	–	–	–	11	10
Barbados	12	17	11	7	7	7
St Lucia	13	13	13	13	12	16
St Vincent & Grenadines	–	–	–	–	14	14
Mauritius	14	15	12	8	6	6
Mexico	15	12	15	14		
Morocco	–	–	–	–	15	12
Antigua	16	18	14	9		
Australia	17	14	17	16		
Cuba	18	20	19	10		

continued

	2000	2001	2002	2003	2004	2005 (up to June)
China	19	19	20	–		
India	20	16	–	20	9	15
Jamaica	–	–	18	18		
Virgin Islands	–	–	–	–	16	19
Tobago	–	–	–	–	26	20
Tanzania	–	–	–	–	25	18
Oman	–	–	–	–	10	8
South Africa				19	13	11
New Zealand	–	–	–	–		

Table 8.1 Top 20 luxury long haul destinations

(Source: Kuoni)

Case study: popularity of long haul destinations

29 January 2006 – Down Under Is Top For Brits

Australia is the British people's most popular long haul destination according to figures released today by tailor-made holiday specialist, Travelbag.

Australia had an amazing five of its cities in the top ten travel destinations for 2005: Sydney, Perth, Brisbane, Melbourne and Cairns.

Malaysia and Thailand also featured for the first time, replacing USA favourites New York and Las Vegas as holidaymakers' love of far-flung, exotic destinations continues.

Despite the tsunami, Thailand fared much better in 2005 than it did in 2004. While Bangkok remained the second most popular destination, Phuket went up from eleventh in 2004 to eighth place in 2005.

The top ten destinations for travel in 2005 for Travelbag were:

- Sydney
- Bangkok
- Auckland
- Perth
- Christchurch
- Brisbane
- Melbourne
- Phuket
- Cairns
- Penang.

For 2006, Travelbag predicts Australia and New Zealand will stay on top, but Thailand could be challenged by other up-and-coming South-East Asia destinations, such as Laos, Vietnam and Cambodia.

China is also being tipped as the destination to watch this year with the country's total inbound tourism set to rise by 8 per cent in the next 5 years, according to a World Tourism Organisation forecast.

Whilst not making the top ten this year, Travelbag also expects Africa to be popular. Last year Travelbag saw a 35 per cent increase in visits to Kenya and emerging destinations such as Mozambique, with its unspoilt beaches, also gathering popularity.

Matthew Foster, Marketing Director, Travelbag says: 'Australia is just huge for the UK at the moment. Whereas it used to be considered a "once in a lifetime" trip, a 2-week annual holiday to Australia is now no more unusual than any other destination.

As more hotel properties open next year and flights remain competitive, we expect Australia to continue its growth.

But the new ones to watch this year are definitely China and Latin American countries such as Costa Rica – for the beaches and eco experience – and Argentina for hip cities like Buenos Aires.

The USA is still incredibly strong and remains popular with British travellers even if other, more exotic, destinations are becoming easier to travel to – and let's face it, most of us like the idea of exploring somewhere new. But the USA is always likely to stay popular with the British because there's just every type of holiday you could possibly want there.'

(Source: http://www.a2mediagroup.com/?c=148&a=2276)

1 **What are the reasons for the rise in popularity of Australia with British travellers?**

2 **Where are Bangkok and Phuket?**

3 **What types of holidays are available in the USA? Give examples.**

4 **Why is China likely to become more popular as a destination? Remember that the 2008 Olympics are in Beijing.** P3 M2

Assessment practice

Locate the following on a world map and provide a brief description of the location:

- The Gold Coast (Australia) popular for its miles of surf beach, lush green rainforest, good hotels and theme parks
- Patagonia (Argentina and Chile) was once a remote backpacking destination, but now attracts cruise passengers, adventure and activity holidaymakers
- Uluru-Kata Tjuta National Park is a World Heritage site in the centre of Australia
- Walt Disney World in Florida and California, USA.

▲ Figure 8.2 Sydney is one of the attractions of Australia as a long haul destination

Long haul travel has become more popular from the UK in recent years as airfares have become cheaper and air travel more accessible.

Nature of long haul travel

When people are planning long haul holidays there are several factors that affect their choice of destination. In this section we will look at these factors and assess their relative significance in customer choice and consider some specific destinations. There has been a change in perception of long haul travel with British tourists. A few years ago long haul travel was considered to be out of reach of most people, reserved for the rich and famous. However, having become used to regular travel and holidays throughout Europe, people are looking for new experiences and want to visit new places.

Many long haul holidays are offered as packages. People are less likely to travel independently as low cost flights from companies like easyJet are not available so customers are unable to save costs by booking flights. However, the trend for independent travel is on the increase. Tailor-made holidays are available, for example tailor-made safari holidays are a popular choice.

Tour operators provide a selection of brochures to help customers choose their trip. These vary from comprehensive brochures showing a full range of long haul destinations to a series of specialist brochures.

Specialist brochures cover specific destinations, for example specialist diving holidays, or there are specialist brochures which appeal to a customer type, for example families.

Long haul operator Kuoni offers a range of brochures.

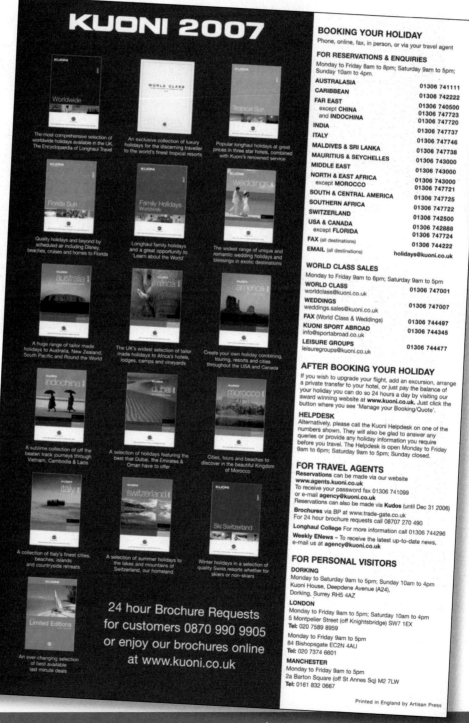

Figure 8.3 Back cover of Kuoni Worldwide brochure 2007 ▶

▲ Figure 8.4 Walt Disney World, USA is a purpose-built attraction

Destination types

Long haul destinations can be categorised as follows:

- Cities – may be visited as part of a tour or for short breaks. The most popular long haul cities visited are New York, Sydney and Bangkok.
- Coastal or seaside resorts – stunning beaches may be a reason for visiting a destination. However, remember that there are many beautiful beaches in Europe so climate is an important factor. In winter, customers have to travel long haul to take a beach holiday.
- Purpose built – all the attractions in Orlando have been built to attract tourists to the area. Although

Disney World was the first theme park in the area this was followed by Universal Studios, Seaworld and several water parks.
- Natural attractions – mountain ranges, rainforests and deserts, etc.
- Historical or cultural areas – sometimes the history and culture of a region are so interesting that the whole tourist industry is based on that culture. The 'Inca trail' has developed as a result of the tourist fascination with Peru's Inca history. See the case study on Machu Picchu on page 296.

When people are considering booking a long haul holiday they are most likely to be thinking first about the type of holiday they would like to take. Of course, different types of customers look for different types of holidays and to make choices even more complex we are all motivated by a different set of factors. For example, a couple who have worked hard all year may want to relax in a beach destination and not be disturbed by children. Another couple might prefer to relax by indulging in watersports.

Holiday types

The type of holiday desired impacts on the choice of destination for the customer. If tourists are looking for a skiing holiday they have to go to a mountain area, for a diving holiday they will be looking for a coastal area with specialist facilities, clear waters and with lots of marine life to see.

Short breaks

Long haul short breaks appear to be a contradiction in terms but are becoming more popular. According to the travel company ebookers, New York was the top destination in 2005, followed by Bangkok and Dubai. The people who take long haul short breaks are usually couples without children; they have money to spend and they can fit in the breaks around their busy jobs. They may be going shopping or for a weekend in the sun but the common factor is a desire to do something different.

Cheaper flights and flexibility on air routes have made long haul air travel easier and hotels are often cheaper than in the UK. Arriving back at work and saying you have been to Hong Kong for the weekend is exciting. In fact, Hong Kong has become a popular short break destination offering shopping and sightseeing. Other exotic weekend destinations include Havana, Buenos Aires and Rio de Janeiro.

Multi-centre

A multi-centre holiday is another name for a tour. Tours may be fly/drive, rail or coach. Tours can be organised

or travellers can hire a car and do their own planning. Tours may take in natural attractions, coastal areas and built attractions such as museums or galleries. Multi-centre tours are very popular with long haul tourists as once they have travelled a long way to arrive at a destination they want to see as much of the area or country as possible.

Those wanting to tour will have to consider the options for local transport very carefully, making sure it suits their needs.

Stopover

Many travellers opt to stop over on long journeys to break the tedium of a lengthy flight. This provides an opportunity to see another place and its culture en route. Traditional stopovers on the way to Australia are Singapore and Hong Kong, both ideal for 2 or 3 days' stay before continuing on. When considering whether a destination has appeal as a stopover, travellers will consider: distance – it's obviously best if it's about halfway, cost and the facilities available. Generally, people on stopovers want short transfers from the airport to their hotel and they usually prefer to avoid complex excursions or activities. They are most likely to enjoy some shopping and local sightseeing. Dubai is proving ideal as a stopover destination as the case study on page 280 shows.

All inclusive

All-inclusive holidays are usually hotel based. They are particularly suitable for families as once they have paid for the holiday there is very little to pay for later, making budgeting very easy. Within the hotel children are free to go and ask for drinks and food as they wish and lots of activities are provided.

The case study on page 281 describes an all-inclusive ship-based holiday. The ship cruises around the islands of the Maldives. Only children of twelve or over are allowed on the trip.

Case study: **Gulf sees stopover boom**

DUBAI and the other emirates have become the 'new Singapore' for air passengers, with millions more expected to choose the Middle East as a stopover in the next few years, Gulf carriers claim.

Huge expansion by Emirates, Qatar Airways and Etihad meant travellers now had an alternative to stopover hubs such as Singapore.

The three carriers have hundreds of aircraft on order and are set to have a big impact on European airlines as travellers switch away from the traditional hubs.

Speaking at an ITB seminar, Geert Boven, Etihad's commercial vice-president, said the introduction of longer-range aircraft, such as the Airbus A380, would change global travelling patterns as onward flights to Australia, for example, could now be made without a stopover.

'The European carriers rested on their laurels. They thought they ruled the world. But because of the new long-range aircraft, traffic flows are being redirected,' he said.

The Middle East's geographical position also gave it an advantage, he said.

'Dubai's success would continue and attract more travellers to consider it as a stopover,' said Keith Longstaff, Emirates' commercial operations vice-president.

'I think Emirates has emulated the success of Singapore Airlines,' he said.

'Singapore has a small population but has been incredibly successful in becoming a worldwide player.'

Longstaff added Dubai's population was expected to grow from 1.4 million to 4 million, and its tourist numbers to rise from 6 million to 15 million, by 2010. In the same period, its hotel bed-stock would rise from 38,000 to 117,000.

(Source: *Travel Trade Gazette*, 17 March 2006)

1 **What reasons are given for the expected rise in popularity of Dubai as a stopover destination?**

2 **Look up details of some routes to Australia. Can you find examples of routes that offer a stopover in Dubai?**

3 **Find out what tourists could do in Dubai for a couple of days.**

▲ Figure 8.5 The beaches in Dubai may be one of its attractions as a stopover destination

Case study: all-inclusive holidays

Draw up a detailed profile of the type of customer the holiday shown in Figure 8.6 is suitable for. Illustrate your profile if you wish.

Figure 8.6
An all-inclusive holiday ▼

MOOR OFF TRANQUIL, DESERTED ISLANDS IN THE MALDIVES

Atoll Explorer
ALL INCLUSIVE

The Atoll Explorer is a small comfortable ship with a relaxed, very informal atmosphere on board and is under the expert Universal Group Management. There is no dressing up for smart dinners or entertainment. Dress code is shorts and swimwear during the day and casual dress in the evenings both on board and on the islands.

Facilities One restaurant usually serving international style buffets with indoor and open-air dining areas, jacuzzi, small gift shop, bar, two sun decks and indoor games. Eurodivers dive school which arranges snorkelling, windsurfing and see page opposite for diving packages to prebook before you go.

Accommodation Just 20 cabins which are small, simply furnished and have either a double bed or two single beds. All are outside cabins with a picture window and have airconditioning, telephone, shower and limited wardrobe space.
Category C cabins: as above located on either upper or lower deck.
Category B cabins: as above on upper deck with small balcony and double bed.
Category A cabins: as above but slightly larger and on upper deck with double bed and balcony overlooking the stern.

NB *Cabin sizes vary.*

Your cruise holiday includes:
• All meals: Full breakfast, lunch and dinner daily.
• All drinks: Beer, house spirits and wine, soft drinks (except champagne) by the glass (alcohol may be substituted for diving, see diving option in Kuoni Plus).
• Watersports: Snorkelling and windsurfing subject to availability.
• Unlimited tea and coffee.
• Indoor games.

NB *Food and beverages consumed on resort islands are not included in the All Inclusive package.*

Your week stay on a resort island may be taken before or after your cruise. Alternatively extend your stay with a second week aboard Atoll Explorer (see Kuoni Plus offer).

UNIVERSAL RESORTS
maldives

ENJOY A BEACH BARBECUE ABOARD ATOLL EXPLORER

DIVE WITH THE MALDIVES' COLOURFUL FISH

(Source: Kuoni Worldwide brochure 2007)

Taking it further

Using brochures, find an example of an all-inclusive long haul holiday that a family would enjoy. Describe the features of the destination and say why it would appeal to a family.

It is usually the natural attractions of a destination that make it suitable for a special occasion such as a wedding. Many special occasion holidays take place in beach resorts. Facilities such as catering and accommodation will also be carefully considered, especially if there are guests and if everyone wants to stay in the same hotel.

According to a Mintel survey one in ten couples get married abroad. This amounts to 35,000 weddings a year; many of these are long haul. This amounts to huge potential business for tour operators. Since 1998, the number of people choosing to marry abroad has risen by more than 50 per cent. There are many reasons for people choosing to have their wedding abroad, one of the main ones is cost. The average cost of marrying abroad is £3000–£4000, which includes the honeymoon, whereas a UK wedding costs on average £15,000.

Consider this

Think about other reasons for getting married in a long haul destination. Discuss the advantages and disadvantages with your colleagues.

When you think about a wedding abroad you are most likely to imagine a beautiful beach setting with hot sunny weather and it is true, this appeals to some couples. If this is what a couple are looking for then they must be aware of climate information for the destination they are considering.

Although popular, beach weddings are not the only option. Tour operators are coming up with new ideas for weddings abroad all the time to try and get a larger share of this lucrative market. All major long haul tour operators offer wedding packages. Here are some ideas:

- Virgin offers a wedding ceremony on the 86th floor of the Empire State building in New York
- Las Vegas is a popular wedding destination – couples can get married in one of the wedding chapels on Sunset Strip and the bride can even get an Elvis look-alike to give her away.
- Kuoni offers the possibility of marrying in Sydney on a sunset harbour cruise or outside the famous opera house
- Most of the beautiful Caribbean islands are geared up for weddings on perfect sandy beaches.

Some tour operators have a wedding list service where family and friends can contribute to the cost of the wedding in lieu of a wedding gift or can buy add-ons to the holiday, for example a yacht trip, a helicopter ride or a special dinner for two.

ESSENTIAL FACTS FOR WEDDINGS AND HONEYMOONS

How's the weather?

Bali: tropical climate with a dry season during our summer and a rainy season in our winter; year-round showers. Average temperature 30°C.

Caribbean: sunny and warm all the time, but beware hurricane season from late September to early October. Temperatures between 25°C and 30°C.

Cyprus: very hot in the summer, mild the rest of the year; lots of sunshine. Temperatures between 15°C and 35°C.

Florida: sunny all year round, very hot and humid in the summer but can be chilly in mid-winter, particularly in Orlando. Temperatures between 15°C and 40°C.

Greece: very hot in the summer, mild in winter, year-round sunshine. Temperatures between 5°C and 30°C.

Kenya: year-round warmth, with a dry season in our winter and a rainy season in our summer. Temperatures between 25°C and 30°C.

Las Vegas: sunny all year, extremely hot in the summer and cold in the winter. Temperatures between –5°C and 40°C.

Mauritius: year-round tropical warmth. Temperatures between 25°C and 30°C.

Maldives: warm all year, with a rainy season during our summer. Temperatures between 30°C and 35°C.

New York: very cold and snowy from November to March, steaming hot in mid-summer. Temperatures between –5°C and 35°C.

Sri Lanka: hot and humid all year round with two distinct monsoon seasons from May to July and December to January. Average temperature 30°C.

Sydney: seasons opposite to the UK so warm in our winter and cooler, though never really cold, in our summer; can rain in winter, but consistently sunny in summer. Temperatures between 12°C and 25°C.

Figure 8.7
Information for people planning to wed abroad

(Source: *Travel Trade Gazette*, January 2005)

Theory into practice

Plan a wedding holiday for a special client – you! Imagine you are going to get married abroad. Think of all the features you would like your holiday to have and select several possible destinations. Use the climate information on page 282. Take a blank world map and label all the destinations with notes about the features of each one. Make a poster of your wish list and the holiday you would choose.

Activity holidays

Customers may choose their destination because it allows them to pursue a particular interest or hobby. They may choose an activity such as cycling, diving or trekking. Cycling holidays account for about 5 per cent of activity holidays taken. Serious cyclists can take their own cycles by air and then carry their gear on their bike or on their back when they reach the destination. All specialist cycling operators will provide bikes for those who want them and most offer a range of different cycling holidays ranging from extremely taxing mountain bike tours to gentle rides through the countryside. A wonderful example is Cycle Cuba, where people go on a cycling holiday in Cuba that is demanding but at the same time raises money for charity through sponsorship. Climate is an important consideration for customers taking a cycling holiday. If it is too hot then the cycling is uncomfortable and too taxing. The landscape of the destination must be carefully considered to suit the cycling ability of the group.

Cruising

For those with lots of time to spare, cruising is an option. Usually a holiday in itself, it is also a means of travelling to a destination. A popular holiday for UK travellers is crossing the Atlantic on a liner, spending a few days in New York and returning by air.

All the major cruise lines offer fly cruises and that means that the prices quoted usually include the flight and all the arrangements are made for the passenger. Flights may be charter where the ship is large enough to warrant charters arriving from various departure airports, or they may be scheduled. The more expensive cruises often use scheduled flights because of the extra flexibility and the perception of luxury. Also included in the price are the accommodation, meals, activities and entertainment on board and usually room service.

World cruises appeal to a lot of people but they can't usually afford the time or the money to do them! Prices start at around £11,000 per person and can be two or three times that depending on choice of accommodation. Also, it obviously takes some time to sail around the world so work commitments might get in the way. The customer profile tends to be older retired people – with plenty of money!

Type of booking

Remember that how you book a holiday affects your choice. If you want to book a tour as a package, you are limited to the tours that the tour operator has put together. This may be convenient and easy to book but may mean you are on the 'tourist trail' with many others. If you book independently, you can choose exactly what you want, but it may cost more and you will have to do a lot of research. Many tour operators and some travel agents now offer tailor-made bookings where you tell them what you want and they arrange and book it for you.

Visitor motivation

Why do people travel? Why do people go on holiday? A great deal of research has been done into motivation for travel, but consumer behaviour is a difficult area to research as sometimes we ourselves don't know exactly why we do something. There are probably as many reasons for going away as there are tourists who go. Tourists on holiday together at the same resort do not necessarily have the same motivation for being there.

Activity

For this activity you are in the very fortunate position of going on lots of holidays. Imagine you are taking each of the following holiday types. For each one you must find a suitable long haul destination that suits *you*. Repeat the activity and imagine that you are finding destinations for the same holiday types for your grandparents or a much older couple. Use brochures to help you and ensure you are able to locate each of the destinations.

Holiday type	You	Older couple
Short break		
Multi-centre tour		
Stopover to Australia		
Hotel based		
All inclusive		
Special occasion (wedding)		
Activity based		
Visiting friends and relatives		
Cruising		
Touring and sightseeing		

When you have finished, compare your choices with a colleague's and discuss their differences and similarities.

Theory into practice

Think about your last trip away. What motivated you to travel? Was it to visit friends or relatives? In that case your motivation might have been a desire to reinforce friendship or family bonds. Perhaps you were motivated by a sense of duty to visit an elderly family member.

A trip or holiday may have more than one motivating force behind it. Football fans who visited Germany for the 2006 World Cup might have been motivated by a desire to see their team win and also a wish to see a new country.

Types of motivation for travel and tourism include the following.

Lesiure and relaxation

Tourists may be motivated by the need for rest and relaxation, having worked hard all year. This motive could manifest itself in the choice of a simple beach holiday for relaxation in the sun. It might be reflected in the choice of a spa holiday where rest and well-being are emphasised.

Culture and history

Those who visit a destination to study the historic architecture, the arts and music are motivated by a desire to experience culture. In its wider sense many tourists want to experience the language, lifestyle and food and drink offered by another culture. We often describe those who like to travel further and further afield in search of new experiences as having 'wanderlust'. Gap-year students often express a wish 'to travel' and what they usually mean is that they want to meet new people, see places and enjoy new experiences. Typical travel destinations on a student tour will be Australian cities, Thailand, Fiji and the USA.

Business

People on business have to travel to specific destinations to attend meetings or events. They may combine their trip with leisure activities. Hong Kong is a good example. Whilst being an important business destination because of its location and access to Asia, it also has culture and shopping to offer.

Education

Many tourists visit the UK in order to participate in English-language courses, and many language schools have opened up to cater for them – language courses can be found in all major cities.

Many UK students undertake educational trips abroad as part of their courses, including learning a language. South America is popular for those who want to learn Spanish and want to travel further afield than Spain.

Cost of visiting

Some tourists are on a limited budget so will have to choose a holiday that is cheap.

A favourable exchange rate also increases our motivation to travel. Over the past few years the US dollar has been very weak against sterling. This has led to increased tourism to the USA from the UK. In the first four months of 2004, UK arrivals to the USA jumped by 16 per cent, compared with the same period the previous year.

Media influences

A popular film attracts people to its location. *Reservoir Dogs* drew people to visit Los Angeles and the surrounding countryside.

Social reasons

Some tourists take a holiday in order to meet new people. This is especially true of singles holidays or 18–30-type holidays. Some people combine their love of activity holidays with meeting a new group of people, perhaps by joining a walking or cycling tour.

Theory into practice

Find three examples of long haul holidays arranged particularly for singles or young people. Choose one and say why it might appeal to you.

Desire for adventure

Some tourists want to spend their time away enjoying new experiences and may opt for adventure holidays ranging from safaris to white-water rafting. Tanzania is a popular safari destination and offers adventure too, being a developing African country.

Escape

Often tourists want to escape from their busy lives at home or work, and that in itself is motivation to travel. It is also common for tourists to want to escape the British climate, hence the sale of winter sun holidays. The Caribbean is a great choice for winter sun as it has a hot climate all year and in winter the hurricane season is over.

Push and pull factors

Those motivators which arise from our own needs and desires or our own experiences at home can be described as 'push' factors in tourist motivation. We can also be motivated by external factors, which are known as 'pull' factors. Examples of pull factors include advertising of particular destinations, seeing holiday or other television programmes about resorts, or even copying our favourite celebrities. *The Times* newspaper runs a column entitled 'How to holiday like a celebrity'.

Decreased motivation

There are some factors which decrease our motivation to travel to a destination. High levels of crime dissuade tourists. Reports of terrorism may put an end to tourism in an area for a period of time, as happened to the holiday destination of Bali after an appalling bomb attack on a nightclub in 2002. Pollution or natural disasters, such as floods or earthquakes, also decrease motivation to travel to a destination. The 2004 tsunami impacted heavily on tourism in affected areas although most are now recovering.

Theory into practice

Make a small survey of some friends or colleagues. Ask them to think about a recent trip away. It doesn't have to be a holiday – it might be a day out or a visit to friends. Ask them why they chose that particular trip. What motivated them?

Categorise the motivating factors and ask about the external motivators. Did someone else's experience or an advertisement motivate them? Remember that there may be more than one motivator.

Put your results in a table – it might look like this:

Traveller	Push motivation	Pull motivation
Susie – hen night in London	Social – to support her friend	All her girlfriends were encouraging her to go

Motivation is difficult to assess and categorise.

- People have a complex set of motivations, not just one. Motivating factors can be internal or external (push and pull).
- Different motivation does not necessarily mean a different destination. Some destinations have so much to offer that they are suitable for all types of people.

Having decided what kind of holiday they would like to take, potential tourists will then consider other factors before booking. These include the possibility of jet lag, climate or possible political problems. We will look at some of the factors that might help or hinder a booking decision.

Travel factors

Time zones and jet lag

Greenwich Mean Time (GMT) is a term used for world standard time. Each time zone to the east of Greenwich time zone is ahead of GMT, that is +1 hour, +2 hours, etc. Each time zone to the west is behind GMT, that is −1 hour, −2 hours, etc. Going eastwards you add hours to GMT, and going westwards you subtract hours from GMT. GMT is also known as Zulu. Another term you may hear more commonly is Co-ordinated Universal Time.

■ Daylight-saving time (DST)

Daylight-saving or summer time has been adopted in most regions of the world. In the UK it is known as British Summer Time. At 1.00 am GMT on the last Sunday in March, the clocks go forward by one hour, and on the last Sunday in October they revert to GMT. Other countries may introduce daylight-saving time on different dates.

The purpose of the change is so that the hours when people are working or studying better match the period of available daylight. When travelling, people must ensure that time changes are included in time calculations.

Theory into practice

You are going to New York for Christmas shopping at the beginning of December. Your flight leaves the UK at 9.30 am and the flight takes 7 hours. What time is it in New York on arrival?

■ International Date Line

The International Date Line is the imaginary line on the Earth that separates two consecutive calendar days. Travelling east across the line takes the traveller back one day; travelling west takes the traveller forward one day. Cruise passengers crossing the Pacific will be affected by the date line most.

On a map it is shown as 180° away from the meridian that goes through Greenwich, on the line of longitude.

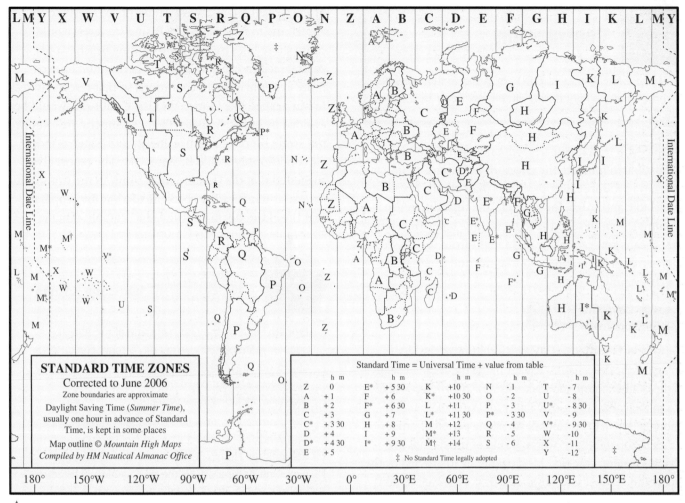

Figure 8.8 Time zone map

(Source: HM Nautical Almanac Office, © Council for the Central Laboratory of the Research Councils)

Standard Time = Universal Time + value from table

	h m		h m		h m		h m		h m
Z	0	E*	+ 5 30	K	+10	N	- 1	T	- 7
A	+ 1	F	+ 6	K*	+10 30	O	- 2	U	- 8
B	+ 2	F*	+ 6 30	L	+11	P	- 3	U*	- 8 30
C	+ 3	G	+ 7	L*	+11 30	P*	- 3 30	V	- 9
C*	+ 3 30	H	+ 8	M	+12	Q	- 4	V*	- 9 30
D	+ 4	I	+ 9	M*	+13	R	- 5	W	-10
D*	+ 4 30	I*	+ 9 30	M†	+14	S	- 6	X	-11
E	+ 5							Y	-12

‡ No Standard Time legally adopted

STANDARD TIME ZONES

Corrected to June 2006

Zone boundaries are approximate

Daylight Saving Time (*Summer Time*), usually one hour in advance of Standard Time, is kept in some places

Map outline © *Mountain High Maps*
Compiled by *HM Nautical Almanac Office*

Case study: jet lag

New Zealand has one time zone, which is 12 hours ahead of GMT. DST is in effect from mid-October until mid-March. The clocks advance by one hour for DST.

Crossing time zones can cause 'jet lag' – usually going east is worse for this than going west. The reason for it is that inbuilt bodily rhythms have been disturbed and it can take a few days for the body to readjust to the new time zone. The 12-hour difference in New Zealand could mean it takes several days to return to normal. Travellers may find that they are falling asleep during the day and staying awake at night.

1 **Find out what can be done to alleviate jet lag.**

2 **Produce a short information sheet that could be given to air passengers before their flight.**

Taking it further

1 Find out what other health problems may occur or be aggravated through flying.

2 What health advice is generally given to travellers by tour operators and airlines? Collect some examples and discuss.

Consider this

If you leave Sydney at 6.00 am in the winter, consider how it can be light nearly all the way by air to London.

People who travel regularly will understand that it is possible to mitigate the effects of jet lag and some journeys produce fewer problems than others. If you travel to Cape Town, for example, the time difference is minimal, even though the flight is quite long. Travelling east means you can take a night flight from the UK yet still arrive in Singapore before sunset and experience a lovely evening.

Deep Vein Thrombosis

Deep Vein Thrombosis (DVT) is a clotting of the blood in any of the deep veins – usually in the leg. It can be fatal if the clot breaks off and makes its way to the lungs where it can then affect the lung's ability to take in oxygen. It is thought that being immobile for a long period of time is a risk factor and that is why any kind of travel – not just flying – can increase risk. Most people are unaffected by the possibility of DVT and unworried by it. However, certain people may be at more risk and may decide not to travel on long journeys. Those with increased risk are those who have other risk factors such as varicose veins or obesity.

Climate and seasons

Tourists need to be aware about climate zones and seasonal variations when arranging trips. This sounds obvious, but many tourists arrive in Thailand, for example, and find it is the monsoon season and they didn't check first. The problem of encountering poor weather, unexpected by the tourist, has increased as people have ventured further afield.

In 2006, the Holiday 2030 report was produced for the Halifax Travel Insurance Company. It looked at global climatic conditions and likely changes and impacts up to 2030. The report suggested that global average temperatures are likely to rise by 1°C to 2°C. This would impact on sea levels and make them up to 72 mm higher but in addition accelerated melting of the Greenland and West Antarctic ice sheets could contribute to rises of 25 cm. Rising sea levels would cause shore lines to diminish, eroding beaches and coastal facilities such as hotels. There would be even more extreme weather conditions so that resorts subject to hurricanes, like Florida and the Caribbean, would be avoided by holidaymakers. Higher temperatures would put strain on resources like energy and water as more air conditioning would be necessary. The report also suggested that the trend to head south to the sun would reverse as temperatures become too hot for people so that they head north instead for a bearable climate.

Case study: hurricane Katrina

Ernesto became the first hurricane of the Atlantic season yesterday with winds of 75 mph. Forecasters said it would strengthen as it headed toward the Gulf of Mexico, where it could menace a wide stretch of coastline, including New Orleans.

The storm could grow into a category three hurricane with winds of at least 111 mph by Thursday, said the US National Hurricane Centre in Miami. Category three hurricane Katrina struck the city a year ago tomorrow. Visitors to the Florida Keys were ordered to leave the island chain yesterday and tourists planning to visit were told to postpone trips. Emergency officials claimed the New Orleans levée system was ready for another major hurricane. 'I think we're in good shape,' said Don Powell, co-ordinator of Gulf Coast rebuilding. 'There's no question in my mind, we're ready.'

(Source: http://www.travelindustryreview.com/news/2856; *Travel Industry Review* 28 August 2006)

1 **It was summer 2005 when New Orleans was devastated by hurricane Katrina. Find out how the region fares today and how much renovation and repair has been carried out. How open is the city to tourists today?**

2 **Produce a short newspaper article on your findings.**

Taking it further

Research figures for tourism in New Orleans and make a comparison of figures pre and post hurricane Katrina. What is the current trend?

Documentation

Depending on destination, tourists may require various documents including visas and vaccination certificates. These can take time to acquire and therefore will prevent travellers choosing some destinations at the last minute. In addition, visas or vaccinations can add an extra cost to the holiday.

Travel and health restrictions

Travel restrictions are put in place when it is dangerous for tourists to visit a destination and will usually occur because of a dangerous political situation or an outbreak of disease. If tourists have already booked a holiday when restrictions are levied then a tour operator will offer an alternative holiday or a refund. With independent travel the situation can be more serious as even if a tourist has travel insurance it is very unlikely to provide cover for an outbreak of war or terrorist activity. You can find about any current restrictions on outbound travel from the UK from the Foreign Office website at www.fco.gov. uk. Health restrictions usually relate to vaccinations. Some countries will not permit entry without typhoid and yellow fever vaccinations, for example, and a certificate must be shown to prove they have been done. Occasionally, outbreaks of disease prevent people travelling. The SARS outbreak of 2004 led to the World Health Organisation adding Toronto and Beijing to its list of places that travellers should avoid.

Consider this

At the time of writing the Foreign Office advises against all travel to the Ivory Coast, Lebanon and Somalia. Do you know why? Go to the FCO website to find out whether the advice remains the same.

Social situations

When considering where to go on holiday, tourists may well decide against travel to a certain area for ethical reasons, for example it is hard to enjoy a luxurious holiday in a resort when you know that people nearby are living in extreme poverty. This might occur in, for example, the Gambia or parts of India. Of course, the opposing view is that your money can help to alleviate poverty. An example of two very different worlds colliding was when holidaymakers camping on the beach in Tenerife in 2006 found that refugees from Africa were swimming onto the shore. A group had arrived from the African mainland in three boats. They were exhausted so the holidaymakers pulled them from the water and gave them food, water and clothing.

Consider this

If you are interested in trying to alleviate poverty when you travel, support Pro Poor Tourism. Find out about its projects at www.propoortourism.org.uk.

Customer types

In this unit you are often asked to consider what types of customers particular destinations appeal to. You have to consider the needs of families, young and old couples, backpackers, those seeking adventure and retirees. You must also consider those visiting friends and relatives (VFR) or business travellers.

For VFR travellers, their destination is determined by the place of residence of those whom they want to visit. Similarly, business travellers will have their destination determined by the location of a meeting or conference. The business traveller looks particularly at access in terms of convenience and at the facilities available in the destination such as easy transport, accommodation and food. The VFR traveller will be also considering accessibility but may not require accommodation at all.

There is a tendency to think of gap-year travellers as those between school and university and indeed that is where the term came from. However, there is a growing trend for older people to take a sabbatical, that is a break from work, later in life. These people are sometimes known as 'SKIs' (Spending the Kids Inheritance)! There is a further group, in their late twenties, who having finally paid off their student debts, take a year out before settling down and having families. These are known as 'QRCs' (Quarter Life Crisis).

According to Mintel ('Independent Travel UK' 2006), by 2010, there will be around 2 million gap-year travellers around the world. Mintel calls older travellers 'career gappers' and even older ones 'denture venturers'!

Consider this

How would the needs of gappers like SKIs, QRCs or denture venturers differ from traditional gap-year travellers? When do you think is the best time to take a gap year?

8.3 Understand the features which make long haul destinations appealing to different visitor types

In this section, we will explore the features of long haul destinations, how they are suitable for different types of holidays and how destinations appeal to different customer types. You should remember that people may look for varying types of holiday to fulfil their needs at different times of the year. For example, a couple with children may take a family holiday in the summer, a skiing holiday at spring half term and a short break for shopping in New York before Christmas for just the two of them.

Remember that tourists will be thinking about the type of holiday they want and their own particular needs alongside the features of the destination which will include:

- accessibility
- facilities available at the destination
- culture to be experienced.

Accessibility

Routes by air

Most long haul travel is by air for reasons of time and convenience. More direct flights are now available too.

Airline routes are very complex as each airline has its own routes, but enters into different types of partnership with other airlines to extend its networks. British Airways (BA) is one of the world's major airlines so it serves as a good example.

BA flies to many destinations worldwide. Most long haul flights are from Gatwick and Heathrow but regional airports are beginning to offer long haul flights, particularly Manchester. This is good news for people who may have had to fly from regions to a London airport and then change to a direct flight. Here is a news item about Thomson starting up long haul holiday flights from Robin Hood airport, Doncaster.

Long haul holiday flights to the Caribbean, Florida and Mexico are soon to go on sale from Robin Hood Airport Doncaster Sheffield for the Summer 2006 season. The new long haul routes will be bookable from Thursday, 28 April, when the Summer 2006 holiday brochures are launched.

(Source: Robin Hood Airport Media Centre http://www.robinhoodairport.com/page.php?p=3&archive=2005&offset=30&media_id=21)

Even if a tourist decides to travel by air there are still decisions to be made about which class to travel in. Scheduled flights offer business and first class although airlines use different names for their services. Even charter flights offer premium class for those who are prepared to pay a bit more.

The following example shows what Thomson offer in its premium class.

*On selected **long haul** flights we are pleased to offer our **Premium Service**, our features include:*

- *Wider seats with extra recline*
- *Up to 5 inches extra legroom*
- *Upgraded menus*

- *Free drinks (except champagne)*
- *Free in-flight entertainment with seat-back video or personal DigEplayer.*

Premium Seats prices start from £150.00 per passenger per return flight.

(Source: http://www.thomsonfly.com/en/flywithus_1878.html)

Cruise

Cruising is very suitable for long haul. Passengers can opt to join a ship in the UK – Southampton is often used for embarkation – and sail to their cruise area. Those with less time to spare will fly to a port, for example Miami, where they can join their cruise ship.

Travelling time and cost

Most tourists do not want to travel too far from their country of origin for trips, for reasons of time, cost and convenience. Tourists choosing to travel long distances, for example to Australia from the UK, make that trip infrequently and tend to go for a longer period of time. The Caribbean is more popular with US tourists than those from the UK as the flight times, and therefore costs, are lower. However, developments in air travel routes have led to an increase in long haul travel and if your special interest lies in seeing elephants in their natural habitat then you will take the trouble to travel to do it.

Travellers will also take into consideration how much further they have to travel to the destination having arrived at the gateway airport or port. Until a few years ago tourists visiting Tobago had to change to a local flight in Port of Spain, Trinidad, as the runway could not accommodate large jets. Since the runway was extended to cater for jumbos, the provision of direct flights has brought about an increase in tourism. In general terms, access to worldwide destinations has become easier and cheaper.

Suitability for the traveller

In the same way that planes have different classes, ships offer larger cabins with more facilities: these are correspondingly more expensive. Each customer has to decide how much they are prepared to spend, what facilities are essential and which ones merely desirable.

Theory into practice

Imagine you are going shopping with friends to New York for 4 days. You are flying with Virgin Atlantic. Visit its website and find out how much extra per person it will cost to fly in premium economy or upper class. What extras do you get for this money? Make some notes. Is it worth it?

Destination facilities

People look for particular facilities at destinations according to their needs. Here are some of the things that might appeal:

- Natural attractions such as mountains, national parks and beaches
- Built attractions such as theme parks and museums
- Climate
- Local transport
- Accommodation range and cost
- Sport and entertainment
- Food and drink
- Culture – festivals, events, arts, local customs.

We will study some particular destinations and examine the features to determine who they might appeal to and what holiday type they are suitable for.

■ Natural attractions

One way of experiencing natural attractions is to go trekking. Trekking is a popular activity to undertake on holiday as it offers adventure yet can be tailored to the ability and wishes of different groups of travellers. Families can trek together in destinations such as the Atlas Mountains in Morocco. Experienced climbers can visit steep and tricky mountains such as the Karakoram range in Pakistan or the sheer-sided Mount Roraima in Venezuela. Billed as the ultimate wildlife experience, a trek to the gorilla sanctuary in the Parc du Volcan rainforest in Rwanda offers excitement and helps ensure the survival of the gorillas.

Best for Families – High Atlas, Morocco

Why? Child-friendly culture, no problems with altitude, short flight time and little travelling on arrival; mules are available for tired little legs.

When? May to October.

The Big Ticks: Mount Toubkal, the highest peak in North Africa at 4165m; staying in a Kabash; seeing snake charmers and acrobats in Marrakesh.

Short-haul Alternative: The Corfu Trail (11 days) is accessible by cheap flights and has *My Family and Other Animals*-inspired nature.

Best for Culture – The Inca Trail, Peru

Why? Machu Picchu isn't the only Inca ruin here: the whole four-day trail is lined with the Inca equivalents of motorway services – inns, rest houses and other, mysterious ruins. Local guides expertly bring these to life.

When? April to November.

The Big Ticks: Dead Woman's Pass (4198m); the first view of Machu Picchu from the Sun Gate; spending the day exploring Machu Picchu; time in Cuzco.

Short-haul Alternative: Northern Romania maintains a traditional life village – try the Maramures region.

Best for Nature – Torres del Paine, Chile

Why? Condors, guanaco (a cousin of the llama), rheas (giant, flightless birds), armadillos and possibly the odd puma, all set among the most diverse and astonishing scenery on Earth with blue lakes, calving glaciers, huge forests and vertical peaks.

When? November to March.

The Big Ticks: The Paine Circuit (eight days) – a complete circling of the massif; the Torres walk to the base of the iconic rock spires (one day).

Short-haul Alternative: The Alpujarras, southern Spain, are carpeted with flowers in the spring, and still have a healthy population of boar and snakes.

Best for Softies – Annapurna Treks, Nepal

Why? Facilities in the Annapurna foothills are second to none. Stay in hotels the whole way and have your daypack carried by your own porter while trekking amid some of the most exciting scenery in the world.

When? March to May; October to December.

The Big Ticks: Views of Machhapuchare (Fishtail) one of the most beautiful mountains in the world; sunrise over the Himilaya from Poon Hill (3210m, six days); the flowering forests of rhododendron in May.

Short-haul Alternative: Tuscany is a lovely base for gentle walking – spend a week in the hills around Sienna.

Best for First-Timers – New Zealand

Why? If you're at all active, New Zealand delivers on every level; sublime scenery, great facilities and it's compact enough to do a couple of different treks in one trip.

When? December to March, but expect rain.

The Big Ticks: The Tongariro Crossing, possibly the best day-walk in the world; the Milford Track (four days), for big peaks, fjords and waterfalls (but be sure to book now for next year); the Abel Tasman Coast Track (five days) for fantastic, sunny coastal walking.

Short-haul Alternative: The central section of the GR10 long-distance path in the French Pyrenees (five–twelve days) for good food and easy access.

Best for Photographers – Everest Base Camp, Nepal

Why? The biggest collection of neck-cricking peaks on the globe; Sherpa culture, yeti skulls in monasteries and beautiful lively villages.

When? March to May; October to December.

The Big Ticks: Kala Pattar (5545m), a hill above base camp that delivers the classic view of Everest, Everest Base Camp (5300m, 14 days), only there in spring, the most famous campsite in the world.

Short-haul Alternative: The Tour of Mont Blanc (11 days) for close-up views of an extraordinary mountain seen from three different countries.

Best for Altitude Junkies – Mount Kilimanjaro, Tanzania

Why? At 5896m it is the highest point in Africa. As it is a fairly easy-angled volcano, it is as big a mountain as you can climb without crampons.

When? June to February.

The Big Ticks: Standing atop one of the seven continental summits; seeing snow on the equator; nipping off for a quick safari afterwards.

Short-haul Alternative: Corsica's GR20 long-distance path – there's nowhere steeper (but it's worth it).

(Source: *Wanderlust*, April/May 2005)

 Figure 8.9 Trekking holidays

1 **Locate all the trekking destinations mentioned in Figure 8.9 on a world map.**

2 **Choose one of the treks and do some research to find out more about it. Describe the features of the destination and explain why those features make the destination suitable for this type of trek. Consider climate, landscape, transport routes and accessibility, accommodation, local services, attractions, local culture and facilities.**

Present your work in the form of a leaflet which includes all this information and can be used to promote the destination. **P3 M2**

Taking it further

Draw up a detailed profile of the type of customers your trek would appeal to. Add this to your leaflet.

◀ Figure 8.10 A visit to a gorilla sanctuary is an exciting wildlife attraction

Potential trekkers have to decide whether to arrange their trek independently or book with an operator. It is a good idea to book with a reputable operator if you are inexperienced as they will provide a local guide and will ensure that no risks are taken with health and safety. An example of a trekking operator is Exodus Travel which has over 30 years' experience and organises travel to Europe, Africa, Asia, South America, North America, Australasia and the Antarctic. An independent trek might work out cheaper but could be difficult to organise, as a guide would have to be located and transport in remote areas might be difficult to find.

■ Built attractions

Havana, the capital city of Cuba, is located in the Caribbean. Cuba's natural attractions include long stretches of beautiful beaches but the appeal of Havana lies in its architecture and history.

The city is in the process of restoration and is a World Heritage site. There are plenty of museums including the famous Museum of the Revolution. The climate is hot all year round but subject to hurricanes in the late summer. Local transport is difficult for tourists as there is little public transport but taxis are widely available. Accommodation in Havana is available at a range of budgets from basic to five star. There are several recently restored boutique hotels, these are small and individually themed rather than part of a chain. The city is renowned for its salsa music and this can be heard in many bars and on the streets. Havana can be visited as a short break but many tourists take a couple of days out of a longer holiday on Cuba to visit the capital.

Theory into practice

Use brochures to find an example of a short break to Havana. Describe the features of Havana in detail, including facilities, accessibility and culture, saying why it is suitable for a short break and what type of customer it would appeal to. Draw up a fact sheet of your findings of not more than one side of A4. **P2**

■ Local transport

Case study: what's the best way to travel around Oz?

Car rental

It's an obvious choice as driving is on the left and Australia's laws are broadly similar to those in the UK. The minimum age for renting is 21, with surcharges sometimes payable by the under-25s. A British driving licence is sufficient.

But beware – random breath tests are carried out, and the legal alcohol limit is only 0.05 per cent. Petrol prices are roughly half those in the UK.

Driving in the outback requires planning – always carry plenty of water and food, and consider taking a satellite phone for journeys to very remote areas.

Car rental companies sometimes impose a free mileage limit in Northern Territory and Western Australia, so check when renting.

Always hire a 4x4 vehicle in the outback or anywhere where you intend travelling on unsealed roads, and check whether driving along unsealed roads is covered by insurance for standard vehicles.

Simon Drew, manager of specialist operator Anzcro, says: 'I always advise agents to up-sell the vehicle group size to the client. Most clients will automatically go for the smallest car to save money, but Australia is a huge country and a larger car will certainly be more comfortable.'

Coach travel

Appealing mainly to backpackers, this is a popular and economic option for getting around Australia.

Passes are available covering the Greyhound and McCafferty's coach networks, and are usually for a fixed number of kilometres. Some regional passes are also available.

Oz Experience is a scheduled express coach operator aimed at backpackers and the youth market, available between main cities in the south and up the east coast.

Anzcro's Simon Drew says: 'Greyhound Aussie Explorer Passes are the cheapest way to get around Australia. You can choose from over 20 routes, and they are ideal for backpackers wanting to take up to one year to complete their route.'

Campervans

Campervans are a popular choice with a network of overnight-stay locations where you can use showers and toilets, and meet other roadies.

Clients can pre-purchase commissionable daily packages that offer excess reduction and a high level of insurance cover, plus extras such as gas, picnic tables and chairs.

Travel 2 assistant product manager Fiona Sharp advises: 'Encourage clients to spend more time on the road as great discounts of up to 20 per cent are available on daily rates for rentals of 21 days or more.

'Britz Campervans has introduced dynamic rates, offering further benefits for early bookers – so the longer the lead time, the better the deal,' she adds.

Rail travel

Many UK visitors opt for popular tourist trains such as the Ghan, Indian Pacific and Sunlander, which are widely sold by operators. They run on selected dates only, but passes are available for extensive rail travel.

Australia's rail network is fairly extensive between major south-east population centres, while Queensland Rail's Tilt Train operates from Brisbane to Rockhampton and Cairns.

Tourism Australia chairman Tim Fischer, a former deputy prime minister, is a great exponent of rail travel, and has written a book on the subject called *Transcontinental Train Odyssey.*

'Trains offer the chance to experience our unique nature and wildlife, fantastic food and wine, indigenous heritage and vibrant cities,' he says.

(Source: *Travel Trade Gazette*, 14 July 2006)

1 **Four types of local travel are featured in the article. For each one discuss what type of customer it is most suitable for and say why.**

2 **Make an oral presentation to your group on your findings.** P2 M1 D1

Accommodation, sport and entertainment, food and drink

Case study: each to their own in India

Family adventures

Mauritius

With the Indian Ocean being heralded as an up-and-coming destination for families, tour companies recognise the need to find options for all ages.

Rob Sanday, Hayes & Jarvis product manager for the Indian Ocean says: 'In Mauritius there are now hotels to suit everyone's budget and tastes. We've added lots of all-inclusive four-star hotels aimed at families.'

A range of resorts in Mauritius now offer activities for the little ones, meaning families can enjoy a long-haul destination that caters for everyone's needs.

La Pirogue has a free kids' club for children up to the age of eleven, which aims to include aspects of Mauritian culture.

During the 12 hours of opening, kids can go on glass-bottom boat rides, learn to dance the sega, snorkel or take part in mini-Olympics. Special menus are prepared for children, and they can even help the chef make their pizzas.

Meanwhile, adults can enjoy the spa and comprehensive range of watersports. Accommodation is laid out in the style of a traditional fishing village with thatched chalets.

Unique experiences

Maldives

The Maldives has used the fact that the islands are so low-lying to its advantage – by pioneering the use of water bungalows in many of its finest resorts.

This type of accommodation has really caught the imagination of honeymooning couples.

At the top end of the market, Club Rannalhi's individual water bungalows have their own private sun deck, glass panel floor and personal breakfasts.

Kuoni has some more budget-friendly options for those who want to experience the uniqueness of the Maldives at a lower cost. It offers the Full Moon resort, which has all the luxury and appeal of the pricier resorts, but without the risk of bankrupting the average holidaymaker.

Linda Pedler, product manager for Kuoni Maldives and Sri Lanka, says: 'Following the tsunami, many hotels have taken the opportunity to upgrade, which means that often three and four-star resorts are being overlooked. But it's vital to support the charter market too.'

The Maldives also has a reputation for being a centre for underwater activities. Diving and snorkelling continue to be popular pursuits, with many resorts offering tuition in their packages.

It is even possible to dine underwater. The Ithaa Underwater restaurant at the Hilton Rangali Island hotel sits 15 feet below the Indian Ocean and has panoramic views of the coral reef surrounding it.

(Source: *Travel Trade Gazette* 30 June 2006)

1 Why do all-inclusive hotels appeal to families?

2 What are water bungalows? Why do they appeal to couples?

3 Why are some of the hotels particularly expensive?

4 What sports and entertainment are on offer for children in Mauritius?

5 What sports are available in the Maldives?

6 Evaluate the suitability of each of the resorts listed for a group of 19-year-old college leavers.

7 What measures could be taken to increase the appeal to the college leavers? **P**3 **M**2 **D**1

Taking it further

Carry out some research and find out what food and drink are the local specialities in Mauritius and in the Maldives.

■ Culture

Many tourists hope to experience local culture when they are on holiday and of course this is one of the benefits of travel. Destinations may have cultural attractions built for other purposes, such as the Taj Mahal in India or ancient temples such as those in Sri Lanka. The cultural experience may be provided by local events or festivals demonstrating the music and dance of a destination. It is important that tourists show respect for the local culture and tour operators can help with this by giving information to holidaymakers before they travel.

Some destinations offer a cultural experience along with the possibility of seeing wonderful natural attractions and beautiful coastlines.

The following extract from the Kuoni Indochina brochure demonstrates the diversity of experience available in Vietnam and gently reminds tourists about respecting local culture.

> *Vietnam offers a fantastic mixture of places to see and visit, whether you are looking for sightseeing, beaches or a touring holiday. In city locations an organised tour is a good idea to help with your orientation, after this if you want to explore independently there are a whole array of taxis, and 'cyclos' which are rather like a modern-day rickshaw which offer a novel and fun way to get around. When visiting ancient sites light cotton clothes and sensible walking shoes are a real asset. It is important to respect local customs and beliefs with regard to dress when visiting religious sites and your local guide will be happy to advise on what is acceptable.*
>
> *World events have inevitably cast their shadow across this country, which was for so many years the subject of news bulletins rather than travel brochures. In the last 20 years this charming and resilient nation has opened its doors to visitors.*
>
> *Not only does Vietnam have a rich diversity of places to see, but also enjoys a vast and beautiful coastline, mist-shrouded mountains, mighty rivers and cascading waterfalls. Whether your passion is for history, scenery, food or culture the delicate tapestry of this nation will offer you all of this and much more besides.*

(Source: Kuoni Indochina, 6 July 2006)

Case study: Machu Picchu

Hiram Bingham, an American explorer, first discovered Machu Picchu in 1911. It is an Inca city located 120 kilometres north west of Cusco in Peru, and before discovery it was hidden by dense jungle on the mountains where it is located, 2400 metres above sea level.

The city's stone constructions are spread over a narrow and uneven mountain top, bordering a sheer 400-metre drop over the Urubamba River canyon. Because of the fascinating architecture the site has been designated a Unesco World Heritage site and has become one of South America's major travel destinations.

Many adventure holiday companies offer tours there, and local operators sell day tours from Cusco. The only means of transport is a train from Cusco to Aguas Calientes, the nearest town to Machu Picchu. Then there is a 20-minute bus journey up the mountain to the ruins.

The popularity of the site has led to problems – it is in danger of being destroyed because of the large number of visitors. In the late 1990s visitors were restricted to 500 per day to protect the site. Unesco is considering a further restriction to 100 visitors per day.

1 **Find out more about Machu Picchu by researching on the internet and in other resources. Report your findings.**

2 **Present the arguments for and against restricting visitor numbers. You could use your ideas for a debate in your group.** P3 M2

Taking it further

Find out about three more long haul destinations that are based on a historical or cultural attraction. Produce a brief fact sheet for each one, illustrating the appeal of the destination. Choose one of these destinations and evaluate how it could capitalise on its facilities to influence future development. D2

▲ Figure 8.11 Machu Picchu is a UNESCO World Heritage site

8.4 Be able to plan a long haul tour

When you plan a long haul tour you will be considering all the factors discussed so far in this unit to determine what to include in the tour.

Visitor needs

First, establish what kind of customer you are dealing with and establish their needs by questioning. You will need to find out:

- who is travelling
- their budget
- their motivation – are they looking for relaxation, culture or adventure
- restrictions in terms of time they can travel, length of tour and any special needs.

Travel

Once you have established the customer's needs think about the tour options and what will suit them. Decide on:

- mode of travel – air, rail, self drive
- distance to travel and journey times – to get to the starting point and then from place to place on the tour
- classes of travel – depending on facilities required and budget.

Accommodation

Consider your customer's preference for:

- motels
- hotels
- campervans
- camping.

Here you will ensure that you include all the customer's preferences in the tour so that they see the sights that interest them and enjoy new experiences.

Use appropriate reference sources to find all the relevant information for the tour. Now you are ready to put together an itinerary for a long haul tour.

At its most basic the itinerary gives details of the journey to be undertaken, in order to arrive at and return from the destination. However, for a multi-centre holiday the itinerary may be much more complex as it must give details of times and accommodation in each centre. An itinerary for a tour must have departure times and details of journeys and activities for each day of the tour. We will consider some examples before you make up your own itineraries.

A basic itinerary for a journey to a destination includes:

- passenger details
- departure date
- departure time
- departure point, e.g. airport
- mode of transport, e.g. airline
- arrival point
- arrival time
- contact details in case of enquiry.

An itinerary for a tour must include more detail:

- client details
- check-in details
- flight (service) numbers
- transport operator, type and class
- tour operator
- departure and arrival in local time
- intermediate stops
- transfer details
- additional services, e.g. trips booked, car hire
- accommodation details, e.g. room type, level of service, extras

Key term

Itinerary – a detailed plan for a journey.

Ms GILLIAN DALE is flying on:

Thursday 07 December

London Gatwick to New York JFK; Fledgling flight 1223 dep. Thu 07 Dec 14:15;
arr. Thu 07 Dec 17.20

Check-in opens Thu 07 Dec 11:15; Closes Thu 07 Dec 13:15

Sunday 10 December

New York JFK to London Gatwick; Fledgling flight 1224 dep. Sun 10 Dec 18:45;
arr. Mon 11 Dec 06.15

Check-in opens Sun 10 Dec 13:45; Closes Sun 10 Dec 15.45

Hold baggage and sports equipment

One hold bag per passenger only. The one passenger on this booking may only check in a total of one bag. If you need to take more, please add the relevant charges to your booking.

Passports and ID

Approved photographic ID is required on all flights, including domestic services.

Pack safely!

Take care when you pack your bags. No dangerous goods may be taken in baggage, and some other items may only be carried in certain parts of the aircraft. New security measures in the UK and at other European airports also strictly limit what you can carry in your hand baggage; these limitations are currently subject to change at short notice. Please ensure you check our online travel update for the latest information before flying.

Baggage allowance

Each paying passenger may take one standard piece of hand baggage, dimensions 45 x 35 x 16 cm, and one piece of standard checked-in hold baggage weighing no more than 20 kg. Additional charges apply if you exceed this allowance.

▲ **Figure 8.12 Basic itinerary for a flight**

- passport, visa and health requirements
- activities planned
- procedure for enquiries or amendments.

Case study: tour itinerary

The Malaysian Explorer itinerary gives details of all the sights and attractions included in the tour and tells the customer where they will stay each night. However, there is still a lot of information needed – more detail would be sent to the customer when booking.

1 **Using the itinerary checklist make notes of what extra information the customer would need.**

2 **Produce a new itinerary with all the extra information included. You will have to research suitable flights.** P4

3 **Describe the type of visitor this tour is suitable for and explain why.** M3

Figure 8.13 ▶ Malaysia Explorer

(Source: Qantas Asia brochure. © QH Tours (UK) Limited)

✈ **Holidays**

Escorted Touring - MALAYSIA

PRICE INCLUDES
Operated by: Hibiscus Holidays

▶ Accommodation with private facilities

▶ Transportation by air-conditioned coach

▶ Services of an English-speaking Tour Escort

▶ Porterage of one piece of luggage per person

▶ Meals as specified (B: Breakfast, L: Lunch)

Khoo Kongsi

Malaysia Explorer

❶ ❷ Overnight stopovers

■ 10 days/9 nights
Singapore - Singapore
Malacca (1) Kuala Lumpur (2)
Cameron Highlands (1) Penang (2)
Kota Baharu (1) Terengganu (1)
Kuantan (1)

■ 7 days/6 nights
Kuala Lumpur - Singapore
Cameron Highlands (1) Penang (2)
Kota Baharu (1) Terengganu (1)
Kuantan (1)

■ 5 days/4 nights
Singapore - Penang
Malacca (1) Kuala Lumpur (2)
Cameron Highlands (1)

ITINERARY

■ ■ □ **Day 1: Singapore - Malacca**
Approximate distance travelled: 260km
Depart from Singapore at approximately 8.00am via the causeway. En route to Malacca you will pass lush tropical jungles, rubber and oil plantations and 'kampongs' or Malay villages. After lunch, enjoy a tour of Malacca's historic sights - St Paul's Hill, Porta de Santiago, Cheng Hoon Teng Temple and Jonkers Street also known as antique street.
Overnight: Renaissance Hotel or similar - Gold; Hotel Equatorial or similar - Silver L

■ ■ □ **Day 2: Malacca - Kuala Lumpur**
Approximate distance travelled: 155km
After breakfast your journey continues to Kuala Lumpur, via Seremban. On arrival enjoy a city tour, including the National Monument, Sultan Abdul Samad Building, the Selangor Club and the National Palace.
Overnight: Hotel Istana or similar - Gold; Park Inn International or similar - Silver B, L

■ □ □ **Day 3: Kuala Lumpur**
Breakfast is followed by a visit to the Batu Caves reached by a straight flight of 272 steps where you will have the opportunity to see how Malaysian handicrafts and pewter wares are made. There will be time this afternoon to explore the city of Kuala Lumpur.
Overnight: Hotel Istana or similar - Gold; Park Inn International or similar - Silver B, L

■ ■ ■ **Day 4: Kuala Lumpur - Cameron Highlands**
Approximate distance travelled: 255km
7 day passengers join tour.
Head north to the Cameron Highlands, the centre of Malaysian tea production, located around 1800 metres above sea level. En route, you will see the 'Orang Asli' (indigenous Malaysians), complete with their blowpipes, and stop for lunch in the highlands.
Overnight: Heritage Hotel or similar - Gold and Silver B, L

■ ■ ■ **Day 5: Cameron Highlands - Penang**
Approximate distance travelled: 310km
Your day begins with a pleasant downhill drive to Ipoh, the 'city of millionaires' which made its fortune from rich tin mines. Visit the famous Cave Temples followed by lunch at a local restaurant before proceeding to Kuala Kangsar with its unique Ubudiah Mosque, a magnificent building with a golden dome. A drive across Penang Bridge, the longest bridge in Asia, brings you to Penang Island.
5 day passengers depart tour.
Overnight: Penang Parkroyal Resort or similar - Gold; Copthorne Orchid Penang or similar - Silver B, L

■ □ □ **Day 6: Penang**
Sightseeing this morning includes the Penang Snake Temple, Khoo Kongsi clan house and the Thai Temple of Wat Chayamangkalaram, which houses a 33 metre reclining Buddha. This afternoon enjoy a swim or perhaps go shopping at your leisure.
Overnight: Penang Parkroyal Resort or similar - Gold; Copthorne Orchid Penang or similar - Silver B, L

Penang

■ ■ ■ **Day 7: Penang - Kota Baharu**
Approximate distance travelled: 375km
Start off early today across the Malay peninsula. Observe the contrasts in lifestyle, as you head from the west to the east coast. Arrive in Kota Baharu, a centre for Malay culture, crafts and religion.
Overnight: Renaissance Hotel or similar - Gold: Pool View; Silver: Town View B, L

■ ■ ■ **Day 8: Kota Baharu - Terengganu**
Approximate distance travelled: 245km
Begin your day with a visit to the famous market of Kota Baharu before proceeding southwards to the state of Terengganu. Check in to your resort and enjoy the rest of the afternoon free for your own activities.
Overnight: Primula Parkroyal or similar - Gold; Grand Continental or similar - Silver B, L

■ ■ ■ **Day 9: Terengganu - Kuantan**
Approximate distance travelled: 250km
A scenic drive along the coastal road will bring you into the state of Pahang where you will see Malay villages built in 'kampong' style. On arrival in Kuantan you will be treated to lunch and the rest of the afternoon is free for you to relax on the beach.
Overnight: Hyatt Regency Kuantan or similar - Gold; Swiss Garden Resort or similar - Silver B, L

■ ■ ■ **Day 10: Kuantan - Kuala Lumpur or Singapore**
Approximate distance travelled: 259km (To Kuala Lumpur), 380km (To Singapore)
The 7 day tour passengers are transferred direct to Kuala Lumpur.
The 10 day passengers see the palace of the Sultan of Pahang, as you depart Kuantan. After lunch in Mersing, you pass Ulu Tiram and Johor Bahru, before crossing the causeway back into Singapore. Arrive at your hotel or Singapore airport at about 6.00pm. B, L
IMPORTANT NOTES: Connecting outbound flights on Day 10 of the tour, must not depart Singapore any earlier than 9.00pm.

ACCOMMODATION: All hotels have at least one restaurant and a coffee shop, air-conditioned rooms with private facilities and televisions, swimming pools and great locations. Hotel tax and service charges are included.

Passengers may take this tour in its entirety or enjoy a shorter duration tour. Choice of pick-up or drop-off at Qantas Holidays accommodation in Singapore, Kuala Lumpur and Penang.

Departures: Thursday from Singapore, Sunday from Kuala Lumpur
All tours operate subject to a minimum of 2 passengers travelling

QANTAS HOLIDAYS VIEW
A comprehensive tour taking in the best of Malaysia, its cities, major cultural centres and its picturesque rural areas.

79

Knowledge check

1 Name three useful reference sources for long haul travel information.

2 Explain the difference between tourist arrivals and receipts.

3 Why is Australia a popular long haul destination for British people?

4 Why is Florida suitable for families?

5 Why are people travelling so far for short breaks?

6 Give two examples of cities suitable for long haul short breaks from the UK.

7 How does education motivate people to travel?

8 What is Greenwich Mean Time?

9 How can jet lag be alleviated?

10 Why might the government put travel restrictions in place?

11 Give an example of how looking for a certain type of holiday affects customer choice.

Preparation for assessment

You work as an assistant for the training officer of a long haul tour operator, Paul Richards: Paul's job is to visit travel agents and train them to sell the company's long haul holidays. This means ensuring the agents know the location of long haul destinations and understand how to meet customer needs by selecting appropriate products. He is currently preparing material for his next series of training events and has asked you to help. He needs to prepare maps, presentation notes, information sheets and exhibition material.

1 Prepare a series of maps – you will need outline world maps for this task. **P1**

a) Map A: locate and mark:

- the continents of Asia, North America, South America, Africa, Australasia, Europe
- ten major tourist-receiving areas and ten major tourist-generating countries.

b) Map B: accurately locate four examples of each of these five destination types: cities, coastal, purpose built, natural, historical or cultural.

Grading tip

Use a key to distinguish different destination types.

2 a) Select one long haul destination from each of the following categories, ensuring that each of your examples is from a different country:

- cities
- coastal
- purpose built
- natural
- historical or cultural.

b) For each of your chosen destinations produce an information sheet which Paul can use for training purposes which includes:

- a description of the types of holidays provided for different types of visitor
- consideration of the factors affecting customer choice
- consideration of different travel motivations. **P2 M1**

Grading tip

To reach Merit level, key motivators for each destination should be explained, showing how they attract visitors and the types of holiday on offer. A detailed explanation of the significance of travel factors and how they affect choice and appeal will also provide evidence for a Merit.

3 Assess the success of long haul destinations in meeting the needs of different kinds of visitors. Make recommendations on how a destination could minimise the effects of factors which negatively affect its popularity. Produce this information as notes or slides for a presentation. **D1**

Grading tip

You will find this task easier if you use the same destinations that you used in task 2 as examples. To assess success, think of gaps in provision of facilities for tourists. Explain how these might be provided, for example improved public transport or evening entertainment.

4 Choose one long haul destination. Describe all the features that contribute to the appeal of the destination in detail. You could present this as a detailed poster for exhibition. **P3**

Grading tip

Make sure you include accessibility, for example methods of transport, their frequency and examples of costs, together with a description of all the other features and destination facilities which contribute to appeal for different types of visitor. Cultural aspects, way of life, traditions and values must also be included. Make sure you choose a destination that has examples of all these features.

5 Assess which of the features described in task 4 are key in appealing to visitors and say why. Link the features to specific visitor types. Write a report on your findings. **M2**

Grading tip

You might support your evidence by researching visitor numbers and showing how a particular feature such as improved transport access has increased numbers.

6 Evaluate how your chosen destination could capitalise on its facilities in order to influence its future development. Add this information to your report. **D2**

Grading tip

To achieve Distinction level you should consider what improvements the destination could make to facilities it already has to attract tourists.

7 Paul wants the travel agents to be able to produce an itinerary for a multi-centre tour. He has produced the following scenario and wants you to produce an exemplar itinerary.

A group of four friends in their mid-twenties wish to arrange a multi-centre holiday. They are two couples, Marsha and Frederik, Carla and Pedro. They are all working in the UK, in London. Frederik and Pedro are both archaeology graduates although they now both work in the city. Marsha and Carla are lecturers at a college of further education. Marsha lectures in communications and Carla in art.

The four have decided that they want to visit South America. All have very busy lives and they need to incorporate some relaxation and rest into their holiday but they also want to visit different places of interest. They are high earners so they can afford luxurious surroundings. They want to have the opportunity to visit historical sites and the men would like to pursue their interest in archaeology. Carla would like to look at local arts and crafts and may want to buy some pieces to bring home. All are agreed that they want some time to rest on a beach in the sun and to wine and dine in the evenings but it is also important to them that they get to know the local culture. They can travel in March or April – around Easter time – for 2 or 3 weeks.

Produce an itinerary for this multi-centre tour.

Grading tip

To reach Pass level, you should make sure that the tour contains at least four centres. The tour should include transport arrangements between the centres, including journey times, distances and options available. It should also include accommodation to be used en route and at each centre, as well as the attractions/events available to the visitor at each centre.

You must devise the tour yourself and note reference sources used.

8 Justify your selections for the two couples saying how you met their needs. Add this information as notes to your itinerary. **M3**

Grading criteria

To achieve a pass grade the evidence must show that the learner is able to:	To achieve a merit grade the evidence must show that, in addition to the pass criteria, the learner is able to:	To achieve a distinction grade the evidence must show that, in addition to the pass and merit criteria, the learner is able to:
P1 identify and locate continents, major long-haul tourist receiving areas, countries and destination of the world using appropriate reference sources **Assessment practice page 273**	**M1** explain in detail why different long-haul destinations attract visitors with different motivations, and how travel factors can influence choice of destination **Case study page 294**	**D1** assess the success of long-haul destinations in meeting the needs of different types of visitors, and make feasible recommendations as to how a destination could minimise the effects of the factors that negatively affect its popularity **Case study page 294**
P2 select and describe different types of holidays offered by long-haul destinations for different types of customers identifying both travel and motivating factors **Theory into practice page 293**	**M2** assess the significance of the key features that influence the appeal of a selected long-haul destination **Case study page 275**	**D2** evaluate how the selected destination could capitalise on its facilities in order to influence its future development **Taking it further page 296**
P3 describe the features that contribute to the appeal of a selected long-haul destination **Case study page 275**	**M3** independently plan a detailed multi-centre tour, clearly justifying selections for the chosen visitor profile **Case study page 299**	
P4 plan a multi-centre long-haul tour to meet a given client brief, showing references used **Case study page 299**		

Retail and business travel operations

Introduction

When you finish your studies you may opt to work in the retail or business travel sector. They offer many advantages as a career; you can choose to work in either sector, and there are travel agencies in all localities so it is a flexible option in terms of location. You will have the opportunity to practise your customer service skills at first hand with people who are excited about booking travel or holidays. There are plenty of incentives for staff who work hard, including educational trips to holiday destinations.

The retail travel sector is in a period of dynamic change as new technology is introduced and the nature of the service offered by travel agents is changing.

In this unit you will find out about how both retail and business travel operate, the relationship between agents and other businesses in travel and tourism and how they co-operate or compete with one another.

We will examine the impact of advances in technology on the sector and how retail agents in particular fight to have competitive advantage.

You will learn how to select different products and services to meet customer needs and how to develop itineraries to meet customer needs.

After completing this unit you should be able to achieve the following outcomes:

1   Understand the retail and business travel environments

2   Understand how advances in technology have affected retail and business travel operations

3   Understand how retail travel organisations seek to gain competitive advantage

4   Be able to produce complex itineraries for retail and business travel customers.

Thinking points

This account gives you a flavour of what it's like working in a travel agent. Remember that travel agents do not travel that much! They spend most of their time finding holidays for other people.

Shireen left college in 2006 having completed a BTEC National Diploma. She explains what her job involves.

A day in the life of a travel agent

I start at 9.00 am – the first thing is to put the kettle on. I am the most junior member of staff but they all take turns to make the tea!

I begin with admin – there's filing to do, checking the post and matching up details on our travel system. If payments arrive I enter them on our system too. This is the time to send out letters – I don't have to write them, I call them up from our computer depending on what is needed. Sometimes there are tasks to do from the previous day when we have been busy.

From about 11.00 am it gets busy with customers. We sell a lot of coach tickets as we are the only agent in town to sell them. Whenever customers come in and are looking at the brochures, one of us gets up to greet them and ask if we can help them.

A lot of customers make enquiries and we look up holidays for them on the Viewdata system. This is my favourite part of the job – it's lovely talking to customers and finding out where they want to go and why. Sometimes I get business customers but they are more likely to telephone than come in.

In between customers, I deal with other telephone enquiries and sort out brochures – we have cupboards full downstairs. I have to produce tickets and I have to make up files for each client and record when they have booked and when the tickets were sent out, etc.

At about 4.30 pm I do the banking. The computer has details of all payments made and I reconcile that with our takings and put any cash and cheques in the safe.

Role of a travel agent

The role of a travel agent is to act as an intermediary (middleman) between the customer and the supplier. The supplier is usually a hotel, transport company, tour operator or insurance company, among others. The travel agent does not buy the products or services of the supplier and sell them on; rather, travel agents work on a commission basis. This means the supplier pays them a percentage of the value of the sale. The commission is variable between suppliers.

It is possible for travel agents to charge customers for their services and this is becoming more common and more acceptable to customers.

The travel agent provides a range of products and services including:

- information on holidays and travel
- booking of holidays
- booking of travel
- booking of other services, e.g. parking or excursions
- sale of insurance
- currency exchange
- tailor-making packages.

Types of retail agency

The Association of British Travel Agents defines a retail travel business as follows:

> *Retail business is business transacted in the capacity of a travel agent, i.e. a person carrying on business, in whole or in part, as agent for a principal remunerated by commission or otherwise, in respect of the sale or offer for sale of travel arrangements. Retail businesses are not in contract with the client.*
>
> (Source: http://www.abta.com)

Retail travel agents specialise in leisure travel, that is, mostly holidays, but some do cater for business customers. There are different types of retail travel agents. The main categories are shown below.

Multiples

Multiples are large chains of more than 100 branches – some have hundreds of branches. They are to be found on almost every high street. They are usually public limited companies who prefer, and can afford, prime locations.

Holiday hypermarkets are a type of multiple first introduced by First Choice, the tour operator. They have some very large retail travel agencies and the staff are specialised, with expertise in particular holiday types. They tend to be located in large shopping centres like Bluewater in Kent, where there is a lot of passing trade. They have many promotions but are expected to hit high sales targets. First Choice's own products are heavily promoted and you will find it difficult to see other operators' brochures.

Independents

An independent travel agent is often owned by a family or partnership. These outlets are more likely to be found in smaller towns as it is difficult for them to afford the high rents of prime locations. Many independents have been bought out by multiple chains, but those that remain have a reputation for good personal service.

Northenden Travel (www.northendentravel.co.uk) is an example of a family independent. You will see in the following extract that it is a sizeable business employing over 20 people, but is nowhere near the scale of the multiples.

A Family Business

Northenden Travel was established in 1983 and is still family owned and managed. The company incorporates separate business-travel and tour-operating departments alongside a high street retail holiday shop. As an independent travel specialist and still family-owned business, we are proud to be trusted with the travel arrangements of many leading UK businesses, universities and chambers of commerce.

Directors Nigel and Jeni Schofield are supported by a team of over 20 people. Each member of staff is highly experienced in sourcing the best value from

	2001	2003	2005	% change 2001–05
Thomson (incl. Callers Pegasus and James Travel)	785	770	776	–1.1
Advantage	812	725	744	–8.4
Going Places (incl. Travel World)	705	698	566	–19.7
Thomas Cook	692	649	612	–11.6
Worldchoice (incl. Premier and Let's Go)	756	585	479	–36.6
First Choice (incl. Hays and Holiday Hypermarkets)*	336	420	435	+29.5
Co-op: Other CTTG Members	236	236	390	+65.3
Co-op: Travelcare (CTTG)	359	393	380	+5.8
Mid Consort	164	116	96	–41.5
Carlson Wagonlit	106	91	91	–14.2

*Formerly Travel Choice

(Source: Annual Company Reports, Accounts & Websites/Mintel 2006)

Table 9.1 Leading travel agents, by number of outlets, 2001–5

the world's leading operators, airlines, and travel suppliers. They have built the business by trading with integrity and offering a better service where quality, creativity, flexibility and value for money are the watchwords.

(Source: https://secure.nortravel.co.uk/ntg.htm)

E-agents

Many of the major tour operators have set up travel agents online. They recognise that internet access and use are growing, and that they have to be part of the internet revolution or they will be overtaken by it. There are also companies that trade as online travel agencies without any retail shop presence. They sell packages, flights or accommodation. Examples include Expedia and Lastminute.com.

Specialists

There are agents who specialise in selling particular types of holidays or cater for a specific group. An example is STA, which specialises in travel for students and young people. STA has over 80 agents across the UK.

Homeworkers

Many people enjoy the flexibility of working from home, especially those with family commitments. They can work full time or part time as they choose. There are several companies operating in this market with a network of homeworkers. Examples include Travel Counsellors and Holidays by Phone. Holidays by Phone is a fairly small business with about 40 homeworkers in the UK in addition to its own call-centre staff, whereas Travel Counsellors has about 400 agents.

Activity

Harvey World Travel is an Australian-owned travel agency company that now trades in the UK. In 2006, Harvey World opened its first agency within a Virgin Megastore. This was advertised by a 5-week television, radio, and press campaign. Following this, Harvey World hoped to extend its retail network into branches of Boots the chemist.

1 What are the benefits to Harvey World Travel of opening branches within other stores?

2 Are there any benefits to the store?

Taking it further

Find out how Harvey World started operating in the UK. You will find information on its website and by searching the archives of the trade press (www.ttglive.com).

Business tourism includes:

- conferences and meetings – with an estimated value to the UK economy of £10.3 billion in 2005 according to the British Conference Venues Survey 2006
- exhibitions and trade fairs – estimated to be worth over £2 billion annually
- incentive travel – this is a sector of business travel that arranges events and travel for companies to offer to employees as rewards for good performance
- corporate events – estimates value this segment at between £700 million and £1 billion annually
- general business travel.

The role of business travel agents is to book accommodation and travel for business travellers. There is little leisure travel to be arranged, however business travellers may ask for leisure travel such as flights and hotels to be organised for accompanying partners.

Although the role is similar to that of a leisure travel agent, the hotels booked are likely to be in cities and offer business services. Flights are likely to be scheduled rather than charter as business travellers are looking for convenient times and departure points.

Types of business agency

General business

General business travel agents are often independent agents who have chosen to specialise in the business market. They are frequently located in business parks so that they can capture local business. There are also some large organisations operating in business travel. An example is American Express. The parent company provides global travel and financial services but the business travel agent is known as American Express Corporate Travel. Services include:

- account management
- ticket reservations for all modes of transport
- emergency travel services
- meeting and events organisation
- travel services such as airport chauffeur parking, chauffeur-driven cars, etc.
- foreign exchange.

Another major player in business travel is Carlson Wagonlit Travel (CWT). This company provides business travel services to over 50,000 corporate clients worldwide, about 2100 of whom are from the UK. In 2003, CWT was voted national business travel

▲ Figure 9.1 Delegates attending a conference

agent of the year. Through the CWT Corporate Select programme, clients are offered a complete range of travel and value-added services. Some of these include:

- domestic and international air reservations
- hotel reservations through the company's Corporate Hotel Programme. It usually gets about 40 per cent off standard rates
- reservations and ticketing for UK rail and Eurostar
- reservations and ticketing for UK and UK–European ferry routes
- car rental reservations
- chauffeur parking at London Heathrow
- management information reports including travel expenditure summary reports and air travel analysis.

Corporate hospitality

Corporate hospitality is the provision of entertainment to clients by a business. A company specialising in corporate hospitality will be able to acquire tickets for major events such as rock concerts and sporting events like Wimbledon. It will also provide catering and transport if required. An example of a UK company specialising in corporate hospitality is Keith Prowse. It offers:

- hospitality packages at events
- on-site facilities at events
- experienced event managers
- dedicated account managers to give advice about corporate hospitality.

Incentive travel

Incentive travel is very similar to corporate hospitality but is usually offered by an employer to employees rather than to customers. For example, a successful sales team may be taken away for a weekend's leisure to celebrate their success or motivate them for the future. Conferences are often held in smart locations in top hotels so that people are keen to attend.

An example of a company operating in the incentive market is Kuoni Events. Kuoni Conference and Incentive division is part of Kuoni Travel Limited and is based in Dorking, Surrey. It offers dedicated project teams who will research and develop events. Examples include an incentive to Dubai, a management meeting in Gstaad, a product launch in Gleneagles and a conference in Singapore.

Theory into practice

Find out what business travel agents operate in your area. If possible, ask an agent to come and talk to your group about what it does. Draw up a table comparing its role and responsibilities with those of a retail travel agent.

E-agents

Business travel agents operate online in just the same way as retail agents. In fact, it is becoming essential to offer online services. According to American Express 42 per cent of companies have introduced online booking systems since 2004.

Theory into practice

Find out what kind of online services American Express offer to business travellers. Are they similar to the services you would expect to find in a high street travel agency?

Travel agents do not operate in isolation. There is a range of organisations which can offer advice and support and represent the interests of the sector to government.

Trade associations and memberships

ABTA

The Association of British Travel Agents (ABTA) is the UK's best-known trade association for tour operators and travel agents. Of holidays sold in the UK, 85 per cent are sold through ABTA agents.

It cost about £1500–£2000 to join ABTA initially but it is important for agents to join as the public will look for an ABTA travel agent when booking travel and holidays. It gives them a sense of security, knowing that the travel agency follows ABTA's code of conduct and is bonded.

However, membership is not compulsory for travel agents.

The main benefit to consumers of booking through an ABTA travel agent is that in the event of the agent or tour operator going bankrupt, ABTA will ensure that people can continue their holiday arrangements with another operator or be repatriated.

Travel agents who wish to join ABTA must comply with four main requirements:

1 **Financial** The requirements are that members should have a minimum paid-up share capital or owner's/partners' capital of £50,000. There must also be net assets of at least £50,000 excluding intangibles. Retail members must have at least £15,000 working capital (net recoverable current assets).

2 **Bonding** ABTA requires that all members protect their clients' money, so providing a bond is a condition of membership. The amount of the bond is calculated by ABTA. It is issued by a bond obliger, which is a bank or insurance company.

3 **Staffing** Retailers must have at least one qualified member of staff at each office. There are additional requirements for those selling travel insurance.

   To be considered as qualified, the person concerned must within the 5 years before any point of time during their employment have had:

   – at least 2 years' practical experience, or

   – at least 18 months' experience plus ABTA Travel Agency qualifications at Level 1 or primary level, or

   – at least one year's experience plus ABTA Travel Agency qualifications at Level 2 or advanced level.

4 **Conduct** Members must adhere to ABTA's Memorandum of Association and Articles of Association and Code of Conduct.

All these requirements are explained in detail on the ABTA website (www.abta.com).

Key term

Bond – a formal undertaking from an approved bank or insurance company to pay a sum of money to ABTA in the event of the member's financial failure, primarily for the purpose of reimbursing customers who would otherwise lose money they have paid.

ABTA provides a range of services to its members, including:

- technology advice
- legal services
- research publications
- financial advice
- seminars
- advice on employment issues
- consumer arbitration.

Case study: Scottish miniple goes bust

Seven-branch Perrin (Goods & Services Glasgow), trading as Prentice Travel and Sunsavers, has become the fourth ABTA member to fail in less than a week.

ABTA said the company, which traded as an agent and operator, was unable to meet its liabilities and ceased trading on Friday.

The company's head office was at 3 Princes Square, East Kilbride, Glasgow, and its seven branches were in Falkirk, Hamilton, Alexandria, Livingston, Irvine, Kilmarnock and Rutherglen.

(Source http://www.travelmole.com)

1 What type of claims would go to ABTA and why do you think they would pay out?

2 What measures can you take as a customer to ensure your holiday is covered in the event of company failure?

3 How could this company trade as an operator and an agent?

Write down your answers and compare them with others in your group.

■ ABTA Code of Conduct

All members of ABTA, travel agents and tour operators alike, agree to abide by ABTA's Code of Conduct. This code was rewritten in 2006. The aim was to write it in plainer English so that it would be easier to understand. Figure 9.2 shows an extract – you can see the whole thing on the ABTA website.

Any company in breach of the code is reported to a Code of Conduct Committee. If a case is found against the member then disciplinary action may be taken. This could result in a reprimand, a fine or even expulsion.

Association of Train Operating Companies

The Association of Train Operating Companies represents the interests of train operating companies to the government, regulatory bodies and the media on transport policy issues. The organisation is also responsible for licensing travel agents to sell rail tickets and other rail products.

Consortia for independent agents

Independent travel agents usually seek to maintain control of their own businesses, yet they can lose out on the buying power of a large group and find it difficult to compete against the big four tour operators – TUI UK, Thomas Cook, First Choice, MyTravel – who all have their own travel agencies.

One means of gaining support for such independent agents is joining a consortium. Consortia allow the travel agents to gain the benefits of being in a group yet retain their independence. Some consortia give the agents the option of using the consortium brand name, which gives the benefit of recognition by the public.

Some of the consortia have grouped together to form the Independent Travel Agents Alliance. This is made up of the consortia Midconsort, Travelsavers, Worldchoice and the Travel Trust Association.

Other consortia in the UK are Freedom Travel and Advantage.

CODE OF CONDUCT

2. MAKING THE BOOKING

What is this section about?	Who does it apply to?
It's about the booking process and it ensures that all Clients are given the correct information relevant to their particular booking.	Agents and Principals

ABTA MEMBERS SHALL:

Suitable Arrangements

2A) Make every effort to ensure that the Travel Arrangements sold to their Clients are compatible with their Clients' individual requirements.

Booking Procedures

2B) Ensure that satisfactory booking and documentation procedures are followed and, where appropriate, that such procedures are in accordance with the procedures laid down by the Principal. See *Guidance on the Application of the Code of Conduct.*

Financial Protection

2C) Inform Clients about any arrangements that apply to their booking for the protection of their money.

Data Protection

2D) Comply with relevant data protection requirements and ensure that they have in place an effective policy for protecting the privacy of Clients, which shall be available to Clients. See *Guidance on the Application of the Code of Conduct.*

Booking Conditions

2E) Ensure that their Clients are aware of booking and other published conditions, including Agents' terms of business, applicable to their Travel Arrangements before any contract is made and that all Clients have access to a set of booking conditions in written or other appropriate form. See *Guidance on the Application of the Code of Conduct.*

Health Requirements

2F) Before a contract is made, inform their Clients of health requirements that are compulsory for the journeys to be undertaken. Members must also advise Clients travelling abroad to check recommended practice with their GP, practice nurse or travel health clinic. See *Guidance on the Application of the Code of Conduct.*

Passport and Visa Information

2G) Before a contract is made, advise their Clients of passport, visa and other entry and transit requirements for the journeys to be undertaken where it is reasonably practicable for the Members to obtain this information. In other cases, Members shall offer Clients reasonable assistance in obtaining such information. See *Guidance on the Application of the Code of Conduct.*

FCO Advice

2H) Before a contract is made, advise their Clients of the availability of any advice issued by the Foreign & Commonwealth Office. This can be viewed at www.fco.gov.uk/knowbeforeyougo. See *Guidance on the Application of the Code of Conduct.*

Association of British Travel Agents

1 September 2006
Page 3 of 18

▲ **Figure 9.2 Extract from ABTA Code of Conduct**

(Source: http://www.abtamembers.org/pdf/codeofconduct.pdf)

Theory into practice

If you were setting up your own travel agency you might decide to start as a franchise so that your risk was reduced. Visit the website of one of the franchises, for example www.freedomtravelgroup.com, and find out the ways that belonging to the franchise helps reduce risk, for example offering ABTA membership. Make some notes on your findings.

International Air Transport Association (IATA)

Travel agents who want to sell or issue international airline tickets must be accredited by IATA. There are detailed criteria for accreditation. You can look at these on the IATA website (www.iata.co.uk).

Licensing

Licences are needed for certain aspects of a travel agent's business.

Air Travel Organiser's Licence (ATOL)

ATOL is the government's licensing and bonding scheme for tour operators selling holiday packages that include flights, and flight specialists selling charter and discounted scheduled airline tickets. If a firm fails, the Civil Aviation Authority (CAA) will protect customers overseas and provide a full refund to those unable to travel.

Travel agents who sell only package holidays would not require an ATOL bond but, increasingly, travel agents are offering dynamic packaging, and they need to apply for an ATOL bond to protect themselves and their customers.

Key term

Dynamic packaging – industry jargon for tailor-making a package for a client.

Rail

Travel agents must apply for licences to sell inclusive rail tours such as those offered by Rail Europe.

Legal framework

Most of the legislation covered in this unit is of greater relevance to tour operators than to travel agents. However, when travel agents tailor-make packages for customers, they act as tour operators and therefore must be aware of and abide by all the relevant legislation.

Agency agreements

Travel agents work on behalf of principals or tour operators. If both travel agent and tour operator are ABTA members they will be bound by the ABTA Code of Conduct. The legal relationship between the tour operator and the travel agent is based on agency law.

An agency agreement will lay out the terms and conditions of the contract, including commissions. If a travel agent stocks a tour operator's brochure and sells from it, there is an implied contract between them, even if there is no written agreement. The travel agent does not have a contract with the customer; the customer has a contract with the principal or tour operator. ABTA provides a model contract for its members to use with their suppliers.

The Package Travel, Package Holidays and Package Tours Regulations 1992

These regulations impact on retail travel agents as they cover not only the organisation of package holidays but also the selling of them. Travel agents need to understand and adhere to these regulations when they sell, and also when they tailor-make packages for clients. The regulations are aimed primarily at tour operators.

Contract law

When a customer books a holiday with a travel agent they enter into a legally binding contract with the tour operator offering the holiday. Travel agents ask the customer to read and accept the tour operator's booking conditions before booking, but do not enter into a contract with the customer themselves. They may ask the client to sign a document allowing the travel agent to act on their behalf.

Consider this

Do you think people read the booking conditions when they book a holiday? Do you read them?

Make a list of the kind of thing you think is covered in booking conditions. Compare your list with that of a colleague. Then compare your list with the actual booking conditions given in a brochure or on a flight booking.

Consumer protection

There are many laws in place to protect consumers. These are not specific to travel and tourism or travel agents but apply generally across all industries. However, it is important that travel agents are aware of them and ensure they abide by them.

Trade Descriptions Act 1968

Descriptions given must be truthful and accurate. This primarily affects tour operators as they have to be careful that brochure descriptions adhere to the act. However, it affects a travel agent too, as any agent making a false verbal statement will be liable under the Trade Descriptions Act.

Supply of Goods and Services Act 1982

The section of this act which is important is the one relating to a contract being carried out using 'reasonable care and skill'. Travel agents have to ensure that they carry out the bookings correctly.

Unfair Terms in Consumer Contracts Regulations 1999

If customers think that any contractual term is unfair or unreasonable, they have a right to challenge it. The terms of the contract should be written in clear, understandable language.

The Office of Fair Trading (OFT) has written guidelines on the interpretation of this act. The guidelines are aimed primarily at tour operators rather than travel agents as they enter into the contract with the customer, but the travel agent might have to liaise with the tour operator on the customer's behalf in a situation where a contract is challenged by the customer.

In 2003, the OFT held an investigation into travel websites. It found that almost half of the websites surveyed were in potential breach of consumer legislation, because they contained claims that the public might find misleading. Most examples were prices advertised that were not really available. The investigators found more than 100 potential breaches under the Electronic Commerce Regulations 2002, Unfair Terms in Consumer Contracts Regulations,

Package Travel Regulations and Consumer Protection (Distance Selling) Regulations 2000. Companies that break such rules are pursued by local Trading Standards Officers or by the OFT.

Theory into practice

Visit four airline websites – choose those that are advertising cheap airfares in the newspapers. Carry out a small survey and see how often you are able to access a flight at the advertised fare. Discuss your findings with your group.

Financial Services Authority (FSA)

The FSA, set up in 1997, is a non-governmental agency responsible for the regulation of much of the UK Financial Services Industry. Insurance bought from a travel agent is exempt from FSA regulation. However, ABTA requires members selling insurance to pass an examination proving that they are competent to do so. All ABTA staff selling insurance are required to pass a Level 1 examination, and one staff member in each outlet must pass the more difficult Level 2 examination. Insurance must be sold along with travel, not as a stand-alone policy, and the FSA does spot checks to make sure that agencies are not selling stand-alone policies.

Relationships with other organisations

Travel agents have to work with other organisations. Remember that they work on a commission basis, they do not buy and resell products like other kinds of retailers. This means that the relationships they have with others are very important. These relationships may take the form of trading agreements or they may be part of the same trading group, for example Thomson travel agents belong to TUI UK.

The sectors that travel agents deal with are:

- hotels and other accommodation providers
- transport providers

Figure 9.3 Purple Parking promotion

Figure 9.3 shows how one parking company aims a promotion at travel agents to persuade them to sell its parking services to customers. It claims it is offering good rates of commission. Other companies may attract the interest of travel agents by offering training or competitions.

Imagine you are a travel agent dealing with a business client. He has booked a flight from Heathrow. He has not asked about parking but it is part of your role to sell 'add ons'. Take it in turns with a colleague to be the agent and the customer and practise selling on the add-on of parking.

Taking it further

In 2007, TUI UK and First Choice merged, as did MyTravel and Thomas Cook. Carry out research and redo Table 9.2 for the two new organisations. **P1**

- ancillary providers such as insurance companies
- car-hire companies
- tour operators.

Vertical integration

The principle of vertical integration was explained in Unit 1. It occurs forwards or backwards in the chain of distribution when an organisation takes over another company or role in the chain. It gives the advantages of control and of economies of scale.

The major multiple travel agents in the UK are owned by vertically integrated companies.

Remember that these companies operate internationally and therefore have retail travel operations in other countries too.

Parent company	Retail travel brands	E-brands
TUI UK	Thomson Callers Pegaus – Travel House	Austravel Thomsonfly Skydeals Team Lincoln
Thomas Cook AG	Thomas Cook	Thomascook.co.uk and websites for each tour-operating brand
First Choice	First Choice Travelshops First Choice Holiday Hypermarkets	First Choice and websites for each tour-operating brand
MyTravel	Going Places Travelworld	goingplaces.co.uk mytravel.com fly cheap and websites for each tour-operating brand

Table 9.2 Major multiple travel agents in the UK

The integration of companies in one group allows the tour operators to control, to an extent, the distribution of their products. Although all agencies sell each other's products, Thomson gives preference to TUI or Thomson brands, First Choice to its own brands and so on. This will be evident in the brochures racking policy, where more of the own-branded products will be on display, and in selling, as agents receive larger commissions on their own products. A policy of promoting own brands is known as 'directional selling', and critics say that it means customers are not given a full choice.

Since a Competition Commission inquiry into this and other practices by the major tour operators, travel agents are supposed to make their links to tour operators obvious to the general public. They do this by displaying notices with parent group details and by sharing the logo, if not always the name, of their parent. You can read the report from the Competition Commission inquiry by going to its website at www.competition-commission.org.uk and searching reports from 1997.

However, a survey by United Co-op Travel Group in 2004 claimed that a third of customers do not know that multiples are vertically integrated.

Key term

Competition Commission – an independent public body established by the Competition Act 1998. It conducts inquiries into mergers and the regulation of industries in response to requests or complaints from another authority.

Horizontal integration

This occurs when companies are bought out or merged at the same level in the chain of distribution. An example is when one travel agent buys another.

In 1999, Martin Morgan sold his Travel House retail chain to TUI UK. This was an example of horizontal integration on the part of TUI. However, in 2004, Morgan bought half of his shops back from TUI for significantly less than he sold them for. Now he has a small chain of 26 outlets in Wales.

9.1

Assessment practice

It is very difficult to keep up with changes in ownership in travel agents. Do some research to find out what recent changes there have been. Look for examples of:

- a travel agent taking over another
- a travel agent being bought by a tour operator
- a travel agent going out of business
- the opening of e-agents.

Look in the trade press for your examples and make a display of your findings. Specify whether your examples are about horizontal or vertical integration. **P1**

Consider this

Before you began this course, did you know which tour operator owned which travel agent? Do you know now?

Agency agreements and preferred operators

When a travel agency sells products and services on behalf of another organisation, for example a tour operator, an agreement is made. In general, the agreement covers selling the principal's products and giving advice to customers about the products. ABTA provides a template for such an agreement. You can study this at www.abtamembers.org/reference/agencyag.doc.

A travel agent may make an agreement with a tour operator to promote its products over those of another operator. Such an agreement will impact on its racking policies and commission levels. Business travel agents may form agreements with companies to provide their travel services.

Racking policies

Racking refers to the practice of displaying brochures on shelves for customers to browse. Vertically integrated travel agents give prominence to their own products. Independent travel agents select the range of products

▲ Figure 9.4 Racking in a travel agency

and services they want to offer based on the quality of the offering and customer demand. Day to day, the agent must make sure that there are enough brochures on display and order them (usually from a central supplier) as needed. Preferred operators are those who work closely with the agency, perhaps providing staff training posters and better commissions. Their brochures will be more prominently displayed.

If a brochure is not stocked by an agency its customers will not have access to that product or holiday. However, with the advent of e-brochures, agents will be able to access information about holidays and other products online.

Commission level

Commission is paid monthly and depends on bookings made. The commission differs with each product or company – higher commissions are paid on own-branded products.

Airline commissions can be as much as 9 per cent, for airlines like Emirates, or zero, for the low-cost airlines. Some travel suppliers operate a tiered system where agents are categorised. Top agents – those who do a lot of business for the supplier – can negotiate high commissions.

Theory into practice

Find out current comssions from www.abtamembers.org/commissions/index.htm.

Some retail travel agents, for example Travelcare, do not pay commissions to staff to sell or promote one supplier rather than another. They say such a practice is not in the customer's interest.

Financial bonding

Earlier we discussed the importance of bonding through ABTA or the ATOL schemes. Travel agents must deal with these organisations in order to get their bonds.

Assessment practice

Summarise how a chosen business travel agent relates to other travel and tourism organisations, for example accommodation providers. Evaluate the effectiveness of the agent and its operations. **M1 D1**

In this section we will examine advances in technology including:

- the impact of the internet
- transport
- reservation systems
- communication systems.

We will examine the effect of each type of advance on sales, products and services, administration and operations.

Internet and other direct booking

Direct booking with operators or principals is currently the main development impacting on retail travel agents. This can be done through call centres, the internet or other booking channels.

A 2004 ABTA report showed that 63 per cent of travellers used the internet to get travel information and 40 per cent used it to book travel.

Consider this

A MORI poll in 2004 showed that young people found it 'uncool' to book with a travel agent; 18- to 24-year-olds prefer to book online. The same survey showed that retired people also search online.

Do you agree that it's uncool to book with a travel agent? How did you book your last holiday? Why is it important to mention that retired people search for travel online?

The debate continues on the future of the travel agent. There are those who think that they will disappear from our high streets and that we will all book over the internet, and others who think that retailers have a future.

Case study: online bookings

American Express business travels survey reveals online air bookings outstripping offline for first time

The American Express European Travel Management Technology Survey 2006 shows European online adoption catching up with US.

London, March 16, 2006 – Latest research from American Express, the leading travel management company, has revealed the incredible pace in the adoption of online travel booking and expense reporting tools since 2004. The survey also uncovers the company's intentions to continue the trend in 2006, as a means to drive cost and process efficiency.

Key findings from the report were:

Internet booking flying high – Europe is embracing online technology; the average number of air tickets booked online has increased by 70 per cent from 2004.

Nearly half look-to-book online – 42 per cent of companies have introduced online booking systems since 2004 and another 25 per cent are planning to buy travel management systems within the next year.

A business travel first – European-headquartered companies report that for the first time online air bookings and travel expense reports will account for the majority of their company booking and expense reports.

Although the business travel market is increasingly moving online, American Express recognises that online adoption requires comprehensive online customer support and advisory services.

(Source: http://home3.americanexpress.com/corp/uk/2006/online_bookings.asp)

1 Why do you think business travellers book online?

2 What are the benefits of agents like Amex of offering online booking?

3 What is meant by 'online customer support'?

4 Why is it needed?

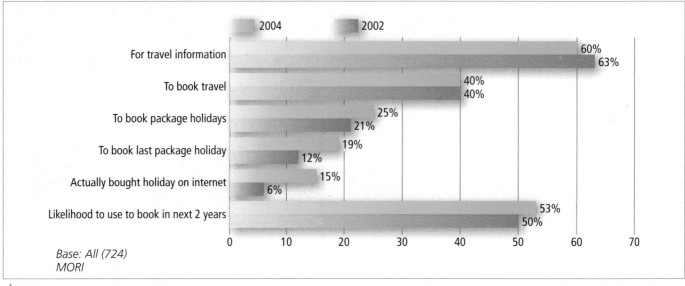

Figure 9.5 Use of the internet

(Source: http://www.abta.com)

One way of responding to the rise in independent travel is to try to cater for a niche market. This means exploiting the demand for independent travel instead of trying to sell packages. Travel agents could specialise in certain areas of the world and develop an expert knowledge of that area. Many industry experts think that those retail travel agencies which do survive will have to offer a personal service with expert knowledge of destinations and products.

It is also the case that there will always be some people without internet access, and people who demand personal service or just can't cope with booking their own holiday arrangements.

Some travel agents are looking for a new source of primary income and are considering charging service fees. Where a fee is charged the service offered has to be excellent or customers will go elsewhere – it cannot be just a booking service.

A typical service charge is £20–25, and if the customer makes the booking then the charge can be credited against it. The system does have the advantage of dissuading time wasters.

Most travel agents will charge for booking flights from low-cost airlines on the internet for customers, as many of the low-cost airlines do not pay commission to travel agents.

Consider this

How likely is it that you would pay for service in a travel agency? One agent told of a booking for easyJet where she booked online for four people and charged them £80. They could have booked it themselves and saved the money. Why do you think they didn't?

Advances in transport

The new giant aeroplane, the Airbus A380, will have an impact on travel. Travel agents will need to be up to date on facilities offered on board the aircraft and these will differ from airline to airline. It is likely that part of the aircraft's cabin will be dedicated to business class with state-of-the-art facilities.

Travel agents must be aware of other developments in air travel. For example, British Airways spent £100 million in 2006 overhauling long haul business class. There are two airlines, Maxjet and Eos, which only offer business class on their flights – operating between Stansted and New York.

Developments such as the new Channel Tunnel rail link extension will take high-speed trains into St Pancras for the first time. It will only take a couple of hours to get to

Paris or Brussels, so demand for Eurostar services should increase. Virgin Trains has introduced a new fleet of 'Pendalino' trains designed to travel at higher speeds.

Travel agents will find it easier to sell business travel as new features such as e-mail access, DVD players and mobile phone use on planes become available.

Travel agents have to keep abreast of changes in road and sea transport, too. This means being aware of changes in coach and ferry services.

For example, agents would want to be aware of improved services for disabled travellers such as this new product from National Express offering services to enable disabled travellers to get to airports (www. nationalexpress.com/utilities/press.cfm).

> *The new generation easy access coach features a wider entrance and a completely flat floor throughout the coach to aid mobility for all. Other features include reclining leather seats, air conditioning and a large toilet. A programme of other coach routes around the UK is being put in place which will see the entire UK-wide National Express network being fully accessible in time for the 2012 London Olympics and Paralympics.*

(Source: http://www.nationalexpress.com/utilities/press14.cfm)

Reservation systems

Front-office procedures are to do with dealing with customers and selling products. Back-office procedures are to do with the suppliers of the products and the running of the office: following up bookings, making payments, banking, ordering brochures, stationery and currency. These procedures do not involve the customer.

All selling procedures used to be done manually with a basic Viewdata system and a great deal of paperwork, but now competitive travel agents use highly sophisticated technology for all procedures. There are several systems on the market and independent agents choose the system they think best meets their needs.

Of course, any system used is only as good as the person operating it, so extensive training is required. Be aware also that computerised systems do not do away with paperwork altogether.

You should be familiar with the terminology used to describe the technology that travel agents use.

Key terms

Viewdata – the interactive screen system that travel agents use to access the tour operators' reservation systems.

CRS (Computer Reservation System) – each tour operator, airline, cruise line, etc. has a computer reservation system accessible by the Viewdata system.

GDS (Global Distribution Systems) – more sophisticated developments of the computer reservation services. They might combine several computer reservation systems from different suppliers and offer other travel services also. Examples include Amadeus, Galileo, Sabre and Worldspan.

The early CRS and Viewdata systems had some drawbacks for travel agents:

- They were not 'real-time' systems, which means the information was not bang up to date and the agent had to telephone reservations departments to confirm.
- The agent could search only one tour operator at a time, which meant the process of finding a suitable holiday was very slow; the customer's preferences had to be keyed in to each new reservations screen.

Most travel agents are switching to the latest systems which are much more advanced and can offer:

- real-time availability
- 24-hour access to the system
- multi-operator searches.

FACT SHEET

New technology	Impact on agent's operation

Some Global Distribution Systems (GDS) include fully integrated back-office systems. This means that all the travel agency's booking and accounting procedures can be automated. Examples are TravelPower and TravelCat. TravelCat is produced by Comtec, a company based in Wales and founded in 1995. The company has received business support from the Welsh Assembly and the Welsh Development Agency. This is significant as it reflects the importance given by government to developing the tourism industry.

The company also produces EasySell, a multi-operator holiday search. EasySell is used by MyTravel, TUI, Thomas Cook and First Choice. Like the Galileo Leisure product, this dramatically reduces the searching and booking time for holidays.

TravelPower and TravelCat systems also allow reconciliation of banking as all transactions are entered into the system and the system tells you what the takings should be at the day's end.

Comtec, the company that produces TravelCat, has brought out a new product which gives travel agents their own website. Of course, travel agents often have websites already but this is different as it allows customers to interact and manage their own bookings online. The customer is given a booking number to enter online, with personal details, which allows access to their booking. Customers can make payments online and get receipts through e-mail.

There is an initial set-up charge to travel agents and then each transaction carries a small fee. There is no charge to customers. The purpose of the new product is to give a means of internet interaction to travel agents and help them be competitive. It could save money in administration if successful.

Alternatives to GDSs include G2 SwitchWorks. G2 is available today in the USA and offers a ready-to-use graphical desktop, G2Agent, that replaces the need-to-know traditional GDS formats. Its search and price functionality provides users with over 300 fare options in a single display and G2Agent requires very little training to become an expert user. It also automates administrative tasks like ticket exchanges and refunds.

Current G2 SwitchWorks customers in the USA include Carlson Wagonlit Travel,

Pricline.com, Disneyland Resort and Trisept Solutions who use G2 booking technology to power air bookings on VAX Vacation Access.

Consider this

Do you think travel agents should encourage their customers to use an online facility like the new TravelCat product? Do you think it will encourage even more people to use the internet and cut out the travel agent?

Communication methods

The new reservation systems are themselves a means of communicating with suppliers for travel agents. They save hours of hanging on the telephone making an enquiry with tour operators or airlines. The TravelCat system allows interaction with customers online.

Where agents are using online technology to sell their products, it is important to provide customer support and this means having telephone contact available.

Effect of new technology

As travel agents invest in new technology they should in return get an increased volume of sales. Bookings should be made more quickly with the new systems – less time is spent waiting on the telephone and it should be possible to have up-to-date information on availability.

Agents have greater awareness of new products and services available from principals as improved communication methods mean there is speedy access to information. Administration procedures are less susceptible to human error and procedures are less time consuming than manual methods.

Technology also impacts on operations, as newer distribution methods are used by travel agents, for example the Travelcat system. However, the impact on travel agents can be detrimental in terms of operations as customers can easily buy products and services direct over the internet and can miss out the travel agent altogether. Customers can now be confident that paying online is secure.

The issue of independent booking is probably the greatest threat to travel agents' survival. In the next section we look at competitive advantage and study the measures that travel agents can take to ensure business thrives.

9.3 Understand how retail travel organisations seek to gain competitive advantage

Methods of gaining competitive advantage

Whatever the type of agent, multiple or independent, in order to gain competitive advantage over other retailers, either of the same type or different types, a travel agent has constantly to develop and be innovative. Travel agents often try to gain that competitive advantage by:

- level of service
- staff training
- promotional activities
- developing the range of products and services
- add-on sales
- vertical integration
- horizontal integration
- increasing market share.

This is of the utmost importance. When customers book online, the element that is missing is that of face-to-face service. If travel agents can make sure that customers receive superb service in their retail outlets, then that becomes a reason to use the agent rather than book direct. This can be achieved through good staff training.

■ Staff training

A trained staff is the best means of being competitive. Through training, agents develop their selling skills and their destination knowledge and are thus able to provide personal service to customers.

There are different types of training, ranging from induction for new staff, to ongoing training to update skills and knowledge and weekly sessions given by the manager for all staff. Training is discussed in more detail in Unit 6.

Promotional activities include any activity that encourages customers to buy. For example, competitions can be held in agencies so that customers want to come in. STA has offered instant prizes on scratchcards which are given when customers buy foreign currency. Another means of promoting the agency through competitions

is by providing a prize – perhaps a voucher towards a holiday – in a competition promoted by another organisation. This can lead to good publicity.

Some travel agencies use professional marketing organisations who will provide promotional materials. At a basic level they provide a central brochure-ordering service so that the agent doesn't have to contact each individual operator for brochures. They will also provide a documentation service providing tickets, invoices, welcome-home letters, confirmations, and so on. The case study below gives an example of a year-long promotional campaign.

It is important that the agency looks good and that the window display appeals to passers by. Late deals are a common merchandising tool to attract people and these are often displayed on cards in the window. These are compiled by staff who search for the offers on Viewdata. They will be informed directly of offers from their own company. Posters are easily obtained and often used to advertise destinations. It is part of the job of the travel agent to arrange attractive window displays.

The large chains may run a discount promotion to encourage sales in times of poor trade. Some travel agents ensure competitiveness by constantly checking offers in their competitors' shops and matching the prices if

Case study: short breaks

Haymarket Travel announced plans to increase its sales in the UK domestic market, as it seems that many customers are booking directly rather than through agents. The agency worked with domestic tour operators and the London Tourist Board. The plan was to bombard customers visiting its London flagship store with information on British short breaks. The campaign began on 1 September 2004 and was planned to last for 12 months.

The store had agents in traditional costumes serving customers, and Morris dancers on summer weekends

outside the shop. Customers were shown videos of British seaside resorts, posters were on display and existing customers received flyers offering discounts off UK breaks.

1   **Why do you think Haymarket Travel chose to focus on short breaks?**

2   **This campaign has to last a year. Perhaps customers will tire of the Morris dancers after a while. Think of at least five other activities which could be used in this promotional campaign at different times of the year. P3 D2**

appropriate. Others offer a facility of paying low deposits for a limited period to entice people to book immediately.

Developing the range of products and services

Travel agents can develop their range of products and services by introducing those from tour operators and promoting them. Sometimes they branch out into different areas. For example, one travel agent now sells a range of luggage. The owner's theory is that customers are thinking about holidays when they come in through the door and they will need luggage.

Add-on sales

Add-on sales are a vital part of a travel agent's business. They include all the extras like travel insurance, parking, currency exchange, excursions and many others. Staff are trained to make these add-on sales.

Consider this

Thomas Cook is planning to sell financial services in its shops. A joint venture is planned with Barclaycard which would involve Thomas Cook selling car insurance and home loans. It is also looking at opening foreign exchange kiosks at airports. There will also be a Thomas Cook credit card. Why do you think Thomas Cook is entering into this deal with Barclaycard?

Dynamic packaging

An important extra service offered by agents is that of tailor-making packages for customers, known as 'dynamic packaging'. This means that instead of selling the customer an 'off-the-shelf' package, the agent puts together the different components, tailoring them exactly to what the customer wants. This service is perhaps the most significant in terms of competitive advantage as it offers a very personal service to customers and saves them the time and effort of doing it themselves. It is more exacting for the travel agent

as they have to know where to find all the information for the different components of a holiday, whereas when booking a package the tour operator has done the groundwork.

Offering tailor-made services can lead to an increase in sales, especially if low-cost airlines are used as a component. Using them brings the cost down for the customer and gives the possibility of regional departures.

There are a number of booking systems now available to travel agents which bring together databases of accommodation, flights and transfers and help agents to research and book tailor-made packages. The travel retailer adds a margin to the prices charged by the suppliers and invoices the customer. Travel retailers are generally happy with this arrangement as it means they determine the commission. Examples of systems are Holidaysandmore.com (a Lastminute.com trade operation), Holiday Brokers and Cultura Trips, a Thomas Cook subsidiary. These are sometimes called dynamic packaging tools. To use these systems you have to register. Unless your college or school has its own travel agency you will be unable to register, but you will be able to practise with similar booking services such as onlinetravel.com, which is used by agents and consumers.

Theory into practice

You work in a travel agency. You and your colleagues have been making many more tailor-made bookings recently in response to demand from customers and also to a request from your manager to increase sales by any means possible. You are finding researching and booking these packages interesting but time consuming.

You have heard that there are several online systems now available which would make your job easier. Your manager has agreed that you should research some and give her information about the benefits and drawbacks in a short report. Look at www.holidaybrokers.co.uk and work through the 'User's Guide', making notes on the advantages and disadvantages of the system as you go. Write up your findings in a report for your manager.

Integrated organisations

Integrated companies are so large and powerful that they are able to adapt to a changing market by developing different means of distributing their products and services. Besides having retail outlets, they have developed call centres and websites, and they sell on television, some even having their own television channels. The following case study gives an example of how TUI UK has developed one of its brands.

Increasing market share

■ Joining a trade association

One way of increasing market share is to join a trade association. Most UK travel agents are members of ABTA. There is no doubt that ABTA travel agents have a competitive advantage over non-ABTA agents as the name is well known and holiday makers have been educated to look for evidence of ABTA bonding when booking.

Case study: Thomson – distribution

Traditionally, Thomson (a tour operator) has been dependent on travel agents to sell the majority of its products, with Portland Direct representing its direct sell business. Its preferred travel agents are its own Thomson shops. However, market changes have forced the company to reconsider its distribution methods. In 2000, Thomson announced the launch of a new national call centre in Glasgow, creating up to 1000 jobs. By 2006, this was set to change dramatically as Thomson axed 450 jobs at the same call centre saying that the losses were necessary as customers switched to internet booking. The move was reported in the press as follows.

Further blow to independent travel agents as Thomson announces more commission cuts

Thomson has dealt independent travel agents a further blow by announcing more cuts to commission. The news is part of a major shake-up in the way the company sells its holidays, flights and hotels.

Thomson chief executive Peter Rothwell said the company is not prepared to pay travel agents high commission fees and wants to channel sales directly through its own high street shops, website and call centres.

In the past, travel companies such as Thomson have relied on agents as one of the main distribution channels. But as consumers become increasingly confident to buy holidays directly through the internet, Thomson is forcing the pace of change in the travel industry.

The latest move will see Thomson end its relationship with selected independent travel agents altogether and reduce commission payments with others.

Since Thomson launched its first round of commission cuts six months ago the company has invested more in marketing directly to consumers. Around 75 per cent of Thomson's business now comes through its own website, call centres and holiday shops. The company expects web sales in particular to accelerate over the next few years.

(Source http://destinations.thomson.co.uk/devolved/about-thomson/ press/further-blow-to-independent-travel-agents-as-thomson-announces- more-commission-cuts.htm)

1 **Describe the three methods of distribution used by Thomson.**

2 **Explain why these methods of distribution are used and why changes have occurred.**

3 **How does being part of a vertically and horizontally integrated company help Thomson gain competitive advantages?** **P3**

Taking it further

Carry out research to find out what distribution methods are most popular for another large tour operator. You might investigate MyTravel. Compare the distribution methods with those of Thomson. How important are travel agents to the tour operator? **M2**

How do the consortia in travel and tourism help the travel agents become more competitive? There are benefits and a few drawbacks to joining one of these associations. The benefits include:

- the consortium negotiates deals with suppliers, such as hotels and airlines
- there is a recognised brand name, e.g. Advantage
- travel agents can retain their own name if they prefer, e.g. those joining Midconsort do not adopt that name
- use of technology systems
- conferences and events
- bonding schemes, e.g. Global has its own scheme as an alternative to ABTA bonding.

The disadvantages include the cost, although it varies a lot between consortia. With Global it costs £25,000 to join and then a percentage of commission, but this includes the technology system and training. However, Global also has another division, Independent Options, and membership of that is free. A consortium like Global operates as a franchise, so the agent is not completely in control of the business.

Another way of increasing sales and gaining competitive advantage is to introduce sales incentives and sales targets to encourage staff to sell more. Incentives can be financial, such as a bonus or commission. In the travel and tourism business incentives are often travel-related. Suppliers such as tour operators send agents on 'educationals'. These are trips to destinations to explore what is on offer and increase the agents' knowledge of the destinations.

Some companies hold parties as incentives for staff. *Travel Trade Gazette* reports on these; one was held by a north-eastern travel agency owner and staff were plied with champagne and Pimms and entertained by a string quartet.

Call centres often make extensive use of incentives to encourage staff to make more sales. It makes the job more interesting if the staff have something to work towards.

An agency has its sales target set by head office or by its owner if it is a small business. The target is subdivided between the staff. It isn't divided equally; more experienced staff are expected to sell more than juniors, and part-timers naturally have smaller targets. In many agencies, staff are paid a bonus when they reach their targets. This bonus is separate from the commission earned.

Theory into practice

Here are some typical questions overheard in a day's work at a travel agency. Can you answer them? You might have to do some research.

- What do I do if my baggage is overweight at the airline check-in?
- Can I get a visa on entry to Kilimanjaro?
- What is different about going first class on Eurostar?
- I am leaving Heathrow at 10.00 am. I want to take the airport bus from Stansted. What time should I take the bus?
- Can you take hand luggage and a handbag on a plane?

Theory into practice

Imagine you are managing a call centre. Sales have dropped and morale is low. You need to think of incentives to motivate staff and increase sales. You have a budget of £500 per week for 2 months. There are 30 staff working in teams of five. Decide on a range of incentives and decide what the staff have to do to earn them. Present your ideas to your group.

We have seen that, traditionally, the role of travel agents has been to sell package holidays on behalf of tour operators. Throughout this unit we have noted that this role is changing, and although travel agents must still know how to select and process a package holiday, there is a greater emphasis on arranging complex itineraries to meet different customer needs.

A retail itinerary may be for a package holiday or a tailor-made holiday put together by the travel agent. It will include all the details shown on a basic itinerary but will also have any passport, visa and health requirements. It should include details of accommodation and any additional services booked. A business itinerary has the same details but is more likely to have sector changes for flights and private transfer arrangements.

In this section you will gain some practice on putting together itineraries. You will practise both retail and business itineraries.

A basic itinerary for a journey to a destination includes:

- client details
- departure date
- departure time
- departure point, e.g. airport
- mode of transport,
- e.g. airline
- flight details
- arrival point
- arrival time
- contact details in case of enquiry.

Figure 9.7 shows an example of a basic itinerary.

Holiday Reference number: 5947832				
Your Flight Details		**Flight Number:**	**Departing:**	**Arriving:**
Departure Date: **Departure Airport:** **Airline:**	Fri 17 Nov 2006 Heathrow to Prague Czech Airways	CZ409	12:30	15:30
Return Date: **Return Airport:** **Airline:**	Thu 23 Nov 2006 Prague to Heathrow Czech Airways	CZ649	17:35	18:35
Your Accommodation:	St. Wenceslas Hotel Coach transport to hotel provided			
Contact number:	0227 1234567			

 Figure 9.7 Basic itinerary

Key term

Itinerary – an itnerary is a detailed plan for a journey.

At its most basic the itinerary gives details of the journey to be undertaken, in order to arrive at and return from the destination. However, for a special interest holiday the itinerary may be much more complex as it must give details of times and locations for each activity that is to take place and must accommodate the customer's needs. An itinerary for a tour must have departure times and details of journeys and activities for each day of the tour. We will consider some examples before you make up your own itineraries.

Activity

Produce a basic journey itinerary for Julian Selzer and Christian Murray who will be travelling from Gatwick to Brussels for a weekend cultural break. They are travelling on Friday evening next week and returning on Monday morning. Find suitable flights from Gatwick and write out an itinerary for the pair.

The itinerary in Figure 9.9 shows a full itinerary for a cycling tour. This is more difficult to produce because of the amount of detail needed and the complexity of planning to ensure that everything goes smoothly for the customers.

Figure 9.8 Cycling tour ▲

In the example you will note the following details:

- departure date and time (local time)
- departure point
- arrival details (local time)
- arrival point
- flight details
- accommodation for each night
- board basis.

This type of itinerary needs a lot of work. Although the cycle tour will remain more or less the same for each client, different clients may request specific hotels or longer durations in a hotel so the itinerary is tailor made according to their wishes. Bookings must be made in each hotel, meal arrangements have to be made and then the necessary flight bookings and transfers added. In this case bicycles and the services of the tour representative must also be organised.

A good itinerary for a holiday is one that is accurate and detailed and manages to accommodate the individual needs of the customer. All tourists have basic needs: transport, accommodation and food. In addition they have needs relating to their special requirements, whatever these may be, and also their need to be able to relax. They also might require particular facilities such as five-star accommodation, or alternative activities for different members of the party.

Cycling tour itinerary 10–14 July 2006

Outward flight London Gatwick to Toulouse

British Airways	BA345
Departing	10 July 08.20
Arriving	10 July 10.30

Hotel accommodation (half board)

Hotel Belle Vue (2 nights)
Hotel Principia (2 nights)
Transport to and from accommodation included

Return flight Toulouse to London Gatwick

British Airways	BA346
Departing	14 July 9.30
Arriving	14 July 11.40

Representative   John Taylor 08765 322831

 Figure 9.9 Itinerary for a cycling tour

Assessment practice

1 You work in a travel agency and have a customer who wants to take her two children to Lapland in December to meet Father Christmas. She will be travelling with the two children, whose ages are six and nine. They want to go for 2 nights from any London airport and on any dates in December. The parent wants meals included as far as possible. Tailor make a holiday for the trio and prepare an itinerary. (Unless you really want to go to Lapland, don't actually book anything!)

2 Make up some customer details and requirements that you can present to another member of your group. These should be for customers who are looking for a UK domestic holiday in the summer. In turn, accept a customer profile and requirements from a colleague and put together a suitable domestic holiday. Produce an itinerary.

These scenarios could be role-played, with one person acting as the customer and another as the agent. **P4**

Assessment practice

Rohan Bhalinder is travelling to Sydney to speak at a medical conference. He has decided to ask his girlfriend, Maria, to go with him. Prepare an itinerary for them taking the following into account.

- They will be travelling from London on a Saturday and returning 2 weeks later
- They want to spend one night in Singapore on the way.
- They require a hotel in Singapore and one in Sydney (five star).
- Rohan will travel in business class but his girlfriend has to pay so she will go in economy.
- Rohan has an Indian passport and Maria has a British passport.
- They will need a taxi in Singapore to get to the hotel and back.
- Rohan is diabetic.

Knowledge check

1 Identify the different categories of retail travel agents.

2 Name three services a business travel agent might offer.

3 What is meant by 'racking policy'?

4 How does ABTA help travel agents?

5 What are the benefits to a travel agent of joining a consortium?

6 What are add-on sales?

7 Identify three types of promotional activity a travel agent might use.

8 How does the Trade Descriptions Act 1968 affect a travel agent?

9 Give an example of a reservation system.

10 What is a Global Distribution Service?

11 What is dynamic packaging?

12 Give an example of an advance in transport technology that will impact on travel agents.

Preparation for assessment

Part 1

You have recently gained a position as an assistant in the offices of ABTA. Your department deals with travel agency support and is preparing for a conference entitled 'The Future of the British Travel Agent – Strategies for Survival'.

There will be a number of speakers from ABTA and from other organisations in travel and tourism. All ABTA members have been sent invitations to the conference and a good response is anticipated. The purpose of the conference is to help members stay up to date with developments in, or affecting, the retail travel sector and show them how they can remain competitive in a rapidly changing environment.

You are not required to give a presentation but to carry out research. Your findings will form the basis of the presentations from ABTA personnel.

Your findings should be presented as detailed sets of notes with illustrations as appropriate. Make sure the notes are clearly presented with suitable headings and sub-headings.

1 Describe the retail and business travel environment of today, including a description of at least three types of business and three types of retail leisure agents. Explain the relationship between travel agents and other sectors of travel and tourism. Give examples. **P1 M1**

Grading tip

To reach Pass level make sure your description includes:

- the type of market each agent attracts
- the products and services sold
- the role of the different agents
- descriptions of trade associations, consortia, memberships and licensing in relation to travel agents, giving at least two examples of each
- key legislation affecting travel agents
- role of the Financial Services Authority in relation to selling travel insurance
- links between travel agents and other travel and tourism organisations.

To reach Merit level, you need to show how the relationships between travel agents and other sectors impact on the industry as a whole. For example, what happens if airlines reduce commissions to travel agents. You must show a good understanding of vertical and horizontal integration.

2 Evaluate the effectiveness of retail and business travel agents and how they operate in the travel and tourism environment. **D1**

Grading tip

To reach Distinction level, you need to assess the strengths and weaknesses of specific agents. You could discuss how they have responded to changes in the industry such as greater internet booking.

3   Describe how advances in technology have affected the retail and business travel operations.   **P2**

Grading tip

To reach Pass level, you must include a variety of technological advances in terms of the effect on operation, including at least three distribution methods. Discuss the effect on booking systems too.

4   Explain how retail travel organisations seek to gain competitive advantage.   **P3**

5   Compare the effectiveness of two retail travel organisations seeking to gain a competitive advantage. Recommend what other steps these agents could take to improve competitiveness.   **M2 D2**

Grading tip

Make sure your evidence is specific and up to date. Use the travel trade press to help you keep aware of new developments. To reach Distinction level make sure your recommendations are justified.

When you are considering competitive advantage remember to include examples of level of service: staff training, promotional activities, the range of products and services on offer, add-on sales; dynamic packaging; integrated organisations; market share as appropriate.

Part 2

ABTA has sent you to work in a travel agency on a month's placement. The purpose is for you to experience working practice so that you understand the environment and problems which travel agents face.

In your last week you are allowed to deal with customers and sell products and services. You deal with four different sets of customers. For each one you must select and process an appropriate product meeting the needs of the customers. Present your findings as itineraries with relevant brochure pages, forms and computer printouts attached.

To complete this part of the assessment you will need access to brochures, relevant forms and the internet. Ask your teacher or tutor if you do not know how to access these resources. If your college or school has a travel agency, you should complete the assessment in the agency. Role plays can be used. Alternatively, this part of the assessment could be carried out on a work placement with appropriate supervision.

1   Mr and Mrs Fremantle are retired and in their sixties. They wish to spend 6 weeks in Portugal, on the Algarve, for a winter break. They can go in October or November but insist on being home at least a week before Christmas. They want a quiet resort and want to stay in a hotel on a bed-and-breakfast basis so that they can go out for dinner to local restaurants. They want to make sure the hotel has a heated pool and some entertainment. They would prefer a sea view and will pay extra for it. Cost is not an issue. They will fly from the local airport.

Find a suitable holiday and produce a complex itinerary that fits the Fremantles' requirements.   **P4**

2   Sayid wants to arrange a surprise for his fiancée's thirtieth birthday. He is very concerned that you don't contact her about arrangements or send any documents to their address. He wants to go to Paris

on Eurostar from Waterloo and stay in a 'posh' hotel. He lives in Norwich so he wants you to arrange his transport to Waterloo and the transfer from Gare du Nord in Paris to the hotel. He has asked for a bed-and-breakfast arrangement and flowers to be in the room on arrival with a message from him. The break is to take place over the actual birthday weekend with a 2-night stay. The birthday is in 6 weeks' time. Sayid has told you he can spend up to £1000.

Research and produce a complex itinerary for all the elements of this tailor-made holiday. **P4**

3 Benjamin Sims has to arrange a business trip to Tokyo. He is currently in Stockholm but will return briefly to the UK to visit his mother on his way to Tokyo. He has asked you to arrange the following:

- a morning flight next Tuesday from Stockholm to London
- car hire from the airport in London for 3 days – make sure pick-up and drop-off are at the right airports
- flight to Tokyo some time on Friday arriving back the following Wednesday
- car hire on return from Wednesday until Friday
- return flight from London to Stockholm
- hotel for the stay in Tokyo – at least four star with gym and business centre.

Benjamin wants to travel business class on the Tokyo flights. You need to know that he is vegetarian, has a British passport and wants to know if there is any visa or health information he should be aware of.

Produce Ben's itinerary.

4 Produce an itinerary meeting the needs of the following clients.

Sarah and Joyce are musicians based in Manchester. They have been asked to join the Birmingham Symphony Orchestra on tour but for two dates only. They need to travel from Manchester to Vienna on a Thursday ready for a concert that evening. Rehearsal starts at 5.00 pm at a venue in the centre of Vienna. Their next concert is in Paris the following Saturday. Again rehearsal time is at 5.00 pm at a central venue. They will return to the UK on the Sunday having spent Saturday sightseeing.

You must arrange the following:

- appropriate flights with pre-booked seats if possible
- extra seats for their cellos
- hotels
- local transfers.

Grading criteria

To achieve a pass grade the evidence must show that the learner is able to:	To achieve a merit grade the evidence must show that, in addition to the pass criteria, the learner is able to:	To achieve a distinction grade the evidence must show that, in addition to the pass and merit criteria, the learner is able to:
P1 describe the retail and business travel environment including the relationship between retail and business travel agents and other sectors of the travel and tourism industry, giving examples where appropriate **Taking it further page 316**	**M1** explain how relationships operate in the retail and business travel environment and its impact on the travel industry as a whole **Assessment practice page 318**	**D1** evaluate the effectiveness of retail and business travel organisations and how they operate in the travel industry environment **Assessment practice page 318**
P2 describe how technological advances have affected retail and business operations **Assessment practice page 322**	**M2** compare the effectiveness of two retail travel organisations seeking to gain a competitive advantage **Taking it further page 326**	**D2** recommend how two retail travel agents can gain a competitive advantage **Case study page 324**
P3 explain how retail travel organisations seek to gain a competitive advantage **Case study page 324**		
P4 use appropriate resources to produce two complex travel itineraries for retail travel customers to given client briefs **Assessment practice page 330**		
P5 use appropriate resources to produce two complex travel itineraries for business travel customers to given client briefs **Assessment practice page 330**		

11 Sustainable tourism development

Introduction

In this unit you will find out what is meant by sustainable tourism development and why it is important at local, national and international levels. We will investigate the impact of tourism development and find out the ways in which the positive impact can be maximised whilst minimising the negative impact.

We will examine agents involved in tourism development and their roles in the development process. You will discover how the public, private and voluntary sectors play different parts in development.

We will look at the objectives of tourism development in destinations with some specific case studies as examples.

We will look at how the principles of sustainable tourism are put into practice and how the travel and tourism industry supports sustainable tourism development.

After completing this unit you should be able to achieve the following outcomes:

1 Understand the impacts of tourism development in selected destinations

2 Know the roles of the agents involved in sustainable tourism development

3 Understand how the objectives for sustainable tourism development are put into practice

4 Understand how the travel and tourism industry supports sustainable tourism development.

Thinking points

What do you think is meant by tourism development? Tourism development can be defined as the process of providing facilities and services for visitors to a destination in order to gain economic and other benefits. Although it occurs throughout the world, it does not occur at the same rate. In some countries and destinations tourism development is in its early stages whilst in other destinations it is well established. Tourism development is complex. It may mean a local area opening up to visitors, or the development of a specific resort or hotel, or a country setting up policies and tourist board structures to promote tourism. On a national level, tourism development is driven by governments setting a policy for tourism and creating a structure that promotes tourism.

Economic impact

Positive economic impacts

■ Improved infrastructure

Development may bring about improved infrastructure which tourists and local people can both use. For example, improvements in roads allow people to travel more easily – this brings more tourists to remoter areas and improves transport for local people or there may be improvements in plumbing which will provide clean water supplies.

■ Increased income

Tourism development brings economic benefits in terms of increased expenditure in an economy. This may come from domestic or inbound tourism. Inbound tourism brings with it increased earnings from foreign currency exchange. In developing nations, investment from foreign companies helps build the infrastructure and the facilities needed for tourism.

The government also benefits from increased revenue as it receives taxes from businesses earning revenue from tourism and in VAT from goods and services bought by tourists.

■ Increased employment

Tourism is not a statutory duty for local authorities, that is, they don't have to spend money on it – but they do, an estimated £90 million per year. In Birmingham, they claim that their tourism business has provided 31,000 jobs and a return to the local economy of £1.13 for every 87p of council tax spent on generating tourism (*Sunday Times*, 21 November 2004). Greenwich also used tourism to regenerate the area. It had very high unemployment in the 1990s as it lost traditional jobs. Now, after the programme of regeneration, 25 per cent of jobs are provided by tourism and £327 million is generated for the local economy.

Case study: Eurostar train services

In 2007, Eurostar train services will move to the newly completed St Pancras station in London instead of Waterloo. This is part of the plans for development of the new high-speed line between London and the Channel Tunnel. Eurostar prefers St Pancras for its operations because it has more underground lines and direct rail links to the Midlands and the north of England and Scotland. It is hoped that these links will encourage travellers from those areas to use Eurostar and increase custom. It is even possible that direct Eurostar trains could operate from northern towns without changes in London. Two new Eurostar stations will be built: in Stratford in east London and Ebbsfleet in Dartford, Kent. These two stations will serve the east and south east of London. The high-speed line to the channel will cut the journey time from London to Paris to 2 hours 15 minutes and the journey to Brussels from London will take under 2 hours.

1   **Discuss how these improvements in journey time and infrastructure will provide economic benefits in the UK.**

2   **Are there any negative impacts you can think of?**

Taking it further

Find out what other partners are involved in the high-speed train link development. How will the 2012 Olympics aid the development?

Negative economic impacts

Leakage

Economic benefits can be lost if goods and services used in the tourism industry are imported rather than local goods and services used: for example, imported food and drink for hotels or materials and workers brought in from outside the area for construction projects. These are examples of leakage, where the local economy does not benefit.

Key terms

Enclave tourism – occurs when tourists spend the whole holiday in their hotel resort or when on a cruise ship all the activities and meals take place on board. In these circumstances, the local population does not benefit from the tourists being there.

Leakage – the amount of money for supplies and services paid for outside a region: money that does not, therefore, benefit the local economy.

Tourism Concern estimates that 89 per cent of money from holidays stays in the UK. Leakage can be prevented by sourcing local materials, using local produce, allowing people to sell crafts in resorts and employing more local people. However, if tourists spend all their time in a hotel resort, for example (enclave tourism) they will not benefit the local economy.

Increased living costs for the local community

When tourists arrive in an area, particularly a developing area, they can have an impact on costs. Restaurateurs find that tourists are able to pay higher prices than locals and so can put prices up. Taxi drivers can charge tourists more. Retailers can sell more expensive goods. In the worst cases this can produce a two-tier economy. When tourists buy second homes in a locality there is often an impact on house prices, which means that local people can no longer afford to buy houses in their own area.

Decline of traditional employment

Traditional industry can be penalised by tourism if workers choose to leave their employment in search of jobs in the tourist industry. This often occurs in developing economies where the jobs in tourism may initially provide more pay. When tourism is regionalised in a country, people may leave their homes and communities to take up jobs in tourism. More serious displacement occurs when whole communities are moved on to make room for tourism development. In the late 1980s, people were evicted from the Mkomazi Game Reserve in Tanzania: tourists are allowed in to view the wildlife but the indigenous people are confined to a narrow strip of land along the Pangani River. This has happened in several locations in East Africa in the name of conservation. Tourism Concern runs campaigns to help such displaced people.

Overdependence on tourism

Economic distortion can occur when one region of a country is highly developed for tourism and other areas have none. This occurs to an extent in the UK where the south east and London receive far more tourists than other regions. It is a greater problem in countries where there is little other industry. Overdependence on tourism is a potential problem. Tourists are fickle and fashions change quickly. An economy dependent on tourism will suffer if tourists leave or if a natural disaster occurs, like the hurricane that devastated New Orleans in 2005.

Environmental impact

Positive environmental impacts

■ Conservation and preservation of natural and built environment

Sites and properties are protected and preserved for the enjoyment of visitors and to conserve the heritage. Tourism contributes enormously to this conservation in several ways:

- the fact that a site is a tourist attraction means it is recognised as warranting preservation

- National Parks and other conservation bodies provide information and education for tourists, thus helping tourists' environmental awareness
- revenue from entrance fees to attractions pays for conservation activities
- conservation holidays are a growing market sector as offered by BTCV and the National Trust.

■ Regeneration

Both the built and natural environment benefit from upgrading and regeneration when a tourist opportunity is uncovered by local and national government. Examples include the Liverpool and Salford dock areas. Salford has a theatre and museum besides new residential and shopping developments.

■ Use of renewable resources

Development of tourist facilities in an area has a direct impact on natural resources, both renewable and non-renewable. Land is used for building, impacting on

▼ Figure 11.1 Wind turbines

wildlife and forestation. Water is used for hotel facilities and watering gardens and golf courses. However, it is possible to use renewable resources, as the following case study shows.

Case study: an ecolodge

The Inn at Coyote Mountain is an ecolodge built on a private nature reserve in Costa Rica. Its aims are to:
- encourage sustainable use of the local environment
- minimise negative impacts of tourism on the local environment and culture
- maximise the benefits of tourism on the local economy and society
- encourage use of renewable resources.

To achieve its aims, The Inn at Coyote Mountain has implemented the following:
- a gravity-fed fresh-water system, with no electricity or pumps
- all water comes from local springs
- wind power is used for energy needs
- more than 1000 new trees a year are planted
- employees are local
- glass and paper are recycled
- guests are asked to reuse towels
- washing is line dried not put in driers
- a waste treatment facility is in use which fertilises an orchard.

(Source: http://www.cerrocoyote.com/id18.html)

1. **Explain how these measures help The Inn at Coyote Mountain achieve its aims, giving examples of maximising positive impacts and minimising negative impacts. P1 M1**

2. **Suggest at least five other policies the ecolodge might introduce to help achieve its aims.**

Taking it further

Find your own example of an ecolodge with similar aims. Explain the elements of good practice evident and make recommendations for further improvements.

Negative environmental impacts

Traffic congestion

Within the UK, most day visitors and domestic holidaymakers travel by car, causing traffic congestion and pollution at destinations and attractions. Some villages in Yorkshire and in the Lake District are now closed to traffic, whilst large car parks have been built on the outskirts to accommodate the visiting coaches and cars.

Pollution

In coastal resorts, jet skis and motor boats cause noise pollution and environmental pollution from the petrol fumes produced. The noise causes distress to wildlife and the petrol fumes can destroy marine life.

Another pollution problem is the disposal of sewage, particularly in developing destinations where sewage plants either do not exist or are not able to cope with the extra waste. The cruise sector is booming but cruise ships produce tonnes of waste. Sewage pollutes seas and rivers, damages wildlife and encourages the growth of algae which in turn damages coral reefs.

Coral suffers damage in many ways including trampling by snorkellers and divers, destruction by anchors from boats and in some instances mining for building materials.

Loss of natural habitats

Even protected areas can be lost for tourism development. A part of the Pembrokeshire coastline in Wales has National Park status, yet in spite of this developers have managed to obtain permission for the building of an all-weather holiday village, complete with a snow dome. A watchdog body, the Council for National Parks, is going to the High Court in London to attempt to stop the development, but the reasons why the development was approved initially were the 600 permanent jobs it will create plus a further 300 jobs in the wider economy. Also, its investors say they will build to the highest environmental standards.

Consider this

What is more important – preserving the National Park or creating jobs?

Erosion of resources

A problem in many destinations is that the influx of tourists puts pressure on scarce resources. Water is a scarce resource in many places and tourists tend to use up more than local people. Where there are golf courses and gardens even more water is used.

Land is taken for development of hotels, airports and roads causing loss of natural habitats. Soil is eroded for development resulting in a change in the landscape. Forests are cleared for ski-resort development.

Case study: China's Great Wall

Tourists spell ruin
The Great Wall of China is more than 200 years old and once stretched almost 6500 kilometres. It is now much shorter as millions of tourists and related developments have left their mark, causing damage to entire sections of the wall. Only 2500 kilometres of wall are left in place.

One of the most accessible and popular parts of the wall to visit is at Badaling. Here tourists clamber over the wall and any local hawkers follow them trying to sell their wares.

It is not only walkers who contribute to the damage, television programmes have been filmed at the wall and even rock concerts have taken place there. Some sections of the wall have been demolished to make way for motorways. Conservationists are increasingly concerned that the wall will suffer more and more damage unless action is taken soon.

(Source: Adapted from *The Times*, 11 April 2005)

1   **Why do you think this situation has been allowed to develop?**
2   **What measures could be taken to protect the wall whilst still allowing tourists access?**
    For ideas on how to do this, research measures taken at Stonehenge in the UK. P1

▲ Figure 11.2 A loggerhead turtle

Trampling occurs on well-trodden trails spoiling the countryside that people have come to see. Walkers are encouraged to stay on paths in order to reduce the erosion.

Effects on wildlife

The presence of tourists can be detrimental to wildlife which can be frightened away from its natural habitat by noise and disturbance. The Greek island Zakynthos is the home of the loggerhead turtle. The female turtles come back each year to the beaches to nest and lay eggs in the same place where they themselves hatched. The males stay in the sea. The species is under threat because Zakynthos is also a vibrant tourist destination. The turtles are prevented from coming onto the beach by the noise from nightclubs and from beach parties. The eggs that do get laid may be inadvertently smashed by tourists. Those babies who do manage to hatch get confused by the bright lights and instead of heading for the sea and moonlight, go the wrong way. In spite of a European Court judgement condemning Greece for not protecting the turtles' breeding grounds, action has not been taken. The World Wildlife Fund has launched a campaign to help protect the turtles.

Consider this

What do you think the Greek government could do to protect the turtles without losing their tourism business? Discuss your ideas with your group.

Social impact

Positive social impacts

■ Community facilities and services

Roads and rail networks may be introduced to cater for tourists but are also of benefit to locals. Sport and leisure facilities may be introduced and the standard of living for the host community may generally improve.

■ Education and training

Jobs in tourism are generally desirable in developing destinations. Employees may be able to undertake professional training and improve their job prospects. The quantity and quality of training naturally varies across countries and companies. In areas of good practice, line staff may receive weekly training and support for higher education programmes.

■ Improved social status

The status of local people can be improved when tourists recognise and respect the culture of the community they are visiting. Also, gaining a job in tourism can lead to enhanced status in the community.

■ Improved standards of living

Regular wages, clean water, effective sewage systems and road and rail networks improve quality of life for local people as well as providing facilities for tourists.

Negative social impacts

■ Crime and anti-social behaviour

Increases in tourism numbers are often accompanied by a rise in levels of crime. Tourists may carry expensive cameras and wear expensive clothes and jewellery so they become targets for criminals. Resorts may be built in enclaves next to poor areas and tourists may become afraid to leave the resort for fear of crime. The host population then becomes resentful of tourists who do not mix with their society or spend their money in the community. General resentment may be expressed by rudeness towards tourists and even hostility. This was a particular problem in Jamaica and in Florida several years ago but education programmes for tourists in the form of advice brochures given out before arrival have helped improve safety.

■ Sex tourism

Tourism has encouraged the growth of prostitution in destinations as young women are willing or persuaded to sell their bodies to provide an income. There are several organisations that are fighting against sex tourism. One is ECPAT (End Child Prostitution, Child Pornography and Trafficking of Children for Sexual Purposes) which is a network of organisations and individuals working together to eliminate the commercial sexual exploitation of children. In 1998, it produced a code of practice for endorsement by tour operators and other travel organisations. The code aims to prevent sexual exploitation of children in tourism destinations. The code is implemented by 45 countries across the world.

It is not only men who engage in sex tourism. Many middle-aged white women visit Jamaica to be entertained by young local men. Commonly known as 'milk bottles' they are willing to spend money on the men in return for nights out and sex.

■ Conflict with host community – demonstration effect

Western tourists visiting developing countries represent an entirely different and sometimes unknown society. Members of the host community may try to copy western behaviour or dress, resulting in changes to their traditional way of life or causing conflict between the hosts and the visitors. Tourists sometimes fail to respect the customs and traditions of the host country causing irritation. The host population may feel resentful about the wealth of the incoming tourists. Even though the tourists may not be wealthy in western terms they have a lot more disposable income than the people in the developing destination. This resentment can lead to crime.

You may have heard of the term 'lager louts'. This mainly originated in Spain and the Balearic islands and was used disparagingly about British male tourists who, after drinking copious amounts of cheap drink, behaved irresponsibly, annoying the local population. Such behaviour has give British holidaymakers a poor reputation in some areas.

Consider this

Think of and discuss other instances of similar behaviour by British people abroad.

■ Displacement

When tourism is regionalised in a country, people may leave their homes and communities to take up jobs in tourism. More serious displacement occurs when whole communities are moved on to make room for tourism development. Recently, there was contention as hundreds of people were displaced from Chattisgarh in India to make room for a National Park aimed at bringing tourism to the area.

■ Seasonal employment

Although seasonal employment affects the local economy, it also has a social impact as those who find themselves out of work for part of the year must find some other form of employment. They may turn to a black-market economy to find work.

Cultural impact

Positive cultural impacts

■ Preservation of traditional customs and crafts

Traditional crafts, such as lace making in Malta, are revived because the tourist trade makes them viable again. In some destinations, hotels have now adopted a policy of inviting local people into their complex on a particular evening each week to sell their crafts to the tourists staying there. The EUROTEX project, funded by the EC, aims to develop textile-related cultural tourism in disadvantaged areas of Europe. The aim is to encourage tourists to buy local textile crafts not only to preserve the crafts, but also to strengthen the local economy. The pilot regions for this project were Alto Minho in Portugal, Lapland and Crete.

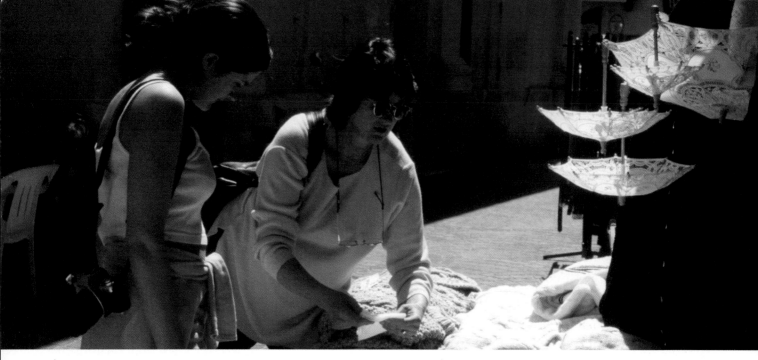

▲ Figure 11.3 Lace-making in Malta

■ Cultural identity

Travelling to new places can bring about a better understanding of different cultures. In the best case scenario, tourists learn about the food and traditions of their destination and the hosts learn about their visitors. Having visitors interested in the host culture can reinforce the cultural identity of the nation as they proudly show it to visitors.

Negative cultural impact

■ Dilution of cultural identity

As it becomes easier, faster and cheaper to travel the world, so each destination begins to look something like another. For example, McDonalds can be found almost anywhere including eastern Europe and Africa. Some tourists want to live exactly as they do at home – but with sunshine; in many resorts in Spain you see English pubs and English food advertised for sale. This kind of development results in a loss of the destination's cultural identity.

In the southern resorts of Tenerife, there are beautiful hotels with excellent facilities and good food but there isn't anything remotely Canarian, even the hotel workers are from mainland Spain. You have to hire a car and travel away from the purpose-built resorts to find the Canarian culture.

Case study: tourism in Libya

Libya has introduced a 20-year plan for tourism and hopes to entice developers to Libya by giving them free land and tax incentives. Investors would need to improve the infrastructure as well as build new hotels. The existing hotels need updating to bring them up to western standards. Many small tour operators have started up and hope to offer tourist packages.

The country has great potential – there are old towns to explore, deserts to cross and beaches to lie on. In addition, there is the attraction of the ruins of a lost Roman empire.

Slight problems for tourists are that the signs are all in Arabic and an entry visa is needed.

Also, it is not envisaged that alcohol will be served anywhere but within enclosed resorts as it is important the Islamic culture is maintained.

1 **Check the location of Libya and name its capital city.**

2 **Find out why there has been no tourism to Libya for the past 20 years.**

3 **Discuss the potential positive and negative impacts of western tourism on Libya.** **P1**

Put all your information together in an information sheet.

What do we mean by 'sustainable tourism development'?

Sustainable tourism means developing and managing tourism in such a way that the positive economic and socio-cultural benefits to the environment, the host community and the visitor are maximised without using up or abusing precious natural or cultural resources.

You will come across other terms relating to sustainability in tourism:

- green tourism
- responsible tourism
- ecotourism
- fair trade tourism.

Key term

Ecotourism – the Ecotourism Society defines it as 'responsible travel to natural areas which conserves the environment and improves the welfare of the local people'.

These forms of tourism all follow the same basic principles:

- Minimise negative economic, environmental and socio-cultural impacts
- Create economic benefits for local people and improve their quality of life
- Promote the conservation of natural and cultural heritage
- Promote respect between tourists and local people.

Consider this

Think about the last time you went on holiday. Were these principles put into practice? How?

In this part of the unit you will learn about the many different kinds of organisations and agencies involved in sustainable tourism development. You will learn about their roles and their reasons for being involved in tourism development. These organisations represent the public, private and voluntary sectors. They are sometimes described as 'stakeholders'.

Roles of agents

The roles of agents vary according to their objectives, status and funding. They may provide finance or marketing for sustainable tourism development, or they may facilitate partnerships. You will understand more about the roles as we study the different stakeholders.

Key terms

Public sector – organisations which are owned by the state and receive their funds from local or central government and usually aim to provide a service. Their policy will be directed by national or local government.

Private sector – organisations which are owned by shareholders or individuals rather than the state. They are commercial companies and usually aim to make a profit.

Voluntary sector – organisations which are often charities or pressure groups. They do not always make a profit but put funds into the company activities, for example conservation.

Private sector agents

■ Landowners

Landowners and owners of stately homes are not always cash rich and seek to develop their properties and land to benefit from tourism. Most British stately homes are open to visitors for some part of the year. Many welcome film crews to their parks and houses and then benefit from increased tourism as the films gain publicity.

Figure 11.4 Access to beaches in Barbados is a subject of contention ▲

Case study: beach policy in Barbados

In Barbados, all beaches are public. Everyone is entitled to access. However, access to beaches has become an issue of contention in recent years because:

- there is a lack of vacant coastal land
- when land is available it is very expensive
- landowners want properties which reach to the sea to have boundaries which prevent access
- new beach land with disputed ownership has appeared through coastal works.

The declared policy is that all citizens and visitors alike must have access to all beaches, including, where possible, windows to the sea.

1 **Do you think the policy should be changed? What would be the benefits/disadvantages to tourists, landowners and local people of changing the policy?**

2 **Draw up a chart illustrating your findings.**

In developing countries, land owned by local people is often bought up cheaply by developers. If local authorities are powerful enough they can prevent this happening and ensure that local people are involved in development. Where locals own the land they can make money from tourism and stop the advent of large hotel chains. In Tobago there are very few large hotels as local people own the land – and want to keep it. They welcome tourists and cater for them with local produce. Some of the hotels are all inclusive and these are not so beneficial to the economy as tourists have all their needs catered for in the hotel.

■ Property developers

Property developers may be individuals who decide to open a hotel or major international companies responsible for developing whole resorts. Property developers are in business to make money out of their developments and are often in conflict with host communities who do not want to lose their land or see overdevelopment. The public sector has to take responsibility for overseeing development and ensuring that community needs are met and that development is sustainable. The Bahamas provides a good example.

The government policy is to extend the economic benefits derived from tourism and to have a hotel sector that is private sector led. In the UK, it is the norm for hotels to be privately owned but in 1992, 20 per cent of hotels in the Bahamas were government owned. In the last 10 years or so, most of these have been privatised. Many hotels were bought and refurbished by international investors and developers. New hotels have also been built and redevelopment of resorts has taken place. A consortium of American, British and South African investors recently bought four hotels on Paradise Island and redeveloped them at a cost of over $250 million. The government gave exemptions from property tax and customs duty for companies investing in hotel and resort development. The purpose was to inject capital investment from the private sector into development, rather than the government providing the capital from taxes.

■ Tour operators

Tour operators have a major role to play in sustainable tourism development as they are instrumental in introducing large numbers of people to destinations when they organise package tours. Their decisions to operate in new destinations have tremendous impact. Many are very aware of sustainable tourism and have policies demonstrating their good practice. One way that a tour operator can try to practise sustainable tourism is by joining the Tour Operators' Initiative. This is an organisation of like-minded tour operators whose aim is explained on the organisation's website. Note that tour operators are in the private sector yet this initiative is voluntary, non-profit making and open to all tour operators.

With this Initiative, tour operators are moving towards sustainable tourism by committing themselves to the concepts of sustainable development as the core of their business activity and to work together through common activities to promote and disseminate methods and practices compatible with sustainable development.

(Source: http://www.toinitiative.org/about/about.htm)

■ Hotel chains

The Accor group of hotels (Sofitel, Novotel, Ibis) is a member of the Tour Operators' Initiative. The group aims to follow the principles of sustainable development and it demonstrates what can be done by hotel chains.

The group gives financial support to charities such as the World Wildlife Fund and to UNESCO restoration projects. Accor aims to educate customers in environmental awareness by publishing literature on preservation of the marine environment in the Red Sea and a comic book for children on environmental issues. Hotel managers and staff are trained on the group's environmental policy and follow a training guide on use of electricity, etc. There are policies to improve practice in waste management and recycling.

Theory into practice

1 Choose a hotel group, for example Marriott or Hilton. Visit the hotel chain's website and find examples of managing hotels following sustainable principles.

2 Have you stayed in a hotel? Can you think of examples of sustainable tourism policies from your stay?

Taking it further

Suggest further ways of practising sustainability in the hotels you studied.

■ Airlines

In 2006, European MPs proposed a tax on aviation fuel and the creation of an emissions trading scheme for airlines. This was not a popular proposal for most airlines who feel they are unfairly targeted and that an emissions trading scheme would prevent growth of airlines. There is also a fear that an aviation tax would result in higher fares.

Key term

Emissions trading – companies are given permits to pollute. If they create less pollution than their permit allows then they can sell the remaining allowance on to another company who is creating more pollution than their allowance.

The pressure is on airlines to clean up their act. The following case study shows how Thomson aims to do so.

Case study: Thomsonfly opts for greener aircraft

14 Aug 2006

TUI's Thomsonfly is to acquire three new Boeing 737-800 aircraft direct from the manufacturer in the first quarter of next year.

No financial details of the deal were given.

The airline will also acquire two B737-300s from an unspecified source, as part of a series of investments aimed at increasing the efficiency of its operations. With the addition of the five aircraft, Thomsonfly will dispose of two of its B767-200s to business-class carrier Silverjet …, while two 737-500s will leave its fleet in the spring of 2007.

In a statement the airline said the new aircraft would be more fuel-efficient and therefore more cost-efficient, cleaner and quieter than those they replace. It added that Boeing aircraft are 70 per cent more fuel efficient than 40 years ago, while Thomsonfly – formerly Britannia Airways – is 50 per cent more efficient than 30 years ago.

Thomsonfly currently operates an all-Boeing fleet of 47 aircraft from 24 UK airports to 80 destinations worldwide.

(Source: http://www.e-tid.com/pma/25641)

Another aircraft that claims to be cleaner is the Boeing 787-8 *Dreamliner*. Find out what benefits this new aircraft promises to airlines and passengers.

Taking it further

Carry out research to find out more about aviation and pollution. Think about noise pollution as well as aircraft emissions. Prepare for a debate where the motion is 'There should be an aviation fuel tax'. Prepare arguments for or against the motion in two teams and debate the issue. You will find lots of information in the travel trade press.

■ Entertainment companies

Entertainment companies usually enter into a development in the later stages and choose a location where they will benefit from the advent of tourism. Examples include cinemas, casinos and leisure centres. Like hotels, they can aim to use renewable resources.

Theory into practice

Think about the last holiday you went on. What were the leisure and entertainment centres in your resort? Did they add to or detract from your holiday experience? Why? Discuss your ideas with your colleagues.

■ Travel publishers

Publishers of travel guides, in particular, can influence the popularity and subsequently the number of travellers to a destination. They have a responsibility, therefore, to raise awareness of environmental issues and encourage travellers to behave in a responsible way.

Public sector agents

The public sector role is of utmost importance as it is responsible for setting policy on tourism and for putting in place the legislation needed to implement policy. In a developed country like the UK the public sector structure is well established and works in harmony with the private sector to develop and monitor tourism. In countries where the tourism industry is in its infancy, the government may have less control over development than private enterprises and has to begin the process of establishing national tourism organisation networks.

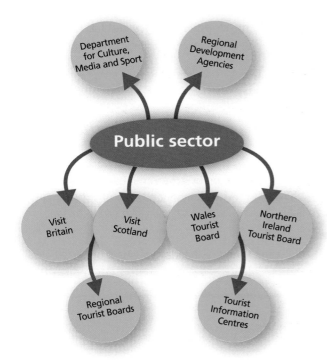

▲ **Figure 11.5 Public sector tourism in the UK**

■ National, regional and local organisations

The structure of public sector tourism in the UK is shown in Figure 11.5.

The Department for Culture, Media and Sport (DCMS) set down its strategies for tourism in the UK in 1999 in *Tomorrow's Tourism Today*. Fifteen action points were at the core of this document:

1. *a blueprint for the sustainable development of tourism*
2. *initiatives to widen access to tourism*
3. *more money for a more focused and aggressive overseas promotion programme*
4. *new internet systems to deliver more worldwide tourist bookings for the UK*
5. *new computerised booking and information services*
6. *a major careers festival and image campaign*
7. *a hospitality industry programme to sign up 500 employees to work towards Investors in People standard*
8. *a new strategic national body for England*
9. *a new grading scheme for all hotels and guest houses*

10. *new targets for hotel development in London and a further £4.5 million for marketing*
11. *more integrated promotion of our wonderful cultural, heritage and countryside attractions*
12. *the development of innovative niche markets, such as film tourism and sports tourism*
13. *encouraging the regeneration of traditional resorts*
14. *more central government support for the regions*
15. *a high profile Tourism Summit bringing together industry and government.*

(Source: Extracted from *Tomorrow's Tourism Today* 1999)

These targets are still valid but in July 2004 an updated *Tomorrow's Tourism Today* was published, reporting on progress and establishing further targets under categories of marketing and e-tourism, product quality, workforce skills, improved data and advocacy across government.

Theory into practice

Divide up the action points from *Tomorrow's Tourism Today* equally between your group. Work in pairs if you prefer. Find out whether the targets have been implemented. Gather information on progress and make a presentation to your group. Use the websites for DCMS and VisitBritain to help you.

■ National tourist offices and Regional Tourist Boards

VisitBritain and the other national tourist offices are responsible for implementing government policy nationally and the Regional Tourist Boards are responsible for implementing it in their regions alongside the Regional Development Agencies. The tourist boards have to promote their areas as destinations and work to influence government policies. They also advise businesses in their area about government policy.

■ Regional Development Agencies (RDA)

These agencies were set up by the government to promote sustainable economic development in England. They have a remit that extends beyond tourism, but since 2003 they have had strategic responsibility for tourism in their regions. They work in conjunction with the tourist boards. Whilst the development agency determines policy, the tourist board is responsible for delivering it. The tourist board develops its business plans with the development agency and has them approved by the development agency board members.

Key term

Quango – an acronym which stands for Quasi Autonomous Non Governmental Organisation, otherwise known as a non-departmental public body. Quangos are set up by government with government funding but they work independently of government.

Case study: sustainable tourism development in Wales

Visit Wales is the Welsh Assembly's tourism team, within the Department of Enterprise Innovation and Networks. Visit Wales has taken over the functions of the former Wales Tourist Board. The role of Visit Wales is to support the tourism industry and to provide the appropriate strategic framework within which private enterprise can achieve sustainable growth and success, so improving the social and economic well-being of Wales. The mission of Visit Wales is to 'maximise tourism's contribution to the economic, social and cultural prosperity of Wales'.

To encourage quality product development, Visit Wales operates various grant schemes. Business consultants provide specialist financial and business development advice to tourism businesses interested in making an application for a grant.

In addition, four Regional Tourism Partnerships (RTPs) were set up in 2002 to cover north, mid, south-west and south-east Wales. Their principal role is to lead the implementation of four regional tourism strategies which seek to improve the competitive performance of tourism so that it makes a better contribution to the economic and social prosperity of Wales. The RTPs work in partnership with Visit Wales, local authorities, National Park Authorities, tourism businesses and with other organisations to undertake a range of marketing, product investment and business support activities on behalf of the tourism industry.

Tourism Membership Bodies in Wales provide a wide range of benefits to member businesses, such as providing information and advice, lobbying government, discounts on purchasing goods and services, and networking opportunities. The Wales Tourism Alliance is the officially recognised umbrella body for tourism industry consultation and representation. It comprises national and sectoral membership bodies, together with representatives of regional and local trade membership bodies.

There are around 80 Tourist Information Centres in Wales. These TICs are managed by a number of different organisations including Local Authorities, National Park Authorities, regional tourism companies and tourism associations.

(Source: Adapted from http://www.industry.visitwales.co.uk/)

1   **Describe the roles of agents involved in sustainable tourism development in Wales. You will need to do some further research to find out how the different bodies consider sustainability. Start at www.industry.visitwales.co.uk/.**   **P2**

2   **Explain how the agents invoved in sustainable tourism developement in Wales could have conflicting objectives.**   **M2**

3   **Assess the effectiveness of measures taken in Wales to put the objectives of sustainable tourism development into practice.**   **D1**

Consider this

Examples of quangos include the Regional Development Agencies. Can you think of and name any others?

■ Local authorities

Local authorities provide the infrastructure for tourism. This includes roads, lighting, water and sewerage, public transport systems and signs. These facilities need to be well managed to ensure an area is fit for tourists.

Local authorities own visitor attractions such as museums, art galleries, swimming pools, parks and gardens. Public spaces must be clean and attractive to attract tourists.

Many local authorities carry out marketing activities and provide visitor information through Tourist Information Centres and other bodies.

Theory into practice

Find out what your local authority's role is with regard to tourism. Make a poster outlining its role and include a diagram showing how the local authority relates to other agents of tourism.

■ Conservation organisations

English Heritage is an example of a conservation organisation in the public sector. This body is sponsored by the DCMS and is an executive non-departmental public body. Its official name is the Historic Buildings and Monuments Commission for England. The organisation also works with other government departments as their work also affects heritage. An example is the Department for Environment, Food and Rural Affairs (DEFRA), which takes care of policy on rural issues. The government provides funding for English Heritage but it also earns revenue from the historic properties.

The role of English Heritage is described on its website.

English Heritage works in partnership with the central government departments, local authorities, voluntary bodies and the private sector to:

- *conserve and enhance the historic environment*
- *broaden public access to the heritage*
- *increase people's understanding of the past.*

(Source: http://www.english-heritage.org.uk)

The organisation looks after over 400 properties for the nation and maintains registers of England's most significant historic buildings, monuments and landscapes.

Public sector organisations develop tourism to take advantage of the economic benefits to the community or region, in terms of jobs or increased revenue. Organisations like English Heritage aim to preserve the heritage and culture for all to enjoy.

Theory into practice

Find out more about the role of conservation at English Heritage. What partners does the organisation work with? How does it fund projects? You might choose a particular project to report on. Write up notes on your findings.

Voluntary sector agents

Many voluntary sector organisations are charities and pressure groups. Probably the best known in tourism is the National Trust. However, there are several voluntary organisations related to sustainable tourism development.

■ Campaigning charities

The purpose of campaigning charities in travel and tourism is to promote responsible and sustainable tourism. They may do this through education programmes which raise awareness, by advising businesses on how to practise sustainable tourism or by lobbying government to change policies.

Case study: Tourism Concern

Tourism Concern has been working since 1989 to raise awareness of the negative impacts of tourism, economic, cultural, environmental and social. Advocacy is a major part of our work and time and again the message from our Southern (Third World) partners is the same: 'We want tourists, but at the moment we don't benefit from them.' Communities often find they have tourism imposed on them by governments and foreign developers and tourism businesses; that there is little linkage between tourism especially at a mass scale – and local industry, such as agriculture; that land and natural resources are frequently co-opted, often illegally; and that their cultural traditions are appropriated and commercialised.

Our links with communities and agencies working in developing countries show that there is great concern that the trend in tourism is towards greater control by multinationals, more all-inclusive tourism which excludes local people and businesses, and greater numbers. The consequence of such a trend proving true could prove disastrous for local people.

(Source: Reproduced by kind permission of Tourism Concern from http://www.tourismconcern.org.uk. Tourism Concern is a campaigning NGO registered as a charity (1064020) and a company limited by guarantee (3260052))

1 **Visit the Tourism Concern website and choose one current campaign. What is the role of Tourism Concern in this campaign?**

2 **How do the objectives of Tourism Concern in your chosen campaign conflict with those of government or developers?** P2 M2

Fair Trade

Oxfam defines Fair Trade as paying poor producers a fair price, and helping them gain the business skills and knowledge to work their way out of poverty. Tourism Concern tries to apply these principles to travel and tourism.

■ Conservation organisations

- The Landmark Trust acquires historic properties and renovates them so that they are suitable for holiday lets.
- The Churches Conservation Trust cares for 300 churches which might otherwise have fallen into disrepair. Some of these are open to visitors.
- The National Trust is another example of a conservation organisation. It is similar to English Heritage but differs in that it is completely independent of government and receives no funds from it. It is a registered charity and therefore a voluntary organisation. It was founded in 1895 by three Victorian philanthropists who were concerned about industrialisation and set up the trust to acquire and protect threatened coastline, countryside and buildings.

This is still the role of the National Trust today. It protects over 200 historic houses and gardens and 49 industrial monuments and mills. It also owns more than 248,000 hectares of countryside and about 965 kilometres of coast for people to visit and enjoy. The Trust also has a role in managing the environment, developing best practice and acting as a source of advice on environmental issues. The National Trust has over 3 million members. The Trust is funded by membership fees, revenue from entrance to properties and donations.

- The National Trust for Scotland is a similar organisation and cares for over 100 properties.

■ Community groups

Community groups may be formed specifically to deal with proposed tourism (or other) developments or may have been formed for a different purpose but then become involved in tourism development. Local people wish to be consulted on possible developments to protect their personal and community interests. Community groups can also act as pressure groups.

Theory into practice

Organisation	Role	Public	Private	Voluntary
English Heritage				
Visit Britain				
Yorkshire Forward				
National Trust				
Hilton Hotels				
Tourism Concern				
British Airways				
Blackpool Pleasure Beach				
Thomas Cook				
DCMS				
British Airports Authority				

Copy and complete the table, deciding whether the organisations are public, private or voluntary. Try to summarise the role of each organisation.

Theory into practice

Summarise the reasons why voluntary organisations become involved in tourism development. Consider the following factors: encouraging responsible tourism, education and raising funds. **P2**

Political objectives

Tourism is related to politics in that it is the government of a country that determines tourism policy. The policy is often to use a national network of tourism organisations to attract greater numbers of tourists to generate revenue or to manage tourism in a sustainable way. There may be other political objectives too.

Creating a national or regional identity

National identity comes from images and experiences within a country but also from how others perceive the country. How a country is perceived is often related to tourism and based on the perceptions of visitors. A country may present itself in a certain way in its publicity and on its website to promote a particular identity and therefore attract visitors. For example, what do you think of when you think of Holland? Windmills, bikes and tulips? Cheese? If you look at the banner on the Holland website you will find all these traditional images. It reinforces people's perceptions of what Holland is like and what they hope to find if they visit.

Theory into practice

Choose three countries. Discuss your perceptions of those countries as a tourist. How do you think tourists see the British? Are these perceptions correct? What gives the UK its national identity?

Consider this

We also have perceptions of people from different regions. Think what your perceptions are of a Londoner, a Glaswegian or someone from Yorkshire. How do regions present a united front to tourists?

Raising the profile of an area

Where a country has suffered conflict and is in the stage of recovery, tourism can be a means of proving to the international community that the country is stable and safe. Croatia provides a good example. As part of the former Yugoslavia the area was a very popular tourist destination. The civil war in the 1990s meant that the tourism industry was devastated. Although a lot of Croatia was unaffected by conflict, tourists naturally stayed away. Now tourism is an essential part of the country's regeneration.

Environmental objectives

Environmental improvements

Investment in tourism can bring about improvements to areas which benefit local people as well as visitors. This might include cleaning buildings, providing riverside and canal walkways and getting rid of litter.

▲ Figure 11.6 The Holland website banner

(Source: http://www.holland.com; reprinted with permission of the Netherlands Board of Tourism and Conventions)

Habitat and heritage preservation

Precious natural habitats and heritage sites have to be conserved or they will be lost to future generations. It is often difficult to balance conservation with allowing the public to view or enjoy their heritage and parklands. National Parks are heavily protected and although people are allowed to enjoy them, there are restrictions on the types of activities that can take place. Historic buildings, such as the colleges in Cambridge and Oxford, are often open to the public but access is restricted by time and numbers so that too many tourists are not detrimental to the buildings' structure.

Revenue from tourism can be used to preserve heritage sites. Ironically, the preservation is sometimes necessary because of increased tourism. Tourists wandering around a site cause erosion and litter.

It should not always be assumed that the objective of tourism is to maximise visitors. Where resources and space are limited the aim is to manage visitors and prevent negative impacts which occur through erosion of paths, buildings and overdevelopment. Examples of such visitor management occur in many historic towns and at historic sites such as Stonehenge.

Another means of attempting to control the flow of visitors is through ecotourism. Ecotourism represents the ideal of minimising negative impacts and practising sustainable tourism as tourists and service providers actively strive to minimise the negative impacts. The idea is to bring small numbers of people to enjoy the natural resources and culture of a destination without changing the basic culture or ecology.

In the UK industrial regeneration is a common theme as the following case study shows.

Case study: Salford

Salford is being transformed. Three new heritage walks have been introduced with maps and guides to accompany them. Chapel Street is included in the walking tour, the first street in the country to be lit by gas and the scene of one of the first battles of the Civil War. There have been walking tours for some time but the new ones incorporate Salford Quays, Worsley and Chapel Street. The council – through its marketing and tourism department – aims to promote the town as a heritage town rather than a dirty old town. The council say that the city has 60 per cent green space and the entire docks area has been regenerated. Salford Quays boasts modern apartments amid the remains of the old docks.

Find out more about regeneration, either in Salford or in your own town if appropriate. Find out who are the stakeholders involved in regeneration projects and their role in the regeneration. How do you think the regeneration will impact on the economy? Present your findings to your colleagues. **P2 P3**

▲ **Figure 11.7 Salford Quays**

Environmental education

Visitor centres are usually a source of information for tourists and school groups. Such information helps the tourists understand the reasons for conservation and encourages them to respect the environment. It also allows children and students to learn about the environment in a practical way. Some National Parks provide information and fact sheets for students that can be downloaded from the internet.

Environmental auditing

Environmental auditing should begin with analysis of the environmental resources in the area. Careful planning a long time in advance can help ensure that environmental resources are protected and conserved during development. Green building helps decrease the negative impact of tourism on the environment.

Case study: discover Coral Reefs School Program

Our award-winning program provides every 4th grade student in the Florida Keys with an introduction to the coral reef. Educator Joel Biddle begins with a video/talk at the Reef Relief Environmental Center (for Lower Keys students) or the John Pennekamp Coral Reef State Park Visitor Center (for Upper Keys students), an excursion to the reef aboard a Glassbottom Boat, a follow-up slide show entitled 'We All Live Downstream' and use of printed materials including the 'Coral Reef Guide for Kids of All Ages' and 'South Florida's Water Wonderland'. The Reef Relief Teacher Kit enables educators around the world to introduce their students to coral reefs.

(Source: http://www.reefrelief.org)

Reef Relief ran this programme for 10 years and in 2005 held teacher workshops so that the local county school teachers could provide the programme to their students directly, using the materials.

1 **Do some research and find out your own example of a coral reef audit or conservation programme.**

2 **Produce a poster with an explanation of the programme.**

▲ Figure 11.8 The coral reef is an important example of an environment that needs protection

Examples of environmental auditing include several programmes which aim to protect coral reefs throughout the world. These involve monitoring the state of the reefs and education programmes to help conserve them, as shown in the case study above.

Socio-cultural objectives

Development of community facilities and improving quality of life

Sometimes planning permission is only given to developers as long as they provide facilities for the host community alongside or as part of their development. Examples include leisure facilities or even schools. In addition, the host community has a better standard of living because of the increased revenues from tourism.

Planning controls

Restrictions on the quantity and type of building help prevent a destination becoming overdeveloped. In Majorca, tourism has become the most important source of revenue to the economy. Parts of the island have become overdeveloped due to mass tourism. Eventually action had to be taken to try to reverse the decline in the island's image as a cheap destination for low-spending, heavy-drinking tourists. Building restrictions were imposed on hotels throughout the island and the capital, Palma, was restored.

Promoting cultural understanding

Welcoming visitors to a country or community can promote mutual understanding, it can inspire people to learn new languages and to try new foods and experiences. On a global level such interaction can help promote peaceful societies. This works both ways. Hosts must have a positive attitude to visitors and be encouraged to welcome them and take part in community tourism initiatives. On the other hand, visitors must respect the people and the culture of the destination they are visiting. Responsible Travel is working on a community-based tourism project database (www.responsibletravel.com/TripSearch/

Cultural%20tours/Activity100044.htm). This features examples of community tourism projects. This extract from the website explains how a project in Thailand works.

> You will have an opportunity to stay with a family as one of the members, you will experience the local food that is unique in taste and style. Our tour leaders have been working closely together with the community and understand the community's lifestyle and customs. The guides are members of the local community. They will demonstrate their daily work.

> The organisation that operates this trip was established in 1994 by a local charity, Thailand Volunteer Service (TVS) to provide benefits to rural communities from tourism. Our aims are to strengthen the community. Decisions are made by the community and programmes are managed by the community for the community, so that the community are the owners of the programme and have rights over the way it is managed, with the purpose of encouraging sustainability and enabling learning among visitors to the community.

(Source: http://www.responsibletravel.com/Trip/Trip100789.htm)

Maintaining traditions or beliefs

Traditions may be lost as younger generations lose interest in preserving them. The objective of tourism may be to preserve such traditions and in fact cultural and heritage tourism are rising in popularity. For example, in Mexico, Zapotec weavers from Oaxaca live in a 'craft village' known for specialising in certain textiles. They are able to demonstrate and sell their work to tourists while preserving an ancient craft.

Economic objectives

In most cases economic objectives are the aim of tourism development. This is not surprising as worldwide tourist arrivals and receipts are increasing, and all countries would like a piece of the action. The World Tourism Organisation reported record numbers of international arrivals in 2005. The number of international tourist arrivals recorded worldwide grew by 5.5 per cent and exceeded 800 million for the first time ever.

According to VisitBritain, in 2004, total expenditure on UK travel and tourism was £70.08 billion, a rise of 4.8 per cent on 2003. In 2004, a total of 239.8 million visits and 1.35 billion overnight stays were made.

The economic objectives of tourism development include:

- employment creation
- revenue generation – the multiplier effect
- increasing foreign currency earnings
- economic regeneration.

Employment creation

Tourism creates jobs both directly and indirectly. Direct employment occurs in hotels, airports, airlines, tour operators, travel agents and tourist offices.

Indirect employment occurs in industries and businesses that service the travel and tourism industry. For example, construction workers are needed to build the infrastructure that supports tourism such as roads and rail networks, hotels and gas and electricity services. Also, local shops and services benefit from tourist business and will be able to employ more people.

Revenue generation

■ The multiplier effect

Key term

Multiplier effect – the additional revenue created in an area as a result of tourism expenditure.

Direct tourism expenditure has a wider impact on the economy. If a tourist visits a destination and stays in a hotel, the hotel then spends money on local services and provisions to run the business and provide food and facilities for guests. Staff working at the hotel receive wages which are then used to buy further goods and services. Thus, the impact of the initial spend is 'multiplied' throughout the economy.

The multiplier is expressed as a ratio. It can also be applied to jobs, as the building of the hotel leads to direct employment in the hotel but also to extra employment in the construction and service industries. The World Travel and Tourism Council estimates that tourism generates an indirect spend equal to 100 per cent of direct tourism spend. The multiplier effect can be maximised by avoiding leakage.

Where tourist facilities are owned by local people, more of the income from tourism is retained in the community. This can be achieved in various ways:

- regulation on ownership of hotels so that they cannot be entirely foreign owned
- encouraging the development of small businesses
- encouraging partnerships between local people.

Hotels should be encouraged to buy produce locally wherever possible rather than importing. This may mean that support has to be given to local producers to help them meet the needs of large hotels. Hotels or local government may supply seeds and agrochemicals on credit to producers to help them set up. In some cases hotels have participated in 'adopt a farmer' projects.

Where tourism takes place in particular geographic regions, tours should be set up to other areas to allow other communities to benefit from tourism. A good example of this is 'agro-tourism' where local people turn their farmhouses into tourist accommodation or restaurants. The restaurants provide meals serving traditional local delicacies. The aim of these projects is to help local people benefit from tourism, especially when they are no longer able to make their living from agriculture.

Increasing foreign currency earnings

Tourism generates foreign exchange earnings. Tourism is an invisible export. This means if tourists spend their money in the UK it brings the same benefit to the economy as if they buy goods exported from the UK in their own countries. By the same token, when UK residents travel abroad they spend their money in another country and this equates to buying imported goods in the UK.

Inbound tourists spend money whilst in the UK and some also spend money on travel with UK carriers. The more tourists who come into the UK the more the spend increases and the more revenue the economy gains. The

Tourism New Zealand has identified its ideal visitor – 'the interactive traveller' – as it chases a rise in tourism earnings rather than volume. Interactive travellers tend to be well-educated, travel internationally on a regular basis and have relatively high levels of discretionary income.

Tourism minister Mark Burton said: 'These guests are exceptionally valuable, as they spend more, visit outlying regions and are as keen as us to interact with, and protect, the environment and heritage that have drawn them here.' Wally Stone, chairman of Tourism New Zealand, added: 'Tourism is New Zealand's largest export industry. Visitor spending grew 4 per cent in 2003 against 2002.'

New Zealand's tourism industry generated £2.19 billion in 2003 – a 4 per cent increase on 2002. Of this, the inbound market from Australia accounted for NZ$1 billion (£346 million) for the first time. Burton called this a 'milestone', and added: 'Without these visitors, New Zealand would have to double the size of its dairy herd, add 5.3 million hectares in forest and expand the wine industry by 23 times to compensate. I am confident that the sector will continue to be an economic powerhouse.'

(Source: *Travel Trade Gazette*, 4 June 2004)

1   Do you think that interactive travellers are 'responsible'? If so, why?

2   Explain how tourism is an export industry.

3   What is meant by 'discretionary income'?

4   Why are tourism earnings of more interest to New Zealand than volume of visitors?

Taking it further

Find out about the role of Tourism New Zealand. Is the organisation in the public, private or voluntary sector? What are its objectives?

impact on the economy of incoming and outbound tourism is recorded in the travel balance, a section of the balance of payments. Each sector of the economy is measured in terms of its imports and exports. A happy situation for an economy is where there is a surplus in the balance of payments rather than a deficit, that is, more money coming in than going out.

Key term

Balance of payments – one of the UK's key economic statistics. It measures the economic transactions between the UK and the rest of the world. It indicates the difference between spending on imports and exports.

The balance of payments was £26.6 billion in the red in 2006. The UK government hopes that increased inbound tourism will help to reduce this deficit and aims to increase the value of tourism to £100 billion by 2010.

Economic regeneration

Tourism development is often used as a tool for regeneration both in cites and in coastal resorts in the UK. Dockland areas in Manchester and Liverpool have been regenerated with housing, restaurants and tourist facilities. The Lowry Centre in Salford (near Manchester) is a good example. Areas which are in decline, perhaps because traditional industries like mining have closed down, are in need of employment and investment. Tourism can be a means of injecting new life into an area. Grants from Regional Development Agencies and the EU can help and local authorities will invest funds.

Income from tourism should be reinvested in social and public projects. Tourism taxes are often in place for such purposes. In The Gambia, tourists are subjected to a £5 tax on arrival. This money is earmarked for improving the infrastructure of the country and for training local people to enable them to work in tourism.

In this part of the unit we will examine how different sectors of the travel and tourism industry support sustainable development.

Travel and tourism industry

Tour operators

Private organisations, such as tour operators, working in destinations abroad are in a position to influence responsible tourism and there are many examples of good practice. In the UK, in line with the Sustainable Tourism Initiative, 25 different tour operators have banded together to develop 'The Tour Operator's Initiative' discussed on page 347.

Many specialist tour operators have been keen to follow sustainable development policies and mass market operators are now following this lead. Some tour operators, for example Thomson, support the Travel Foundation, a UK charity that claims to help protect the natural environment, traditions and culture.

You might send for the insider guide published by the Travel Foundation. This is a leaflet aimed at tourists and gives tips for responsible travel. It can also be downloaded at www.thetravelfoundation.org.uk/our_insider_guides.asp.

First Choice is one of the tour operators keen to develop a sustainable tourism strategy. Its vision and policy are shown opposite.

Case study: Travel Foundation

The Travel Foundation is an independent UK charity that aims to help the outbound travel industry manage tourism more sustainably.

It offers a unique resource to the tourism industry, helping to safeguard resources on which business depends and balancing the need for sustainability with profitability.

The Foundation's focus is on protecting and enhancing the environment and improving the well-being of destination communities, thereby enriching the tourism experience, now and in the future.

The development of the Foundation helps enable a real breakthrough for sustainable tourism and is good news for consumers, companies, destination communities and policy makers.

- Consumers get greater quality and an enriched holiday experience, as well as the reassurance that their favourite destinations will be protected for generations to come.

- Businesses are better able to meet the needs of the customer, at the same time as protecting the resources on which their future depends.

- Destination communities receive greater benefit from tourism, with a boost to their local economy and conservation of the natural environment, local traditions and culture.

- Local and national governments have evidence to develop effective tourism policies and support destination communities and environments

(Source: http://www.thetravelfoundation.org.uk)

1   Find out three ways in which the Travel Foundation helps businesses practise sustainable tourism.

2   Find out how the Travel Foundation is funded.

3   Give examples of partners with whom the Travel Foundation works.   **P3 M3**

First Choice

Group sustainable development policy

Our Policy was developed following a series of internal workshops in 2003 and updated in 2004 and in 2005.

As one of the leading leisure travel companies, we recognise that the environment, the communities and cultures within which we operate and our relationships with key groups and individuals are vital to the success of our business. We therefore commit in the long term to:

- *Minimising the direct environmental impact of our operations and being proactively involved in activities and projects that work to protect and restore the natural environment*
- *Working with customers, employees, shareholders, suppliers, industry partners, local communities, and other relevant interested parties, to understand and respect their needs and also supporting them in delivering our commitments*
- *Using the collective influence of the First Choice Group responsibly to create momentum to make the tourism industry more sustainable*
- *Being open, honest and realistic about our environmental and social impacts, targets and achievements in the context of our business objectives*

In support of the above we will work to:

- *Engage First Choice employees and gain their commitment to action, by raising awareness of this Policy and increasing their understanding of sustainable development and the benefits of addressing it*
- *Prevent pollution wherever possible and continually improve our environmental performance by setting and measuring objectives and targets that address our environmental impacts – principally aircraft noise and emissions, waste, procurement, use of energy, paper and water*
- *Promote fair working conditions throughout our own business and our supply chain*

- *Comply with all relevant legislation, act in advance of it where possible and keep pace with best practice*
- *Report current business practices and ensure plans are in place to embed the Company's sustainable development vision*
- *Deliver long-term strategic benefit and shareholder value by maximising the synergies that sustainable development provides*

(Source: http://www.fcenvironmentandpeople.com/fcenviro/progressing_aims/sustainable_development.html#policy)

In addition the tour operators should give guidance to their customers on how to behave responsibly on holiday.

Thomas Cook takes 'responsible tourism' initiative

Thomas Cook has begun highlighting hotels with responsible tourism policies in its latest Summersun and Tropical Shores brochures.

The eighteen hotels that have been awarded this new logo have demonstrated that they take environmental and social issues seriously.

Criteria include responsible approaches to laundry, use of hot water, beach cleanliness and the local environment.

Each hotel achieved a perfect score on a checklist, taken from the Supplier Sustainability Handbook and formulated by Thomas Cook in partnership with the Federation of Tour Operators, and also has independent accreditation from a body such as Green Globe, EMAS and ISO 140001.

Tony Hopkins, director of product and publishing, said: 'Responsible tourism is increasingly on the agenda in the UK, and we wanted to highlight the fact that this is something that Thomas Cook and its hotels take seriously.'

The hotels include the Olympic Lagoon Resort, Cyprus; Sol Milanos Pinguinos, Menorca; Xanadu Resort Hotel, Turkey; Villa Hotels Holiday Island, Maldives, and the Iberostar Creta Marine, Crete.

(Source: http://www.travelmole.com)

You can download the Supplier Sustainability handbook from www.fto.co.uk/responsible-tourism/sustainability-guidelines/. Download one copy that can be kept for reference in your classroom.

Assessment practice

1 Look at some Thomas Cook brochures and find an example of its new policy of highlighting environmentally friendly hotels. Discuss with colleagues what kind of difference this makes to bookings or to the holiday experience.

2 Just how committed to raising awareness about responsible tourism are tour operators? Carry out a survey of brochures using a selection of tour operators. Go through the brochures and find examples of tips similar to those printed by First Choice. Discuss your findings in your group.

3 There are other tour operators who support sustainable tourism. One such is Discovery Initiatives. Have a look at its website at www.discoveryinitiatives.co.uk and find at least five examples of how it contributes to sustainable tourism in destinations. Draw up an information sheet of your findings. These examples of good practice may help you with your assessment. **M3 P3 D2**

Hotel companies

One way hotels can practise sustainable tourism is by employing local people where possible. Where local people lack the necessary skills, training programmes should be implemented. Some large hotel groups have a good record of doing this. An example is Sandals in the Caribbean which claims to have obligatory training for 120 hours per year for line staff in its hotels.

Case study: Sandals

All Sandals and Beaches Resorts have been awarded the coveted Green Globe Award for environmental stewardship. From recycling to conserving, ecological responsiveness is a Sandals commitment. Because at the resorts made for love, loving the environment has become second nature.

All our Resorts are Green Globe Certified
Our mission is to offer the ultimate Caribbean vacation experience by innovatively, reliably and consistently providing the safest and highest quality services and facilities to guests, while attaching a premium to our human resources and being among the most environmentally responsible and community friendly groups in the hospitality industry.

- Staff Awareness
  Team members, participation in workshops and seminars conducted by the environmental committee, local government organizations, and also by non-governmental environmental organizations.
- Water Conservation Program
  Monitoring of total water use on property (pools, guestrooms, kitchen, dining room and garden areas).
- Energy Management Program
  Use of timers on electrical equipment such as:

Jacuzzi blowers, steam rooms at the spa, outdoor lighting for walkways, refrigeration equipment in the kitchens, etc.

- Waste Management Program
  Waste disposal practices and procedures at the hotel such as recycling of linen and bed spreads, food, office paper, and packages.
- Control of Hazardous Substances
  Hotel determines suitability of product before any purchase is made and provides full training for staff whenever new chemicals or equipment are purchased for use in the hotel.
- Social and Cultural Development and Interaction
  Promoting and selling local tours and attractions with special recognition of 'Green tours' at the tour desks. Inviting local craft vendors to the hotel at least once per week to display and sell their craft items.

(Source: http://www.greenglobe.org)

1 **What is the 'Green Globe' Award? (See www. greenglobe.org.)**

2 **What is the Green Globe based on?**

3 **Find an example of another company awarded the Green Globe and explain why.**

Airlines

Airlines are often lambasted for being environmentally unfriendly and yet some of them have made tremendous efforts to contribute to sustainable tourism. Such practices include respecting local restrictions on noise and pollution, buying newer, quieter and more efficient aircraft and investigating emissions trading.

Charitable foundations

Charitable foundations such as Tourism Concern have worked hard to produce advice and examples of good practice for sustainable tourism.

Tourism Concern's ten Principles for Sustainable Tourism were produced to coincide with the Rio Earth Summit 1992 and aim to influence the policies and programmes adopted by the travel and tourism industry worldwide.

- *Using resources sustainably – the conservation and sustainable use of resources – natural, social and cultural – is crucial and makes long-term business sense.*

- *Reducing over-consumption and waste – reduction of over-consumption and waste avoids the costs of restoring long-term damage and contributes to the quality of tourism.*

- *Maintaining diversity – maintaining and promoting natural, social and cultural diversity is essential for long-term sustainable tourism, and creates a resilient base for the industry.*

- *Integrating tourism into planning – tourism development which is integrated into a national and local strategic planning framework undertakes environmental impact assessments, increases the long-term viability of tourism.*

- *Supporting local economies – tourism that supports a wide range of local economic activities and which takes environmental costs and values into account, both protects those economies and avoids environmental damage.*

- *Involving local communities – the full involvement of local communities in the tourism sector not only benefits them and the environment in general but also improves the quality of the tourism experience.*

- *Consulting stakeholders and the public – consultation between the tourism industry and local communities, organisations and institutions is essential if they are to work alongside each other and resolve potential conflicts of interest.*

- *Training staff – staff training which integrates sustainable tourism into work practices, along with recruitment of local personnel at all levels, improves the quality of the tourism product.*

- *Marketing tourism responsibly – marketing that provides tourists with full and responsible information increases respect for the natural, social and cultural environments of destination areas and enhances customer satisfaction.*

- *Undertaking research – ongoing research and monitoring by the industry using effective data collection and analysis is essential to help solve problems and to bring benefits to destinations, the industry and consumers.*

(Source: http://www.tourismconcern.org.uk)

Key term

PHARE (Pologne, Hongrie Assistance à la Reconstruction Economique) – the main channel of European assistance to countries in central and eastern Europe.

The case study on page 364 outlines the objectives of increased tourism in Albania.

Case study: sustainable tourism in Albania

In 2004, World Day of Tourism was celebrated in Albania by a special event to highlight the country's potential as a tourist destination. The event was hosted by travel and tourism organisations and organised by Albania's Tourism Industry cluster. Foreign journalists were invited to report on the event and on the types of holiday available in Albania. These included spa packages, city breaks, historical attractions and outdoor activities. The country also boasts beaches, mountains, and archaeological sites.

The Tourism Minister reported a 15 per cent increase in visitors to Albania in 2004 to 355,000. The tourists are mainly from Kosovo and other parts of Europe.

Albania is just beginning to develop tourism as for years development was prevented by the prevailing communist regime. A digital postcard campaign, supported by US Peace Corps volunteers, with cards offering 'Greetings from Albania' promoted the country. Education in tourism has begun with a programme at the University of Tirana. It is hoped that tourism will become a major source of revenue for Albania.

With funding from the European Bank for Reconstruction and Development the Albanian ministry has outlined a detailed set of guidelines for the tourism industry which includes long-term plans for environmental protection. Part of the development efforts include the creation of national parks and protected areas. Some of Albania's natural attractions, such as the lagoon at Diviaka, the marsh areas of Butrint Lake, and the inland forests at Lura will receive protected designation. On the industry side, a PHARE program for tourism in Albania is providing grants and loans to entrepreneurs who want to develop basic services and lodgings. Foreign investors have investigated development opportunities, particularly in the hotel industry in coastal areas.

(Source: Adapted from an article in Travelwirenews (http://www. travelwirenews.com), 12 December 2004)

1 **Explain how the travel and tourism industry can support the development of sustainable tourism in Albania.** **P4** **M3**

2 **Make recommendations on how the travel and tourism industry in Albania could adapt to support sustainable tourism development, giving examples of good practice elsewhere.** **D2**

Support

Development of the tourism product

You have read how many organisations have tried to introduce sustainability into their products and services by joining together with other tourism organisations and by seeking advice. There is still a lot of work to be done however.

Guidance to tourists

Guidance to tourists on sustainable tourism may come from tour operators, airlines, voluntary organisations or from government. The Foreign Office devotes part of its website to sustainable tourism:

Just simple things can make an enormous difference when you travel. The following tips are based on guidelines produced by the Rough Guide, Lonely Planet and the Travel Foundation. Think how you can have a positive impact on the people and places you visit, and help ensure that they inspire future generations of travellers.

If you think you are too small to make a difference, try sleeping with a mosquito.

(Source: http://www.fco.gov.uk/servlet/Front?pagename=OpenMarket/ Xcelerate/ShowPage&c=Page&cid=1100182468244)

Activity

Visit the Foreign Office website (www.fco.gov.uk) to find out more.

Sustainable tourism policies

The DCMS is committed to sustainable tourism and seeks to promote it by working closely with other government departments such as the Department for Transport, the Department for Communities and Local Government (DCLG) on planning issues and DEFRA on countryside and wildlife issues.

Sustainable tourism was established as a priority for the UK in the government publication *Tomorrow's Tourism Today* in 1999. The policy followed a consultation exercise with a wide range of organisations.

Action points were developed into a strategy, 'Time for Action', by the English Tourism Council (now VisitBritain). The strategy had three objectives for sustainable tourism:

- *to benefit the economy of tourism destinations*
- *to support local communities and culture*
- *to protect and enhance the built and natural environment.*

These were then expanded into objectives and targets for the national tourist boards. Regional Tourist Boards and local authorities must also be aware of these objectives and incorporate them into planning.

You can see that the basis for planning exists internationally and in the UK throughout the public sector but it is essential that foreign governments also adopt the principles of responsible tourism in their planning and also that private organisations are committed to it.

Planning and management

In recent years the importance of sustainable tourism has been increasingly recognised and, in developed destinations especially, an integrated approach to development is either in place or being put into place. This means that partnerships are essential in planning so that all parties are aware of the issue of responsible tourism. For tourists to engage in responsible tourism it has to be an issue at all planning levels, from international to local, and across sectors so that planners, transport departments, marketing agencies

Key term

Sustainable Tourism Initiative – a multi-stakeholder partnership seeking to introduce sustainable tourism practice in the UK outbound tourism industry.

and economic development units are all party to it.

The Sustainable Tourism Initiative was developed in 2003 in preparation for the World Summit on Sustainable Development. The aim was to encourage sustainable tourism practice in the UK outbound tourism industry, acknowledging that there is a responsibility to sustainability, not just in the UK but in the destinations visited by UK residents. The organisations subscribing to the initiative included government, tour operators and other industry members.

The objectives of the Sustainable Tourism Initiative are to:

- *raise awareness amongst the industry and the public about the issues of tourism and sustainable development via clear communications and training programmes*
- *research, develop and demonstrate best practice initiatives for companies to adopt.*

You can find out more at www.fco.gov.uk.

Knowledge check

1 What is meant by 'sustainable tourism'?

2 What is a major difference between English Heritage and the National Trust?

3 Can a host community benefit culturally from tourism?

4 Give two examples of agents of tourism development in the private sector.

5 What is the role of a Regional Development Agency in tourism?

6 What is the government role in policy formulation for tourism?

7 Explain the role of Tourism Concern.

8 How does tourism development create jobs?

9 Explain 'leakage' and how it occurs.

10 What is meant by 'enclave tourism'?

11 Give examples of the negative social impact of tourism development.

12 How can leakage be avoided?

13 Give two economic objectives of tourism development.

14 Give two examples of political objectives of tourism development.

15 Give two examples of good practice in sustainable tourism in specific destinations.

Preparation for assessment

You have been invited to contribute to a seminar on sustainable tourism. Sustainable tourism has been designated a priority for your local authority and members of the tourism department at the council will be presenting their ideas for a forthcoming strategy. To add interest to the debate they want to look at examples of tourism development in other countries. This will give them more depth of knowledge and possibly give them some examples of good practice. You have been asked to research a developed and a developing destination in terms of their tourism development and to report on your findings. You will prepare materials for a presentation including handouts and visual aids.

The destinations you are to research are St Lucia and Lithuania. Background on both destinations is given here but you should be prepared to do further research. Remember that you must research both destinations. However, for some of the grading criteria, you only need to discuss one destination. These are P2, P3, M1, M2, D1 and D2. This means for these tasks you can choose to discuss either St Lucia or Lithuania.

St Lucia

St Lucia is an island in the Windward Islands of the eastern Caribbean. It is volcanic with high rainfall and dense forests. It also has beautiful beaches, natural harbours and coral reefs. The population is over 160,000 inhabitants.

The labour force is distributed as follows:

Agriculture	21.7 per cent
Industry, commerce and manufacturing	24.7 per cent
Services including tourism	53.6 per cent

(Source: *The World Factbook*, CIA, figures for 2006)

St Lucia's traditional export crops were coffee, sugar cane and bananas. Bananas are still the main crop but exports are threatened by the loss of preferential trading agreements with the UK due to changes in EU policy. The government wants to revitalise the banana industry but must also look to other industries for income. The island is becoming increasingly dependent on tourism but has also attracted foreign investment into offshore banking.

Tourism has transformed St Lucia in the last 20 years. Beach resorts and marinas have been built on the west coast. Cruise ships visit almost daily to purpose-built facilities in Castries. Tourism is the main source of foreign exchange and the main contributor to gross domestic product. Over 10,000 people are employed in tourism.

The formulation of policy for tourism is the responsibility of the Ministry of Tourism. The St Lucia Tourist Board is responsible for marketing. The St Lucia Hotel and Tourism Association and the Chamber of Commerce and Industry represent the private sector. The Heritage Tourism Association (HERITAS), is a group of eighteen owners and managers of heritage sites made up of community-based organisations as well as government and non-governmental organisations. One of the organisations' main objectives is to develop and advance the island's heritage as a product for sale to locals and visitors.

Two major hotel developments, the Hyatt Regency and the Rosewood, were completed in 2000. These two hotels cost more than US$ 34 million. The St Lucia Sandals was also expanded in that year. Land and sea transport and restaurants also benefited from greater investment in 2000.

Identified positives

In 2004, plans for establishing, upgrading and implementing quality standards for the island's tourism product were made. Tourism officials have developed five draft standards for the tourism sector in the areas of accommodation, food and beverage, vending, water-based tourism, and ground transportation. Workshops are being held to develop the plans further.

St Lucia is able to welcome large numbers of cruise passengers, over 400,000 per annum, berthing has been created at Port Castries for large cruise ships.

	2001	2002	2003
Tourists stayover	250,132	253,463	276,948
Excursionists	6422	7712	12,817
Visitor arrivals	256,554	261,175	289,765
Cruise ship passengers	489,912	387,180	393,240
Cruise ship calls	327	245	262
Yacht passenger arrivals	–	–	–
Average hotel occupancy	57.0	56.1	62.7

(Source: http://www.stats.gov.lc)

Table 11.1 Overview of tourism statistics for St Lucia

NB Excursionists are day visitors whereas tourists stay at least one night.

A successful campaign has already been mounted to encourage hotels to buy more of their produce from local farmers.

Identified problems

- Land and habitat have been lost to hotel and infrastructure development.
- Coral reef has been destroyed through increased sedimentation from land clearing and beach maintenance. Anchoring of boats has also caused damage.
- Waste management is not sufficient for the needs of hotels, causing pollution to areas of coastline and land pollution from waste sites.

- The government is concerned that the number of all-inclusive hotels is too high and that local people are not benefiting from the tourism they attract. The government needs to find ways of reducing the estimated 60 per cent of leakage from these hotels and encourage tourists to leave the hotels and visit the rest of the island spending their money more widely.
- Local people have a poor perception of enclave resorts.
- Tourism is dominated by large operators and it is very difficult for small businesses to enter the market.

New developments

- There was a proposal to redevelop the area of Soufrière following the inscription of the Pitons Management Area as a World Heritage Site in 2005. The area includes the Piton twin peaks, the Sulphur Springs and the Diamond Falls, all of which attract thousands of tourists.
- The government has developed national policies on waste management using funds from a tourism tax.
- The government decided to introduce a Heritage Tourism Programme. The aim was to achieve more equitable and sustainable tourism development and to enhance the impact of tourism.
- The programme is funded by the government of St Lucia and the EU. Ten sites and attractions were identified to be marketed as heritage attractions. Jobs have been created for tour guides and craft producers as well as employees at the attractions. The owners of the attractions are members of HERITAS.

Useful websites

www.globaleye.org.uk
www.stlucia.org
www.intracen.org
www.heritagetoursstlucia.com
www.infoplease.com
www.stats.gov.lc
www.geographia.com

1   Describe the impacts of tourism development in
    St Lucia. **P1**

2   Describe the roles of agents involved in
    sustainable tourism development in St Lucia. **P2**

3   Explain how the positive impacts of tourism
    development have been maximised and the
    negative impacts minimised in St Lucia. **M1**

4   Explain how the objectives for sustainable tourism
    development are put into practice in St Lucia. **P3**

5   Explain how the agents involved in sustainable
    tourism development in St Lucia could have
    conflicting objectives. **M2**

6   Assess the effectiveness of measures taken in
    St Lucia to put the objectives of sustainable
    tourism into practice. **D1**

7   Explain how the travel and tourism industry
    supports the development of sustainable
    tourism in St Lucia. **P4**

8   Analyse how the travel and tourism industry is
    supporting sustainable tourism development in
    St Lucia. **M3**

9   Recommend how the travel and tourism
    industry could adapt to support tourism
    development in St Lucia, drawing on examples
    of good practice. **D2**

Lithuania

Lithuania is one of the Baltic states, formerly part of the USSR. It shares borders with Belarus, Latvia, Poland and Russia. The population is 3.4 million. The capital city is Vilnius.

In 1990, Lithuania declared its independence from Russia. However, independence was not finally achieved until 1991 as the Moscow administration turned troops on Lithuanian demonstrators.

English is widely spoken and Lithuanian is the mother tongue, although Russian and Polish are also spoken.

The country has a good transport network so it is relatively easy to get about. It has 90 kilometres of coast. There are no mountains or forests but there are hills and pleasant countryside. Art festivals are an attraction. The food tends to be heavy with meat and potatoes, pancakes, dark bread and cakes and fried cheese. The local beer is good. The currency is the litas.

The labour force is distributed as follows:

Agriculture	20 per cent
Industry, commerce and manufacturing	30 per cent
Services including tourism	50 per cent

(Source: *The World Factbook*, CIA, figures for 2006)

Since independence, more than 80 per cent of businesses, previously state owned, have been privatised. Foreign investment is helping to boost the economy and Lithuania is forging trade links with the west. Unemployment is high at over 10 per cent.

Tourism is seen as a means of growth to the economy and a major tourism offensive was launched in 2003 by the State Department of Tourism. Lithuania has joined the World Tourism Organisation and was the first Baltic state to do so. The country became a member state of the EU in 2004. Many steps have already been taken to develop tourism:

- a law on tourism has been approved
- a National Tourism Development Programme has been prepared
- an information system on tourism in Lithuania was prepared
- a marketing plan was developed, funded by state and local authorities and representatives of the tourism industry. Part of the plan concerned presenting a positive image of Lithuania. Various publications were marketed in languages such as Latvian, German, English, Polish and even Esperanto. Lithuania was represented at nineteen International Fairs on Tourism.
- Tourist Information Centres have been opened in Helsinki and in Warsaw
- sightseeing tours have been arranged for journalists and travel organisers from Finland, Germany and the USA
- three hotels have been awarded the 'Green Key Award' for meeting over 70 environmental criteria in three categories including decreased power and water consumption, economic use of heating energy, waste separation and the possession of an environmental policy.

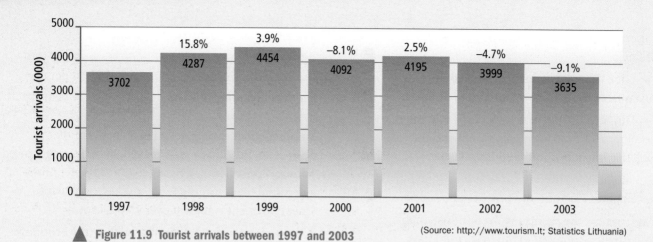

Figure 11.9 Tourist arrivals between 1997 and 2003

(Source: http://www.tourism.lt; Statistics Lithuania)

Figure 11.9 shows the numbers of tourist arrivals between 1997 and 2003. Figures are in thousands.

Most visitors are from neighbouring countries and they travel by car. However, numbers of visitors from western Europe are increasing.

Websites

Useful websites for further research:

www.tourism.lt

www.neris.mii.lt

www.travel.lt

www.lonelyplanet.com

www.cia.gov

1 Describe the impacts of tourism development in Lithuania. **P1**

2 Describe the roles of agents involved in sustainable tourism development in Lithuania. **P2**

3 Explain how the positive impacts of tourism development have been maximised and the negative impacts minimised in Lithuania. **M1**

4 Explain how the objectives for sustainable tourism development are put into practice in Lithuania. **P3**

5 Explain how the agents involved in sustainable tourism development in Lithuania could have conflicting objectives. **M2**

6 Assess the effectiveness of measures taken in Lithuania to put the objectives of sustainable tourism into practice. **D1**

7 Explain how the travel and tourism industry supports the development of sustainable tourism in Lithuania. **P4**

8 Analyse how the travel and tourism industry is supporting sustainable tourism development in Lithuania. **M3**

9 Recommend how the travel and tourism industry could adapt to support tourism development in Lithuania, drawing on examples of good practice. **D2**

Grading tip

Remember, for some of the grading criteria, you only need to discuss *one* destination. These are P2, P3, M1, M2, D1 and D2. This means for these tasks you can choose to discuss St Lucia *or* Lithuania.

To reach Merit or Distinction level in this assessment you will need to use the reference sources given to find further information. Find more of your own if you can and remember to keep a bibliography. Be very specific about your examples, giving names of agents, etc.

Grading criteria

To achieve a pass grade the evidence must show that the learner is able to:	To achieve a merit grade the evidence must show that, in addition to the pass criteria, the learner is able to:	To achieve a distinction grade the evidence must show that, in addition to the pass and merit criteria, the learner is able to:
P1 describe the impacts of tourism development in one specific short-haul and one specific long-haul destination **Case study page 338**	**M1** explain how the positive impacts have been maximised and the negative impacts minimised in a selected destination **Case study page 340**	**D1** assess the effectiveness of measures taken in a destination to put the objectives of sustainable tourism development into practice **Case study page 350**
P2 describe the rules of agents involved in sustainable tourism development at a selected destination **Case study page 350**	**M2** explain how the agents involved in sustainable tourism development could have conflicting objectives in a selected destination **Case study page 350**	**D2** recommend how the travel and tourism industry could adapt to support sustainable tourism development in a selected destination, justifying recommendations by drawing **Assessment practice page 362**
P3 explain how the objectives for sustainable tourism development are put into practice at a selected destination **Case study page 355**	**M3** analyse how effectively the industry is supporting sustainable tourism development in two destinations **Case study page 360**	
P4 describe how the travel and tourism industry supports the development of sustainable tourism at one specific short-haul and one specific long-haul destination **Case study page 364**		

Work experience in the travel and tourism industry

Introduction

Work experience is a valuable addition to your programme of study. It helps you to apply your knowledge of travel and tourism in a work context and to develop your practical skills. You will experience the world of work and appreciate the code of behaviour and skills essential to the effective running of the workplace.

Your work experience may take place in a block of two or more weeks or on a day-release or weekend basis. This unit will help you prepare for your placement, give you opportunities to consider the skills, qualities and behaviours relevant to the workplace and help you review the effectiveness of your work placement.

At the end of this unit you should be able to:

1   Know how to prepare for a work experience placement in the travel and tourism industry

2   Be able to demonstrate the skills, qualities and behaviours needed for effective performance in the workplace

3   Understand the nature of the chosen work experience organisation

4   Understand the factors contributing to an effective work experience placement.

Thinking points

The value of work experience is widely acknowledged. Most schools and colleges incorporate work experience into their programmes – not just for travel and tourism but for all vocational subjects. While it is great that most students get an opportunity to do work experience it also means that there is a lot of competition for places. If you have a particular sector of the industry that you would like to work in, don't wait for someone else to find you a placement. Follow the guidance and advice given in this unit and take the initiative to find a placement that is just right for you. Start looking early – you need to be first and you need to be the best!

How to find a work placement

Potential work placement organisations

Think about what kind of organisation you would like to work in. All towns and cities have travel agents and hotels but if you want to work for a tour operator you may have to travel. Your Tourist Information Centre will normally accept students for placements but there will be a lot of competition for places.

- **Co-ordinator** – many colleges and schools have a work-experience co-ordinator whose role is to help students find a work placement. But the co-ordinator will have to find placements for many students, so you might decide to find your own placement.
- **Contacts and networking** – use any contacts you can to find a work placement. Perhaps you have a family member or friend who works in travel and tourism.
- **Database** – your college or school should have a database of work placements previously used by travel and tourism students. This may be held by the co-ordinator or the teacher or tutor. If a placement on the database appeals to you, notify your teacher or tutor and find out what the procedure is for making contact with the organisation. Often, colleges and schools prefer students not to contact organisations on the database directly, as they want to ensure that these organisations are not inundated with requests.
- **Careers advisers** – they may be based in your college or school or in another centre, for example Connexions. They do not find work placements but they will help you decide what type of placement will be suitable for you with your career goals in mind.
- **Newspapers** – look at job advertisements in the local newspaper to get ideas of organisations in your area which are suitable for work experience.
- **Resource centres/websites** – if you are looking for a work placement in a specialist area such as the airport sector, you will find that there is often a job centre or website for recruitment. Examples include Manchester and Stansted airports. These centres will be advertising jobs, not placements, but will give you ideas on whom to contact.

Constraints

Once you have found a placement, you need to make sure you are fully prepared to start work. Spend some time finding out about the following issues.

Location of placement and travel arrangements

Make sure you have the address of your organisation. Companies with their own websites often provide a location map which you can download. Find out the times of buses or trains before you start the placement and see how long the journey takes. It may take longer in the rush hour. See if you can buy a weekly ticket to save money. Many students do a practice run of their journey so they do not have to worry about the journey on the first day.

Hours of work

If you had an interview your hours will probably be explained to you. If not, telephone and ask. Find out also to whom you are responsible. It is embarrassing to arrive on the first day at the wrong time and not know who to ask for. Remember you need to know your hours to fit in any other commitments and to arrange your travel.

Personal commitments

If you have personal commitments which affect your availability for work experience, you must inform your tutor and your employer and negotiate suitable hours. Acceptable commitments include an existing part-time job or family responsibilities. Do not expect employers to accommodate your social arrangements.

Accommodation

Most students take up work placements in their own locality. If yours is not in your own area, you will have to consider where you will live. Sometimes, although it is unusual, students find placements in resorts and are provided with accommodation. Over-eighteens finding placements with Butlins are offered accommodation. If you have family or friends to stay with in another area, you can think about taking up a placement in their area.

Equipment and clothing

Your employer will tell you if you need any special equipment or clothing. If a uniform must be worn, it will be provided. If you are unsure about what to wear, telephone and ask about the dress code. Do this in good time as you might have to buy some suitable clothes.

Always carry a pad and pen to write notes on what you are doing at work. You may have been given a log to complete as well. Consider taking an audio/video recorder or a camera to work. Tapes and photos will add interest to your project, but it is very important to remember to ask permission before taking any pictures or recordings.

Documentation

Letter of enquiry or application

A letter of enquiry is a speculative letter asking if there are any job opportunities; a letter of application relates to a specific job which has been advertised. You are most likely to be sending a letter of enquiry.

Make sure any letter you send:

- is addressed to the relevant person, for example, the human resources manager or agency manager, by name if possible
- contains details of your course
- contains the dates of your work placement
- has a sentence or two on why you would like to have work experience in that organisation
- is word-processed in a business format
- has been checked by your teacher or tutor.

Travel and tourism organisations receive hundreds of requests for work experience. To increase your chances of success, try the following:

- send out a lot of letters to different companies – some will not reply at all

Activity

1 Study the press release below. Produce a press release for yourself which you can send to prospective work placements.

2 Hold a discussion with your colleagues. What other ways can you think of to get your details noticed by employers?

38, St John's Street, Powertown, Lancs LA4 5DE
1 March 2005

PRESS RELEASE

Travel and tourism student seeks work placement!

An ideal opportunity for you to acquire the services of

Gemma Hudson

who is conscientious, reliable and enthusiastic

AND …

will cost you nothing!

Gemma is available for work placement from 17 May to 25 June 2007. The work placement is an important part of her Travel and Tourism BTEC course at Trinity and All Saints College, Lancaster.

Further information about Gemma is attached in her CV.

Interested? Please contact Gemma on 0776———, at the above address, or by e-mail at gemma_123@yahoo.co.uk

---

- include a stamped addressed envelope to encourage a reply
- instead of a letter, try sending something different that gets you noticed – what about a press release stating you are available for placement, or a tape or CD about yourself?
- visit the organisation personally, wearing suitable business clothes, and take your CV
- send out letters early before the organisation has its full complement of work-experience candidates.

▲ Figure 21.1 Interview in progress

Set objectives

What do you hope to achieve from your work experience? Objectives can fit into different categories. You should expect to develop personal skills, for example punctuality, and you will gain experience that should benefit your future career. In addition, think about what the placement will help you achieve in the curriculum areas of your programme.

Developing new skills

In the work environment you will have an opportunity to develop some or all of the following skills:

- **Customer care** – you will be dealing with members of the public, suppliers and colleagues, and the customer care skills you develop will be of use whatever career you choose in the future.
- **Technical/practical** – you may learn to use specialist equipment and resources, for example reservation systems, other IT systems or you might be finding your way around directories.
- **Social/personal** – when you go to work you leave your personal problems at home. Develop a professional attitude showing respect and consideration for customers and colleagues alike.
- **Analytical/critical/problem-solving skills** – your work experience will present you with real challenges. Use your initiative to deal with any problems or incidents that occur. Bear in mind your limitations and refer issues to relevant managers if appropriate.
- **Prioritising tasks** – you will be given various tasks to do, sometimes from different members of staff. Learn how to judge which tasks are more important or urgent and do those first. If in doubt, ask.
- **Time-keeping** – punctuality shows your commitment to the placement. Remember to return punctually from breaks as well as arriving on time for the start of work.

Consider this

How many students from your college/school are looking for work experience? How can you make sure you stand out from the rest?

CV and interview

Unit 6 explains how to produce a CV and prepare for an interview. It is highly likely that employers will ask to see your CV and they may invite you for an interview. You should keep an electronic copy of your CV and update it regularly so that it is always available. If you are invited for interview, prepare as you would if the interview was for a permanent job. Carry out research into the company, prepare questions for them and answers to their possible questions to you. Wear appropriate business clothes.

Letter of acceptance

Once you have been offered a work placement, whether by letter or verbally, write a letter of acceptance confirming the dates you will be attending the placement.

- **Self-motivation** – always ensure you have tasks to do. If necessary, ask for something to do or ask staff for an explanation and demonstration of what they are doing.
- **Action planning/research techniques** – you will have an assignment to complete on your placement. Use the resources available while at work, including people, to develop your planning and research skills.

Developing your career

Your work experience is the first step of your career – whether you eventually go into travel and tourism or not.

- You will gain knowledge and experience in a sector of the travel and tourism industry – this will help you decide whether your career lies in that sector.

- If you perform well on your work experience, your employer should agree to provide a reference for future jobs.
- You will start to build up a network of contacts who might help you in your future career.
- Employers often offer jobs – full- or part-time – to those people who perform well on work experience.
- You will build up experience, skills and possibly qualifications which can be included on your CV.

Curriculum

- Plan ahead to decide which units you should be able to collect evidence for.
- Collect evidence whist you are at your placement.
- Ask if you can come back in the future if you need further evidence.

Assessment practice

Study this example of Bijan's work placement at the local Tourist Information Centre. The centre puts all new staff through the 'Welcome Host' training programme. Bijan prepared some objectives before he went on his placement – these are shown below.

Bijan's objectives are useful as they remind him of the purpose of his work placement and give him a focus while he is there. They will also help him when he carries out his review of the work placement, as they provide a measure for his achievement.

Prepare your objectives for work experience under the headings used by Bijan in the example below. Do not complete the comments sections at this stage. If you think you need more information about the placement to do this, discuss the types of activities you will be doing at work with your teacher or tutor and carry out some background research into the organisation. **P2**

Personal objectives	Comments	Career objectives	Comments	Curriculum objectives	Comments
Develop new skills with new colleagues Learn how to use accommodation reservation system Develop customer care skills Develop action-planning and problem-solving skills		Gain 'Welcome Host' qualification Gain useful contacts for the future Determine whether this sector is for me		Collect evidence for completion of Work Experience unit Collect evidence for Preparing for Employment and Customer Service units	

Code of conduct

Those students who have a part-time job will already understand that the world of work demands different behaviour from that in a college or school. Think about:

- **Time-keeping** – it is unacceptable to be late. Plan to arrive at least 10 minutes before your starting time. Your employer will be asked to comment on your punctuality.
- **Attendance** – in a short placement, there is no reason why you should not attain full attendance. If exceptional circumstances occur (for example sickness) telephone your placement and your teacher or tutor at the earliest opportunity. Have contact details for work readily available. Make sure you are fit for work by avoiding late nights and drinking before and during the placement.
- **Demonstrating honesty and reliability** – of course you are honest and reliable, and these are qualities you will demonstrate in the workplace. However, be aware that you will be working with people who do not know your qualities and behave in an open and honest way at all times.
- **Accepting authority and responding to instructions** – think about how you respond to authority. Are you able to accept that your immediate supervisor will tell you what to do? How do you respond to instructions? On work experience you should not question authority; you should graciously accept instructions and carry them out to the best of your ability. If you are not clear about what to do or need help, ask.
- **Accepting responsibility** – if you are asked to do something, however small, do it carefully and take responsibility for doing it properly – this does not mean that you can't ask for help when you need it.
- **Adhering to dress code** – you may be given a uniform to wear. If not, you will be given advice about what to wear. Even if it is not what you normally like to wear, respect the dress code and remember that it is there to project a certain company image.

- **Being courteous and using appropriate language** – on your course you will study ethics in the workplace. Think about your attitudes to other people. Do you treat everyone with courtesy? Do you act and speak in a non-discriminatory manner? Set yourself high standards and adhere to them.
- **Adhering to rules and procedures** – consider your reactions to rules and procedures; most workplaces keep rules to a minimum, but there will necessarily be some as they are essential to health and safety, and you must accept them.

Demonstration of skills

The skills you are hoping to develop were outlined in the 'Setting objectives' section of this unit. Keep these in mind when you are at your placement. Each day try to think of situations where you have demonstrated these skills and reflect on how you might have improved. Write notes in your log including your reflections on your performance.

Monitoring progress

Keep careful records as described above. If possible, review your progress with the employer or your teacher or tutor as you go along. You may have been issued with a log book by your tutor. If so complete it as instructed. Your teacher or tutor is likely to visit you on work experience and will talk to you as well as asking for feedback from your employer.

Assessment practice

Make a list or table of potential contacts/resources you can use to find your work experience placement. Make sure you take into account your personal constraints. **P1**

Explain how two placements might help you meet the objectives you identified in the assessment practice on page 377. **M1**

Analyse the career progression within your two potential placements, and from those organisations into other areas of travel and tourism. **D1**

Whilst on work experience you will be expected to undertake research to produce a report about your work experience organisation.

Finding out about your organisation

Your placement may be day release or an intensive block of work. Whatever the format, you should start your research immediately and put some time aside each day to work on it. If you leave it until the end of the placement, you will not be able to collect all the relevant information. This is a common problem – don't let it happen to you!

Make sure your employer and the staff at your placement are aware of your assignment and then they will be prepared to help you. If there is not enough time during the working day to carry out your research, spend a short time each evening working on it, and make a list of information you need to collect the following day.

How to find relevant information

- **Interviews with staff** – most people are glad to talk about themselves. Take notes or make recordings of their responses (with their permission).
- **Resources** – make the most of the resources available at work, especially training manuals and information on policies and procedures.
- **Observation** – this is a very useful tool, particularly for looking at customer service. However, if you are observing the way staff operate, be discreet. Write notes later.
- **Keeping records** – you should keep notes on all aspects of your research as you work on it. Note points still to be carried out. Keep copies of relevant documents for inclusion as appendices to your assignment.

What you need to find out

The following checklist is designed to help you. It includes examples of the kind of information you are expected to find out.

- **Description of organisation** – summarise what it does. Example: Tourism Concern is a registered charity which encourages sustainable tourism in destination countries by working with communities and trying to find ways of reducing the social and environmental problems connected with tourism and increasing local benefits.
- **Sector** – here you indicate whether your organisation is in the public, private or voluntary sector. Example: Tourism Concern is in the voluntary sector.
- **Ownership** – who owns the organisation? Is it a Public Limited Company, a sole trader or a partnership, for example? Example: Thomson Holidays is a Public Limited Company owned by shareholders.
- **Size** – you can indicate the size of the company by the number of employees, by the revenue of sales or by its locations.
- **Organisation chart** – draw up an organisation chart of your work experience placement. This should clearly show key roles and line management. If the organisation is very large, just draw up a chart for your department. Add a description to your organisation chart saying who does what and how they link with others.
- **Key activities** – what is the main function of the organisation? For example, a Tourist Information Centre seeks to promote tourism in the local area and provide information for visitors.
- **Products and services** – what does the organisation actually provide? For example, a travel agent provides the following services:
  - books holidays, acting as intermediary between the customer and the tour operator
  - sells flights and other travel services

- sells travel insurance
- books excursions
- sells currency
- organises itineraries
- gives travel advice.

Detail specific products and services, for example listing the tour operators the travel agent represents or the destinations it specialises in.

- **Health and safety issues** – these include legislative and regulatory requirements, specific policies and procedures and security. When you undertake your work experience you will find out how they apply in practice. These requirements are covered in detail in Unit 6 about preparing for employment.

  When you arrive at work you will be given induction training; this is essential for all new staff and will introduce you to basic policies and procedures relating to your work environment. Basic health,

safety and security requirements will be included in induction. Other procedures will be explained to you if they are relevant to the work you are doing.

All health, safety and security requirements will be published in a manual or displayed in the workplace. You should make sure you are familiar with all the procedures.

- **Own role** – describe your own role whilst on work experience. What are your duties and responsibilities? Who do you report to and how do you link with others? Place yourself on the organisation chart.
- **Other staff roles** – you could find out about the roles of others in the organisation by interviewing them. Try to interview at least three people. Devise some questions to ask them. Find out what are their duties and responsibilites. Who do they report to? Find out about the progression opportunities within the company. **P4**

21.4 Understand the factors contributing to an effective work experience placement

Factors

How have you benefited from work experience? Has it been successful?

You should consider:

- the new skills and knowledge you have gained
- how they can be used in the future
- attendance and punctuality
- behaviour in the workplace
- the personal contacts you have made
- references
- possible career pathways and plans for future employment
- other opportunities for progression such as part-time employment.

Before you complete your review, make sure you have the following information to hand:

- log book
- any interviews or witness statements
- employer review
- personal SWOT analysis (strengths, weaknesses, opportunities and threats)
- attendance and punctuality records.

Supporting evidence

Once your work-based experience is at an end you will carry out an evaluation. You need certain tools to help you do this and these should be used during the placement itself to monitor your activities and performance.

Case study: log book extract

Here is an extract from a log book kept by Bijan while working in a Tourist Information Centre.

Tuesday 26 April 2007

Activities
First 4 hours of the day spent on the desk with Janine. Had to answer customer queries.

Given time in the afternoon to work on my project – used the intranet and accessed a lot of Regional Tourist Board information on structure and policy.

Skills developed
Customer care – learnt a lot from watching Janine and then dealing with customers myself.

Research – found out a lot about the Regional Tourist Board.

IT – used the intranet.

Problems and solutions
Had to help a German customer and I couldn't communicate at all! Managed to find a staff member who spoke some German.

Action points
- Acquaint myself with all the TIC leaflets and literature so I don't have to ask Janine for obvious things.
- Learn German?

1 **How do you think the headings help Bijan?**

2 **What could Bijan do if he found he was writing 'made tea' or 'stamped brochures'?**

3 **Design your own log page.**

4 **Discuss your ideas with your group.**

You may have been provided with recording documentation by your college or school. Otherwise, develop your own. You could include:
- a diary or log book
- attendance records
- a witness statement
- records of employer feedback
- an interview record sheet
- a skills audit.

Keep all the documentation in a portfolio alongside the materials (letters, CV, objectives chart) that you completed before the placement.

The log book

The first page of the log book should show your name, your employer's details including contact names and telephone numbers, and your teacher's or tutor's name and telephone number.

Allocate a page for each day of your placement. It is important that the log is not merely a diary, but records the skills you are developing and any problem-solving you are involved in.

Witness statements

Witness statements could be used to provide evidence of skills you have demonstrated, for example dealing with a customer. The witness must have observed you and will comment on your performance.

Employer feedback

Your employer will be asked to complete an evaluation sheet on your performance. It is often a series of tick boxes with space for brief comments. Your school or college will provide this and it will either be included in your log book or sent directly to the employer.

Interviews

You might have carried out some interviews during your placement. Remember that interviews can be written, or recorded on audio or videotape. All types of records are valid.

Interviews might be useful to collect evidence for other units as well. Can you think of contacts in travel and tourism whom you could interview? Which units would the information be useful for?

If you have kept detailed records during the placement, carrying out a skills audit will be straightforward.

The first stage could be a SWOT analysis. Evaluate the strengths and weaknesses you demonstrated in your work experience. Identify any opportunities that arise from the experience. It is unlikely that you will find any threats, unless your experience was completely unsuccessful!

Activity

Placement:			
Dates:			
Strengths	Weaknesses	Opportunities	Threats
Full attendance	Struggled with the database	I was offered help with future assessments	

1 Copy and complete the table above. Some examples have been entered for you.

2 The next stage of the audit is to measure your achievements on work experience against the objectives you set yourself earlier. Return to the table you completed before your placement. Consider each of the objectives set and whether you met them. Complete the table with your comments. **P5** **M3** **D2**

Preparation for assessment

Prior to the placement

1 Describe at least five opportunities for work placements in the travel and tourism industry. **P1** You should include:
- a description of each organisation
- your potential role
- any constraints.

Make sure that you record all the sources you use to show you have used a wide variety.

2 For two of the opportunities identified in task 1 explain how the placement will help you meet your personal, career and curriculum objectives. **M1**

3 Analyse the career progression potential of the two opportunities identified in task 1 both within the organisation and beyond into other areas of travel and tourism. **D1**

Grading tip

To reach Distinction level, you need to evaluate whether the career progression prospects are good or bad, what type of roles might be achieved and how long it might take.

4 Prepare the following documents:
- a letter of enquiry or application
- an up-to-date CV
- an interview checklist
- a letter of acceptance.

All the documents should be prepared and suitable for sending to prospective work experience employers. **P2**

5 Set objectives for your work placement (use the table on page 377 if you wish). **P2**

Grading tip

You should include at least two each of personal, career and curriculum objectives.

During the placement

6 Monitor your progress on work placement by keeping a daily log of activities undertaken. Make sure you include sections on the skills you develop and on how you adhered to an appropriate code of conduct. **P3**

7 Describe the nature of the work experience organisation, including your own role and responsibilities. **P4**

Grading tip

Include all the factors listed on page 380. You should also draw up an organisation chart – if the organisation is very large, just draw up the chart for the department you work in.

8 Show how you demonstrated effective skills, qualities and behaviours in your work placement and explain how the work that you did on placement contributed to the key activities of the placement organisation. **M2**

Grading tip

You need evidence for this task – at least a tutor review and employer feedback – saying how you managed to contribute.

9 Describe factors that contribute to a successful work experience placement. **P5 M3**

10 Produce an action plan with justified recommendations for future personal development. **D2**

Grading tip

Relate this to your own placement, tracking how you achieved your objectives. To reach Merit level you must explain which aspects of the placement you thought were successful and why. You must have evidence, for example employer feedback, that demonstrates your personal effectiveness on the placement. To reach Distinction level, you need to ensure that your evaluation analyses your strengths and weaknesses, whether you met your original objectives and whether you performed in accordance with the code of behaviour you set. You must also add the action plan to your evaluation.

Grading criteria

To achieve a pass grade the evidence must show that the learner is able to:	To achieve a merit grade the evidence must show that, in addition to the pass criteria, the learner is able to:	To achieve a distinction grade the evidence must show that, in addition to the pass and merit criteria, the learner is able to:
P1 use different contracts and resources to identify and describe potential work experience placements in the travel and tourism industry, taking into account constraints **Assessment practice page 378**	**M1** explain how two potential work experience placements could provide opportunities to meet personal, career and curriculum objectives **Assessment practice page 378**	**D1** analyse the career progression potential of roles within the chosen work experience organisation and from that organisation into other areas of the travel and tourism industry **Assessment practice page 378**
P2 prepare for work experience by completing relevant documentation and setting objectives for the placement **Assessment practice page 377**	**M2** demonstrate effective skills, qualities and behaviours in a work placement, explaining how work undertaken has contributed to the key activities of the placement organisation **Case study page 381**	**D2** evaluate own performance on work experience and produce an action plan with justified recommendations for future personal development **Assessment practice page 382**
P3 undertake work experience, monitoring progress of activities including skills used and adherence to code of conduct **Case study page 381**	**M3** explain the factors that contributed to the success of the work experience placement and provide supporting evidence to demonstrate personal effectiveness **Assessment practice page 382**	
P4 describe the nature of the work experience organisation, including own roles and responsibilities **Case study page 381**		
P5 describe factors that contribute to an effective work experience placement, including supporting evidence used to track this **Assessment practice page 382**		

Residential study visit

Introduction

This section of the book will help you organise a residential study visit. This unit is one of the most exciting and challenging of the programme; students always enjoy it, not only for the visit itself but also the organisation and preparation.

In the unit you have to determine the aims and objectives of your visit, ensuring that you consider how it will benefit you in terms of personal development, the research it will allow you to do and the opportunities it will present for collecting evidence for this and other units. You will produce a detailed proposal for the visit and then participate in it. On your return, you will have the opportunity to evaluate the visit and see whether you met your original aims and objectives.

Throughout this work you will be able to develop your organisational and teamwork skills, show your initiative and solve problems. By working conscientiously, paying attention to detail, considering other team members and evaluating the experience carefully, you can hope to achieve a Distinction.

At the end of this unit you should be able to:

1 Understand the aims and objectives of residential study visits

2 Be able to produce a suitable proposal for an effective residential study visit

3 Understand the process of risk assessment

4 Know the factors that contribute to a successful residential study visit.

Thinking points

Residential study visits are a feature of many educational programmes. For you, though, studying for a BTEC travel and tourism qualification, they are extra special. You not only get the chance to go away with your group and see one of the places you have been learning about, but you will also have the opportunity to organise the trip and find out for yourself how different transport systems compare, how to budget and how difficult it can be to accommodate the needs of a diverse group of people.

Think about day visits you have already been on as part of your course. Did you contribute to the organisation of those in any way? What were the objectives of the day visits? How useful were they? Use your previous experience to help you plan this residential study visit.

Remember that your trip is a study visit and, although it should be enjoyable, it is not a holiday! You can determine the aims and objectives before you know exactly where you are going – in fact your objectives will have an impact on the decision about where you go. If you want to do team-building activities, for example, you might choose an outward-bound centre. Once you know where you are going you can refine your objectives and ensure they are relevant to the destination.

Setting aims and objectives

Start by discussing the aims and objectives as a group, but make sure you record them yourself as you will need them for your portfolio. You should also add some objectives that apply just to the small group you are working in. Some of your objectives will be educational as they will relate to what you are studying and you may be able to use the visit to do research for another unit.

Show initiative from the start by setting some personal objectives for yourself. These could relate to being more independent or increasing responsibility for yourself and others. The aim summarises the purpose of the trip, and here you have a chance to apply your marketing knowledge and write out the aim as a mission statement for the trip. The following example is the mission statement of a study trip to Amsterdam. You'll hear more about this and other trips as you work through this unit.

> *Our mission is to organise a trip abroad that is educational and enjoyable. We want to achieve high standards of teamwork, initiative and assignment work.*

Objectives are more specific and help you achieve your aim.

Make sure all your objectives are SMART, that is:

- Specific
- Measurable
- Achievable
- Realistic
- Timed.

Here are some ideas to consider when drawing up your objectives.

- Use the study visit to help you collect information for another unit.
- The preparation for the visit can also be used to collect evidence for units: for example, finding out about the features of different types of passenger transport.
- Think about how the trip may help your personal development. There may be opportunities to be independent. Away from home for the first time, you may be able to demonstrate qualities of initiative, teamwork or leadership.
- Use the opportunity to get to know your colleagues better and develop good working relationships.
- Consider whether the visit will aid your career development, perhaps by meeting people working in travel and tourism or by practising language skills.
- Determine the outcome and presentation of your work with your teacher or tutor – it could be a portfolio of work, a report or an oral presentation.

Case study: study trip to Amsterdam

▲ Figure 22.1 Amsterdam is an ideal destination for a study trip for travel and tourism students

Here are the objectives determined for a study trip to Amsterdam. Remember that students can add their own group or personal objectives to the general list.

Objectives for study trip to Amsterdam

- To achieve excellent grades in this unit.
- To enjoy our visit to Amsterdam.
- To get practical experience of organising a trip.
- To learn about a different culture.
- To apply knowledge and skills from other units.

- To work together successfully as a team.
- To show initiative and work independently.
- To gain wider key skills, especially improving own learning and working with others.
- To ensure the visit is affordable.

Look carefully at this group's objectives. Decide whether each one is a SMART objective. Discuss this in your group. P1

Deciding where to go

Your residential study visit may take place in the UK or abroad. It may be located in an activity centre or in a holiday resort; you might visit a city or a beach. Whatever the destination, it needs to be decided quickly so that you can get on with the organisation.

When you are deciding on the destination, bear in mind the following:

- you can't please all of the people all of the time – you will have to compromise
- some students spend months arguing about where to go – then it's too late to organise the trip!
- decide whether to book using a package holiday company – it will affect how much work there is for you to do
- if your teacher or tutor has decided on the destination, accept graciously and be positive about the choice – they probably know what they are doing!
- be adventurous and look forward to new experiences
- accept that you will probably have to pay to go.

Considerations for choosing the destination

■ What type of study visit do you want?

You could include:

- visiting attractions
- investigating local tourist facilities
- looking at hotels and their operation
- taking part in sports and leisure activities
- finding out about the local culture.

■ How long will you stay?

Your visit should last at least 3 days but of course you can choose to go for longer.

■ Where will you stay?

This could be:

- hotel
- hostel

Consider this

One residential study visit to Amsterdam was also a race (organised with parents' permission). A group of fifteen students researched all the routes from their home town to Amsterdam. They found four different air routes which were accessible and a boat/train route. They could also have gone by car and Channel crossing, but no one wanted to drive. They travelled in small groups, each group on a different route. A rendezvous was arranged at the hotel. On the journey they made notes on customer service, punctuality, prices of food, and so on, and health and safety issues.

The advantages of the race were that the students had to travel independently, including one who was flying for the first time, and they were able to compare all the different routes taken. Of course, they had plenty to do in Amsterdam as well.

If you are thinking about having a race you will have to be over 18 years old and you will have to find out your college policy on travelling.

- student residences
- campsite.

Hotels often offer good deals for groups of students, so don't assume you can't afford to stay in a hotel. Student residences will be available only outside term time.

You can use the following sources of information about accommodation:

- telephone reservations departments of large chains, e.g. Novotel
- internet sites of hotel chains
- specialist accommodation websites, e.g. Expedia (which has pictures) or Octopus
- destination guides (books or internet)
- local universities.

▲ Figure 22.2 Young people on a winter sports holiday

Theory into practice

Find out about different types of accommodation in Amsterdam. Cost each of them for a group of fifteen students arriving on a Monday in April and leaving the following Thursday. Make sure you know what is included in the price and how many boys and girls are in the group. **P2**

■ How will you travel?

You will need to think about the following:

- What transport will you use – air, train, coach or sea?
- What is the cost of each route?
- How will everyone get to the departure point, and how much will that cost?
- How will you get from the point of arrival to the destination?
- How will you travel within the destination?
- How easy or difficult will it be to book?
- Which route offers the best convenience and comfort?

You can use the following sources of information about travel:

- travel websites like Traveljungle or Travelsupermarket
- a travel agent
- enquiries office at the railway station
- coach companies
- airline websites.

Consider this

Booking over the internet requires a credit card or debit card. Also, there is an extra charge for using a credit card.

Theory into practice

Find three different routes to Amsterdam from your college or school. Cost each route for a group of fifteen students travelling from Monday to Thursday in April. For each route point out any particular benefits or constraints. **P2 M1**

To help you determine the suitability of the destination you should consider location, climate, safety and security. Some examples are shown in Table 22.1.

Location	Barcelona	Paris	London
Accommodation	Wide range of inexpensive accommodation – affordable for students	Some reasonable two-star hotels	Very expensive to stay in hotels
Climate	Mild climate in the spring	Less predictable than Barcelona	Who knows?
Access	Close to an airport	Several options for travel, air or Eurostar	Easy access by bus or train
Transport within destination			
Health, safety and security issues			
Seasonality			
Opportunities for learning			
Educational visits or talks			
Nightlife			

Table 22.1 Factors indicating the suitability of a destination

Assessment practice

1 Find out about Berlin and whether it is suitable for a 3-day visit for a group of fifteen students. Draw up a table like the one above, comparing the suitability of the destination with that of London.

2 Find out what suitable activities could be included on the trip. At least some of the activities should have an educational benefit. You can add these activities to your table and compare with similar activities in London.

3 Prepare a 3-day itinerary of the activities showing all departure and arrival points and times. **P2**

Figure 22.3 Berlin is a popular destination for a city break

Constraints

When researching destinations for your proposal you must consider constraints that will affect your choice.

Financial

Have you managed to get any funding for your trip or do you each have to pay for yourself? How much can you afford – what is your budget? What can you get for this budget in your chosen destination? What will you need to spend when you get to?

Practical

■ Distance

Some potential destinations may be out of the question because they are too far away. They may cost too much and take too long to get to. It is best to decide on a location which will give you enough time to get there and enjoy a few days in the destination in the time you have allowed for your visit.

Administrative

■ Permissions

You must find out what documentation has to be completed in your school or college to organise a visit. Complete the documentation and ask your teacher or tutor to check and sign it. Expect the following as a minimum:

- school/college trip form – details of the trip, participants, staff, dates and costs
- parental consent form – for under-eighteens
- risk assessment form
- list of participants and next of kin
- list of telephone numbers in case of emergency.

Remember to keep copies of all these documents for the group.

■ Insurance

If you are travelling within Europe, make sure each person has a valid European Health Insurance card. This entitles the holder to medical treatment within the EU. Ask to see the cards, which are available from the Post Office or can be acquired online.

You should also have a group travel insurance policy. Your school or college can arrange this for you through its own insurers – this will be the cheapest option. Otherwise, shop around with insurance companies.

Legal

■ Passports/visas

If the trip is abroad, each student will require a passport. Make sure they are applied for in good time – it can take a few weeks to process a passport. Some destinations, for example the Caribbean, require there to be at least six months left to run on a passport from arrival.

Check whether visas are needed, particularly if you have non-UK passport holders in your group. If you are responsible for passports, ask to see each student's passport before the trip and check it.

Remember to check on what you can and can't do in your chosen destinations – for example, in the USA you won't be able to drink unless you are 21.

To do with risk

■ Medical information

Any student with a medical condition should ensure the group leader is informed. This should also be declared for insurance purposes.

■ Safety

Is the destination safe? If there has been a natural disaster such as a flood, you may want to discount it from your options. Some destinations have a high crime rate – how safe would you and your possessions be? It may be that the destination is unsafe because it is politically unstable.

Theory into practice

You can find out about the safety of a destination by visiting the Foreign Office website at www.fco.gov.uk. Find out what it says about travel to the following cities: Barcelona, Beirut and New York. **M1**

Presenting the proposal

Your proposal should be written and should include the following information:

- Aims and objectives
- Chosen destination and its location
- Means and range of transport
- Accommodation
- Activities to be undertaken
- Curriculum opportunities
- Full costs
- Full itinerary including arrival and departure points, times, distance and transport.

You should add to your proposal an account of how you have considered constraints, the features and benefits of the proposal and why you think your choice of destination and activities meets the aims and objectives you set. **P1 P2 M1**

A feature is a fact about a destination, and a benefit is what this means for visitors. Some examples are shown in Table 22.2.

Feature	Benefit
Wide range of inexpensive accommodation	Affordable for students
Mild climate	Suitable for sightseeing in the spring
Close to the airport	Easily accessible
English widely spoken	Easy to communicate

Table 22.2 Features and benefits of a destination

22.3 Understand the process of risk assessment

Reasons for risk assessment

Part of your proposal should include a risk assessment. This will help you determine the suitability of your destination, and it should increase the likelihood of success.

Carrying out a risk assessment is a legal requirement under the Health and Safety at Work Act 1974 and colleges and schools organising visits have a policy of completing risk assessments to determine whether a visit should go ahead. It is their responsibilty to ensure the safety of all participants, staff, students and any others such as parents or drivers. If risks are identified then it may still be possible for a visit to go ahead as long as the risks are considered and minimised. Of course, it is impossible to eliminate all risk. You should allocate roles and responsibilities for carrying out the risk assessment or elements of it and decide who is responsible for any contingency plans.

Key term

Risk assessment – the process of identifying what could go wrong, deciding which risks are important and planning how to deal with those risks.

Content of risk assessment

These are the steps to follow when carrying out the risk assessment:

- identify the risks surrounding your project – these may relate to travel and transport, the destination itself, activities to be undertaken in study time or free time
- assess the likelihood of each problem occurring
- decide on action to be taken to reduce risks
- put in place systems to deal with the problems
- monitor the risks throughout the project.

The possible responses to risks are shown below.

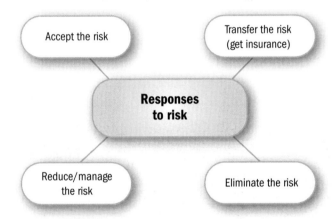

Figure 22.4 Responses to risk

Key term

Contingency plan – a plan made in advance to deal with anything that might go wrong.

Here are some contingency plans you can implement when planning and preparing your study visit to reduce risk.

- Write up a code of conduct that everyone agrees to follow.
- Prepare advice sheets on suitable clothing, climate expected, costs, etc.
- Hold a meeting to give verbal advice and discuss any potential issues.
- Use reputable travel companies.
- Ensure you have enough staff accompanying the visit.
- List the group's mobile numbers so that any lost member of the group has access to others.
- Record any necessary medical details.

Think of all the risks associated with organising and participating in a residential study visit. Here are some situations that might occur – in fact, they have all occurred on student trips!

- A student joins the trip without a passport.
- A student arrives at Dover with a passport – but it is Australian and a visa is needed.
- A student is taken ill on the first day.
- Two students crash on jet skis.
- A fight breaks out with a security guard.
- Students fail to meet at the check-in desk at the airport.
- A drunken party takes place in the hotel in spite of a no-alcohol rule.
- It rains every day.
- A bag is stolen from a student.
- A bad storm causes diversion of the plane to a different airport.
- A ferry strike means the whole group is stranded in Calais.

Theory into practice

Copy and complete the following risk assessment table. You can use the examples given, adding your own, or just use the form to take you through a risk assessment for your own trip.

P3 M2

Risk	How likely?	Response	Action/contingency plan
Student joins trip without passport	Not very	Reduce risk	Check all passports prior to trip and issue reminders
Visas needed	Not very	Eliminate risk	Check passports and apply for visas in good time

Assessment practice

Complete a risk assessment for your proposed trip. Explain how hazards identified will be minimised.

Explain why risk assessments are carried out and what content is covered.

22.4 Know the factors that contribute to a successful residential study visit

Participation in the planning of the visit

Who does what?

Your participation is very important. This means not only going on the trip with a positive attitude, but fully participating in the organisation of and preparation for the visit.

You are likely to be assigned responsibility for a particular aspect of the study trip. This may be an individual responsibility or a small-group responsibility. Your responsibilities will include aspects of organisation, but also ensuring that documentation is completed.

Your teacher or tutor will make sure that each group or individual has an equal workload. However, be prepared to show initiative and to help out where needed as well as undertaking your own tasks. Once you know your particular responsibilities you can set objectives for yourself or for your group, in addition to those set earlier.

The whole group will have meetings, perhaps weekly, to report on how they are progressing with their objectives and to pass on information to each other. Students may take it in turns to chair and minute those meetings.

Whatever your individual or group responsibility, you should be thinking about how you can participate effectively in the residential study visit.

The residential study visit can be successful only if each person completes the tasks set by the agreed deadlines. It is a useful exercise to determine all the deadlines as a group.

Regular meetings help with time management. If you have to report back to your group, it is very difficult to confess that you haven't done anything!

The group that organised the Amsterdam visit used a technique called 'critical path analysis' to determine the priority and length of tasks. The concept behind critical path analysis is that you cannot start some activities until others are finished. These activities are sequential, with each one being more or less finished before the next one starts. Some activities are not dependent on completion of others – they can be done at any time during the project. These are called parallel tasks.

Critical path analysis:

- helps to lay out all the tasks that must be completed as part of a project
- helps to identify the minimum length of time to complete a project.

The group started by brainstorming all the tasks they had to do and listing them. They worked out which tasks were dependent on others and therefore sequential. They also tried to decide how long each task might take.

You will note that dates are not used, but the numbers of days or weeks needed to complete the tasks. The completed critical path diagram is shown below. Although critical path diagrams look fairly complex they are easy to do once you have understood the concept. If you prefer, you can produce a flow chart with dates.

Theory into practice

In your own study visit, can you differentiate between sequential and parallel tasks?

	Task	Length	Type	Dependent on
1	College permission	1 week	Sequential	
2	Consent forms	3 days	Sequential	
3	Code of conduct	3 weeks	Parallel	
4	Passports	3 weeks	Parallel	
5	Set budget	2 weeks	Sequential	1, 2
6	Book hotel	8 weeks	Sequential	1, 2, 5
7	Book flights	1 week	Sequential	1, 2, 5
8	Insurance	1 day	Sequential	5, 6, 7
9	Business plan	2 months	Parallel	
10	Log	2.5 months	Parallel	
11	Go to Amsterdam	4 days	Sequential	1, 2, 3, 4, 5, 6, 7, 8
12	Evaluation	1 week	Sequential	9, 10, 11

Table 22.3 List for critical path analysis

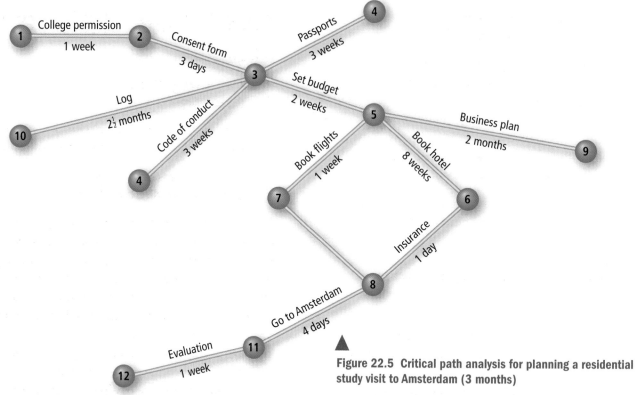

Figure 22.5 Critical path analysis for planning a residential study visit to Amsterdam (3 months)

Case study: responsibilities for organising a study visit

Study these examples of group responsibilities for a study visit to Barcelona.

Transport group – responsible for:

- transport to and from the airport in the UK and overseas
- air route research and booking
- transport to all visits in Barcelona.

Administration group – responsible for:

- code of conduct
- letters to parents
- permission documents
- checking passports/visas
- any other internal documents
- insurance
- lists of telephone numbers.

Marketing group – responsible for:

- publicising the arrangements to all participants
- sending out press releases to gain press coverage
- internal newsletter coverage
- photographic record of the study trip.

Finance group – responsible for:

- collection and recording of deposits
- collection and recording of balance
- fundraising – if relevant
- setting budgets
- payments
- keeping accounts.

Health and safety group – responsible for:

- risk assessment
- information on personal safety and security
- European Health Insurance cards
- medical emergencies.

Itinerary group – responsible for:

- researching speakers on the visit
- organising activities and entertainment
- producing itinerary.

Choose one of the groups listed above and produce a list of objectives for that group. Remember these could be added to the original group objectives.

Devising a code of conduct

Most schools and colleges issue a code of conduct for study visits which students must sign. Why not produce your own code for your visit? Negotiate the terms and conditions with your teacher or tutor. **P4**

Producing an information sheet

Produce an information sheet reminding participants of essential facts and what they need to bring with them. **P4**

Include:

- essential clothing items suitable for the climate at the destination
- comfortable walking shoes
- passports and other documents as appropriate
- currency information and suggested amount to allow for spending
- accommodation address and telephone numbers
- safety information
- suitable places to eat and drink
- special events or attractions.

Producing itineraries

Each student must be issued with a copy of the itinerary including travel details, accommodation and activities.

Personal responsibility prior to the visit

Even if you are not a member of the group responsible for administrative arrangements you must take responsibility for your own personal documentation. This will include:

- consents
- passport/visa
- medical information
- emergency contact details.

Participation during the visit

Responsibility to self

You are responsible for your personal health, safety and security. This means respecting the code of conduct.

Adherence to the code of conduct

You agreed to a code of conduct before you left school or college so remember that. It may have aspects of time management in it. We have discussed time management in planning but you must also consider your punctuality and reliability on your visit. Your tutor or group may set a curfew at night and will almost definitely require you to start work punctually in the morning. (Your teacher or tutor may not care whether you get up for breakfast!) You will also have set meeting points during the day and you will upset the whole group if you are not punctual. The code of conduct may specify suitable clothing and what behaviour is allowed. For example, it is usual to agree that food and drink (especially alcohol) will not be taken into rooms.

Budgeting

You will have paid for your transport and accommodation prior to the visit. However, you will need spending money whilst you are away. You will have decided as a group how much money will be needed for food, travel within your destination and spending money. Try to allocate an amount to spend each day and do not be tempted to overspend. Don't carry all your money on you all the time. Think about safety and use a safe if you can.

Responsibility and giving consideration to others

Whenever you make contact with an organisation outside your college or school, you are representing your educational establishment, your course and ultimately yourself. Remember to:

- be polite

- greet the contact appropriately
- introduce yourself and your course/school/college.

Sometimes, unfortunately, you might have to deal with someone who does not have your high standards of customer service. Continue to be polite whatever the response. If you are meeting face-to-face:

- dress in a suitable manner
- speak and act courteously
- introduce yourself
- consider your personal hygiene
- use the host language if at all possible.

Theory into practice

You are arriving at your hotel in Paris as a group of fifteen students.

Practise greeting the receptionist and introducing your group, saying where you are from. Use French as much as possible – even if just for the greeting and to say thank you. **P4**

Awareness of needs of others

You also need to show consideration and courtesy to other members of your group, your tutors and your coach driver if you have one. Remember to think about how your behaviour and attitude impacts on fellow passengers and other guests in your accommodation. People who are travelling on business or on holiday do not want to hear loud groups of young people on public transport and at night it is likely that they will want to sleep rather than listen to you wandering from room to room and partying.

Being aware also means remembering your duty of care to your colleagues and looking out for their health, safety and security as well as your own.

Consider this

Nick was a very responsible young man and he had been forewarned about the dangers of petty theft in Barcelona. In a bar with a large group of his schoolmates, he noticed that a young couple whom he did not know were hanging around the group and picking up a handbag left by the pool table. He stopped the couple from leaving and called out to all his group to ask if they all had their bags. They said they did so he apologised to the couple for stopping them and they left the bar – with the bag. Then, a young girl appeared from the ladies room and realised her bag had been stolen!

Barcelona is notorious for this type of theft. Did Nick do the right thing? How could this situation have been avoided?

Cultural awareness

Be aware that different countries have different expectations and rules. In some places there is a public smoking ban, for example Ireland. Be aware that some areas of cities may be dangerous for tourists or that women in particular may feel unsafe. It is recommended that you always stay with another member of your group whilst out on your visit. Take the opportunity though to try to converse in the local language and be appreciative of differences in religion, dress and food. Try new things and don't look for English food.

Gathering evidence of your participation

While participating in the residential study visit you will gather evidence so that you can succeed in this unit and possibly others. You should keep a log of every task that you carry out, with records of telephone calls and copies of documents.

Table 22.4 shows an example of a log. You could follow the same format for your log – note how it mentions problems and their solutions, and is not just a diary of events.

Date	Task	Problems encountered	How dealt with	Comments
1/10	Go to Premier Travel agent in Cambridge to pick up Amsterdam brochures	Hotels were too expensive	Now looking at youth hostels	Very helpful travel agents
4/10	I was chairperson for the first meeting. Natalie booked flights on the internet with Buzz	Didn't know Claire's surname	Rang Charlie to see if she knew and she did	Poulter
10/10	Research hotels on Buzz website	Youth hostels were too cheap!	Now looking for 3-star hotels	Found Hotel Barbacan. Accommodation budget limit £1200
11/10	Check Buzz website for Hotel Barbacan			Price has gone down to £948
11/10	Decide who is sharing with whom			3 singles, 4 twins, 2 triples
17/10	Telephone the hotel	Could not find telephone number	Looked again on Buzz. Had to contact international enquiries	The group decided to book directly

Table 22.4 Extract from Rebecca Hammond's personal log, taken from her Residential Study Visit portfolio for Amsterdam

Key term

Log – this should record not only what you do, but all the problems you encounter and how you deal with them.

In addition, you should prepare a checklist of evidence which you hope to collect for other units.

For example, Celine is participating in a residential study visit to Paris. While in Paris she hopes to collect evidence for her Customer Service assessment. She has made a list of the basics she will collect in Paris. Further research before and after the trip will ensure she provides detailed evidence.

She has chosen three attractions from the itinerary.

1 **Disneyland Paris**
   - collect leaflets on products and services
   - make notes on interpretation techniques
   - impact – make notes on transport routes, surrounding retail/industrial activity
   - visitor types – research on internet, observe while there

2 **Palace of Versailles**
   - collect leaflets on products and services
   - make notes on interpretation techniques
   - make notes on impact and transport routes
   - visitor types – ask at the information desk if any stats are available – observe visitors

3 **River Seine**
   - collect leaflets on river boat trips
   - find out what is available on the banks of the Seine, for example, the Paris beach, restaurants
   - take photographs of the river

Success criteria

How do you decide if your residential study visit was a success? You may have had a wonderful time but that does not necessarily mean that you successfully completed this unit. You now need to carry out an evaluation and in your evaluation you should consider the following:

- How suitable was the destination for your group and the activities you planned?

The next stage of group evaluation is to meet as a group and decide whether you have met your objectives. List all the objectives and go through them commenting on how successfully each was met.

Make notes and make sure you include recommendations for improvements in the future.

You can use the questions under 'Success criteria' on pages 401–2 to help you and add extra questions if you think they are appropriate. Here are some examples.

- Were you able to work as a team?
- Did the weather affect the success of your visit?
- Were there any health, safety or security problems?
- What would you do differently next time?

Here is Rebecca's summary of what she thought should be done differently next time. It followed a full SWOT analysis.

> *If we were to do the trip again or a similar project, I think we should keep having a weekly meeting because it showed that everyone knew what he or she was doing and everyone had to communicate with each other. Working in small groups within the whole group works well as every group has allocated tasks. We need to concentrate more on keeping to deadlines to avoid stress and I think we should interact more between groups. Having a strong chairperson in the meetings is vital. Rotating the chair is fair and democratic.*

Key term

Rotating the chair – taking it in turns to chair a meeting. The chairperson has to produce the agenda and run the meeting properly. Someone else should take minutes.

Small-group evaluation

If you have worked in small groups your performance also needs to be evaluated. Peer evaluation can be carried out where each group evaluates another group. Decide whether the group you are evaluating met their objectives by completing an evaluation form. Present the evaluation to the evaluated group, explaining what they think could be improved next time.

Theory into practice

Design an evaluation form for a small group including:

- objectives and whether they were met
- comments on teamwork
- comments on time management
- comments on communication skills
- recommendations for improvement. **M3 D2**

Tutor evaluation

Your teacher or tutor will have been monitoring your progress during planning and when on the residential study visit. They will have observed your contribution to meetings and how you interact with other team members. It is likely, too, that your tutor has accompanied you on the visit and has been able to see if you acted responsibly whilst away and carried out your tasks efficiently. Remember that your tutor will also be marking the unit assessment.

Your teacher or tutor may decide to complete a witness statement giving evidence of your participation in the study visit.

Self-evaluation   **P5 M3 D1**

You don't have to share your self-evaluation with the group, so be very honest with yourself.

Again, you or the group can design a form if you wish, but make sure you ask yourself the following questions:

- Did you achieve your personal objectives? List them and comment.
- How much did you contribute to the group objectives?
- Did you attend all the planning sessions?
- Did you meet deadlines?
- Have you improved your communication skills, and how?
- Did you work well in a team?
- Did you work well independently?
- Did you show initiative?
- What would you do differently in the future?

Give examples of all your skills and successes.

Preparation for assessment

Produce a report on a residential study visit you have participated in. If a written report format is chosen, ensure that the correct layout, appropriate headings and sub-headings are used. The itinerary and log may be attached as an appendix if your report is a written one. Your report should contain the following sections.

1   Common aims and objectives for study visits. There should be at least two aims and five specific objectives including at least one educational and one personal.   **P1**

Grading tip

Although you may decide on these as a group, you must present them individually. Remember to add some of your own personal objectives as well so that your work is more individual to you.

2   Proposal for a study visit including specific aims and objectives, full itinerary with details of transport, accommodation, day visits, entertainment and constraints and considerations. Include also the features and benefits of the destination and the curriculum opportunities.   **P2**

3   Explanation of how your choice of destination and itinerary allowed objectives to be met and how constraints and considerations were taken into account.   **M1**

4   Description of the process of risk assessment and a risk assessment for the proposed study visit. The completed risk assessment must include at least six potential hazards; the controls put in place to reduce each risk must be clearly identified. Your evidence must include potential hazards relating to travel to, from and within the destination, activities to be undertaken during the visit and hazards associated with free time.   **P3**

5   Explanation of how hazards identified in the risk assessment will be minimised.   **M2**

Grading tip

Use the checklists in the text to help you but make sure your risk assessment is specific to your group and your visit.

Explaining how hazards will be minimised lends itself well to a table but must be detailed enough to evidence the Merit criterion.

6   Log of participation in the study visit and in the planning process.   **P4**

7   Description of factors that contribute to the success of a residential study visit and methods of evaluating the success.   **P5**

8   Evaluation of the success of the study visit, including personal contribution and using a range of feedback sources.   **M3**

9   Evaluation of your own contribution to the planning of and participation in the study visit, with recommendations for improvement.   **D1**

10 Evaluation of the study visit and the group's performance, with justified recommendations for future learners.   **D2**

Grading tip

If you use all the evaluation methods suggested in the text you should have a very thorough evaluation. Understanding what could have been improved upon and why and making appropriate recommendations will enable you to reach Distinction level.

Grading criteria

To achieve a pass grade the evidence must show that the learner is able to:	To achieve a merit grade the evidence must show that, in addition to the pass criteria, the learner is able to:	To achieve a distinction grade the evidence must show that, in addition to the pass and merit criteria, the learner is able to:
P1 describe common aims and objectives for residential study visits **Case study page 389**	**M1** explain how their proposal meets aims and objectives for a study visit and how constraints and considerations have been taken into account **Theory into practice page 391**	**D1** evaluate your contribution to the planning of and participation on the study visit and explain areas for improvement **Text page 403**
P2 propose a study visit taking into account constraints and considerations **Theory into practice page 391**	**M2** explain how hazards identified in the risk assessment will be minimised **Theory into practice page 396**	**D2** evaluate the success of the study visit and make recommendations for future learners, justifying their recommendations **Theory into practice page 403**
P3 describe the process of risk assessment, including reasons and content, and complete a risk assessment for the proposed study visit **Theory into practice page 396**	**M3** use different sources of feedback and evaluation techniques to explain how your own efforts contributed to the success of the study visit **Theory into practice page 403**	
P4 participate in a study visit including involvement in appropriate planning processes **Theory into practice page 400**		
P5 describe the factors that contribute to the success of a residential study visit and identify evaluation methods that will be used to see if these have been met **Text page 403**		

Index

Page numbers in *italic* type refer to illustrations and tables, those in **bold** type refer to key terms.

▲ Figure 22.6 For visitors to Paris the Palace of Versailles is a popular attraction

- Was the accommodation good value for money?
- Did all the travel arrangements work out efficiently?
- Did you manage to find your way around the destination?
- Did the destination have the facilities you needed, for example medical, currency exchange, shops?
- Was the visit the right length?
- Were your aims and objectives met?
- Did you all stay within your budget?
- Did you adhere to the group's code of conduct?
- Were your learning opportunities successful?
- Did you collect information as evidence for other units?

You have thought about success criteria as you have gone through the organisation of and participation in the study visit. You have set aims and objectives, both for your group and for yourself. You have made checklists of materials to research and collect for your assessments. You should also have made a log showing how you came up against problems and dealt with them. All of this information can be used in your evaluation.

Evaluating the residential study visit

The following ideas for evaluation take you through the full process of group and individual evaluation and will ensure you do the work thoroughly.

Group evaluation

Consider carrying out a group evaluation half-way through the project. This is called a formative evaluation and it will help you tackle any problems which are apparent. At the end of the project it is called a summative evaluation.

The easiest way to do this is to carry out a SWOT analysis as a whole group. Remember that this means identifying the strengths, weaknesses, opportunities and threats for the group so far.

Repeat the SWOT analysis at the end of the project and keep records of both.